THE
WORST DISASTER

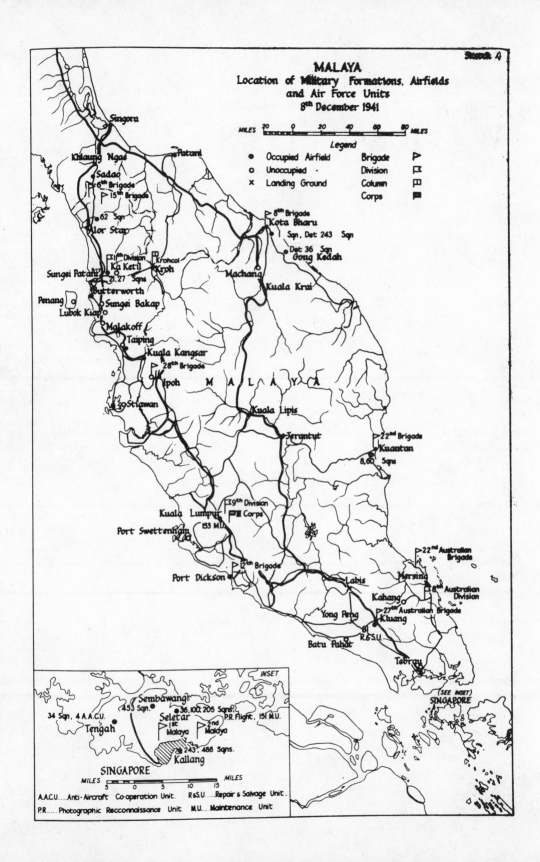

MALAYA
Location of Military Formations, Airfields
and Air Force Units
8th December 1941

THE WORST DISASTER:
The Fall of Singapore

Raymond Callahan

NEWARK
UNIVERSITY OF DELAWARE PRESS
LONDON: ASSOCIATED UNIVERSITY PRESSES

OTHER BOOKS BY Raymond Callahan

The East India Company and Army Reform
1784 — 1798

©1977 by Asssociated University Presses, Inc.

Associated University Presses, Inc.
Cranbury, New Jersey 08512

Associated University Presses
Magdalen House
136-148 Tooley Street
London SE1 2TT, England

Library of Congress Cataloging in Publication Data

Callahan, Raymond.
   The worst disaster.

   Bibliography: p.
   Includes index.
   1. Singapore, Siege, 1942. 2. World War,
1939-1945 — Campaigns — Malay Peninsula. I. Title.
D767.55.C34   940.54'25   75-29730
ISBN 0-87413-112-X

PRINTED IN THE UNITED STATES OF AMERICA

to Mary Helen

. . . Singapore . . . if attacked — which is unlikely — ought to stand a long siege.

> — Churchill to the Prime Ministers of Australia and
> and New Zealand, August 11, 1940

We are ready. We have had plenty of warning and our preparations are made and tested.

> — "Order of the Day" issued by Air Chief Marshal
> Sir Robert Brooke-Popham, Commander-in-Chief,
> Far East, on December 8, 1941

This Japanese attack is just a flash in the pan. They won't cause us serious trouble.

> — A British divisional commander, Cairo,
> c. December 10, 1941

It shouldn't have happened.

> — General Sir Archibald Wavell, February 10, 1942

. . . we were frankly out-generalled, outwitted and outfought.

> — Lieutenant General Sir Henry Pownall,
> February 13, 1942

. . . the fall of Singapore . . . was . . . the worst disaster and largest capitulation of British history.

> — Churchill, 1950

Singapore was hopeless from the beginning of the campaign.

> — Lieutenant General Sir Ian Jacob, 1971

CONTENTS

PREFACE   9

ACKNOWLEDGMENTS   11

1   SINGAPORE: February 13-15, 1942   15

2   YEARS OF ILLUSION: 1919-1940   21

3   INSOLUBLE PROBLEM: May - June 1940   39

4   PAPER SOLUTION: July - October 1940   46

5   FINAL DECISIONS: November 1940 - July 1941   74

6   COUNTDOWN: July - December 1941   139

7   CATASTROPHE: December 6 - 15, 1941   190

8   AFTERMATH AND BEGINNINGS: 217
         December 1941 - February 1942

EPILOGUE   269

BIBLIOGRAPHY   276

INDEX   286

PREFACE

Singapore fell on February 15, 1942. To Winston Churchill the surrender of the great naval base, and 85,000 British and imperial troops, was the greatest disaster in British military history. Later writers have seen it as a condemnation of interwar British defense policy, or of wartime strategic direction, or of both. In a larger perspective it was clearly the event that destroyed the prestige on which British rule in the East had rested. To Asian historians it will doubtless assume great symbolic importance: the moment when the curtain began to come down on the era of European dominance. The passage of time has gradually made available to historians most of the surviving documents on the strategic policy that led to the fall of Singapore, as well as on the event itself. A few remain unavailable, but for personal rather than policy reasons in most cases, since, as this writer was forcefully reminded many times, the fall of Singapore is still a very sore subject. That is doubtless the reason why studies of it are so few, compared with the care that has been lavished on chronicling the ultimately successful desert battles against Rommel. It is not the purpose of this book to reopen old wounds or condemn the guilty, of whom in any case there were fewer than is popularly supposed, but rather to analyze how and why such a disaster happened. For that reason there is little tactical detail, an omission compensated for by the many excellent accounts of that sort which are readily available. The focus here is on the high-level decisions, most of them taken well before December 8, 1941, that made the war in Malaya "hopeless from the beginning," in the words of a former member of Churchill's staff. Not villains, but inescapable dilemmas prepared the way for this most spectacular of British military disasters. One of the most remarkable aspects of the story is the unanimity with which, in retrospect, everyone agrees on the inevitability of the catastrophe. Yet, as in a nightmare, the British were powerless to escape. Their Victorian and Edwardian predecessors had handed on to them a position in the East that they could no longer defend, yet could not abandon. They could only hope — hope that Japan would not attack, that America would prevent the worst consequences if it did. These hopes were disappointed; the consequent losses, irreversible. Perhaps the obsession with the desert campaign is not so surprising after all.

ACKNOWLEDGMENTS

I have been very fortunate in the assistance I have received, and I would like to express my gratitude to the following: the Library of Rhodes House, Oxford; the Public Record Office; the Imperial War Museum, and especially to Mrs. E. Hook of its Department of Documents; the Liddell Hart Centre for Military Archives at King's College, London and its most helpful archivist, Miss J. Sheppard; and the Library of the Royal Commonwealth Society and its librarian, Mr. D. H. Simpson. In addition, the following individuals greatly facilitated my researches: Lieutenant General Sir Ian Jacob, G.B.E., not only gave me access to his papers and a number of long interviews, but warm hospitality on several occasions at his lovely home. My debt to him is very great. Dr. T. C. Carter generously spent an evening with me discussing his experiences in Singapore. Mr. W. C. S. Corry, formerly of Malayan Civil Service, put me in touch with a number of retired M.C.S. officers who were kind enough to answer various questions I put to them: Mr. W. L. Blythe, C.M.G.; Mr. H. P. Bryson; Sir William Goode, G.C.M.G.; Mr. A. H. P. Humphrey, C.M.G.; and Sir Robert Scott, G.C.M.G. Mr. Bryson and Mr. Humphrey both gave me long and illuminating interviews as well. To all of them I am most grateful. Colonel G. A. Shepperd, during the course of a pleasant day spent as his guest at Sandhurst, provided several interesting sidelights to the Singapore story, and Professor Richard Storry of St. Anthony's College, Oxford, made some very helpful observations about Western attitudes toward Japan. Professor Hugh Thomas kindly allowed me to examine the papers of his uncle, Sir Shenton Thomas, in the pleasant atmosphere of his London home. Colonel J. F. Worth, O.B.E., discussed with me some of the problems created by the rapid growth of the Indian Army in 1941.

I am grateful to the following for permission to make use of unpublished material to which they hold the copyright: the Controller of Her Britannic Majesty's Stationery Office for the use of unpublished Crown Copyright material from the Public Record Office; the Trustees of the Liddell Hart Centre for Military Archives for the use of material from the Brooke-Popham and Ismay Papers, as well as from Mr. C. A. Vlieland's typescript "Disaster in the Far East 1941-42"; Mr. Hugh Bryson for the use of material from the Bryson Collection in the Royal Commonwealth Society Library; Dr. T. C. Carter for permission to quote from his papers, now in the Imperial War Museum; Major A. J. Mac G. Percival for permission to examine and quote from his father's papers, also in the Imperial War Museum; Professor Hugh Thomas for permission to examine and quote from those of his uncle's papers in his custody as well as those deposited in the Library of Rhodes House, Oxford; and Colonel B. H. Ashmore, O.B.E., for permission to quote from his reflections on the Malayan campaign, a copy of which is among the Percival Papers.

The maps in this book are reproduced from S. W. Kirby et al., *The War Against Japan: Vol. 1 The Loss of Singapore* (London: H.M.S.O., 1957), by the kind permission of the Controller of Her Britannic Majesty s Stationery Office. The illustration used on the dust jacket is reproduced courtesy of the Imperial War Museum.

Thanks go to Cassel and Company LTD in London for permission to quote from Winston Churchill's *The Second World War.*

There are several people to whom my indebtedness is very special. George Basalla made the time in a busy schedule to read, and comment upon, the entire manuscript. Bill and Ann Reader were the kindest of hosts while I did the last of the research for this book. Needless to say, none of those who have helped me are in any way responsible for what I have written, although I hope they will feel that it is some recompense for their generosity with their time. The greatest of my obligations is expressed in the dedication.

Raymond Callahan
Newark, Delaware

THE
WORST DISASTER

1
SINGAPORE:
February 13-15, 1942

On the afternoon of Friday, February 13, 1942, exhausted British, Indian, Australian, and Malay troops stood in their last-ditch positions on the outskirts of the city of Singapore, waiting for the final Japanese thrust that would inevitably break through into the thirty square miles, crammed with over a million people, that was all that remained of the British empire in the Far East. The city's water supplies were failing; food distribution and civil defense alike were collapsing. The city, burning and disintegrating, was full of stragglers, deserters, and looters in numbers that defied military police control. The great naval base on the north shore of Singapore Island, whose defense had brought together over 100,000 British and Imperial troops, was already in Japanese hands. The vast stores of fuel, accumulated for a fleet that had never come, were on fire, and the clouds of oily smoke that drifted over the island provided an appropriately funereal backdrop for a conference of senior officers that was scheduled for two o'clock at Fort Canning, the headquarters of the now so-much-diminished Malaya Command, located in the center of the beleaguered city. Presiding was the commander of the doomed garrison, Lieutenant General Arthur Percival, who bore the resounding title General Officer Commanding, Malaya Command. His authority now extended a maximum of four and a half miles from the Singapore waterfront. Although a soldier of proven valor during the First World War and its aftermath, when he had served in Ireland and North Russia, Percival had spent most of the previous decade in a series of staff positions. A tall, rather scholarly-looking man, he was now ex-

15

hausted by the strain of the previous ten weeks and bowed under the knowledge that upon him would rest the responsibility for the greatest surrender in British military history. His principal subordinates were all present. Lieutenant General Sir Lewis Heath was a soldier of a very different type from Percival. An officer of the Indian Army, the legend-encrusted guardians of the Raj, Heath had seen active service on India's Northwest Frontier and had recently been knighted for his dynamic leadership of the Fifth Indian Division during the campaign that ended Italy's East African empire. He had commanded Percival's chief operational formation, III Corps, during the long retreat that had begun on the Thai border and was now coming to an end in the suburbs of Singapore. Like his Indian troops, he had reached the limit of his endurance. Lieutenant General H. Gordon Bennett commanded the Eighth Australian Division, but his importance at this conference stemmed less from his place in the chain of command than from his role as the commander of an Allied force with the power to refer to his government in any case of serious disagreement with Percival. He represented as well a nation more directly threatened by the apparently irresistible Japanese advance than Britain. All this, and his outspoken criticism of British military leadership and Indian troops (plus the Australian uniforms on many of the deserters and looters roaming Singapore's streets, described by one witness as "an undisciplined rabble, ready to run and desert at the sound of a distant rifle"), gave Gordon Bennett a rather different position at any conference with Percival than his single understrength division might otherwise have warranted. Two other divisional commanders were also present: an Indian Army officer, Major General B. W. Key, whose Eleventh Indian Division was a survivor of the long retreat (it had been virtually destroyed once, and Key was its third commander since December 8), and Major General M. B. Beckwith-Smith, a Guardsman and veteran of Dunkirk, whose Eighteenth Division of luckless East Anglian Territorials had only just arrived at Singapore. Major General F. Keith Simmons, the British regular who was commander of the very misleadingly named "Singapore Fortress" (which comprised the fixed defenses, now mostly abandoned and destroyed, of the lost naval base), and two brigadiers completed the assembly.

In a yellowing exercise book now preserved among his papers, Percival recorded in his clear staff officer's longhand the course of the ensuing discussion. Heath, who had asked for the meeting, put the seriousness of the situation bluntly. "The Japanese had driven us back for 500 miles down the Peninsula and he did not see how we could hope to stop them now that they had arrived within three miles of the center of Singapore City . . . he did not see any use in continuing the struggle." Gordon Bennett agreed with Heath. Percival argued that they were under orders to fight on, and added that he hoped to organize a counterattack. Heath snapped back, "You have already tried one counterattack and it was a complete failure." Gordon Bennett and Keith Simmons agreed that counterattack was out of the question; Heath urged immediate surrender; Percival still resisted the inevitable. "There are other things to consider. I have my honour to consider and there is the question of what posterity will think of us if we surrender this huge army and valuable fortress." Defeat and exhaustion, and a personal antagonism rooted in the longstanding professional antipathy of British service officers and Indian Army officers, fused into a sudden flare of bitter anger. His patience now completely gone, Heath snarled back, "You need not bother about your honour. You lost that a long time ago up in the North." Percival merely reiterated his determination to fight on. The conference then turned, perhaps thankfully, to the task of allotting vacancies on the thirteen small ships that would sail that night — the convoy that everyone knew would be the last chance to escape. At three fifteen the meeting came to an end. A young RAF radar officer, trying to find someone to authorize the evacuation of his invaluable technicians, saw Percival later that evening. The GOC seemed to him a "broken man." That night mobs of armed and drunken deserters tried to rush the last ships, nearly all of which were destined to be destroyed in the next few days by Japanese ships and planes.

Saturday, the last full day of resistance, was unrelievedly grim. The Japanese overran the Alexandra Military Hospital, slaughtering most of the patients and staff. Teams of government employees and Royal Engineers, aided by civilian volunteers, combed the city, destroying all stocks of alcohol (1,500,000 bottles of gin and whiskey alone) to prevent a drunken orgy of massacre by the victorious Japanese. Senior civil servants began to destroy confidential files. At ten thirty in the morning Percival, looking spruce and starched despite his terrible burdens, met the governor, Sir Shenton Thomas, and the Colonial Secretary, Mr. Hugh Fraser, at the Singapore Club, to which the governor had been driven by the bombing and shelling of Government House. The water supplies were failing, Percival told them. The pumping station was in Japanese hands, and, although it continued to operate, there were so many breaks in the mains that much of the water was running to waste and pressure was falling rapidly. Sir Shenton Thomas "said he could not face the prospect of Singapore with its large Asiatic population being left without water. He feared it would lead to riots of the worst order and very possibly to attacks on the European population. . . . . In this situation he advocated immediate surrender." Percival refused to agree but then, revealingly, joined in a discussion of surrender procedure.

Sunday morning the end came. Percival assembled his principal commanders at nine thirty at his headquarters and informed them of the parlous water-and-food situation, which they knew all too well. He then asked for their advice. Heath promptly gave some: "In my opinion there is only one possible course to adopt and that is to do what you ought to have done two days ago, namely to surrender immediately." Percival made a ritual bow toward his orders to resist to the last, but Gordon Bennett and Keith Simmons agreed with Heath, as did most of the other commanders present. Some merely sat silent. Having gotten everyone on the record for surrender, Percival agreed to capitulate. That evening, blinking in the harsh glare of a Japanese cameraman's lights, continuously rubbing his face in a gesture of exhaustion — or did he merely hope to rouse himself from a nightmare? — Percival was recorded for posterity as he signed the document of surrender in the presence of a harshly gesticulating Lieutenant General Tomoyuki Yamashita. Singapore had fallen; the British empire had lost 138,708 men, and an era had come to an end.[1]

Half a world away, Singapore's last agony looked very different. Britain was in its third year of total war, and, while American entry and continued Russian resistance spelled eventual victory, the pressures on Britain and its leader were harsh and immediate. Disaster in the Far East, setbacks in the Western Desert, the grinding battle of the Atlantic, weariness at home and restiveness in Parliament — all this was combined with the problems of dealing with two allies, each more powerful than, and each making urgent demands on, a Britain whose strength and resources were already strained to the breaking point. It was enough to daunt anyone, and it added an edge to Winston Churchill's temper, always ready in any case to flare at the least suggestion of faintheartedness. If Singapore could not be saved, at least something could be salvaged,

2
YEARS OF ILLUSION, 1919-1940

i

On the grey and hazy afternoon of November 12, 1911, the Admiralty yacht H.M.S. *Enchantress* steamed into Portland harbor, where the Home Fleet lay at anchor. On board was the newly appointed First Lord of the Admiralty, thirty-seven-year-old Winston Churchill. Years later he still vividly recalled that moment:

> As I saw the Fleet for the first time drawing out of the haze a friend reminded me of "that far-off line of storm beaten ships upon which the eyes of the grand Army had never looked," but which had in their day "stood between Napoleon and the dominion of the world." In Portland harbour the yacht lay surrounded by the great ships; . . . . On them, as we conceived, floated the might, majesty, dominion and power of the British Empire . . . . Open the sea cocks and let them sink beneath the surface, . . . and in a few minutes — half an hour at the most — the whole outlook of the world would be changed. The British Empire would dissolve like a dream; each isolated community struggling forward by itself; the central power of union broken; mighty provinces, whole Empires in themselves, drifting hopelessly out of control and falling a prey to others.[1]

A few months later he said the same thing, in less emotionally charged language, in a memorandum written to stress the importance of dominion support for the Admiralty's policy of concentrating the Royal Navy's strength at the decisive point — in the North Sea. There was some sentiment in Australia and New Zealand in favor of "local" navies. "The safety of New Zealand and

Australia is secured by the naval power and the alliances based on the naval power of Great Britain," Churchill wrote. "If the power of Great Britain were shattered upon the sea, the only course open to the 5,000,000 of white men in the Pacific would be to seek the protection of the United States."[2]   The two Pacific dominions were as conscious of this fact as Churchill. It bred in them the fear that someday they would need the British Fleet, and that fleet, tied down in European waters by a threat to the British Isles themselves, would not be able to succor them. The growing Japanese navy, the source of their fears, was aligned with Britain by the treaty made in 1902 and recently renewed. "Quite apart from the good sense and moderation that the Japanese have shown since they became a civilised Power," Churchill wrote with that slightly patronizing air that marked Western thinking about Japan until 1941, "and quite apart from the great services mutually rendered and advantages derived by both powers from the Alliance, there is a strong continuing bond of self-interest. It is this that is the true and effective protection for the safety of Australia and New Zealand."[3]   But what if the bonds of self-interest frayed, or Japan ceased to show "good sense and moderation"? "In Australia they feared that a situation would arise in which the Japanese alliance had come to an end, while the danger to the United Kingdom from Germany still prevented the Admiralty from strengthening the British forces in the Pacific adequately," the New Zealand minister of defence told the Committee of Imperial Defence in April 1913.[4]   Such fears seemed groundless in London. Five years later they would have seemed even more so, for the defeat of Germany and the surrender of its fleet seemed to reconfirm British predominance at sea. It did not quite work out that way, however. A new and more formidable antagonist had appeared — the United States of America.

America was determined to have a navy "second to none," which meant a navy equal to the Royal Navy. America was in a position to outbuild Britain, which emerged from the war victorious but shaken and, financially, much weaker than the United States. In the Washington naval treaties of 1922, the British formally surrendered their long tradition of "maritime supremacy." At the same time the Japanese alliance was terminated. Attenuated by Japan's growing assertiveness, it was doomed, like the Royal Navy's superiority, by American pressure — pressure echoed in this case by the Canadians. The demise of both the Japanese alliance and dominance at sea destroyed the basis of British defense

policy in the Far East. It did nothing to lessen British responsibilities there, however. Australia, New Zealand, Malaya, Borneo,
Hong Kong, and the vast commercial interests built up over a century in China — all these still had to be defended. An alliance with
America would have solved many problems, but that was not possible. Therefore the British fell back on a policy made up in equal
parts of promises and hopes. In June 1921 they decided to establish a fleet base on the north shore of Singapore Island. The strategic assumptions behind this decision were simple and superficially
logical. The defense of Britain's interests in the Far East against
Japan required the presence of a fleet. In peacetime the fleet
would normally be "centrally located," that is, in European waters. If a threat should arise in the Far East, the Singapore base
would be ready to service and support the fleet, which would
move east to counter the threat.[5] "Main fleet to Singapore," as
the strategy came to be known, was based on the rather comfortable assumption that when the need arose the fleet would be
free to move east, an assumption that had not passed unchallenged
when first made. The naval staff itself, in December 1920, had
pointed out that an aggressive move by Japan that coincided with
a threat to British security in Europe would pose an insoluble
problem.[6]   Six years later an Australian officer, Lieutenant Colonel H. D. Wynter, delivered a lecture to the United Service Institute of Melbourne in which he questioned whether Japan would
ever make any hostile move unless prior British involvement in
Europe made the dispatch of the fleet to the East impossible. The
lecture was subsequently published in the influential British military journal *Army Quarterly.*[7]   British strategy remained unalter-
ed, however, despite this obvious flaw in its logic, because there
was no alternative assumption upon which to base a defense policy
for the Far East. If the security of British interests there depended on a fleet, and that fleet might not be available when
needed, then those interests were indefensible. Such a conclusion,
however obvious in retrospect, was simply not acceptable in the
twenties. Britain was still a great power, even if a weakened one,
and great powers must continue to behave as such; Europe, moreover, wore an unusually pacific appearance. The "Locarno spirit"
reigned; Germany was still the Germany of Weimar; the British es-
trangement from Italy and the militant expansionism of Japan
lay in the future. It was still possible to believe that the "worst
possible case" would not ever arise. The Far Eastern crisis of
1931-33, which opened with Japan's move into Manchuria, began

the demolition of the assumptions upon which British defense policy in the Far East were based. In 1935 Germany repudiated the limitations placed upon her armaments at Versailles, while the Abyssinian crisis of that same year estranged Britain and Italy. In 1937 Japan began her attack on China proper, signaling her intention to become the paramount power in East Asia. This posed a direct threat to British interests, but, by 1937, the dispatch of the fleet to the East was increasingly problematic. In May of that year, at the last Imperial Conference held prior to the outbreak of the war, the dominions were assured categorically that "in the Far East, the security of Australia, New Zealand and India hinges on the retention of Singapore as a base for the British fleet."[8]   In June, however, the Committee of Imperial Defence warned that in the event of an Anglo-French war with Germany, "the strength of the fleet for the Far East, and the time within which it would reach Singapore, must be variable factors, . . ." The intervention of Italy, the Committee added, "would at once impose conflicting demands on our fleet," but they concluded that "no anxieties or risks connected with our interests in the Mediterranean can be allowed to interfere with the despatch of a fleet to the Far East".[9]   The CID had pinpointed the crucial factor in the destruction of the "Singapore strategy" — the emergence of the Mediterranean as a rival focus of strategic concern. Britain also had massive commitments there, and in the Middle East, whose oil supplies were of vital importance. All this was felt to be threatened by the breach with Italy in 1935. The Admiralty had promptly recognized the consequences of Italian hostility for the defense of Britain's position in the Far East.[10] The focus on the Mediterranean was increased by French concern over the balance of power in the inland sea. In February 1939 the Chiefs of Staff prepared a "European Appreciation" that was really a wide-ranging survey of British strategy in the event of a war against Germany, Italy, and Japan. From the army and RAF point of view, the security of Egypt was given first priority. The navy assumed that in conjunction with the French it could hold the eastern and western basins of the Mediterranean unless a fleet was required for the Far East, in which case Britain might well lose naval control of the eastern Mediterranean.[11]   The Admiralty therefore became increasingly cautious about the possibility of finding a fleet for the Far East. Major General Henry Pownall, the director of military operations and intelligence at the War Office, noted in his diary on February

27, 1939, that "the Navy are beginning to quibble a bit over sending a part of the Fleet to the Far East — saying they can't send so many as they thought, and that they will take 90 days to get there instead of 70. All very well but 90 is a d - - d long time . . . it would upset the dominions there (if they knew) . . . ."[12] The Australians may not have known, but they certainly suspected. The Commonwealth prime minister, J. A. Lyons, asked London early in 1939 whether the assurances given in 1937 still held good. Replying on March 20, 1939, Neville Chamberlain redefined British strategy in the Far East.

> In the event of war with Germany and Italy, should Japan join in against us it would still be his Majesty's Government's full intention to despatch a fleet to Singapore. If we were fighting against such a combination, never envisaged in our earlier plans, the size of the fleet would necessarily be dependent on a) the moment when Japan entered the war and b) what loses if any our opponents or ourselves had previously sustained.
>
> It would however be our intention to achieve three main objects:
> (i)   The prevention of any major operation against Australia, New Zealand or India
> (ii)   To keep open our sea communications
> (iii)   To prevent the fall of Singapore.[13]

This wordy caution reflected the realization in London that the automatic dispatch of the fleet to the Far East was now out of the question.

The date of Chamberlain's telegram is significant. Five days before it was sent, Hitler entered Prague. This precipitated a reappraisal by the Chamberlain government of its foreign policy and led to the British guarantee to Poland at the end of the month. Overnight the British became involved in the creation of an eastern front against Germany, which immediately heightened the importance of Greece and Turkey. In their "European Appreciation" the Chiefs of Staff had already pointed out that a Greek alliance was important to naval control in the eastern Mediterranean, while one with Turkey could strangle Italy's Black Sea trade, including its vital Rumanian oil supplies. After Hitler's coup on March 15, the Chiefs of Staff became even more insistent on the vital nature of alliances with Greece and Turkey. In the two-front war against Germany now envisioned, these countries would be crucial to the success of the economic blockade that was held to be one of Britain's most potent weapons. They were also important to the naval control of the eastern Mediterranean, while their adhesion to the Anglo-French cause would help to encourage and sustain an anti-German Balkan block, which might well deter Italy.[14] This line of thinking quickly produced the British guarantees to Greece (April 13) and Turkey (May 12). (Churchill's government would inherit this concern for the eastern Mediterranean from Chamberlain's, and it would play a decisive role in subsequent British strategy.) The guarantees to Greece and Turkey also put the seal on the growing ascendancy of the Mediterranean over the Far East. During the Anglo-French staff conversations that opened in London on March 29, 1939, it was agreed that while Singapore was "the key to the strategical situation in the Indian Ocean, the Far East and Australasia," the dispatch thither of a fleet could no longer be accorded automatic priority over the Mediterranean. It would be a matter of balancing risks when the time came.[15] On May 2, 1939, the Committee of Imperial Defence stated that in the event of a war with Germany, Italy, and Japan "it is not possible to state definitely how soon after Japanese intervention a Fleet could be despatched to the Far East. Neither is it possible to enumerate precisely the size of the Fleet that we could afford to send."[16] In June the Admiralty found it possible to be more specific: two capital ships were the most that could be spared for the Far East without prejudicing British interests in home waters and the Mediterranean.[17] An Anglo-French conference that met at Singapore that same month expressed "grave concern" over their respective weaknesses in the Far East, and suggested that if naval forces were unavailable, air strength might be increased. In July the Committee of Imperial Defence raised the "period before relief" — the length of time the Singapore garrison would have to hold out on its own — from seventy to ninety days. In September it was raised again, to 180 days.[18] When war came, nothing but the husk remained of the Singapore strategy: the great empty naval base.

The most significant factor in the evisceration of the Singapore strategy was, clearly, the competition between the Mediterranean and the Far East for the second place on the list of Britain's strategic priorities — no one ever questioned the primacy accorded the defense of the United Kingdom itself. From 1937 on it is plain that the Far East was fighting an unsuccessful rearguard action. This balancing of Mediterranean possibilities against Far Eastern risks was inherent in Britain's post-1918 strategic dilemma — a global empire without the resources to match its commitments.

The idea that air power could compensate for inadequate sea power in the Far East had its roots deep in the history of the previous twenty years. In the atmosphere of rigorous financial stringency in Service estimates that set in after 1918, the idea was first advanced in 1920 by Sir Hugh Trenchard, the chief of the air staff, whose motivation was not merely financial economy but the survival of the service he headed. Formed at the end of the first World War from hitherto separate army and navy air services, the Royal Air Force had a long and difficult struggle to maintain its independence in the years of retrenchment that followed. "Air control" was one of many policies Trenchard advocated (strategic bombing was another) that would give the new service a unique role and thus help to consolidate its position. Winston Churchill, the colonial secretary at the time, adopted the idea as a way to cut down the large, and politically vulnerable, bill for garrisoning Iraq. Air control was also tried out in the Aden Protectorate and on the Northwest Frontier of India, and Trenchard tried to take over responsibility for the Persian Gulf and Red Sea from the Navy, claiming that he could police those areas with RAF flying boat squadrons. The attempt to substitute air power for the older services led to the most spectacular interservice quarrel of the 1920's, the lengthy row between Trenchard and the first sea lord, Admiral Lord Beatty, over the defense of the Singapore naval base. Briefly, Trenchard argued that air power was more efficacious than traditional fixed defenses, and cheaper as well, since RAF squadrons designated for Singapore could be used elsewhere until the need arose for them in the Far East. The Navy (supported by the Army, which would man Singapore's heavy guns) retorted that mobility cut both ways: the planes might be busy elsewhere when they were wanted at Singapore. In any case, the Admiralty never fully appreciated the vulnerability of the capital ship to air power until it was painfully demonstrated in 1940 during the Norwegian campaign and again in 1941 in the Mediterranean — or perhaps not until the loss of the *Prince of Wales* and the *Repulse* to Japanese torpedo bombers. The fixed defenses were built, but the RAF remained unshaken in its belief that it could defend Singapore more effectively than the orthodox methods actually chosen. There remained from these quarrels a legacy of tension between the RAF and the older services which was particularly marked in the Far East and was the cause of considerable difficulty later. In 1936-37, as the dispatch of a fleet to the Far East became increasingly unlikely, the Air Ministry, on the advice of the air officer commanding, Far East, Air Commodore S. W. Smith, decided to build a group of new airfields in eastern Malaya. It was becoming obvious that the defense of the naval base involved holding all of Malaya, and from existing airfields in western Malaya the relatively short-range aircraft of the day could neither maintain adequate reconnaissance over the Gulf of Siam nor mount effective air strikes against a Japanese invasion force. It was a perfectly reasonable decision, but unfortunately it was taken without any consultation with the army. As a result the airbases were very badly sited. They were hard to defend against ground attack, while their proximity to the east coast left them vulnerable to just such an attack. This was demonstrated when the GOC Malaya, Major General William Dobbie, conducted exercises during the northeast monsoon of 1936-37 (October-March) that proved that amphibious landings on Malaya's east coast were possible during this period, which had until then been regarded as a closed season for such operations.[19] Since there were not enough troops available to defend anything outside Singapore Island, the question was academic at the time. In 1941 the existence of these exposed airbases fatally unbalanced the military dispositions in northern Malaya.

When the Navy admitted in 1939 that it could not send a fleet to the Far East at any time in the foreseeable future, two threads in the interwar history of the RAF came together — the desire to play a greater role in the defense of Singapore and the practice of offering air power as a substitute for the older services. It is no coincidence that the air officer commanding, Far East, in June 1939 (Air Vice Marshal J. T. Babington), was a disciple of Lord Trenchard, and strongly committed to the view that the RAF could and should play the prime role in the defense of Singapore and Malaya.

Finally, it was in June 1939 that the Admiralty committed itself to the position that two capital ships was the largest force that could be spared for the Far East without compromising British maritime control in the West. This calculation was made at a time when the British were still able to assume French naval help in the Atlantic and the Mediterranean. The collapse of France was to make less difference than has often been claimed to Britain's ability to send heavy fleet units to the Far East. From June 1939 on, two ships were all the Royal Navy could hope to spare for the Far East, and, in the event, two is all that were ever sent.

ii

With the outbreak of war, the Far East inevitably became, for London, a matter of secondary concern. The task of British diplomacy there became one of buying time by avoiding a rupture with Japan while still sustaining China enough to retain American goodwill. Two Far Eastern matters, however, were of prime importance to Chamberlain's War Cabinet: Malaya's dollar earnings and Anzac manpower. Malaya in 1939 produced 38 percent of the world's rubber and 58 percent of its tin, and most of this rubber and tin was exported to the United States. During 1939 Malaya sold more to the United States than any other part of the British Empire except Canada, its exports to the U.S. exceeding imports by twelve million dollars a month. In September 1939 the British government ordered the Malayan authorities to give the highest priority to the maximum production of tin and rubber. Not only were they essential to Britain's own war effort, but, even more important, they were the Empire's principle dollar earners. This was critical, since the legacy of the British "default" in 1933 on her World War I debts was that American supplies were available only for hard cash. Since the beginning of serious rearmament in the mid-thirties, Britain had been dependent on the United States for certain key items, like machine tools. War was bound to increase that dependence. This was well known in Whitehall, and by February 1940 the War Cabinet was being warned that, at the current rate of expenditure, gold and dollar reserves would last two years at most. Malaya's rubber and tin exports were therefore vital, and no interference with them could be tolerated. British personnel employed on the rubber estates or by the tin mines were not allowed to leave their jobs to volunteer for the forces. This directive, which was never altered or revoked (the 1941 target figures called for Malaya to produce nearly double the rubber and three times the tin it had produced in 1939), caused increasing tension in Malaya, where the civil administration was often forced to oppose military demands, made in the name of preparedness, because they were likely to interfere with tin and rubber production. It is important to remember that the Lend-Lease agreements, while relieving Britain's long-term financial anxieties, at least in regard to war supplies, still required Britain to pay for the huge orders placed prior to the passage of the Lend-Lease Act. In fact, Britain paid for the overwhelming majority of the goods received from the United States until 1942. Given the criticism that has been leveled at the civil administration and the business community in Malaya, it is only fair to note that in carrying on business as, or better than, usual, they were simply doing what London had told them to do (even though it doubtless suited the inclinations and bank accounts of many).[20]   The Malayan civil authorities, and through them the business community, were working to one directive; the military, to another. There was no referee for the resulting clashes except London, and there the pressures of war made Malaya's financial contribution paramount and obscured the fact that two contradictory sets of orders had been given to the authorities in the Far East.

The Land Forces Committee of the War Cabinet decided on September 8, 1939, that Britain would create a 55 division army.[21] Nearly a third of these divisions were to come from the dominions and India, fourteen from the dominions (Australia, Canada, New Zealand, and South Africa) and four from India. This decision was to have considerable significance for developments in the Far East. The Indian Army had always been the strategic reserve for the entire British empire in the East. In 1939 that superbly professional force had only recently begun to modernize and mechanize, and both these processes were heavily dependent on a continuing flow of material and technical specialists from Britain, which the war inevitably interrupted. India's prewar commitment to imperial defense was one division, and a brigade group sailed for Malaya on August 1, 1939, but the remaining two brigade groups and divisional headquarters went to Egypt. For the next year Indian Army units moved to the Middle East in a steady stream as soon as (and occasionally before) they were ready for overseas service. Not until October 1940 did another Indian Army unit land in Malaya. With a war in the West and only the possibility of one in the East, this could probably not have been avoided, but it meant that not only was the cream of the Indian Army in the Middle East, but that the whole orientation of that army became "middle eastern" — training, equipment, organization, and tactical doctrine. This was compounded by India's dependence on the United Kingdom for equipment. Whatever thought was devoted there to adapting equipment and methods to operational conditions outside Europe had the Middle East in view.

The use of Australasian manpower led to even greater complications. Unlike India, Australia and New Zealand were independent (if subordinate) partners, with views of their own. This was especially true of Australia, which showed throughout a disposition to deal with the United Kingdom on the basis of an equality which London, especially after Churchill became prime minister, was not disposed to concede. As the price for the use of their troops, the Australians did, however, exact from London a series of reassurances that eventually put the British in a very awkward position.

To begin with, the British government advised Australia and New Zealand not to send any troops out of the country until Japan's attitude was clarified. Neither dominion was in a position to do so in any case, since they were in the process of organizing forces that could be shipped overseas from miniscule regular cadres and large numbers of enthusiastic volunteers. Then, in November 1939, an important meeting was held in London with representatives of the dominions. The British Chiefs of Staff produced an appreciation of the situation in the Far East that admitted the impossibility of concentrating a fleet at Singapore but pointed out that if the Japanese moved, it was likely to be against Shanghai, Hong Kong, or Indochina. "We feel that the immediate danger to Australia and New Zealand is remote." This judgment was reinforced by an opinion from Lord Lothian, the British ambassador in Washington, who felt that America would intervene to stop any southward move by Japan. This would hold good, Lothian felt, even if Japan left the Philippines alone and concentrated on British and Dutch possessions, although, in such a case, American involvement would come more slowly: "I think that long before Japanese action threatened Australia and New Zealand, America would be at war." Both these assurances must have seemed rather tenuous to the representatives of the Pacific dominions. The first lord of the Admiralty, Winston Churchill, evidently thought so, for he drafted a memorandum in characteristically vigorous language:

> We wish to make it plain that we regard the defence of Australia, and of Singapore, as a stepping-stone to Australia, as ranking next to the mastering of the principal fleet to which we are opposed, and that if the choice were presented of defending Australia against serious attack, or sacrificing British interests in the Mediterranean, our duty to Australia would take precedence. It seems very unlikely, however, that this bleak choice will arise during the next year or two, which is what we have to consider at the present time.[22]

The Cabinet, conscious of its Mediterranean commitments, recently extended by the conclusion of a convention with Turkey, found this a bit too clear cut. They insisted that it had to be taken in conjunction with both the CID paper of June 4, 1937, and Chamberlain's telegram of March 20, 1939, to the Australian prime minister. They also seized upon the phrase "serious attack" to define the conditions that would certainly call for sending the fleet east. Churchill's memorandum was duly revised and qualified, and, as communicated to the dominion representatives on the afternoon of November 20, 1939, wore a very different appearance from Churchill's original draft. In the event of war in the Far East,

> the Admiralty would make such preparatory dispositions as would enable them to offer timely resistance either to a serious attack on Singapore or the invasion of Australia or New Zealand. These dispositions would not necessarily take the form of stationing a fleet at Singapore, but would be of a character to enable the necessary concentrations to be made to the eastward in ample time to prevent disaster. With our present limited forces we cannot afford to have any important portion of His Majesty's Fleet idle. All ships must play their part from day to day and there are always the hazards of war to be faced, but the Admiralty can be trusted to make the appropriate dispositions to meet events as they emerge from imagination into reality.[23]

As qualified as these assurances were, they were enough to satisfy New Zealand, always in any case the dominion most amenable to British wishes. On November 20 New Zealand informed London that it would send the first echelon of its expeditionary force to the Middle East. Australia, which had been informed by its representative in London, R. G. Casey, as early as November 5-6 that the British Chiefs of Staff wanted one Australian division in the Middle East as quickly as possible, to be followed by a second to form an Australian corps there, followed suit on November 28.[24]   The buildup in the Middle East, the inevitable consequence of the role assigned to the area in Anglo-French strategy, henceforth had first lien on the military effort of the Pacific dominions.

At this point a certain ambiguity begins to creep into the discussions between the United Kingdom and Australia about the defense of the Far East. From at least June 1937 the British had been slowly backing away from the position upon which their whole strategy in that area had hitherto rested — that a Japanese threat would be met by the eastward movement of the fleet — and edging toward a more "Mediterranean" strategy. By November 1939 the British government would no longer promise to station a fleet at Singapore. Timely preparations to move the fleet eastward to resist a "serious attack" really came down to this: the Royal Navy would send what it could when the need arose. It has been shown how little that was likely to be. The forebodings of the naval staff in 1920 and of Colonel Wynter in 1926 had come true even before the fall of France. The dominions, however, were still clinging to the formulary pronounced'at the 1937 Imperial Conference. It is not surprising that they did so, since they believed that their security depended on the United Kingdom's continued adherence to this strategic principle. But they seem to have missed the change in emphasis that increasingly modified the 1937 commitment. Chamberlain's telegram of March 1939 had placed the prevention of an invasion of either Australia or New Zealand first in the list of British strategic objectives in the Far East. In November 1939 the Chiefs of Staff talked about the unlikelihood of a Japanese invasion of Australia and New Zealand. Churchill's draft memorandum for the dominions had echoed the 1937 statement, but the revised version also stressed invasion, thus reflecting the belief expressed in the Cabinet that this would call for the dispatch of the fleet in any circumstances. A promise to protect Australia and New Zealand from invasion, however, no longer meant a commitment, second in importance only to the defense of the British Isles themselves, to base a fleet at Singapore merely to counter a Japanese threat. Even more significant was Lothian's opinion: " . . . long before Japanese action threatened Australia and New Zealand, America would be at war." Since it was impossible to guarantee when, or even whether, a fleet could be based on Singapore, and equally impossible to leave Australia and New Zealand exposed to Japan (especially if their manpower were to be drawn upon for use in the West), London had evolved a new strategy for the Far East. Hope was still expressed that Singapore could be adequately reinforced in the event of a "serious attack" by Japan, but the security of Australia and New Zealand now rested upon the unwillingness of the United States to stand by while Japan attacked them. The deterrent to Japan was no longer to be a British fleet at Singapore but the United States of America.[25]

Churchill's role here is very important, since this formulation of Far Eastern strategy would be the basis of his own policy after May 1940. In the first volume of his war memoirs he does not mention the discussion with the dominion representatives recounted above, but he does set out his viewpoint in the autumn of 1939, which is obviously based upon what he then wrote.

It did not seem possible to me that the United States could sit passive and watch a general assault by Japan upon all European establishments in the Far East, even if they themselves were not for the moment involved. In this case we should gain far more from the entry of the United States, perhaps only against Japan, if that were possible, than we should suffer from the hostility of Japan, vexatious though that would be. On no account must anything which threatened in the Far East divert us from our prime objectives in Europe.[26]

Indeed, Churchill's views on the defensibility of Britain's Far Eastern interests in the conditions that existed in 1939 had really been set down more than a quarter-century before, as noted above. In the debate within the British government after the First World War over the future of the Japanese alliance, Churchill had un-equivocally chosen America over Japan. "Mr. Churchill welcomed the opportunity of recording his opinion that no more fatal policy could be contemplated than basing our naval policy on a possible combination with Japan against the United States," he told Lloyd George at a Committee of Imperial Defence meeting in December 1920.[27] It was a position he neither altered nor regretted. Thirty years later, looking back on it, Churchill wrote: "It was with sorrow that in 1920 I became a party to the ending of our alliance with Japan from which we had derived both strength and advantage. But as we had to choose between Japanese and American friend-ship I had no doubts what our course should be."[28] As one trenchant analysis of the events of 1918-22 puts it, "the British government was in fact replacing a formal alliance with Japan by a mere understanding with the United States, and assuming that the latter's interests would be served by defending the security of the Pacific dominions, and Britain's own territorial and commercial interests in the Far East . . . . The risks inherent in this decision were obvious."[29] So were the implications, and Churchill was obviously aware of them. Despite lip service to the importance of holding Singapore, it was clear as early as June 1939 that the Admiralty could not spare more than two capital ships for the Far East, as against the figure of nine that was the minimum it believed to be necessary.[30] Thus the security not only of Aus-tralia and New Zealand but of Singapore itself lay in the presumed reluctance of the United States to countenance the southward expansion of Japan. Without prevision of Pearl Harbor, this policy made considerable sense in the circumstances. It is clear both that the policy took shape under the pressure of events before Churchill returned to office, and that it harmonized with his own inclinations. Even before the fall of France, he was committed to a holding action in the East and to reliance on the American deterrent to Japan. It is, however, questionable whether all this was made clear to Australia and New Zealand. Moreover there is in the document communicated to the dominion representatives in November 1939 a note of exasperation, which is echoed in Churchill's memoirs, and was doubtless elicited by Australian questioning. This, too, prefigured the future, for London was never to find quite the right touch in dealing with Australia. To the British, Singapore was "the Far East" — to Australians it was the "Near North."

iii

In January 1940 the first contingents of Australian and New Zealand troops sailed for the Middle East. In the same month Sir Shenton Thomas, the governor of the Straits Settlements (whose most important component was Singapore), asked London to reinforce the RAF in Malaya to compensate for the missing fleet. On March 13 Air Vice Marshal Babington followed this up with a memorandum to the Air Ministry making the same arguments. The Air Ministry replied that they had nothing to spare for Malaya, but pointed out that growing RAF strength in Egypt and India formed a reserve that could be drawn upon for Malaya if the need arose. This was their standard position about the mobility of air power that had first been put forward during the argument over aircraft versus fixed defenses in the mid-twenties. It had the same basic flaw as the Navy's strategy for Singapore: what would happen if, when the need for them arose, the aircraft were committed elsewhere? The following month the Overseas Defence Committee of the War Cabinet sent the governor his answer: there were no forces to spare for areas not immediately threatened. This dispatch also reiterated that Malaya's prime duty was to produce as much rubber and tin as possible. Malaya was not silenced, however. On April 13, 1940, Major General Lionel Bond, the GOC Malaya, sent London an appreciation of the problem of defending Singapore. He noted that Thomas, Babington, and the local naval commander (who bore the title rear admiral, Malaya) were all in agreement with him. Singapore was expected to hold out for six months, the GOC pointed out, but the Japanese could easily assemble an expeditionary force in south China within striking distance of Singapore. They could just as easily seize airbases in Thailand or Indochina to cover such an attack. To hold Singapore, it was necessary to hold all of Malaya, for that was the only way to prevent Japanese aircraft rendering the naval base untenable. To do this, however, massive reinforcements would be necessary: three divisions, two tank battalions, two machine gun battalions, and a pool of reinforcements amounting to at least 20 percent of the force (to compensate for the length of time it would take for men put into the pipeline in the United Kingdom to emerge at Singapore). If it was decided in addition to forestall a Japanese descent on southern Thailand, where they could seize airfields to cover an attack on Malaya, at least two more divisions would be necessary.[31]   At the time that this memorandum was written, the troops available in Malaya (excluding the garrisons of Singapore and Penang Island) amounted to the three battalions of the Twelfth Indian Infantry Brigade. There were only ten divisions and two tank battalions with the British Expeditionary Force in France. Bond's appreciation was the first detailed study of exactly what it would cost to secure the naval base without a fleet, even though it had been realized since 1937 that its defense involved holding all Malaya. The GOC's assessment was considered in London on May 16 — the day Britain's new prime minister, Winston Churchill, flew to Paris for a fateful meeting.

Notes to Chapter 2

1. Winston S. Churchill, *The World Crisis*, 6 vols. (New York: Charles Scribner's Sons, 1923-31), 1: 123.

2. Memorandum by WSC (undated, but Jan.-Feb. 1912), Randolph S. Churchill, *Winston S. Churchill: Companion Volume II*, 3 pts. (Boston: Houghton Mifflin, 1969), pt. 3, pp. 1511-12.

3. Ibid., p. 1512.

4. Public Record Office (PRO), CAB 2/3. C.I.D. Minutes, April 13, 1913. The Committee of Imperial Defence (C.I.D.), established in 1902, was theoretically the focus of the British Empire's defense planning. See N. d'Ombrain, *War Machinery and High Policy: Defence administration in peacetime Britain 1902-1914* (London: Oxford

University Press, 1973). An older account of the C.I.D., Franklyn A. Johnson, *Defence by Committee: The British Committee of Imperial Defence 1885-1959* (London: Oxford University Press, 1960), is also very useful, and much better written.

5. On the origins of the Singapore base, see C. N. Parkinson, "The Pre-1942 Singapore Naval Base," *United States Naval Institute Proceedings* 82 (September 1956): 939-53; W. D. McIntyre, "The Strategic Significance of Singapore 1919-1942: The Naval Base and the Commonwealth," *Journal of Southeast Asian History* 10 (March 1969): 69-94; Raymond Callahan, "The Illusion of Security: Singapore 1919-1942," *Journal of Contemporary History* 9 (April 1974): 69-92.

6. S. W. Roskill, *Naval Policy between the Wars*, vol. 1, *The Period of Anglo-American Antagonism 1919-1929* (London: Collins, 1968), p. 294. The second volume of this study, based on Captain Roskill's long and privileged access to Admiralty records (he wrote the three-volume official history of the Royal Navy in World War II) will be an important contribution to the Singapore story.

7. *Australia in the War of 1939-45*: Series I (Army), vol. 4, L. Wigmore, *The Japanese Thrust* (Canberra: Australian War Memorial, 1957), pp. 7-8. Colonel Wynter's lecture appeared in the April 1927 issue of the *Army Quarterly*.

8. McIntyre, "The Strategic Significance of Singapore," pp. 83-84

9. J.R.M. Butler, ed., *History of the Second World War: United Kingdom Military Series*, "Grand Strategy" series, vol. 2, J. R. M. Butler, *Grand Strategy (September 1939-June 1941)* (London: H.M.S.O., 1957), p. 325. Unfortunately the first volume in the "Grand Strategy" series, which is being written by Norman Gibb, and which covers the critical prewar years, has not yet appeared.

10. Arthur J. Marder, "The Royal Navy and The Ethiopian Crisis of 1935-36." *American Historical Review* 75 (June 1970): 1327-56. This has been reprinted with some additional material, in Marder's *From the Dardanelles to Oran: Studies of the Royal Navy in War and Peace 1915-1940* (London: Oxford University Press, 1974), pp. 64-104.

11. Butler, *Grand Strategy II*, pp. 15-16.

12. B. Bond, ed., *Chief of Staff: The Diaries of Lieutenant-General Sir Henry Pownall*, 2 vols. (London: Leo Cooper Ltd., 1973-74), 1: 190.

13. Butler, *Grand Strategy II*, pp. 325-26.

14. S. Aster, *1939: The Making of the Second World War* (New York: Simon and Schuster, 1973), pp. 117-20. Churchill shared the view emerging in Whitehall on the priority of the Mediterranean over the Far East. See his letter of March 27, 1939, to Chamberlain in P. Cosgrave, *Churchill at War: Alone 1939-40* (London: Collins, 1974), pp. 62-63. The Chiefs of Staff committee was made up at this time of the chief of the imperial general staff (CIGS), General Lord Gort, V.C., the first sea lord and chief of the naval staff (CNS), Admiral Sir Roger Backhouse, and the chief of the air staff (CAS), Air Chief Marshal Sir Cyril Newall.

15. Butler, *Grand Strategy II*, p. 13.

16. Butler, ed., *History of the Second World War.* "Campaigns" series, S. W. Kirby et al., *The War Against Japan*, vol. 1, *The Loss of Singapore* (London: H.M.S.O., 1957), p. 19.

17. Ibid., p. 20. This prompted the Australian government to ask again about the continuing validity of previous British assurances. Chamberlain, in reply, merely reiterated what he had said in March.

18. Ibid., pp. 20-21.

19. S. W. Kirby, *Singapore: The Chain of Disaster* (New York: Macmillan, 1971), p. 31. In this posthumously published book Kirby was more outspoken than he could be in the official history he authored.

20. Kirby et al., *The Loss of Singapore*, pp. 24, 277. Sir Shenton Thomas, "Malaya's War Effort," pp. 16-17. This is a 34-page typescript, dated July 1947. There is a copy in the Bryson Collection in the Royal Commonwealth Society Library, London, and another with the Thomas papers in the Library of Rhodes House, Oxford. Interview with Mr. W. C. S. Corrie (formerly of the Malayan Civil Service), December 12, 1973. A number of former administrators in Malaya have stressed the impact on Malaya's preparedness for war of the orders from London to produce as much rubber and tin as possible: Sir R. Scott, G.C.M.G., letter to the author February 13, 1974; Mr. A. H. P. Humphrey, C.M.G., letter to the author January 22, 1974.

21. Winston S. Churchill, *The Second World War*, vol. 1, *The Gathering Storm* (Boston: © 1948 by Houghton Mifflin Company, Reprinted by permission of the publisher Houghton Mifflin Company.), p. 451; Butler, *Grand Strategy II*, p. 33.

22. Butler, *Grand Strategy II*, p. 324. By this time Gort had been succeeded as CIGS by General Sir Edmund Ironside, and Backhouse by Admiral Sir Dudley Pound.

23. Ibid., p. 326. The last two sentences were almost certainly written by Churchill.

24. *Australian in the War of 1939-45*: Series I (Army), vol. 1, G. Long, *To Benghazi* (Canberra: Australian War Memorial, 1952), pp. 64-65.

25. The first mention of possible American aid in the Pacific occurs in a Chiefs of Staff paper prepared in February 1939, at precisely the time when the eastern Mediterranean was emerging as a dominant factor in British strategic planning. M. Howard, *The Continental Commitment* (London: Temple Smith, 1972), p. 130.

26. Churchill, *The Gathering Storm*, pp. 416-17.

27. Public Record Office (PRO), CAB 2/3, C.I.D. Minutes, December 14, 1920.

28. Winston S. Churchill, *The Second World War*, vol. 4, *The Hinge of Fate* (Boston: Houghton Mifflin, 1950), p. 580.

29. M. Beloff, *Imperial Sunset, vol. 1 Britain's Liberal Empire 1897-1921* (New York: Alfred A. Knopf, 1970), pp. 335-36.

30. COS (41) 230, PRO, PREM 3, 156/4.

31. Kirby et al., *The Loss of Singapore*, pp. 15, 26-30; Kirby, *Singapore: The Chain of Disaster*, pp. 44-46. Dobbie had pointed out the necessity of holding all Malaya in 1937 and had accurately predicted that a Japanese attack would be mounted from southern Thailand and would come south along the axis of the west-coast road and railway; so had General Sir Theodore Fraser, the GOC in 1925 (Kirby et al., *The Loss of Singapore*, pp. 14, 31). It is odd that only in 1940 did London receive a detailed estimate of what it would take to forestall, or frustrate, such a thrust — and even then the initiative came from the local commander.

3
INSOLUBLE PROBLEM:
May-June 1940

Wednesday, May 15, 1940, the fifth day of Winston Churchill's premiership, did not begin well. At 7:30 A.M. he was awakened to take a call from Paul Reynaud, the French premier. Reynaud "spoke in English, and evidently under stress. 'We have been defeated.' " Churchill, perhaps not yet fully awake, or perhaps thoroughly startled, did not immediately respond, and Reynaud repeated, "we are beaten; we have lost the battle." Churchill tried to be optimistic about containing the German breakthrough, but "the French Premier came back to the sentence with which he had begun, which proved indeed only too true: 'We are defeated; we have lost the battle.' I said I was willing to come over and have a talk."[1] Three hours later Churchill met his War Cabinet. There was a discussion of how best to sustain the French. The War Cabinet decided that it could not send to France more RAF fighter squadrons, a measure the French were urgently demanding, but did authorize the bombing of targets east of the Rhine, a policy about which the French were indifferent. Churchill left the meeting with authority to draft a letter to Franklin Roosevelt, which he did in the course of the afternoon, his first letter as "Former Naval Person." After warning the president of the consequences of a German victory — "You may have a completely subjugated, Nazified Europe established with astonishing swiftness, and the weight may be more than we can bear" — he presented the president with a list of immediate needs: destroyers, aircraft, and antiaircraft guns and ammunition. And, finally, "I am looking to you to keep the Japanese quiet in the Pacific, using Singapore in

39

any way convenient.''[2]   That sentence summed up the policy that
had been taking shape in London since early 1939, and which
Churchill was to follow consistently for the next eighteen months,
for he knew that a French collapse would finally undermine the
already shaky assumptions upon which the defense of Britain's
vast Eastern empire rested.

The next afternoon, while General Bond's appreciation was
being considered in London, Churchill flew to Paris and met with
Reynaud and General Maurice Gamelin, the French — and Allied —
Commander-in-Chief. That meeting, held in a ground-floor room
at the Quai d'Orsay, has been described by Churchill in one of the
most vivid passages in his war memoirs. He discovered the dimensions of the German breakthrough, the complete lack of any
reserve in the hands of the French High Command and, most
significant, he sensed the atmosphere of despair and disintegration
that was rapidly paralyzing France.[3] He flew back to London the
next day and promptly created a War Cabinet subcommittee,
presided over by Neville Chamberlain (now lord president of the
council), to consider the questions that would arise if France
collapsed, and the associated problem of withdrawing the British
Expeditionary Force from France. It was apparently on this day
that Churchill asked the Chiefs of Staff for a report on "British
strategy in a certain eventuality," that is, the fall of France.[4]
Roosevelt's answer to Churchill's appeal was received on the following day (May 18). Its tone was friendly, but the president could
not give any specific promises. On this same day a reply to Bond's
appreciation went off to Singapore. Note was taken of his request
for a larger garrison, the GOC was told, but in the prevailing circumstances no reinforcements could be sent. The Chiefs of Staff were
reviewing urgently the whole question of Far Eastern defense, he
was assured. In this same dispatch the importance of Malaya's
rubber and tin was once again underlined.[5]

On Sunday, May 19, the Chiefs of Staff produced the first draft
of the paper that Churchill had called for upon his return from
France. It predicted that in the Far East Japan would follow an
opportunist policy, "but with a watchful eye on the United States
of America." The Chiefs of Staff pointed out Singapore's economic
importance and the need for adequate air and naval forces to
defend it. Then they wrote the epitaph of the twenty-year-old
Singapore strategy.

What forces we can send can only be judged in the light of

the situation at the time. It is most improbable that we can send any naval forces to the Far East. Therefore we must rely on the United States of America to safeguard our interests in the Far East.

With Bond's request in mind, they added, "Australia should be asked to consider a reinforcement of the garrison at Singapore."[6] The War Cabinet approved the final version of this paper on May 27, the day after they had authorized the beginning of the Dunkirk evacuation. The next two weeks, during which the "miracle of Dunkirk" took place, closely followed by the opening of the second phase of the battle of France, the departure of the French government from Paris, and the entry of Italy into the war, left little time to spare for anything but immediate concerns. Not until mid-June were the problems of the Far East again seriously considered.

From the time Churchill sent his first message to Roosevelt on May 15, he waged a persistent campaign to secure from the United States as large as possible a measure of support. His principal bargaining counter, skillfully played over the next few months, was the American fear that the British fleet would pass into German control if Britain fell. The Far East played an important part in Churchill's design, for the British did not want to be distracted from the immediate problems of survival by any Japanese moves there. On June 13, 1940, the Chiefs of Staff drafted a memorandum to guide Lord Lothian in his talks with Roosevelt, which put the matter even more bluntly than their paper on May 19: " . . . we see no hope of being able to despatch a fleet to Singapore. It will therefore be vital that the United States of America should publicly declare her intention to regard any alteration in the *status quo* in the Far East as a *casus belli*."[7] Even though this paper was not formally approved by the War Cabinet for four more days, its substance was communicated immediately to the Pacific dominions, to whom it came as something of a jolt to be told bluntly that the basis of British strategy in the Far East — and with it their security — had dissolved.[8] The War Cabinet, when it finally approved this paper, also had before it a warning from the Chiefs of Staff that French Indochina was now defenseless and that a Japanese occupation of it would directly threaten Singapore.[9] How much real attention the War Cabinet was able to pay to any of this is doubtful. These were the days of the French agony, of Churchill's last visits to France, of the stillborn proposals for an Anglo-French union, and of the desperate attempts to persuade the French to remain in some way in the war. Probably more significant in the long run than these restatements of what had become obvious was a brief debate on the future of the British position in the Mediterranean.

In mid-June the Chiefs of Staff, surveying the host of troubles pressing upon them, suggested that preparations ought to be made for evacuating the Mediterranean. The fleet could retire through the Suez Canal to Aden, and the Canal could then be blocked. On June 17, the day Reynaud fell (to be replaced by Petain), the naval staff suggested that, in order to retain the control of the Atlantic, which was absolutely vital, the Mediterranean fleet ought to be moved from Alexandria to Gibraltar. The first sea lord, Admiral Sir Dudley Pound, telegraphed the suggestion to the commander in chief, Mediterranean, Admiral Sir Andrew Cunningham, the same day. Cunningham immediately replied that it could be done, but only at the cost of losing Egypt and Malta. The prime minister's reaction was equally prompt.

> It is of the utmost importance that the fleet at Alexandria should remain to cover Egypt from an Italian invasion which would otherwise destroy prematurely all our position in the East. This fleet is well placed to sustain our interests in Turkey, to guard Egypt and the Canal, . . .

Cunningham sent a second cable the following day, June 18, to drive home his point. To withdraw the fleet would lead to a "landslide in territory and prestige." The Joint Planning Sub-Committee, to whom the Chiefs of Staff had referred the Admiralty suggestion, reported that the arguments for retaining the fleet in the Eastern Mediterranean outweighed "the purely naval reasons for its withdrawal." On the 18th the Chiefs of Staff deferred consideration of the matter, and it was never heard of again. On July 3 the commanders in chief in the Middle East, as well as India and the dominions, were told that the Middle East would be held as long as possible. [10] Since the decision to keep the fleet in the Mediterranean meant the loss of the last opportunity to free naval resources for an Eastern fleet, it is worth examining why it was taken and how real the alternative possibility was.

It has been argued that the decision to hold the Mediterranean was pure Churchill, and was largely dictated by pugnacity and emotion. Michael Howard has given this position the support of his great authority.

Churchill . . . knew little of the Far East; he had been hostile to the building of the Singapore base; and he may well have felt that in this part of the world British power could never be effective without American support. But he had served with Kitchener in Egypt; he had been one of the architects — indeed he had some claim to be the principal architect — of Britain's Empire in the Middle East after the First World War. This for him was, after India, the very heartland of the British Empire, worth retaining for its own sake irrespective of its significance in the conduct of the war. The generals who failed to defend it earned his malevolence; those who succeeded, his extravagant affection.[11]

This is more colorful than accurate. The Mediterranean was becoming a major concern in British strategy long before Churchill returned to office. Furthermore, the telegram to the commanders in chief in the Middle East gave two sound reasons for the decision to hold on there as long as possible. First, the abandonment of the Middle East would drive an immense hole into the economic blockade that, as the Chiefs of Staff had pointed out to the War Cabinet on May 27, was one of Britain's few remaining weapons. Second, the area's vital oil resources had to be denied to the Axis. (The British consistently overrated Germany's oil supply difficulties in the early years of the war.) It was equally important to keep Middle Eastern oil flowing to Great Britain. Just how important this last consideration was can be seen from a report by the Oil Control Board to the War Cabinet in July 1942, a time when the loss of the Middle East again appeared imminent. The loss of the Abadan and Bahrein oil fields would mean, the Board stated, that an additional 270 tankers would have to be found to carry 13,146,000 tons of oil from the USA.

> The cuts required to free this amount of tanker tonnage are impracticable and the Oil Control Board conclude that the loss of Abadan and Bahrein *would be calamitous inasmuch as it would force a drastic reduction in our total war capacity and probably abandonment of some of our present fields of action.*[12]

There were also important considerations of morale. The Middle East was the only place where Britain could meet either of the Axis powers on land. To abandon the Middle East immediately after their expulsion from Europe might have discouraged the British public and the flickering anti-Nazi forces in Europe. The

willingness of the United States to assist Britain might well have
been affected by what would have seemed a further demonstration
of Axis irresistibility, and, as he showed when he ordered the attack
on the French fleet early in July, Churchill was willing to go to
very considerable lengths to convince everyone, especially the
Americans, that the British would fight on. Finally there was the
hope of rallying the Balkan states and Turkey as barriers to the
southeastward expansion of Germany. This was another policy
inherited, as has been seen, from the Chamberlain government, but
it is one that Churchill certainly made very much his own. Taking
all these things together, there were solid reasons for the policy
that Churchill and his War Cabinet adopted. As Cunningham wrote
after the war, "I do not know how near we came to abandoning
the Eastern Mediterranean; but if it had come to pass it would have
been a major disaster, no less."[13]

The calamitous month of June closed with disappointments in
both the eastern Mediterranean and the courtship of the United
States. Turkey prudently declared herself neutral on the 26th. On
the same day Lord Halifax, the foreign secretary, told the War
Cabinet that "The United States of America had declined to make
any declaration about their policy in the Far East and little could
be expected from them."[14]   In the lull between the end of the
Battle of France and the beginning of the Battle of Britain, the
British government had, therefore, to work out a new approach
to the defense of the Far East that took into account not only
British obligations there but current preoccupations in the Atlantic
and Mediterranean, which prevented any fulfillment of those
obligations. Disappointed in the hope that the United States would
extend a protective shield to cover Britain's Eastern dependencies,
the British government had to fall back on makeshift and bluff.

Notes to Chapter 3

1. Winston S. Churchill, *The Second World War*, vol. 2, *Their Finest Hour* (Boston:
© 1949, by Houghton Mifflin Company. Reprinted by permission of the publisher
Houghton Mifflin Company.), p. 42.

2. Ibid., pp. 23-25.

3. Ibid., pp. 45-49.

4. J. R. M. Butler, ed., *History of the Second World War: United Kingdom Military*

Series, "Grand Strategy" series, vol. 2, J. R. M. Butler, *Grand Strategy (September 1939-June 1941)* (London: H.M.S.O., 1957), pp. 187 fn., 193, 209; Roger Parkinson, *Peace for Our Time* (New York: David McKay Company, Inc., 1971), p. 354.

5. Butler, ed., *History of the Second World War,* "Campaigns" series, S. W. Kirby et al., *The War Against Japan,* vol. 1, *The Loss of Singapore* (London: H.M.S.O., 1957), p. 30; S. W. Kirby, *Singapore: The Chain of Disaster* (New York: Macmillan, 1971), p. 46.

6. Butler, *Grand Strategy II,* pp. 212, 318.

7. Ibid., p. 242.

8. W. D. McIntyre, "The Strategic Significance of Singapore 1919-1942: The Naval Base and the Commonwealth," *Journal of Southeast Asian History* 10 (March 1969): 85. It is interesting that Butler, in the official history of British strategy, does not mention the June 13 telegram to the dominions.

9. Butler, *Grand Strategy II,* p. 229.

10. Ibid., pp. 300-301; Butler, ed., *History of the Second World War,* "Campaigns" series, S. W. Roskill, *The War at Sea,* vol. 1, *The Defensive* (London: H.M.S.O., 1954), p. 297; Churchill, *Their Finest Hour,* p. 639.

11. Michael Howard, *The Continental Commitment* (London: Temple Smith, 1972), p. 141.

12. Butler, ed., *History of the Second World War,* "Grand Strategy" series, vol. 4, Michael Howard, *Grand Strategy (August 1942-September 1943)* (London: H.M.S.O., 1970), p. 54 (italics original); Butler, ed., *History of the Second World War,* "Grand Strategy" series, vol. 3, J. R. M. Butler and J. M. A. Gwyer, *Grand Strategy (June 1941-August 1942),* 2 pts. (London: H.M.S.O., 1964), pt. 2, pp. 654-55. Butler, *Grand Strategy II,* pp. 404-5 discuss the report on German oil supplies made by the Lloyd Committee to the War Cabinet in December 1940, which stressed the paramount importance of denying Middle Eastern oil to the Germans.

13. Viscount Cunningham of Hyndhope, *A Sailor's Odyssey* (London: Hutchinson & Co. Ltd., 1951), p. 242.

14. Public Record Office (PRO), CAB 65, WM 183 (40), June 26, 1940.

4
PAPER SOLUTION:
July-October 1940

i

On a summer evening in 1940 there was a dinner party at King's House, the official residence of the British high commissioner in Kuala Lumpur, the capital of the Federated Malay States. Afterward Stanley Jones, the colonial secretary of the Straits Settlements and currently "Officer Administering Government" (i.e., acting governor and high commissioner) during Sir Shenton Thomas's absence on leave, sat talking with Mr. and Mrs. W. L. Blythe. Blythe and Jones were old friends and had served together in the Malay state of Johore years before. Jones enquired after the Blythe's thirteen-year-old daughter, who was at school in England. They were hoping to get her out to Malaya, the Blythes told him, in view of the grim situation in Europe. Shocked, Jones told them that they must not bring her out East. It was more likely that women and children would have to be sent away from Malaya for safety than it was that it would become a safe refuge from the perils of the European war. Recalling the episode years later Blythe wrote, "this, I think, was the first time that the real seriousness of the situation struck us, but this was not general knowledge, and Government, very rightly did not issue warnings of this sort to the public lest it should create alarm and despondency."[1] While the government in Malaya put on a brave front, mindful of the repeated exhortations from London to get out the rubber and tin, its masters in London were desperately trying to improvise some protection against the looming danger about which Jones warned his friends.

46

The summer of 1940 was unprecedented even in Britain's long history of standing alone against dominant continental powers. The Chiefs of Staff, in their paper on the future of British strategy that the War Cabinet approved on May 27, had pointed to the trinity of bombing, blockade, and subversion as the only available British response to a German-dominated Europe. Above all there was the problem of immediate survival. Amid all these pressures it says a great deal for the central machinery in Whitehall that it was able to produce a new strategy for the Far East — and it is not very surprising that it was far from flawless.

The Chiefs of Staff had suggested in May that the need for additional ground forces in Malaya could be partly met by asking Australia to send a division there. On June 25 they raised this point again. The Australians refused on July 3. Given the strategic revolution that had taken place, and the rather shattering British message of June 13, Australia and New Zealand wanted a full-scale review of Far Eastern strategy before they made any further commitments. The whole Far Eastern situation was making the Chiefs of Staff rather uneasy.

> We are extremely apprehensive of the trend of events in the Far East . . . . We are not in a position to send a fleet there in the present circumstances . . . . If we adopt a policy in the Far East that may lead us to war with Japan, having at the same time informed our Dominions that we are unable to render the assistance that we promised them, it seems to us unlikely that Australia and New Zealand will release any further forces for service overseas.
>
> To sum up we feel that on military grounds we must avoid war with Japan.[2]

Inability to fulfill past pledges and the decision to fight in the Middle East alike pointed to keeping the temperature down in the Far East. The decision to bow to the Japanese demand for the closure of the Burma Road, which the Cabinet took on July 10, and the withdrawal of the remaining two battalions of British troops from China later in the summer both reflect this necessity. Meanwhile the Chiefs of Staff found themselves confronted with yet another eastern problem: the defense of the oil-rich Netherlands East Indies. The Dutch royal family and government had taken refuge in Britain on May 13, 1940. On the preceding day the British had sent troops to secure the small Dutch West Indian island of Curacao and its valuable refineries. The Japanese government had promptly indicated that it did not want a precedent applicable to the East Indies established, and the British readily gave the necessary assurances. The Dutch realized, however, that if Japan moved south they would be involved. Indeed, they would in many respects be the principal target, and they wanted to be sure of British support.

"Far Eastern Policy: Report by the Chiefs of Staff" came before the War Cabinet on July 29. There was no easy solution — in fact no British solution at all — to the problem of defending the European position in the Far East against Japan, and the Chiefs of Staff, deeply divided over what to do, pushed the final decision onto the Cabinet. "We are all agreed that, committed as we are in Europe and the Middle East, we must do everything short of sacrificing our vital interests to avoid an open clash with Japan."[3] But were the Netherlands East Indies a vital interest? All the Chiefs of Staff agreed that, if the United States would promise to come in in the event of a Japanese attack, aid should certainly be given to the Dutch. Sir Dudley Pound, however, held out against coming to the assistance of the Dutch if Britain found herself facing Japan alone. This provoked a discussion in which Pound found himself isolated. The dominions secretary, Lord Caldecote, who had the responsibility for relations with Australia and New Zealand, "said that certain important convoys were shortly due to leave Australia. He thought that Australia and New Zealand would only be prepared to agree to the convoys sailing if they knew we had reached a decision to resist aggression in the Dutch East Indies."[4] This made the connection between dominion fears, defense of the Netherlands East Indies, and the buildup in the Middle East only too clear. Churchill's contribution was relatively noncommittal. "If the need arose we might have to withdraw our Fleet from the Mediterranean in order to station an adequate fleet at Singapore. . . . The final decision taken would, of course, take account of the means at our disposal to resist such aggression."[5] An undated minute by the prime minister attached to the Cabinet minutes at this point, however, reflects some impatience with the whole discussion, for reasons that Churchill would soon make plain. In the meantime the Chiefs of Staff were invited to finish up their Far Eastern appreciation and to prepare another paper on the assumption that Japan attacked the Dutch and Britain went to their aid. The Far Eastern appreciation was circulated on August 5, with a covering note from Sir Edward Bridges, the Secretary to the War

Cabinet, calling attention to the fact that Australia and New Zealand "are becoming somewhat restive and are reluctant to despatch further troops until they have received the military appreciation of the situation in the Far East." It was not only the Pacific dominions who wanted clarification about London's plans for the defense of the Far East. Sir Shenton Thomas, on leave in England, had become aware of the belief — or hope — that Japan would not attack Malaya. In July he had written to the Colonial Office pointing out that this belief was no substitute for a clear policy:

> I submit that it is necessary to decide now what action should be taken in the event of war with Japan. Apparently naval reinforcements are not possible . . . and in the absence of the Navy the RAF *is the only source of help* . . . I know that it will be said that sufficient forces of the RAF cannot be spared today. If, then, Malaya should be attacked by Japan within (say) the next two months, is the territory and Singapore to be left to its fate? If so, let us be told and we will do the best we can; but if not let a decision be taken at once as to the size and nature of the relieving air force and let all preparations for receiving it and enabling it to function with the maximum efficiency be put in hand now.

On August 1, 1940, he had repeated his arguments to the members of the Joint Planning Staff. Obviously it was important to provide some answers to all these questions.[6] On August 7 the Chiefs of Staff completed their paper on the Netherlands East Indies.[7] The following day the whole matter came again before the War Cabinet. These two papers, the decisions taken on them, and the fate of those decisions, are crucial to the story of the British collapse in the Far East and therefore must be considered in some detail.

In the new situation produced by the fall of France, the Chiefs of Staff pointed out that it was necessary to hold all of Malaya (in fact, as has been shown, this had become evident as early as 1936-37). Since a fleet was not available, the main burden of the defense would have to fall on the RAF. The minimum air strength necessary for the security of Malaya, Singapore, and British trade in the Indian Ocean was calculated to be 22 squadrons with 336 first-line aircraft. (The total aircraft requirement was actually much higher, since the first line or Initial Establishment [IE] of a squadron was backed by an Immediate Reserve [IR], usually calculated as 50 percent of the IE. The total would therefore be 336 plus 168, or 504 aircraft.) The total currently in the Far East was

eight squadrons with 88 aircraft, all museum pieces. The Chiefs of
Staff held out no hope of being able to do more in 1940 than reequip the squadrons in Malaya with modern aircraft and add four
more from the United Kingdom. Two of the latter would be fighter
squadrons, since there were currently no fighters at all in the Far
East. The balance they hoped to make up in 1941. When the RAF
reached the prescribed level, a garrison of six brigades (the equivalent of two divisions) would suffice for Malaya. In the meantime,
however, a much larger garrison was needed, not least, although
the Chiefs of Staff refrained from saying so, to protect all the airfields that the RAF had been building until such time as adequate
air strength made them assets rather than liabilities. Bond's estimate
of three divisions plus attached troops was accepted, but the
Chiefs of Staff hastily added that they could not provide even one
division from the United Kingdom, where the army, slowly re-
equipping after Dunkirk, was bracing itself to meet invasion.
The Middle East could not be drawn upon, and India's growing
army was mortgaged to the Middle East. Thus, all that they could
suggest was that Australia be asked again for a division, and the
authorities in Malaya be instructed to prepare for a second division,
if one could be found.[8]

The decision to entrust the defense of Malaya to air power was
inevitable under the circumstances. It was the RAF or nothing.
But was there any more reality to the new strategy than to the one
it replaced? In August 1940 the immediate concern of both the
Air Ministry and the Ministry of Aircraft Production under Lord
Beaverbrook was the production of fighter aircraft for home
defense. In the long run the creation of a great bomber force was
the central aim of the Air Staff. The Middle East, where active
operations had been underway for several months, was making
steadily growing demands on the RAF. The likelihood of the Far
East reaching its target figure for aircraft was thus only marginally
greater than of its getting naval reinforcements. Furthermore, by
accepting the theory that air power could replace sea power, the
new policy automatically made the protection of RAF airfields
the primary duty of the army, despite the fact that the Chiefs of
Staff could not promise more than a third of the forces the GOC
considered minimally necessary to hold all Malaya, and even that
little was contingent on the willingness of the Australian government to find a division for Malaya. The appreciation was far more
an expression of hope than a statement of realistic policy. But,

with massive commitments and inadequate resources, it is hard to see how it could have been otherwise.

The paper on the defense of the Netherlands East Indies did not even exude hope. The Chiefs of Staff were opposed to giving the Dutch a binding commitment without an assurance of American support, because the British simply did not have the resources to fulfill any such undertaking. (In fact, at this date the Dutch, with 144 aircraft in the East Indies, were stronger in the air than the British.) The crux of the problem was Britain's naval weakness, and here it is obvious that Pound had carried the day. "A simultaneous attack on Malaya and the Netherlands East Indies is not a likely contingency," the paper began optimistically, but added that " . . . any attempt to produce an adequate naval concentration at Singapore in the present world situation would be unsound. The most that we could do . . . would be to send one battlecruiser and one aircraft carrier to the Indian Ocean to be based at Ceylon for the Purpose of protecting our vital communications and those round the Cape to the Middle East." Even this, the paper added, would only work if Japan was "unenterprising." There were not enough cruisers and destroyers available to form a balanced Eastern fleet, even if the capital ships could somehow be found. (In the month of July German submarines had sunk 56 ships, and commerce raiders, 11 more — the cruisers and destroyers were desperately needed on the trade routes, as well as in home waters where invasion loomed.) To drive the point home an appendix entitled "Possibility of concentrating Further Naval Forces in the Far East" spelled out the cost of an Eastern fleet: "To produce a fleet for the Far East . . . it would be necessary to abandon both the Eastern Mediterranean and Gibralter and, further, to take one battleship from Home Waters and both from Atlantic convoy work." The conclusion was obvious and blunt: " . . . in the situation today we cannot produce a fleet capable of dealing with the Japanese in the Far East."[9]

Not very surprisingly, Caldecote thought that the two papers put up by the Chiefs of Staff would be very discouraging to Australia and New Zealand. Churchill at this point read the Cabinet a draft telegram to the dominions, which, he said, "would inspire them with a much greater degree of confidence." It was a general survey of the war, and included this: "If a full scale invasion of either Australia or New Zealand was threatened the situation could be retrieved by the intervention of the United States. Indeed, if the

United States had previously made it clear that they would not tolerate the invasion of Australia or New Zealand, the Japanese would never take the plunge."[10] It was clear that, short of a full-scale invasion of the Pacific dominions, Churchill had no intention of abandoning the Eastern Mediterranean.

Even though the War Cabinet did not formally approve the Far Eastern appreciation until August 28, it became the basis for further planning immediately. Similarly, the paper on aid to the Dutch had the effect for which Pound had hoped: no guarantee was given. A year would go by before the question of building up an Eastern fleet was reopened in London. The whole discussion also drove home exactly how dependent Britain was on American sea power to restrain Japan. Interestingly, it assumed that, in any Anglo-American war against Japan, the United States Fleet would be based on Manila and Singapore, especially the latter, as it was deemed more secure from air attack. The possibility that the Japanese would neutralize the American fleet, much less make Manila and Singapore immediately untenable, obviously occurred to no one. Nor, without the benefit of hindsight, is there any reason to assume that it should have.

Churchill sent his telegram to Robert Menzies and Peter Fraser, the prime ministers of Australia and New Zealand, on August 11, 1940. "We are trying our best to avoid war with Japan," he wrote, but

> Should Japan nevertheless declare war on us, her first objective outside the Yellow Sea would probably be the Dutch East Indies. Evidently the United States would not like this. What they would do we cannot tell. They give no undertaking of support, but their main fleet in the Pacific must be a grave preoccupation to the Japanese Admiralty. In this first phase of an Anglo-Japanese war we should, of course, defend Singapore, which if attacked — which is unlikely — ought to stand a long siege. We should also be able to base on Ceylon a battle cruiser and a fast aircraft-carrier, which . . . would act as a very powerful deterrent upon the hostile raiding cruisers. The Eastern Mediterranean Fleet . . . could, of course, at any time be sent through the Canal into the Indian Ocean, or to relieve Singapore. *We do not want to do this, even if Japan declares war, until it is found to be vital to your safety. Such a transference would entail the complete loss of the Middle East, and all prospect of beating Italy in the Mediterranean would be gone* . . . We hope, . . . to keep the Eastern Mediterranean Fleet at Alexandria during the first phase of an Anglo-Japanese

war, . . . If however . . . Japan set about invading Australia or New Zealand on a large scale, I have the explicit authority of the Cabinet to assure you that we should then cut our losses in the Mediterranean and sacrifice every interest, except only the defence and feeding of this island, on which all depends, and would proceed in good time to your aid with a fleet.[11]

This is a fair summary of the discussions in London and is certainly straightforward about the primacy accorded the Middle East. Churchill's reliance on the United States is not, however, as obvious in this telegram as it was in the draft read to the War Cabinet. Nor are there any of the assurances that Caldecote thought the dominions would want about aid to the Dutch. It is absolutely clear, however, on one point: the dispatch of a fleet to Singapore was no longer an automatic response to a Japanese entry into the war, but a last-resort action to counter a large-scale Japanese invasion of Australia or New Zealand. Singapore would still be defended — but by an air force that would not reach the necessary size for at least eighteen months and a garrison that would only be a third of the required force if Australia itself sent a division. What if Japan moved before all these deficiencies could be made up? Moreover, in the back of the most important mind in London lay the hope that even the attenuated assurances given in August 1940 would never have to be made good by the British, since America would prevent any hostile move by Japan. It is questionable just how clearly the Australian government realized the extent to which circumstances had reduced British policy in the Far East to an exercise in hoping for the best.

Nothing in the course of Anglo-American relations during the summer of 1940 gave much concrete support to the idea that America would contain Japan so that Britain could wage war in the West undistracted. A British suggestion in mid-June that the United States announce its determination to support the *status quo* in the Far East met, as has been seen, with no response. When the Japanese demanded the closure of the Burma Road, Lothian was instructed to tell Cordell Hull, Roosevelt's secretary of state, that Britain could not refuse without assurances of American support. Hull could give none, but this did not prevent him from denouncing the three month suspension of traffic on the road as an unwarranted obstacle to world trade.[12] Roosevelt told Lothian in June that he was agreeable to secret air and naval staff talks, and on July 4 the ambassador informed London that the president had approved technical naval discussions in London. But when the

three-man American mission, thinly disguised as a "Standardisation
of Arms Committee," arrived in August, it was quickly made clear
to the British that they were "observers" only, with no authority
to commit the United States. In fact, their real duty was to report
to Roosevelt on the likelihood of British survival.[13] During these
months the United States drove a very hard bargain in the famous
destroyers-bases deal, trying to extract a commitment that the
British fleet would not be involved in any British collapse. This
Churchill would not give — could not, in fact. Nevertheless, the
prime minister was well content with the results of the summer's
negotiations. He knew that British survival, and hopes for victory,
depended on American support and, ultimately, American intervention. Thus he was well content to involve the United States by
trading valuable bases for antique destroyers. As he later put it:
"it was the first of a long succession of increasingly unneutral
acts . . . ."[14] Nevertheless, none of this provided much comfort
about the Far East; neither did the results of attempts to enlist
American backing when it was time to consider the reopening of
the Burma Road. Late in August the American observers in London
were given a copy of the Chiefs' of Staff Far Eastern appreciation.[15]
There should have been no illusions in Washington thereafter about
Britain's nakedness against Japan. In early September the War
Cabinet discussed asking the United States to send a cruiser
squadron on a ceremonial visit to Singapore as a friendly gesture
when the British reopened the Burma Road. In mid-September
Hull told Lothian that the United States hoped that the Burma
Road would be reopened, but on the 30th he was unable to give
any assurances of support if the result for Britain was war with
Japan. The secretary of state did suggest technical staff talks
(i.e., no political commitments would be involved), with Dutch
and Australian representatives also present. The War Cabinet, perhaps remembering the fateful consequences of the Anglo-French
staff talks prior to 1914, leaped at the proposal. On October 3 it
decided to reopen the Burma Road. The next day Churchill wrote
Roosevelt announcing the decision and suggesting that an American
naval visit to Singapore could be made the occasion for talks on
the defense of the Far East, which the Dutch might join. On the
ninth, however, the day after the reopening of the Burma Road had
been announced by the prime minister in the House of Commons,
Lothian reported that Hull had turned very cautious, and now felt
unable to agree to anything but an exchange of naval information
through Rear Admiral R. L. Ghormley, one of the American ob-

servers in London.[16] Undeterred, Churchill minuted to Eden the following day that nothing could "compare to the importance of the British Empire and the United States being co-belligerents . . . . if Japan attacked the United States without declaring war on us, we should at once range ourselves at the side of the United States and declare war on Japan."[17] The real danger, of course, was that Japan would do exactly the opposite. Lothian went wearily back to Hull with the suggestion that, after a preliminary exchange of information in London, "unobtrusive" staff talks should take place in Washington; but the British could have had no hope that much would, or could, come of this until the impending American presidential election was over.[18]

ii

Meanwhile the question of following up the August decisions on Far Eastern strategy by putting some teeth into the almost non-existent defenses of Malaya was under discussion in London. Despite the unwillingness of the Americans to be drawn on the question of support in the Far East, Churchill was determined not to allow any more than a bare minimum of Britain's scanty military resources to be locked up in a theater that was currently inactive and, if his hopes were realized, might well remain so.

Shortly after the Chiefs of Staff had presented their Far Eastern appreciation, they produced a paper on the reinforcement of garrisons abroad. Priority inevitably went to the Middle East. The Air Ministry indicated that its long-term policy was to equip and maintain squadrons in the Far East with American aircraft. In view of shipping problems, this doubtless seemed a reasonable decision in London, but it meant that the most "modern" fighter aircraft the Far East would receive prior to December 1941 would be the Brewster Buffalo, a plane inferior to the Japanese Navy Zero in every respect.[19] It was the question of army rather than air reinforcements, however, and, in particular, the use of the growing Indian Army that touched off the first of a series of rows about the Far East between the prime minister and the Chiefs of Staff.

Almost from the moment of taking office, Churchill had pressed for larger contributions by India to the war effort. On May 18 he minuted to the Chiefs of Staff that all the British regulars in India should be brought home, as in 1914, and replaced by territorials (reservists). He raised the same point again on June 2 and four days later told Eden, the secretary of state for war, that India was not doing anything of value to the war effort. A few weeks later he pressed the same complaint upon Leopold Amery, the secretary of state for India and Burma.[20] In his memoirs he explained that his idea of a worthwhile Indian contribution was the immediate appearance of Indian troops in the Middle East.[21] In fact, India had stripped itself at the beginning of the war, sending a divisional headquarters and two brigades to the Middle East, while one brigade went to Malaya.

> The departure of these first three brigades left the Army in India with barely any modern weapons or vehicles, and the prospect of obtaining them was not favourable. The concentration of supply in Great Britain which had been accepted before the war turned the modernization scheme into a phantom, and it was replaced by what amounted to a monthly improvisation. Great Britain was hard pressed to supply herself and could spare nothing for India, while the problem of dollar exchange seriously restricted demands on America.[22]

Nontheless, India undertook to raise two more brigade groups for service overseas during 1940, and the Government of India was better than its word. In the autumn of 1940 a brigade went to the Middle East to bring the Fourth Indian Division up to strength, and a second divisional headquarters (the Fifth under Major General Lewis Heath) and two more brigades went to the Sudan. Two additional brigades stood ready to go overseas, and five infantry divisions and the personnel for an armored division were being raised.[23] The Indian Army faced shortages of everything but manpower, and this was a truly remarkable feat, more so in many respects than the expansion of the British Army. Yet it still did not satisfy the prime minister. On the first of September (the month that would see three brigades leave India for Middle East Command), he refused Amery's request for aircraft and antiaircraft guns and complained again about the paucity of India's contribution to the war effort. There were at the time 78 obsolete aircraft in the whole subcontinent.[24] In his memoirs he commented critically that the Government of India wanted to take a long term view and build up the Indian Army as far as possible on the basis of a greatly expanded Indian munitions industry.[25] How else India could have made the immense contribution it did to the British war effort is hard to see. In fact, in October 1940 India became the center of the Eastern Group Supply Council, which successfully coordinated and expanded production of war materials in British territories east of Suez, thus easing the strain on British resources and shipping.

Winston Churchill's great blind spot was India. His only acquaintance with it came from his few years there as a subaltern in a crack British cavalry regiment forty-five years before. Like many regular British officers, he had a disdain for the Indian Army that was an odd combination of class prejudice — its British officers did not come from the same social background as the officers of "good" British regiments like his own — and historical memories with racial overtones — Indian troops had been disloyal in 1857. His stubborn attempt to defeat the 1935 Government of India Act, a landmark in India's progress towards independence, should not be confused with any affection on his part for India, affection both real and widespread among the British officers of the Indian Army. India and its army were appendages of British power — so, for that matter, was the rest of the Empire and Commonwealth — and Churchill was above all a great British patriot. Fundamentally he neither understood nor trusted the Indian Army. Thus in the same month that he told Amery that India was not pulling its weight, he wrote another minute, this one complaining that Indian brigades being formed were composed entirely of Indian battalions, thus breaking the rule established after the 1857 Mutiny that one of the three battalions in every Indian Army brigade must be British.[26] How else the Indian Army could expand while the number of British units in India shrank, as he insisted they should, he did not say. The complaint characteristically echoes what he had written as a young man, forty-three years before.[27] Now, in the autumn of 1940, he wanted the two Indian divisions already in the Middle East to be joined by the next two brigades now ready in India for overseas service. He also wanted the second Australian division, now ready to go overseas, sent to the Middle East.

The Chiefs of Staff had other ideas. They had wanted an Australian division for Singapore since June and had reiterated this in their Far Eastern appreciation. They had accepted Bond's figure of three divisions as the minimum needed in the current circumstances. This could be reduced to two divisions, they felt, once RAF strength in the Far East reached its target figure of 336 aircraft. (The Air Ministry had quickly pointed out that this was dependent "on the course of operations in the Middle East. Nothing but a limited measure of reequipment was practicable at present" in the Far East.[28]) Thus on September 4, when the Chiefs of Staff presented a paper on "Future Strategy," they proposed an ultimate figure of three divisions for the Far East and seventeen for the Middle East.[29] The Seventh Australian Division and the two Indian brigades would be the first installment in the Far Eastern buildup. Churchill counterattacked vigorously.

Prime Minister to General Ismay   10/ix/40
    1. The prime defence of Singapore is the Fleet. The protective effect of the fleet is exercised to a large extent whether it is on the spot or not. For instance the present Middle Eastern Fleet, which we have just powerfully reinforced, could in a very short time, if ordered, reach Singapore. It could if necessary, fight an action before reaching Singapore, because it would find in that fortress fuel, ammunition and repair facilities. The fact that Japanese had made landings in Malaya and had even begun the siege of the fortress would not deprive a superior relieving fleet of its power. On the contrary, the plight of the besiegers, cut off from home while installing themselves in the swamps and jungle, would be all the more forlorn.
    2. The defence of Singapore must, therefore, be based upon a strong local garrison and the general potentialities of sea power. The idea of trying to defend the Malay peninsula and of holding the whole of Malaya, a large country four hundred by two hundred miles at its widest part cannot be entertained. A single division, however well supplied with signals etc., could make no impression upon such a task. What could a single division do for the defence of a country nearly as large as England?
    3. The danger of a rupture with Japan is no worse than it was . . . . the presence of the United States Fleet in the Pacific must always be a main preoccupation of Japan.

Therefore, he concluded, the Seventh Australian Division ought to go to the Middle East.[30] This fitted in with the Australian desire to see their forces concentrated, and the Seventh Division duly went to the Middle East. The needs of Malaya could be met, Churchill felt, by four Indian battalions and the two British battalions that the War Cabinet had decided in August to evacuate from China. The Chiefs of Staff persisted. They stressed the importance of defending Singapore with land and air forces until a fleet could arrive, which of course had been the point of their Far Eastern appreciation. Churchill was unmoved. Britain could not afford to divert scarce resources to the Far East. War with Japan was by no means inevitable, and, even if it came, Japan was unlikely to attack Singapore with the American fleet poised on the flank of any southward thrust.[31] There the matter stood. A few weeks later, in mid-October, in discussions about the program for army expansion, Churchill successfully insisted upon the target figure for the Middle East being raised from seventeen to twenty-seven divisions.[32] Since the United Kingdom could supply only fifteen of these, it meant that a dozen would have to come from India, Australia, and New Zealand. Thus, at a stroke, the prime minister had established a claim to every division that India was likely to have ready for service overseas in 1941. New Zealand's single division was already committed to the Middle East, as was everything Australia could send. Concentration could scarcely be carried further. Yet when the next two Indian brigades and a divisional headquarters were wrested from the gravitational pull of the Middle East and sent to Malaya, Churchill grumbled to Eden that "the General Staff continue to press for diversions from the Middle East, such as the Seventh Australian Division to be used for garrisoning the Malay peninsula. Now the two Indian Brigades are to be employed in these jungles against a possible war with Japan, and a still more unlikely Japanese siege of Singapore."[33]

The steadily hardening priority for the Middle East that the prime minister was determined to enforce stands out clearly in these exchanges. It is remarkable, however, that in his minute to Ismay of September 10, Churchill virtually repudiated the Far Eastern appreciation that had been formally accepted by the War Cabinet as recently as August 28. The Chiefs of Staff failed to shake him, and, from this point, there were really two strategies for the Far East. The official one was contained in the Chiefs' of Staff paper; Churchill's personal policy consisted of relying on America and hoping for the best. By virtue of his position as minister of defence, dominating both the War Cabinet and its Defence Committee, Churchill was able to enforce his policy by refusing to allocate the resources necessary to implement the official one. It has already been pointed out that the Australians probably did not fully grasp the significance of the changing emphasis in British strategy after 1937. It is scarcely surprising that they failed to grasp this new distinction between official and actual policy for the Far East. Indeed one prominent member of the Malayan Civil Service, writing years later, claimed that there was conscious duplicity.[34] While this is an exaggeration, there is no doubt that the effect of the duality in British policy was very unfortunate. A strong case can be made for Churchill's

priorities. None can be made for his not conveying them more
clearly, except that his doing so would have dampened Australian
enthusiasm for the Middle East.

The prime minister's assessment of Singapore's powers of
resistance is also noteworthy, particularly the use of the word
fortress, which recurs in his minutes. Singapore was not, and was
never intended to be, a *fortress* in the sense normally conveyed by
that word. It was a naval base with defenses against seaborne
attack. It stood on the north shore of Singapore Island. Any
defense against an overland attack had to be made well north of
the Johore Straits, which separate the island from the mainland.
This was all the more necessary since 40 percent of Singapore's
daily water supply depended upon a reservoir on the mainland.
General Dobbie had recognized this fact in 1937 and had prized
money out of the War Office to begin the construction of a line of
defenses in Johore. His successor, General Bond, abandoned the
project, at least partly because of the growing awareness that it
was necessary to defend the entire peninsula both to protect the
new RAF airfields and to keep enemy aircraft out of range of
Singapore. None of this was properly grasped by Churchill, as his
minutes make clear. When at length, on January 19, 1942, he discovered that Singapore was not a *fortress* like Verdun or Plevna
(to cite the examples he himself used), the shock was one of the
most unpleasant he sustained during the war: "I cannot understand how it was I did not know this . . . . none of my professional
advisers . . . . pointed it out to me . . . . I ought to have known. My
advisers ought to have known and I ought to have been told, and
I ought to have asked . . . . the possibility of Singapore having no
landward defences no more entered my mind than that of a
battleship being launched without a bottom."[35] It is easier here
to agree with Churchill's complaint. He made his conception of
Singapore's defenses plain in his minute of September 10, 1940,
yet the Chiefs of Staff failed to disabuse him of his error. Why?
They may have assumed that he knew the true state of affairs,
although the tenor of his minutes about Singapore should have
convinced them otherwise. Perhaps they themselves were not
clear on this point. One interesting clue lies in the habit of
referring to defended ports as *fortresses* in prewar Committee
of Imperial Defence discussions. This legacy of Victorian military
terminology may have had significant consequences.[36] As late as
1959 Lord Ismay, Churchill's wartime chief of staff, who had
joined the Committee of Imperial Defence in 1936, wrote in the

draft of his memoirs, "I had always visualized that Singapore was a self-contained fortress.[37] This particular question may never be clarified entirely, but it is clear that from September 1940 on, the Chiefs of Staff ought to have been in no doubt about Churchill's assumptions regarding the Singapore *fortress*.

It is also interesting to note Churchill's assessment of Japan. They were as a rule cautious and disinclined to take chances, he declared in the September 10 minute. He told the Admiralty five days later that the naval intelligence division overrated the strength and efficiency of the Japanese.[38] The gambler's throw that erased the American fleet on which Churchill relied so heavily, and over-ran all of the Western Pacific and Southeast Asia in five months was beyond his — and everyone else's — imaginings. It may have been easier to assume that the Japanese would not gamble because their strength and efficiency were more often underestimated than overvalued. The Naval Intelligence Division may have accurately assessed the quality of the Japanese Navy, but other intelligence assessments were far off the mark. Both these factors may have been due to the control of the intelligence-gathering machinery in the Far East (known as the Far East Combined Bureau, or FECB) by the Royal Navy, which weighted it heavily toward collecting the type of information desired by the Admiralty.[39] Moreover, the Far East Combined Bureau, and the intelligence departments in London, drew much of their information on the Japanese army and air forces from observers in China, who consistently under-rated them. The degree to which this was carried often approached the ludicrous, particularly in the Far East. Obviously an element of racial feeling entered into the Western evaluation of Japan. European military powers had dominated Asia for more than a century. Japan, it is true, had beaten Russia in 1904-05, but it was still possible in 1940 to believe that the western fighting man had an inherent qualitative advantage over any Asian opponent. Compounding misinformation and disdain about Japanese military ability was the sheer lack of understanding in the West of how the Japanese government really worked, or of the internal dynamics of Japanese society, particularly the changes after 1930 that led to the ascendancy of those elements which, in Western eyes, were "irrational" — something that Churchill subsequently admitted in his memoirs. "To understand a society such as the Japanese requires exceptional time and effort," and not only were people with the requisite knowledge rare, but "specialists on Japan in Britain and the U.S. and Malaya, etc., in 1941 were sometimes suspect as being faintly 'pro Japanese,' " one British authority on Japan later wrote.[40]   Thus delusions about Japan were born and nourished, and delusions about the Japanese, like those about the strength of Singapore, helped Churchill and his advisers to follow more easily a path to which brute facts were, in any case, constraining them.

Finally there is the interesting question of why the Australians, with their quite natural concern over the defense of the Far East, should nevertheless still have preferred to see their Seventh Division go to the Middle East. The Australians wanted their forces concentrated, which, of course, made administration easier. More importantly, Australia, jealous of its independence and equality within the Commonwealth, assumed that a concentrated block of troops in one theater would give them correspondingly strengthened voice in the formulation of policy. Time would show this to be a delusion. The Australian government also had repeated British assurances on the subject of defense against Japan, reiterated most recently in Churchill's August 11 letter to Menzies. Moreover, there was no conscription for overseas service in Australia, only for home defense. The men in the Australian Imperial Force, as the Australian units serving overseas were known, were all volunteers. An Australian official historian has described their motivation in this way: "War had been declared; Britain was in danger; Australians should be there. To probably a majority of Australians the problem was seen in terms as simple as that."[41]   If these ardent volunteers were kept as a garrison force in a theater that everyone hoped would remain inactive, morale would slump and the flow of volunteers would dwindle. Everything conspired to push the Australians into the Middle East.

iii

Two days after the War Cabinet's Defence Committee accepted the target figure of twenty-seven divisions for the Middle East, Air Chief Marshal Sir Robert Brooke-Popham was appointed commander-in-chief, Far East. This was the result of both the decision to make the RAF primarily responsible for Far Eastern defense, and a parallel series of events in Malaya that pointed to the need for a superior coordinating authority there.

Malaya was, administratively, extremely complex — a legacy of the piecemeal growth of British power there. First, there were the

Straits Settlements (the islands of Singapore and Penang, together with Province Wellesley and Malacca on the mainland, and the tiny island of Labuan off the coast of Borneo hundreds of miles away), which were a Crown Colony directly administered by a governor and British officials. Then there were the Malay States, nine in number. These were not Crown Colonies but protected states that had entered into special treaty relationships with the British government. Their rulers enjoyed a very considerable degree of autonomy in internal affairs, especially in matters concerning land tenure, the Muslim religion, and Malay custom. British residents were attached to each ruler, but it would be a mistake to regard the rulers as puppets manipulated by their residents. They enjoyed a very real degree of independence, guaranteed by treaty and respected by the British administrators with whom they dealt. Four of these states (Perak, Selangor, Negri Sembilan and Pahang) were grouped together as the Federated Malay States, and a federal government, located at Kuala Lumpur, administered matters of common concern. The remaining five (Kedah, Perlis, Trengganu, Kelantan, and Johore) were the Unfederated Malay States. Thus there were a grand total of eleven separate administrations in Malaya. Only two things tied them all together. First, the British administrative personnel in all eleven were drawn from the Malayan Civil Service. The M.C.S., although not as well known as the Indian Civil Service, nevertheless regarded itself as an elite service, administering a very rich country with a complex, multi-racial social structure. "We were proud of it — we preened ourselves on being M.C.S.," one of them later recalled. The second link was at the administrative summit. The governor and commander-in-chief of the Straits Settlements was also high commissioner for both the Federated and Unfederated Malay States, and the point of contact between the various Malayan administrations and the Colonial Office.

In 1939 that point of contact was Sir Shenton Thomas, who had entered the colonial service in 1909, and, after a quarter of a century in Africa, had been appointed to Singapore in 1934. While not a strong or dynamic man, he was amiable, handled the social side of his duties very well, and was a competent peacetime administrator — although, oddly, he never mastered enough Malay to dispense with an interpreter. When the war broke out he was not far from his sixtieth birthday and due to retire in the near future. But Malaya's vital role in financing the British war effort led the Colonial Office to decide that a change at the top was not desirable. On

October 18, 1939, the colonial secretary, Malcolm MacDonald, cabled Sir Shenton:

I have complete confidence in your handling of the many difficult political and economic problems which arise and are likely to arise in that part of the world, and I should like to avoid having to make a change in the command while the war is on.

"I assume in any case you will require to take some leave next year," he added, mindful of Sir Shenton's long tropical service in the pre-air-conditioned era and the ill health he had experienced a year before. The governor immediately agreed to stay on, but he asked for home leave beginning in April, 1940, to which the Colonial Office readily assented.[42]

On the outbreak of war in 1939 there had come into existence at Singapore a War Committee, chaired by the governor, which was, in theory, the highest local authority in defense matters. Although he bore the courtesy title of *commander-in-chief*, another legacy, like the use of the word *fortress*, of the Victorian era, it had no practical significance. The other members of the committee were Bond, Babington, and, when the headquarters of the Royal Navy's China Squadron was transferred from Hong Kong to Singapore, the commander-in-chief, China (Admiral Sir Percy Noble). The secretary for defence, Mr. C. A. Vlieland of the Malayan Civil Service, a capable but rather difficult person, was also a member. Vlieland's position was less grand than his title might imply. He was, in fact, merely the coordinator of the defense activities of all civil government departments. The War Committee had no agenda, kept no minutes, and was purely consultative. Nonetheless, it could have served as a useful clearing house for information and a focus for the discussion and resolution of problems. Instead, largely because of personality clashes, it hampered rather than improved Malaya's preparedness for war. Nothing in Sir Shenton's previous experience had prepared him to preside over such a committee. His own orders from London were clear — production of rubber and tin was paramount. On the military issue of how best to defend Malaya, he found himself caught between the mutual antagonisms of the other committee members. Bond, a taciturn and reserved individual, although conscious of the necessity of holding all of Malaya, quite rightly felt that he did not have the necessary resources and simply refused to consider defending the new RAF airfields on the east coast; Babington aggressively maintained that, since only air power could defend Malaya, it was the army's duty to protect his airfields. He resented Bond's refusal to use his one brigade of disposable troops for this task, and was, moreover, personally jealous of the GOC, who enjoyed both a seat on the Governor's Legislative Council and the courtesy of being addressed as "Your Excellency," privileges that were also Victorian legacies and had not been extended to the senior local representative of the *parvenu* RAF. Vlieland sided with Babington, and the two carried the governor with them.

Then in April 1940 Sir Shenton went on leave. Since he has been heavily criticized for this, it should be pointed out that periodic "long leave" was standard practice in the colonial service to give officials a rest from climates that were often trying and unhealthy, and in Sir Shenton's case the Colonial Office had encouraged him to come home. Travel was by ship, which meant that a considerable amount of time was consumed in getting to and from England. Finally the war looked very different when he left Malaya than it did two months later. As seen above, Sir Shenton did his best while he was in England to impress upon the Colonial Office and the military planners the need for a clear-cut defense policy in the Far East. Should he have hurried back to Malaya after the fall of France had revolutionized Britain's strategic position? At least one of his principal subordinates believed that his lengthy absence subsequently weakened his position by making him appear more complacent about the situation than he in fact was.[43]

Certainly in his absence the atmosphere on the Singapore War Committee deteriorated further. S. W. Jones, the O.A.G., less impressed by Vlieland and Babington, did his best to hold the balance even. He could not, of course, mitigate either the personal antagonisms or the lack of resources that lay behind the Bond-Babington quarrel. Noble, who was considerably senior to either Bond or Babington, held aloof from the squabble, but came slowly to the conclusion that something had to be done. When he returned to England upon his relief by Vice Admiral Sir Geoffrey Layton, Noble sought an interview with the secretary of state for the colonies, Lord Lloyd, and told him that Bond and Babington ought to be replaced by younger men who could work together. He also urged that a senior officer should be appointed commander-in-chief, to control both the civil and the military authorities in the Far East. It is not entirely clear what effect

Noble's representations had on subsequent events, as the timing of his interview with Lloyd is uncertain.[44] Meanwhile, Noble's successor, Layton, had come to a similar conclusion. Early in October he cabled the Admiralty to suggest that Babington, whom he considered most at fault, ought to be recalled.[45] Information about the bickering in the War Committee at Singapore was also reaching London through other channels.[46] The necessity of ending this, and of ensuring that a coordinated defense plan existed to make the best use of the limited resources likely to be available for the Far East, both pointed to the need for an overriding authority. The Government of India would have liked to wield this (since they were providing most of the troops), but the Chiefs of Staff rejected the idea of putting the entire Indian Ocean area under New Delhi in early September, and India was told to keep its eye on the North-West Frontier. The traditional fear of a Russian invasion of India seems a bit misplaced in the circumstances, but giving India control of Far Eastern defense might have distracted the Indian Army from the Middle East. In fact, the acceptance of the doctrine that air power alone could defend Malaya in the existing circumstances virtually decided that the new commander must be a senior officer of that service. The Chiefs of Staff approved a unified command in the Far East on October 12, and they recommended Air Chief Marshal Sir Robert Brooke-Popham for the post. He was duly appointed on October 17.[47]

Brooke-Popham, "Brookham" to his colleagues, was tall, charming, distinguished in appearance, and sixty-two years old. Like all the first generation of senior RAF officers, he had begun his career in one of the older services, in his case the army. He was one of the first army officers to learn to fly (a year before the future Lord Trenchard). Already too old for combat flying in the First World War, he filled a series of increasingly responsible staff positions in the army's Royal Flying Corps and passed into the RAF when that service was created in April 1918 by the merger of the RFC and the Royal Naval Air Service. After the war he rose steadily. He was commandant of the RAF Staff College and the first officer of his service to become commandant of the Imperial Defence College. His last prewar appointment was as air officer commanding in the Middle East, with his headquarters in Egypt. He retired in 1937 and spent the next two years in Kenya as governor. When war came he was recalled to active duty and employed on missions to Canada and South Africa in connection with the establishment of RAF training programs. Why was this elderly officer, with an impeccable career but inevitably somewhat out of touch with recent developments, chosen for a task of great complexity and importance? His own papers offer no clue. A number of possibilities do, however, suggest themselves. He certainly had the necessary seniority. October 1940, with the battle of Britain barely over and the bomber offensive against Germany just beginning, was not a time when the RAF wanted to post one of its experienced senior officers, or one of its rising stars, to an inactive theater.[48] Furthermore, Brooke-Popham had certain assets. He would have to work in close association with the colonial administrations in the Far East and would be much involved in liaison with the dominions and allies, actual or potential, like the Dutch and Americans. His experience as a colonial governor, and his recent missions to Canada and South Africa, did constitute reasonable credentials for this part of his task. One is left with the impression, however, that, as in the case of the Colonial Office decision to extend Sir Shenton Thomas's tour, busy men in London with urgent problems clamoring for their attention, took the easy course and chose a man who was unobjectionable for a post in an area that, however important, was not a matter of pressing concern at the moment.

Brooke-Popham received his directive on October 22.[49] While his selection was not as odd as has often been alleged, there is little that can be said in defense of the instructions he received. He was made responsible for the "operational control" (defined as general direction rather than detailed control) and "general direction of training" of all British land and air forces in the immense arc that stretched from Burma through Malaya to Hong Kong, and of all RAF squadrons stationed anywhere in the Indian Ocean or Bay of Bengal "for ocean reconnaissance in those areas." To do all this, and maintain contact with Australia, New Zealand, and all the colonial governments and British diplomatic representatives in the area, he was given a staff of seven and told "no expansion of this staff is contemplated." He received no authority over naval forces in the area of his command, and therefore none over the FECB, his principal source of intelligence. Unlike the War Office and the Air Ministry, the Admiralty exercised operational as well as administrative control over its units, and Sir Dudley Pound was a strong centralizer. This probably accounts for the decision to withhold the navy (which was, in any case, not much in evidence) from Brooke-Popham's control. It was more important that he was given no control over the civil administration. Even the army and

RAF units he did command remained responsible in matters of administration and finance to London, and for their "normal day-to-day functions," to their respective local commanders. Brooke-Popham was, in fact, not a commander-in-chief in any but the most nominal sense. He was a high-level coordinator and liaison officer, with limited powers and inadequate staff. The verdict of one historian, "he simply became an extra cog in an already cumbersome machine," seems eminently fair.[50] The sheer size of his command was enough to defeat a much younger man with wider powers and a larger staff. Brooke-Popham was to spend a large part of his time traveling, simply to keep in touch with the forces he commanded and the authorities with whom he was to maintain liaison. He was later to complain, with some justice, "the Far East is usually examined on a small-scale map, so people are rather apt to get a false idea of distances."[51] In particular, it was an error to saddle Brooke-Popham, who could have used all his time and energy on Malaya alone, with responsibility for Burma.[52] But the worst mistake was in failing to give him effective control over all the forces and authorities in the area for which he was made responsible.

In defense of the drafters of Brooke-Popham's directive, it should be noted that placing the Malayan civil authorities under him would have been very difficult and, even in the military sphere, his appointment was virtually unprecedented. The integrated theater commands that functioned so successfully later in the war were developed by a process of trial and error, and Brooke-Popham's ill-fated command can be seen as the first step in that process. But perhaps the best explanation for Brooke-Popham's muddled instructions was that the Far East was simply one of many problems pressing for attention in October 1940, and far from the most urgent, however grim the long-range outlook there might be.

Sir Robert's directive was supplemented by a number of briefings before he left London. He met with Major General H. L. Ismay, an old acquaintance from the days when Ismay had been a student at the RAF Staff College during Brooke-Popham's tour as commandant. Currently chief of staff to Churchill in the latter's capacity as minister of defence and the prime minister's representative on the Chiefs of Staff committee, as well as head of the military wing of the war cabinet secretariat, Ismay was one of the most important, and best informed, men in London. It may be that he was instructed to see that Brooke-Popham understood Churchill's point of view on the Far East, for there is no evidence that the prime minister found the time to see Brooke-Popham before his departure. Nor did the new commander-in-chief meet the Chiefs of Staff collectively for a discussion of Far Eastern defense, although he saw two of them, Sir Cyril Newall (who was about to be succeeded as chief of the air staff by Air Chief Marshal Sir Charles Portal) and Sir John Dill, the chief of the imperial general staff, individually.[53] It was a curiously offhand way to treat the man who had been chosen to carry the burden of defending the part of the Empire that still, in theory at least, ranked second only to the United Kingdom itself. He was certainly left in no doubt about the priority the Middle East enjoyed over his theater. He was also told about the charged atmosphere that prevailed in the War Committee at Singapore and assured that "any change which he may recommend in the civil organization will be made at once. Our Far East position is so serious . . . that the risk of possible injustice to an individual should be accepted."[54] The day before he left London, he wrote a letter to the Chiefs of Staff in which he made it clear that he understood all too well Singapore's real place in Britain's global strategy: "I fully realise that at the present time the requirements of Singapore must come a bad third to those of the British Isles and of the Middle East."[55] As a result of the failure to brief him adequately, however, there were important question marks in Brooke-Popham's mind when, on October 28, he left Plymouth on the first leg of his long journey to Singapore. "Was this figure [336 aircraft as the minimum needed in the Far East] really based on a calculation of what was required or merely on what was likely to be available. I never knew."[56]

Two events that bracketed Brooke-Popham's departure illuminate both the dimensions of his problem and the unlikelihood of a satisfactory solution. When the Chiefs of Staff cabled their Far Eastern appreciation to Singapore, they instructed the local commanders to prepare a detailed tactical appreciation based on it, and also on the assumption that the Japanese had complete control of Indochina and had established a base at Camranh Bay (a situation that would, in fact, arise in July 1941). On the day before Brooke-Popham's appointment, Layton, Bond, and Babington sent in their answer. Since a Japanese attack on Malaya would be mounted from Indochina and Thailand, it pointed out, a Japanese entry into Thailand ought to be countered by a British move into the narrow Kra Isthmus just north of the border between Malaya and Thailand. Apart from any troops needed for this operation (and Bond, in April, had estimated that it would require two divisions), the defense of Malaya required 566 aircraft in 31 squadrons. When that number was reached, the garrison could be reduced, but only marginally, from 27 battalions (three divisions) to 23 (roughly two and a half), which was 5 more than the Chiefs of Staff contemplated leaving in Malaya when their own figure of 336 aircraft was reached. The local commanders also wanted three battalions over and above the number needed for Malaya, in order to garrison British Borneo, and three flotillas of motor torpedo boats to keep Japanese from taking advantage of Malaya's long, exposed coastline. At the end of the month, with Brooke-Popham on his way out, a conference was held at Singapore between the local commanders and representatives of Australia, New Zealand, India, and Burma, with an American observer present. The "Singapore Defence Conference" raised the demands already made by adding a fighter squadron for Rangoon and seven more battalions for Burma. The total now stood at 582 aircraft (32 squadrons totaling 878 planes when the Immediate Reserve is figured in) and a *minimum* of 33 battalions (three and two-thirds divisions) plus coastal craft, tank, and antitank units.[57]

The likelihood of these demands being met is illustrated by an incident that took place in London after Brooke-Popham left. In 1938 two Air Ministry scientists, Dr. D. R. Pye and Mr. H. E. Wimperis, had recommended the installation of a radar station at Singapore. At the end of 1940 the Air Ministry finally decided to establish one there. In December the assistant chief of the air staff (Radio), Air Vice Marshal Joubert de la Ferté, briefed a young Flight Lieutenant who had spent an eventful six months since June working on the vital task of keeping radar stations operational in the face of German bombing. He was being posted to the Far East, Joubert told him. The area was virtually defenseless, but would shortly be receiving some poor quality American fighters. That, said the air vice marshal, was better than nothing.[58]

Notes to Chapter 4

1. W. L. Blythe, C.M.G., letter to the author, January 1974. At the time of the conversation, Mr. Blythe was deputy controller of Chinese labor, stationed Kuala Lumpur. The Colonial Secretary was, under the governor, the administrative head of a British Colony.

2. Public Record Office (PRO), CAB 66, WP (40) 249, July 4, 1940. General Sir John Dill had replaced Ironside as CIGS on May 27, 1940.

3. E. L. Woodward, *British Foreign Policy in the Second World War,* 5 vols. (London: H.M.S.O., 1970-),2:91.

4. PRO, CAB 65, WM (40) 214, July 29, 1940.

5. Ibid.

6. Covering note by Bridges, August 5, 1940, to COS (40) 592, in PRO, PREM 3, 156/2; Sir Shenton Thomas, "Comments on the Draft History of the War Against Japan," October 1954, pars. 54, 163, Thomas Papers, Rhodes House Library, Oxford.

7. PRO, CAB 66, WP (40) 308, August 7, 1940.

8. The COS appreciation, WP (40) 302, is paraphrased in J. R. M. Butler, ed., *History of the Second World War*, "Campaigns" series, S. W. Kirby et al., *The War Against Japan*, vol. 1, *The Loss of Singapore*, (London: H.M.S.O., 1957), pp. 33-36.

9. PRO, CAB 66, WP (40) 308, August 7, 1940.

10. PRO, CAB 65, WM (40) 222, August 8, 1940.

11. Winston S. Churchill, *The Second World War*, vol. 2, *Their Finest Hour* (Boston: Houghton Mifflin, 1949), pp. 435-37. Italics mine.

12. Woodward, *British Foreign Policy*, 2: 92-100.

13. Butler, ed., *History of the Second World War*, "Grand Strategy" series, vol. 2 J. R. M. Butler, *Grand Strategy (September 1939-June 1941)* (London: H.M.S.O., 1957), pp. 243, 341.

14. Churchill, *Their Finest Hour,* pp. 403-4.

15. Butler, *Grand Strategy II*, pp. 341-43.

16. Woodward, *British Foreign Policy*, 2:112-13; Churchill's message to Roosevelt is in Churchill, *Their Finest Hour,* pp. 497-98.

17. Churchill, *Their Finest Hour*, p. 675.

18. Woodward, *British Foreign Policy*, 2:114.

19. Kirby et al., *The Loss of Singapore* pp. 506-10, gives performance figures that show that the Zero was superior not only to the Buffalo, but also in most respects to the Hurricane, MK II, which arrived in the Far East in January 1942. The Hurricane's only advantage was a slight edge in maneuverability at heights above 10,000 feet. Only the Spitfire was clearly superior to the Zero, and the first Spitfires did not appear in India until November 1943.

20. Churchill, *Their Finest Hour*, pp. 55, 139-40, 163-64, 173.

21. Ibid., p. 172.

22. C. MacKenzie, *Eastern Epic,* vol. 1, *Defence* (London: Chatto & Windus, 1951), p. 10. It must always be remembered that it was not only material that had to come from England. Despite the beginnings of "Indianization," the officer corps of the Indian Army was still overwhelmingly British, and a steady supply of good junior officers was needed as it expanded. Since the British Army was also growing, this was not always easy to arrange. Even when they were available, their comparative ignorance of Indian languages handicapped them and affected the quality of newly raised units. Technical specialists, like mechanics and radio operators, also had to be drawn from a Britain where they were in short supply.

23. Ibid., p. 13.

24. Churchill, *Their Finest Hour*, p. 666.

25. Ibid., p. 172.

26. Ibid., p. 671. See also Winston S. Churchill, *The Second World War,* vol. 3, *The Grand Aliance* (Boston: © 1950, by Houghton Mifflin Company. Reprinted by permission of the publisher Houghton Mifflin Company.), p. 480.

27. Dispatch to the London *Daily Telegraph*, September 9, 1897, in F. Woods, ed.,

Young Winston's Wars: 1897-1900 (New York: Viking Press, 1972) p. 14.

28. Butler, *Grand Strategy II*, p. 351.

29. Ibid., pp. 343, 347.

30. Churchill, *Their Finest Hour*, pp. 667-68.

31. This discussion is paraphrased in Butler, *Grand Strategy II*, pp. 338-39.

32. Ibid., pp. 347-49.

33. Churchill, *Their Finest Hour*, pp. 499-500.

34. C. A. Vlieland, "Disaster in the Far East 1941-1942", Typescript deposited in the Liddell Hart Centre for Military Archives, King's College, London (referred to hereafter as Military Archive Center). Mr. Vlieland summarized his argument in the *Daily Telegraph*, February 15, 1967.

35. Winston S. Churchill, *The Second World War*, vol. 4, *The Hinge of Fate* (Boston: Houghton Mifflin, 1950), p. 49.

36. Lt. Gen. Sir Ian Jacob, GBE, who joined the CID in 1938 and subsequently served on the staff of the War Cabinet 1939-46, made this point in conversation with the author, October 31, 1973.

37. Ismay Papers, I/14/69, Military Archive Center. King's College, London. On this Sir Ian Jacob, to whom the draft was submitted, commented to Ismay, "Had you really? I never had." Ismay Papers, January 24, 1959, The sentence does not appear in Ismay's published memoirs: *The Memoirs of General Lord Ismay* (New York: Viking Press, 1960).

38. Churchill, *Their Finest Hour*, pp. 667-68.

39. Brooke-Popham (Commander-in-Chief, Far East) to Sir A. Street, January 15, 1941, Brooke-Popham Papers (BPP), vi/1/2, Military Archive Center, King's College, London. Street was the permanent under-secretary at the Air Ministry.

40. S. W. Kirby, *Singapore: The Chain of Disaster*. (New York: Macmillan, 1971), pp. 74-75; Churchill, *The Grand Alliance*, pp. 580-86, 603. The quotation is from a letter from Professor Richard Storry of St. Anthony's College, Oxford, to the author, June 26, 1975.

41. *Australian in the War of 1939-45:* Series I (Army), vol. 1, G. Long, *To Benghazi* (Canberra: Australian War Memorial, 1952), p. 38.

42. MacDonald to Thomas, October 18, 1939; Thomas to MacDonald, October 31, 1939; MacDonald to Thomas, November 27, 1939, Thomas Papers, in the possession of Professor Hugh Thomas. Interview with Mr. A. H. P. Humphrey, C.M.G., June 1, 1975. Mr. Humphrey was Sir Shenton's private secretary, 1936-38.

43. A. H. Dickinson to H. Fairbairn, June 8, 1967, Bryson Collection, Royal Commonwealth Society Library, London. Dickinson was inspector general of the Straits Settlements Police, and chief security officer, Malaya, 1939-42. Mr. H. P. Bryson, in an interview with the author, June 12, 1975, reflected that Sir Shenton's early return from leave might have made an impression on Malaya's civilian population. Mr. Bryson was clerk to the Executive and Legislative Councils in Singapore at the time.

44. Kirby, *Singapore: The Chain of Disaster*, pp. 38-42, 52-53. Kirby claims that Noble's *demarche* came to nothing, since Lloyd was taken fatally ill immediately afterwards. The dates, however, do not fit. Noble was relieved by Layton on September 12, 1940. Lloyd's death did not occur until February 4, 1941, by which time the decisions on the command structure in the Far East had been made. The papers on which Kirby based on this book are in the Military Archive Centre but are not open for inspection at present.

45. Ibid., pp. 53-54. Layton's papers are in the British Museum but will not be opened until the 1990s.

46. See, for example, a memorandum of October 23, 1940, entitled "Malaya: Defence Organisation" in BPP v/4/2.

47. Butler, *Grand Strategy II*, pp. 488-90; Kirby et al., *The Loss of Singapore*, p. 55.

48. In an interview with the author on January 14, 1971, Lt. Gen. Sir Ian Jacob remarked that there was a general reluctance in the services to see first-class officers posted away to the Far East.

49. The directive is printed in Kirby et al., *The Loss of Singapore*, pp. 484-85.

50. Kirby, *Singapore: The Chain of Disaster*, pp. 56-57.

51. Air Chief Marshal Sir Robert Brooke-Popham, "Operations in the Far East, from 17th October 1940 to 27th December 1941," *Supplement to the London Gazette*, January 22, 1948, par. 6 (cited hereafter as Brooke-Popham, *Dispatch*).

52. S. W. Kirby et al., *The War Against Japan*, vol. 2, *India's Most Dangerous Hour* (London: H.M.S.O., 1959), pp. 6-7.

53. Brooke-Popham, *Dispatch*, par. 1.

54. Brooke-Popham, *Dispatch*, pars. 3-4, "Malaya: Defence Organisation," October 23, 1940, BPP v/4/2.

55. Brooke-Popham to the Chiefs of Staff, October 26, 1940, BPP v/1/1.

56. "Comments on the first draft of **The War Against Japan, Volume I**," April 16, 1953, BPP v/9/34. It is odd that Brooke-Popham did not, or was not able to, clarify this in his meeting with Newall. Even odder is the fact that Newall sent a copy of the Chiefs' of Staff Far Eastern appreciation chasing after Brooke-Popham by sea. The ship carrying it fell victim to a U-boat, which recovered the documents. They were found in Berlin in 1945 with a German translation and this covering note: "This is a document of first importance and should be sent to N.[aval] A.[ttache] Tokyo." Squadron-Leader G. H. Wiles to Brooke-Popham, July 15, 1948, BPP v/9/30. This episode is not discussed in the official history.

57. Kirby, *Singapore: The Chain of Disaster*, pp. 50, 58-60. The RAF in the Middle East had only 20 squadrons by the end of 1940. The difference between what the local commanders in the Far East thought necessary and what they had at the same date amounted to 534 aircraft, 19 battalions, plus 144 heavy and 168 light antiaircraft guns and 138 searchlights (not to mention tanks, coastal craft, radar equipment, etc.), Butler, *Grand Strategy II*, p. 492.

58. Squadron-Leader T. C. Carter, "History of R.D.F. Organisation in the Far East 1941-1942," Carter Papers, TCC 2/1, Imperial War Museum, London; interview with Dr. Carter, November 27, 1973.

5
FINAL DECISIONS:
November 1940-July 1941

i

In February 1941 Sir Robert Brooke-Popham wrote Ismay a worried letter. "Out here we suffer from lack of information regarding the lessons that have been learnt from operations in EUROPE and elsewhere, . . . the ignorance of modern war conditions out here does worry me . . . ."[1] At about the same time Flight Lieutenant T. C. Carter, a radar specialist, reached Singapore. It was, he later recalled, "another world" from the bombed and besieged Britain he had left, a world where traditional routines were unchanged. Carter was told that his first duty was to leave his card with the senior RAF officers.[2]

Despite repeated pleas from Brooke-Popham, nothing was done by London during these months to galvanize, or modernize, the defenses of the Far East, and it is this that makes critical the period between his arrival in the Far East and Churchill's departure for the Atlantic meeting with Roosevelt the following August. It took at least three months before a decision to reinforce the Far East took the concrete form of troops, equipment, or aircraft actually present in Malaya, while an even longer period was necessary before they were completely operational there. The decisions taken, or enforced by events, during this period meant that not only would there be no fleet when Japan struck in the Far East, but the chosen surrogate for naval power, the RAF, would be well short of its full establishment, equipped with obsolescent aircraft, and manned by inexperienced personnel. The calamitous nature of the British defeat in the Far East was ensured during these months.

The pivot of events was the course of the war in the Middle East. On October 28 Italy invaded Greece, to whose aid the British were pledged. This, and the German penetration of the Balkans, led to a widening and deepening of Britain's Mediterranean commitment. The RAF in the Middle East had to meet new demands — by the end of the year four of its squadrons had moved from Egypt to Greece and had to be replaced. This led to calls for more aircraft for the Middle East, further reducing the likelihood that the Far East would get its quota. Furthermore, the mounting evidence of a German thrust to the southeast reactivated British hopes of drawing Turkey in and forming a Balkan front. The Chiefs of Staff produced a paper on November 1 in which they discussed the possibility of a German move through the Balkans, aimed at Turkey and the oil fields of the Middle East. From this point on, Turkey was never far from their thoughts or the prime minister's. The fact that Germany was ultimately defeated without Turkish help should not obscure the fact that the policy of trying to engage Turkish support was reasonable enough in 1940-41. Without any major allies the British could not hope to defeat Germany except by a lengthy process of attrition. The Chiefs of Staff had pointed this out as early as May 19, 1940. Indeed, a strategy of containment and attrition was what the British and French governments had agreed upon at the beginning of the war. In such a process it made good sense to interpose any obstacle that could be conjured into existence between Germany and the natural resources of the Balkans. Beyond all this lay the oil of Iraq and Persia, vital to Britain and, the British believed, to oil-poor Germany — if the Germans could lay hands upon it. In December 1940 the War Cabinet had received a report pointing out that in the campaign against German oil supplies, "British control of the Eastern Mediterranean remains of paramount importance." The Turks were rightly cautious and demanded a great deal, and this became yet another argument for building up the forces in the Middle East. They would form a pool from which could be drawn the aircraft, specialist units, and ultimately divisions that would be necessary if Turkey could be brought in. The Chiefs of Staff wanted to build up large enough forces in the Middle East by the spring of 1941 to assist Turkey, or at worst to deny Syria and Iraq to the Germans. It was agreed that the Turks could be told that there would be fifteen divisions in the Middle East by the summer of 1941 and twenty-five by the end of the year.[3] While this discussion was going on, Anthony Eden, the secretary of state for war, arrived back in

London from a tour of the Middle East. He brought with him the
news that Sir Archibald Wavell, the commander-in-chief, Middle
East, was planning a counterattack against the Italian forces that
had crossed the Egyptian frontier in September. Churchill was
delighted: "I purred like six cats." Amid those events (with the
blitz and the worsening situation in the Atlantic also taking up
time and energy) the Far East had to be content with what attention
could be spared from more pressing matters.

When he left England, Brooke-Popham left behind a memorandum for the Chiefs of Staff, calling their attention to the
immense discrepancies between what was agreed to be necessary in
the Far East and what was actually available. Only forty-eight of
the aircraft there could be considered modern, and none of these
were fighters. On the same day they considered this, the Chiefs of
Staff had before them a draft written by Rear Admiral R. M.
Bellairs, the head of the British staff mission that was preparing
to leave for the long-sought talks with the United States. "On the
one hand we shall say to the Americans that the whole safety of
the Far East depends on the arrival of their battle fleet at Singapore. On the other hand we shall also have to say that we have not
placed a garrison in Malaya sufficiently powerful to ensure that
the base at Singapore will be intact when the United States fleet
arrives . . . . " This was a bit too strong for the Chiefs of Staff,
who commented that "there was no real grounds for the view that
our garrison in Malaya was not sufficiently strong to ensure that
the base in Singapore would be intact when the American fleet
arrived," a remarkable statement in view of their recommendations
in August. Bellairs was told to put a more cheerful face on his
memorandum.[4] Nevertheless, the service departments were asked
for a program of reinforcements for Malaya spread over the next
six months. This request was given added point by the arrival on
November 9 of both the tactical appreciation produced by the
local commanders in the Far East and the report of the Singapore
Defence Conference.

After digesting the full extent of the demands from the Far
East, the Chiefs of Staff sent a memorandum to Churchill on the
19th, pointing out the immense deficiencies that existed there
and suggesting some modest steps toward meeting them. Another
Australian division (the Eighth) was preparing for overseas service,
and they suggested that at least a brigade of this division might go
to Malaya until May 1941, when it could proceed to the Middle
East upon relief by a newly formed Indian division. There was no

other way, they pointed out, of providing troops for Malaya. None could be sent from the United Kingdom due to shipping shortages (and, they might have added, the priority accorded the Middle East). India would have nothing more available until the spring. The Chiefs of Staff also wanted to make at least a beginning on the buildup of RAF strength in the Far East. They proposed the immediate dispatch of two squadrons of fighters and a squadron each of torpedo bombers and flying boats. They also recommended that aircraft be sent out to reequip two of the bomber squadrons already in the Far East, which, although classed as having "modern" aircraft, were flying Blenheim Mark I's, already obsolescent in the West, and further handicapped in Far Eastern conditions by their lack of range. This memorandum also called attention to the need to have the forces necessary to hold Malaya on the spot when war broke out, since subsequent reinforcement might be impossible. This was reasonable enough in the light of admitted British weakness in the Eastern seas, but it forecast a grim position in the Far East if war came, even if all the promised reinforcements were sent.[5]

The Australian government, alarmed by the weaknesses revealed at the Singapore Defence Conference, and by the discrepancy between the prewar assurances about Singapore's powers of resistance and the emerging facts, offered to waive temporarily its objections to the dispersal of its forces and allow a brigade group of the Eighth Division to proceed to Malaya as soon as shipping could be found. The Dutch government-in-exile was also unhappy with the ambiguity of its situation in the Far East, and on November 20 asked again for assurances of support if attacked by Japan.

Early in December the Dominions Office drafted a placatory telegram to Australia listing the air reinforcements that were to be sent. At the same time R. A. Butler, parliamentary undersecretary at the Foreign Office, sent a memorandum to the Chiefs of Staff suggesting that the Mediterranean Fleet's brilliant carrier strike against the Italian battle fleet at Taranto (November 11, 1940) might have eased the naval situation sufficiently for a battle cruiser and a carrier to be detached to Ceylon.[6] All this might have been the prelude to the dispatch of reinforcements to the Far East, but these proposals ran into the unswerving determination of the prime minister that Britain's limited resources should be devoted to fighting the present enemy. "A strict defensive in the Far East and the acceptance of its consequences is . . . our policy," he told the first sea lord in late November. He

made haste to bring the Dominions Office into line, minuting to
Caldecote in mid-December that he wished to avoid dispersal of
forces, and that concentration on the Middle East rather than an
increase in the garrison of Malaya and Singapore was his aim.[7]
Churchill would not, therefore, accept the Chiefs' of Staff memorandum of November 19. The telegram that eventually went to
Australia (on December 23) was drafted by him and struck as
optimistic a note as possible, while standing firm on the main
issue.

The danger of Japan going to war with the British Empire is in
my opinion definitely less than it was in June after the collapse
of France . . . . The naval and military successes in the Mediterranean and our growing advantage there by land, sea, and air
will not be lost upon Japan. It is quite impossible for our fleet
to leave the Mediterranean at the present juncture without
throwing away irretrievably all that has been gained there and
all the prospects of the future . . . . We must try to bear our
Eastern anxieties patiently and doggedly . . . . it always being
understood that if Australia is seriously threatened by invasion,
we should not hesitate to compromise or sacrifice the Mediterranean position for the sake of our kith and kin . . . . Apart
from the Mediterranean, the naval strain has considerably
increased. . . . we are at the fullest naval strain I have seen in
this or the former war. The only way in which a naval squadron
could be found for Singapore would be by ruining the Mediterranean position. This I am sure you would not wish us to do
unless or until the Japanese danger becomes far more menacing
than at present. I am also persuaded that if Japan should enter
the war, the United States will come in on our side, which will
put the naval boot very much on the other leg, and be a de-
liverance from many perils.
     As regards air reinforcements for Malaya, . . . with the ever-
changing situation it is difficult to commit ourselves to the
precise number of aircraft which we can make available for
Singapore, and we certainly could not spare the flying boats to
lie about idle there on the remote chance of a Japanese attack
when they ought to play their part in the deadly struggle on
the north-western approaches. Broadly speaking, our policy is
to build up as large as possible a fleet, army, and air force in
the Middle East, and keep this in a fluid condition, either to
prosecute war in Libya, Greece, and presently Thrace, or reinforce Singapore should the Japanese attitude change for the
worse. In this way dispersion of force will be avoided.[8]

Meanwhile the Chiefs of Staff were considering the huge requisitions put in by the commanders in the Far East. They agreed that 582 aircraft was "ideal," but they stood by their own figure of 336 as the maximum likely to be available in 1941 — thus providing a clue as to how the figure was arrived at in the first place. They qualified their commitment even to this figure by noting that it was subject to the war situation as a whole and the supply of aircraft. They did accept the local estimate of the garrison required for Malaya and felt that it could be met by June 1941, although they could not provide seven battalions for Burma (which enjoyed an even lower priority than Malaya). The best that could be done for Burma was to ask the much-tried India Command to earmark a brigade group for it. Nor did the Chiefs of Staff see how they could provide the field artillery, antiaircraft guns, or tanks, all of which the local commanders wanted. Turning to the Dutch request for some indication of the help they could expect, the Chiefs of Staff advised that the question be left open. The Dutch, like the Australians, would have to wait. These recommendations, which amounted to nothing more than a reconfirmation of the policy adopted by the War Cabinet in August, again ran into the prime minister's reluctance to tie up anything beyond the barest minimum in the Far East. "I do not remember to have given my approval to these very large diversions of force. On the contrary, if my minutes are collected they will be seen to have an opposite tendency. The political situation in the Far East does not seem to require, and the strength of our Air Force by no means warrants, the maintenance of such large forces in the Far East at this time."[9]   The Chiefs of Staff replied to this in a note that showed that in some respects they were very close to the prime minister's position.

> The program for the air force expansion in the Far East is a long-term target and we do not propose to make any appreciable diversion of our war effort to the Far East at the present time . . . . In view of the importance of Singapore, our obligation towards Australia and New Zealand, who are pressing very strongly for an increase in our defensive strength in the Far East, and the possible reluctance of the United States of America to despatch a Fleet to Singapore, it seems desireable in our view, to make a small start in our long-term program . . . . There are, at present, no fighters in the Far East and we, therefore, propose to start forming two fighter squadrons there.[10]

Like Churchill, the Chiefs of Staff were content with token forces for the Far East. Unlike him, they wanted the tokens in place. On the immediate issue they got their way, although Churchill, with his remarkable capacity for keeping track of details, monitored exactly what went to Malaya. On January 27, 1941, Colonel R. M. Hollis of his staff gave him a note on air reinforcements for the Far East. Eight experienced pilots and 340 RAF ground staff had sailed on January 7, and six officers and 180 airmen were being sent to establish the radar coverage for Singapore. The remainder of the pilots would come from the Flying Training Schools in Australia and New Zealand, and their Buffalo aircraft direct from the United States.[11] This meant that the inadequate Buffalo would be flown by pilots most of whom had no operational experience at all.

The prime minister's minute scrutiny of the trickle of reinforcements for the Far East was directly connected with the rapidly developing situation in the Balkans and the Middle East. Wavell's offensive against the Italians had been stunningly successful, but, as early as January 6, Churchill had warned the Chiefs of Staff that the need to sustain Greece against the imminent German threat would have to take priority over the desert campaign. As London's attention swung to the Balkans, Turkey loomed steadily larger. Early in 1941 "the thoughts of the Prime Minister and Chiefs of Staff were turning more and more to Turkey, regarded now as the pivot of our Balkan strategy." On January 29 the commanders in the Middle East were warned to be ready to send three fighter and seven bomber squadrons plus 100 antiaircraft guns to Turkey, to be followed by "considerable land forces."[12] Here was an additional reason for pouring all available resources into the Middle East, which automatically depressed Malaya's real priority even further.

Meanwhile Eden (who had succeeded Halifax as foreign secretary in December) had been pursuing desultory conversations with the Dutch over the question of British assistance. Into this leisurely diplomatic saraband a note of urgency was suddenly interjected when the Joint Intelligence Committee reported on February 2 that a Japanese move against the Netherlands East Indies was imminent. Ten hectic days followed. The Chiefs of Staff were adamant that nothing could be done to stop the Japanese, except the application of diplomatic pressure, which would depend largely on the United States. Pound acutely summed up the dilemma that they faced:

In the Pacific the economical method of controlling it is to have one battlefleet at Singapore which is strong enough to fight the Japanese fleet under the relative conditions of strength we should like. Also, unfortunately the Americans will not place their Pacific Fleet at Singapore.

They still balked, therefore, at treating a Japanese attack on the Dutch as a *casus belli* or guaranteeing the Netherlands East Indies. However, they did agree to accelerate the provision of a second Indian division for Malaya. India was also to be asked to provide a brigade for Burma as soon as possible and to send four battalions of the Indian State Forces to Malaya for internal security. To do all this, they instructed India to give Malaya temporary priority over the Middle East.[13]

The crisis faded as quickly as it had arisen, and so did the limelight that was briefly accorded the Far East. It is an instructive little episode, however. No one had any doubt about the critical importance of the Netherlands East Indies strategically or economically (it produced 41 percent of the world's rubber, 9 percent of its tin, and 7.81 million tons of crude oil in 1941). Nonetheless, already chary of their ability to produce an effective defense of Britain's own position in the area, the Chiefs of Staff would not commit themselves to the Dutch — unless they were assured of American backing. The only response they could suggest in the face of possibly imminent hostilities with Japan was to ask India to stretch its forces still further by producing more troops for Malaya, and half the forces for Burma that the local commanders felt necessary. On the key question of air reinforcements, they had nothing to offer. Yet, as the official historian has observed, "this disquieting fortnight might . . . have served as a warning of how quickly a crisis could occur in . . . relations with Japan."[14] On the 20th, however, the War Cabinet gratefully set aside, once more, the question of a guarantee for the Dutch, and the Far East sank again into relative obscurity.

It was easy to forget about the Far East because the question of aid to Greece had become pressing. On January 29 the Greek prime minister had told the head of the British military mission in Athens that an appeal for British assistance would be made when German troops, currently building up in Rumania, crossed the Bulgarian frontier. The War Office estimated that this could happen by February 17. On February 10-11, it was decided that Wavell's victorious advance against the tattered remnants of the Italian army in

Libya would be halted at Benghazi, which had fallen on February 6. A defensive flank would be created there, and all available forces concentrated in Egypt ready to move to Greece. On the 12th Eden set out for the Middle East with the chief of the imperial general staff, Sir John Dill, on a mission whose principal object was to supervise the execution of the plan to aid Greece. With all this in prospect, it is not very surprising that the "February crisis" caused only a momentary, irritated, turning of heads in the direction of the Far East. Yet in January 1941 the Japanese Army had set up at Taipei the "Taiwan Army Research Section" to study the problems of tropical warfare. Included in its brief were Malaya and the Netherlands East Indies, as well as the Philippines and Burma.[15]

Far Eastern concerns were again forced into the forefront by the arrival in London at the end of February of the Australian prime minister, Robert G. Menzies. He had come to discuss the weaknesses in the defense of the area that were revealed at the Singapore Defence Conference the preceding autumn. There was also the long-standing Australian feeling that they were not properly consulted on major issues of war policy by the United Kingdom. The Australians were always the principal complainants on this head. South Africa, not in any case immediately threatened by anybody, had a direct personal link to Churchill through its prime minister, General Jan Smuts. Canada's principal interests were served by the policy that Britain was following, and New Zealand, small and remote, tended to follow London's lead almost automatically. The Australians, ever conscious of Japan looming to the north and of their dependence on British sea power, as well as of their own large contribution to the Imperial war effort in the Middle East, felt neglected and dangerously exposed. The British answer was that the United Kingdom was the backbone of the Empire's war effort, and its War Cabinet, viewing the entire problem, must decide the main outlines of strategy. The machinery for consultation, via the dominion high commissioners in London and the Dominions Office, supplemented on occasion by visits from dominion leaders or special envoys, seemed adequate to Churchill. And, short of physically moving the dominion governments to London, it is hard to see what other machinery could have been devised that would not have led to a great loss in efficiency. The pace of war had increased since the days of Lloyd George's Imperial War Cabinet of 1917-18. The constitutional position of the dominions had also changed greatly, and no dominion government could have agreed to be automatically bound by a representative in London. The real weakness in the system was psychological, not technical or constitutional. Australian amour propre was disturbed by the apparently high-handed way in which London disposed of their troops. Churchill never found quite the right touch in dealing with Australia, perhaps because he did not try very hard. Then there was the divergence of priorities — Britain's vital interests centered in Europe, Australia's in Asia and the Pacific. Resources were scanty, and to the British it seemed only reasonable to concentrate the Empire's strength in warding off a stroke at its heart. The Australians feared that in so doing their own heart might be exposed to a mortal thrust. Finally, there was the fact, unpalatable to Australia, that it was bound to be somebody's junior partner. Australian ability to affect global strategy did not markedly improve with their transfer from the British to the American sphere in early 1942. These divergent views on Australia's place in the war had already led to a clash between Churchill and Menzies at the time of the abortive Dakar expedition (September 1940).[16]   Events in Greece, Crete, and North Africa in the spring and summer of 1941 were to lead to further clashes, and it is against this background of growing mutual irritation that the British and Australian governments argued about the defense of the Far East.

When Menzies first discussed the matter with the Chiefs of Staff and the service ministers on February 27, he stressed the lack of fighter aircraft at Singapore and was told by Sir Charles Portal, the chief of the air staff, that forty-eight Brewster Buffaloes from the United States ought to have reached Singapore. The Buffalo, Portal assured Menzies, was a match for any Japanese fighter. In defense of the Air Ministry's decision to rely on untested American aircraft in the Far East, it was pointed out to Menzies that it would take three months to get Hurricanes out from the United Kingdom. The Australian prime minister was also told that, without American support, a war with Japan would be a bleak proposition. After this Menzies was caught up in the discussion of support for Greece and did not get back to the question of Far Eastern defense for a month. He was present at the March 7 meeting of the War Cabinet, which decided to commit troops to Greece. There was considerable unhappiness in both Australia and New Zealand about both the decision itself and the way it had been taken. The bulk of the force that was going to Greece came from the Pacific dominions. Neither felt that adequate consultation had taken place before the final decision, and, despite Menzies's presence in London, the Australian government cabled that "repetition of such an action might have far-reaching and unpleasant imperial repercussions."[17] This, and the following two months of military disaster, were the background to further discussions both between Menzies and the Chiefs of Staff, and, within Churchill's own circle, on the defense of the Far East. On March 27 Menzies gave the Chiefs of Staff a memorandum on the subject. It was the day of the Belgrade coup which wrenched Yugoslavia briefly out of the German orbit and raised the hope that an effective Balkan front might actually be brought into being. Nearly a fortnight passed before Menzies got an answer. He had asked what was being done to implement the recommendations of the Singapore Defence Conference. He had also pointed out that the Australian government was convinced that "in the absence of a main fleet in the Far East the forces and equipment available for the defence of Malaya were totally inadequate to meet a major attack by Japan." He then posed a very embarrassing question: what would happen if Japan entered the war while America remained neutral?

The facts were that the British government had virtually rejected the recommendations of the Singapore Defence Conference, that Malaya was inadequately defended, and that American abstension would completely destroy what scant hope remained of defending the Far East. It would not do to put the matter quite so bluntly, however — not with an Australian division committed to the highly precarious Greek venture. The Chiefs of Staff prepared a reply for Menzies and sent it to Churchill with a covering note that put their position very clearly. On the critical question of RAF strength, they pointed out that "expansion will be steady, though it is not to be expected that the full number will be achieved until next year. In the meantime the Chiefs of Staff do not think the situation is critical as suggested by the Australian government." Thus they blandly retreated from the promise that a first-line strength of 336 aircraft would be built up in the Far East in 1941, covering their retirement with hope for the best — the basic ingredient in Far Eastern defense policy for twenty years. The naval position was equally bleak. "The Naval Staff have not found it possible to enter into any definite commitment as to the number of capital ships other than RENOWN which they could send to the Indian Ocean in the hypothesis [Japanese intervention coupled with American neutrality] put forward by Mr. Menzies."[18] Almost simultaneously with the production of this note, the Chiefs of Staff gave their approval to a plan put forward by Brooke-Popham for a preemptive attack, to be christened "Matador," on the Kra

Isthmus in southern Thailand if a Japanese attack on Malaya seemed imminent. Foreseeing that this would give the commanders in the Far East a lever with which to try to extract more forces, Churchill immediately riposted: "I view with great reluctance the continued diversion of troops, aircraft and supplies to a theatre which it is improbable will be lighted up unless we are heavily beaten elsewhere."[19]   The Chiefs of Staff had made it plain enough that they were not contemplating any such diversions, but, with the Balkans and the Middle East boiling over, the prime minister was taking no chances.

The Defence Committee formally approved on April 9 the paper that the Chiefs of Staff had prepared for Menzies. Its themes were all very familiar. Resources were urgently needed in the Mediterranean, and it would be a mistake to send them to Malaya instead. If war with Japan broke out, the Admiralty intended to send a battlecruiser and a carrier to the Indian Ocean, but they could make no further promises: everything would depend on the situation in the Atlantic and the Mediterranean. The promise to sacrifice the latter, however, in the event of a serious threat to Australia, still held good. Their response to Menzies's hypothetical case of American neutrality in an Anglo-Japanese war was to deny its validity and to point out that Australia's security had been immensely improved by America's steadily growing commitment to Britain (the Lend-Lease bill had become law on March 11). In an appendix to the paper, the naval staff spelled out exactly how strained British sea power was as a result of nearly a year of single-handed struggle. The Royal Navy's margin in capital ships was four: the two battleships of the "Nelson" class (launched in 1925), the battlecruiser *Renown* (launched in 1916 and twice modernized), and one battleship of the "R" class (laid down before the First World War and never modernized). The question of sending any of these east was highly problematic. "A situation might arise where no heavy ships other than *Renown* could be spared for the Far East . . . . It has always been reckoned that to be certain of getting to Singapore we should have to send a force of nine capital ships, i.e., one less than the force with which the Japanese might oppose us. It is most unlikely that we shall have any such force available in which case our fleet would have to go to Ceylon in the first instance, and then see how the situation stood."[20] Inexorably, "main fleet to Singapore" had dwindled to "*Renown* to Ceylon" — probably. This could have done little to ease the anxieties that Menzies felt about his country's security.

Events in the eastern Mediterranean had meanwhile presented the British commanders there with problems of bewildering complexity. On March 30 Rommel, who had reached North Africa about the time that Wavell's offensive was halted in the interest of aid to Greece, launched his first desert offensive. Wavell's gains were quickly erased. The British were hustled back over the Egyptian frontier within ten days and Tobruk, with its largely Australian garrison, was isolated and besieged. A pro-Axis revolt broke out in Iraq on April 3, and, to extinguish it, London appealed to India on April 8 for troops. The response was, as usual, immediate. The Twentieth Indian Infantry Brigade, already loaded at Karachi for Malaya, was sent to Basra at the head of the Persian Gulf, where it arrived on April 18. It was followed by the other two brigades of the Tenth Indian Division. On April 21 the decision was taken to evacuate British forces from Greece. On the 24th the Australian government asked what plans London had for carrying on the war if Suez and Gibraltar were lost and Japan simultaneously moved south. It was not, perhaps, the most tactful question to put in the circumstances.

General Sir Archibald Wavell was one of the finest commanders Britain produced in the course of the war. Not the least of his remarkable qualities was his habit of putting down on paper the "Worst Possible Case" that could face him. On May 24, 1940, he had written such an appreciation, code-named "Mongoose," and sent it to Sir John Dill. It dealt with two possibilities, the "Worse Possible Case," the collapse of France, and ("Worse Case Still") the fall of the British Isles, and then went on to sketch out how he would carry on in the face of either. As April of 1941 proved itself indeed to be the cruelest month, Dill reread "Mongoose," showed it to Major General John Kennedy, the director of military operations at the War Office, and then asked Wavell if the scheme still held good. Wavell replied that he was revising it to bring it up to date and that a copy would be sent home by liaison officer.[21] On top of this came the Australian request for an appreciation based on their own idea of the "Worst Possible Case." All this was in Kennedy's mind when he motored down from London to the prime minister's official country residence, Chequers, on Sunday evening, April 27. Churchill was in the throes of preparing a major speech, a process that always produced a heightened state of nervous irritability in him. Aimed largely at the United States, it contained the phrase "nothing that can happen in the East is comparable with what is happening in the West," and it ended with lines taken from the Victorian poet A. H. Clough:

And not by eastern windows only,
When daylight comes, comes in the light;
In front the sun climbs slow, how slowly!
But westward, look, the land is bright.

After Churchill had delivered the broadcast speech from his study, the party, which included Ismay, David Margesson (secretary of state for war) and General Sir Alan Brooke (commander in chief, Home Forces), went in to dinner. Kennedy, asked by the prime minister for his views on the situation in Egypt, replied that the Germans might be able to bring such a weight of attack to bear on Egypt, from the north and west, that it could not be held. The prime minister erupted: "Wavell has 400,000 men. If they lose Egypt, blood will flow. I will have firing parties to shoot the generals." Struggling against the tide of Churchill's wrath, Kennedy tried to explain that it was only prudent for a commander to prepare for the worst case as well as the best. Then he let slip that Wavell had a plan for carrying on if he was forced out of Egypt. "This comes as a flash of lightning to me," the Prime Minister declared. "I have never heard such ideas. War is a contest of wills. It is pure defeatism to speak as you have done." Churchill returned to the charge several times later in the evening, repeating to Kennedy that in war it was determination that counted.[22] Brooke, who had been a silent observer of the whole scene, recorded in his diary that Kennedy's disclosure that Wavell had contingency plans for the evacuation of Egypt had so enraged the prime minister that it took the rest of the party to calm him down.[23]

Kennedy's passage at arms with the prime minister was to have momentous consequences. The following day Kennedy reported to Dill what had happened. The CIGS, who had borne the brunt of Churchill's anger on numerous occasions, was at first inclined to treat the whole episode lightly. Already, however, a minute was on its way to him from the prime minister: "The Director of Military Operations yesterday spoke of plans which had been prepared in certain eventualities for the evacuation of Egypt. Let me see these plans, and any material bearing upon them."[24] Later on this eventful Monday, Dill had to attend a War Cabinet meeting at which Menzies was present. Following up his government's request, Menzies pressed for some indication of British plans in the event of disaster in the Middle East. Upon his return to the War Office the CIGS told Kennedy "you have raised a terrific storm, and it was made worse by Menzies . . . . " The storm burst later in the day with the arrival of a directive from Churchill written, according to Kennedy, without the advice of the Chiefs of Staff and as a direct result of the previous evening's stormy session at Chequers.[25] It was one of the most strident documents penned by the prime minister in the course of the war. The first paragraph was critical for the future of British strategy in the Far East.

> Japan is unlikely to enter the war unless the Germans make a successful invasion of Great Britain, and even a major disaster like the loss of the Middle East would not necessarily make her come in, because the liberation of the British Mediterranean Fleet which might be expected and also any troops evacuated from the Middle East to Singapore would not weaken the British war-making strength in Malaya. It is very unlikely, moreover, that Japan will enter the war either if the United States have come in, or if Japan thinks they would come in, consequent on a Japanese declaration of war. Finally it may be taken as almost certain that the entry of Japan into the war would be followed by the immediate entry of the United States on our side.
>
> These conditions are to be accepted by the Service Departments as a guide for all plans and actions. Should they cease to hold good, it will be the responsibility of Ministers to notify the Service Staffs in good time.

After thus making it clear that Australian anxieties would not deflect him, Churchill went to the heart of the matter: "The loss of Egypt and the Middle East would be a disaster of the first magnitude to Great Britain. . . . It is to be impressed on all ranks, especially the highest, that the life and honour of Great Britain depends upon the successful defence of Egypt . . . . No surrenders by officers and men will be considered tolerable unless at least 50 percent casualties are sustained by the Unit or force in question . . . . The Army of the Nile is to fight with no thought of retreat or withdrawal." Finally he dismissed, once and for all, the buildup in the Far East. "There is no need at the present time to make any further dispositions for the defence of Malaya and Singapore, beyond those modest arrangements which are in progress, until or unless conditions set out in the paragraph 1 are modified."[26]

Churchill wrote some years later that the first half of 1941 was the most difficult period of the war.[27] This directive, written with Rommel on the frontier of Egypt, Tobruk besieged, and the evacuation from Greece in full swing, bears witness to the tremendous pressure under which the prime minister was laboring. Endeavoring to coax a steadily increasing measure of support out of the Americans, Churchill was faced with a mounting toll of military setbacks.

It was not yet certain what Hitler's principal aim for 1941 might be, but even if it was Russia, and a mounting number of indications pointed to this, there was no certainty that the Soviet Union would not be smashed as rapidly as France had been. German troops would then be free to redeploy against England — or the Middle East. In any case Churchill meant to bend every effort to holding the Middle East, and the opening paragraph of his directive must be read as a deck-clearing preamble, rather than a well-thought-out position. Even if the shipping had been available to move British troops from the Middle East to Malaya (and, at a later point in the directive, Churchill correctly pointed out that there was nothing like enough to remove even a fraction of the men and stores in the Middle East), it would have been a disorganized remnant if his hope of units sustaining 50 percent casualties had been realized in more than a few instances. The same was true of his remarks about the liberation of the Mediterranean Fleet if Egypt fell. A fortnight previously he had sent a directive to the Chiefs of Staff in which he had called for the interruption of Rommel's supplies at almost any cost, declaring that the blocking of Tripoli was worth a battleship as well as heavy losses in cruisers and destroyers.[28] This document is dated less than a week after the Chiefs of Staff had produced their paper for Menzies demonstrating how finely balanced British naval strength was. The pressure put upon Cunningham to use his irreplaceable and hard-driven ships to cut Rommel's supply route bordered on the reckless. It is clear that what Churchill really counted on in relation to Japan was the American deterrent.

The Mediterranean, as has been described, was becoming a major strategic preoccupation even before the war began. Hope of enlisting Turkish aid and constructing a Balkan Front, the region's vital oil supplies, and, finally, the fact that they were there and could fight the Axis there and nowhere else after June 1940, all strengthened the grip of the Middle East on the shapers of British war policy, while the intensifying struggle there added its own pressures. The Far East, still theoretically second in priority to the United Kingdom, was increasingly in the position of a residuary legatee. The Middle East finally triumphed completely in April 1941. Even the very modest program of defense through air power that was agreed upon the previous summer was tacitly abandoned in the desperate attempt to hang on in the Middle East. The date when the fate of Singapore was finally sealed was April 28, 1941.

Kennedy, the unwitting cause of all this (along with Menzies and his government), put the match to another powder train before the day was over. He wrote an analysis of Churchill's directive for Dill, which correctly pointed out the serious flaws in the prime minister's opening paragraph.

It takes some three months to dispatch and install additional defences in Malaya. It seems to me inconceivable that Ministers are gifted with such foresight . . . as to the possible action of Japan. Moreover, even if they give us three months' notice, it might well be impossible to make available the reinforcements required for Malaya if in the meantime we implement the in-structions given in the remainder of the directive as to the dis-patch of our resources to other destinations.[29]

Before this had time to explode, there was another interlude with Menzies. On April 29 the Chiefs of Staff replied to the request for an examination of Australia's "Worst Possible Case" by simply refusing to accept the hypothesis and pointing out that the war could only be won in and around the United Kingdom, and then only if the necessary resources were not dispersed overseas. This may have been meant as much for their own prime minister as for Menzies. If so Churchill was unabashed. At a Defence Committee meeting that same day Churchill simply restated the position he had developed in his directive of the 28th: Japan would await a success-ful German invasion of the United Kingdom before entering the war. Moreover, they would not move if they thought the United States would come in against them, and it was certain that America would declare war if Japan attacked Britain. This, as will be seen, was a considerable overstatement on the basis of current American attitudes. Menzies did not push the matter further, however.[30] It is not surprising, though, that he returned to Australia dissatisfied with the organization that shaped policy in London, and especially with Churchill's extensive personal powers. It was abundantly clear that the British would not budge on their refusal to make "hypo-thetical" commitments about the Far East, and equally clear who constituted in this case "the British." Menzies's proposed remedy was for the War Cabinet to take in permanent dominion representa-tives and become an Imperial War Cabinet on the 1917-18 model. This was turned down by both Churchill and Canada. Australian irritation with Britain remained, however, and grew sharper over the summer, until it exploded in December.

Having dismissed the Australians for the time being, Churchill could continue to pursue his argument with the Chiefs of Staff, but principally with Dill, about the degree to which British resources were being absorbed by the Middle East. Primed by Kennedy, Dill sent Churchill a long memorandum on May 6, in which he argued that "the loss of Egypt would be a calamity . . . but it would not end the war. A successful invasion alone spells our final defeat . . . . Egypt is not even second in order of priority, for it has been an accepted principle in our strategy that in the last resort the security of Singapore comes before the security of Egypt. Yet the defences of Singapore are still considerably below standard."[31] Dill's fear that the invasion danger was not past, sharpened by Kennedy's concern for the security of both the United Kingdom and the Far East, put the CIGS on a collision course with the prime minister. The next day Churchill received the collective reply of the Chiefs of Staff to his directive. They defended Wavell's contingency planning for the "Worst Possible Case" and poured cold water on the prime minister's passionate commitment to holding Egypt: ". . . we submit that it is an overstatement . . . . Surely our life continues as long as we are not successfully invaded, and do not lose the Battle of the Atlantic." They also repeated Kennedy's warning about the assumptions laid down in the prime minister's opening paragraph. "We wish to emphasise that, when dealing with the Far East, 'good time' means at least three months, since that is the minimum period within which reinforcements and equipment could reach Malaya."[32] Churchill did not reply directly to this, but a week later he wrote to Dill.

> I gather you would be prepared to face the loss of Egypt and the Nile Valley, together with the surrender or ruin of the army of half a million we have concentrated there, rather than lose Singapore. I do not take that view, nor do I think the alternative is likely to present itself. The defence of Singapore is an operation requiring only a very small fraction of the troops required to defend the Nile against the Germans and Italians. I have already given you the political data upon which the military arrangements for the defence of Singapore should be based, namely, that should Japan enter the war the United States will in all probability come in on our side; and in any case Japan would not be likely to besiege Singapore at the outset, as this would be an operation far more dangerous to her and less harmful to us than spreading her cruisers and battle-cruisers on the Eastern trade routes.[33]

But Dill refused to drop the issue. Two days later he was back with another memorandum. He quoted at Churchill his own paper of November 17, 1939, on the strategic primacy of Singapore over the Mediterranean and pointed out that "a small addition at Singapore will make all the difference between running a serious risk and achieving full security," and ended by declaring, "if we reach a point when the maintenance of our position in Egypt would endanger either the United Kingdom or Singapore, we should hold fast to th latter, even if this meant the loss of Egypt. This is my considered opionion . . . ." For good measure he added that "it is . . . in line with your own ideas as expressed in your memorandum of 17 November 1939."[34]   At this point, with the German attack on Crete looming, the exchange of memoranda ceased. Churchill had not budged; if anything, the argument had hardened his commitment to the Middle East. He had pledged himself to give prior warning — which the Chiefs of Staff had defined as three months, and Kennedy as an impossibility — of the outbreak of war with Japan. Meanwhile Dill's fears and those of the Australians were brushed aside with assurances that America would prevent a Japanese attack. The argument with Dill had one additional consequence: it undermined the CIGS's position with Churchill.

"I retained the impression that Singapore had priority in his mind over Cairo," Churchill wrote in his memoirs. "For my part I did not believe that anything that could happen in Malaya could amount to a fifth part of the loss of Egypt, the Suez Canal, and the Middle East. I would not tolerate the idea of abandoning the struggle for Egypt, and was resigned to pay whatever forfeits were exacted in Malaya. This view was also shared by my colleagues."[35] In the previous November the prime minister had minuted to the first sea lord that a strict defensive in the Far East was his policy, and that he was prepared to accept the consequences.[36] Whatever else may be said of Churchill's Far Eastern policy, there can be no doubt that he adopted it with his eyes wide open. But this made the clash with Dill, still arguing as he was for the prewar priorities, all the more sharp. "If you will read the minute Dill sent to Winston in May 1941," wrote the faithful Ismay years later, "you will see what I regard as the most extraordinary document that has ever seen the light of day. Put yourself in the P.M.'s place and ask yourself whether you would have much confidence in the strategic advice of a man who had put his signature to that document."[37] It is not necessary to agree with Ismay's assessment to see that it reflects a sharp decline in the prime minister's confidence in Dill. Since becoming CIGS on the first day of the Dunkirk evacuation, Dill had borne much of the burden of the most difficult year in British military history. He was worn down by successive clashes with Churchill (which, in Ismay's opinion, he took too much to heart) and undermined by private tragedy.[38] He remained CIGS until November, when he was succeeded by the infinitely tougher Sir Alan Brooke, but his relations with the prime minister were on the wane.

Events in the Middle East in late May and June left little time for the consideration of other matters in London. The Germans attacked Crete on May 20, and a week later its evacuation was ordered (on the same day the Home Fleet cornered and sank the *Bismarck*). It was carried through only at the cost of appalling losses to Cunningham's fleet. The revolt in Iraq was collapsing, but London was urging on Wavell a campaign to take control of Vichy-dominated Syria. Wavell was simultaneously supervising the preparations for an offensive against Rommel, code-named "Battle-axe," for which the tanks had been rushed to Egypt through the Mediterranean at the insistence of the prime minister. The failure of this operation (June 15-17) upset Churchill greatly.[39] Wavell's stock, like Dill's, had been declining for some time. "Battle-axe" settled his fate. He switched jobs with General Sir Claude J. E. Auchinleck, the commander in chief, India, whose vigorous response to the request for forces to suppress the Iraqi insurrection had favorably impressed the prime minister. It is revealing of Churchill's attitude toward the whole problem of the Far East that he was willing to put in the key Indian military position a man he felt to be temporarily worn out, rather than face the possible embarrassment of having him unemployed in London. He told Dill that he would not have Wavell hanging about in London living in his club. Far better that he should go to India, and, "sitting under the pagoda tree," regain his strength and balance.[40] Within six months Wavell would be trying to cope with a situation even more calamitous than any he had faced in the Middle East.

It is not surprising that a restatement in mid-June of Dill's position by the Future Operations Planning section of the Joint Planning Staff fell on deaf ears. In a paper put before the Defence Committee, they pointed out Britain's military weakness in the Far East. In the Middle East they agreed that the loss of Egypt must be avoided. "No sacrifice is too great to avoid it, except the sacrifice of the United Kingdom, our vital sea communications, *or of Singapore*." The planners stressed that the loss of Singapore to the Japanese would be disastrous, while, if it could be held, a Japanese intervention "should have no decisive affect on the war in the west."[41] Churchill more or less ignored this. He was, as the official historian of British strategy has written, "reluctant to approve as accepted policy proposals based on assumptions which could only be speculative."[42]   He doubtless also realized that, in the face of his other priorities, there was little or nothing he could do about the Far East. At Kennedy's prompting, however, Dill included the planners' priorities in a letter to Auchinleck on June 26, 1941: "You know what the essentials are in our great picture — to hold England, retain a position in the Middle East, maintain a firm hold in Malaya and keep open our sea communications . . . ."[43] Four days before this was written, the entire face of the war had been altered by the German attack on Russia.

"Barbarossa" relieved, at least temporarily, the fear that Germany would attempt an invasion in the summer of 1941, although the possibility remained that a quick victory over Russia (which was widely expected) would leave the *Wehrmacht* free for an autumn attack on England or the Middle East. Much more important, it created a voracious new claimant for British and American supplies. Churchill was told of the beginning of "Barbarossa" when he awoke at 8:00 A.M. on June 22. His only reaction was to order the BBC to be ready to carry a speech at nine that evening.[44]   In that broadcast he stated flatly: "Any man or state who fights against Nazidom will have our aid." On July 7 the prime minister sent his first message to Stalin, whose reply asked for the immediate establishment of a second front. Churchill could only point to the manifold difficulties that made this impossible, but he realized, as he had already told the Admiralty, that if the Russians could only hold out until winter Britain would gain an invaluable respite.[45]   He therefore followed up his long telegram explaining why the British could not land in northern France with another announcing the dispatch of 200 Tomahawk (P-40) fighter aircraft that had just reached the United Kingdom from America.[46]   It was the first installment in what was to become a steadily increasing series of payments to the exigent Soviets. As the summer wore on, not only did British aid to Russia begin to mount, but Franklin Roosevelt began to move slowly toward the dispatch of aid to Russia — aid that, in the first instance at least, could only come out of material previously earmarked for the British. "In order to make this immense diversion and to forgo the growing flood of American aid without crippling our campaign in the Western Desert," Churchill wrote later, "we had to cramp all preparations which prudence urged for the defence of the Malay Peninsula and our Eastern Empire and possessions against the ever growing menace of Japan."[47]   In 1950 Churchill may have believed this, but, as shown above, it was, in fact, the Middle East that decisively "cramped" the defense of the Far East, and did so months before Hitler attacked Russia. What aid to Russia did was absorb what was left over and ensure that there was no improvement in the quality of the defenses in the Far East. Whether there would have been a quantitative improvement, even without the dispatch of aid to Russia, seems very doubtful in view of the prime minister's determination to stint the Middle East for nothing.

The Middle East was certainly not cramped where air power was concerned. In mid-May the Defence Committee agreed that the RAF in the Middle East should have 40 1/2 squadrons by mid-July. To reach this figure, 862 aircraft would have to be moved to the Middle East by that date. In the first half of 1941 the Middle East in fact received 1300 aircraft (including 724 fighters, 421 light bombers, and 108 heavies).[48] There were, by mid-1941, only two fighter squadrons, with 32 Buffaloes, available in Malaya, four squadrons of light bombers, and no heavies. In early July Brooke-Popham was writing to Ismay " . . . I wish I could see more clearly how to adopt Vildebeestes to attain the object of sinking Japanese troopships if they're escorted by cruisers and covered by fighters off carriers . . . ."[49] The ancient Vildebeeste torpedo bombers made even the Buffalo look modern. Yet these museum pieces were a key element in the RAF striking force that was supposed to protect Malaya. The commander in chief, Far East, got his answer, indirectly, from Babington, now back in England, promoted air marshal and commanding the RAF's Technical Training Command. "On the authority of Pugg [sic] Ismay, the fundamental governing factor would seem to be the Prime Minister's conviction that there will be three months warning of any explosion in the Far East."[50] This is a rather garbled version of the Chiefs' of Staff proviso that they be given ninety days warning of a Japanese war, but it is evidence of the lack of urgency about the Far East felt in London as late as mid-summer 1941. Churchill later wrote, "I confess that in my mind the whole Japanese menace lay in a sinister twilight compared with our other needs."[51]

Nevertheless, one step was taken to improve high level coordination in the Far East. In June the British ambassador to China, Sir Archibald Clark-Kerr, had pointed out that the coordination of civil activities at Singapore was not really adequate.

The problem is complicated as the Dominions, Colonies, and India are all concerned as well as the Foreign Office, and

Treasury and a number of other departments. At present coordination is affected in London, but with increasing difficulty of rapid communication detailed co-ordination from that center as in peacetime is already becoming more difficult and may become impossible. Widely dispersed authorities within the area may then be forced to take decisions without guidance, which may not be in conformity with our interest in the area as a whole, or may run directly counter to action being taken elsewhere.[52]

This telegram was largely responsible for a War Cabinet decision to send a mission of inquiry to the Far East. A different chain of events decided that the mission would be entrusted to Alfred Duff Cooper. Duff Cooper had been a prominent antiappeaser, and had shown great political courage in resigning as first lord of the Admiralty at the time of Munich. He was a man of considerable charm but limited administrative ability. Churchill had made him minister of information, where he had been a rather conspicuous failure. In late July he left the Ministry of Information and became chancellor of the Duchy of Lancaster. The mission to the Far East was a convenient way of using Duff Cooper, whose department, as Churchill well knew from his own unhappy tenure of it in 1915, had virtually no duties. He left England at the beginning of August with instructions to report on how coordination in the Far East could be improved. The idea that sent him east was sound, but he himself was to prove a very unfortunate choice. For one thing he knew little or nothing about the Far East and its problems. His previous record did not indicate outstanding administrative talent — indeed, rather the reverse. He was, in fact, a failed minister being politely shuffled offstage. Since Duff Cooper was ambitious, it is not surprising that he treated his mission to the Far East as a chance to redeem his reputation, and he tried to carve out as wide as possible a sphere of activity for himself there. Since his administrative skills did not match his ambition, it is also not surprising that he failed, with unhappy consequences.

By the time that Duff Cooper left, Churchill himself was preparing to leave England for the first time since his last visit to Reynaud thirteen months before. He would travel secretly by battleship to a rendevous at Placentia Bay, Newfoundland, with Franklin Roosevelt. The two men had many reasons for taking the personal and political risks necessary to bring off this meeting, not least the desire of each to assess the other personally. High on the list of matters to be discussed, however, stood the question of Japan. On July 23 the Vichy authorities had bowed to Japanese demands for the use of ports and airfields in southern Indochina. This placed Japan within easy striking distance of Malaya, and it was evident in London that, if Japan continued to move south, disaster stared the British Empire in the face. "It was evident that existing plans for the defence of Malaya had broken down," writes the official historian blandly.[53] It would be more correct to say that events had finally exposed the fact that there were no effective defense plans in the Far East. On July 25 the United States froze Japanese assets in retaliation for the move into southern Indochina, thus effectively cutting off the export of oil to Japan. Britain, the dominions, and the Netherlands East Indies followed suit. The countdown to war in the Far East had begun. The first Australian reaction was to press London to extract some guarantee of support against Japan from the United States.[54] The Chiefs of Staff warned three days later that the Japanese move into southern Indochina and their consequent ability to put pressure on Thailand "has created an overland threat to Malaya against which even the arrival of the fleet would only partially guard." The air force that was supposed to be the first line of defense had reached a total of 80 (mostly obsolescent) aircraft. "In fact, the policy of defence by air power was . . . dead," writes the official historian, for once mincing no words.[55] High time indeed for Churchill to seek from the United States a firm commitment that it would fulfill the role for which he had always cast it in the Pacific — the deterrent to Japanese action, or, in the last resort, the shield against the worst consequences of such action.

Yet, on the very eve of his departure for the Atlantic meeting, Churchill held a conference at Chequers on August 2, which demonstrated that not even the ominous transformation of the Far Eastern situation had affected the magnetic attraction the Middle East exerted on British resources. A new round of talks was about to open with the Turks, and Auchinleck, home for consultations, was told to treat Turkey as second only to the Western Desert in priority. He was to make an immediate offer of a hundred 3.7-inch heavy antiaircraft guns.[56] (Malaya, at the time, had less than half of its approved scale of heavy antiaircraft weapons.) At 1:30 P.M. the next day the prime minister boarded his special train at Wendover, near Chequers, for the first leg of his momentous journey west.

ii

Churchill's search for American support against Japan, which had begun in May 1940, was unceasing. Strategy was hammered out between Churchill and his service advisers, but relations with the United States were always the prime minister's special province, in which neither the War Cabinet nor the Chiefs of Staff interfered. Until the autumn of 1940, however, Churchill had little to show for his persistent wooing of the United States, at least as far as Asia and the Pacific were concerned. Shortly after the German attack in the West, a significant portion of the United States Fleet, then on maneuvers in Hawaiian waters, was ordered to remain at Pearl Harbor instead of returning to its west-coast bases. When Churchill appealed to Roosevelt on May 15, 1940, for aid in keeping Japan quiet, the president had pointed to this action. For some months this was all the comfort the British got in the Pacific. On July 2 Roosevelt signed an act that allowed him to prohibit the export of anything deemed essential to national defense. He used these powers to embargo the sale abroad of both aviation gasoline (on July 26) and scrap iron and steel (on September 24). In both cases the weight of the State Department had been thrown into the scales in favor of moderation in the use of embargoes, lest they goad rather than restrain Japan. As has been seen, the Roosevelt administration refused to be drawn when the question of closing, and later reopening, the Burma Road arose. An inquiry from the Navy Department in October about the facilities that could be made available at Singapore was treated by Churchill as very important, but it came to nothing. No American squadron came to Singapore to mark the reopening of the Burma Road in October. America was represented at the Singapore Defence Conference that same month, but only by the naval attaché to Thailand who was present as an observer. Undaunted, the Chiefs of Staff on November 8 pressed Lothian, who was home for consultations, to discuss with the president sending that part of the United States Fleet then at Pearl Harbor to Singapore.[57]

Three days before Lothian met the Chiefs of Staff, Franklin Roosevelt had been reelected for an unprecedented third term. The momentum of Anglo-American contacts thereafter began to increase perceptibly. In particular, the military conversations that the British had long wanted rapidly took shape. On November 12 Admiral Harold Stark, the chief of naval operations, addressed a memorandum to Roosevelt, in which he urged the president to approve formal staff talks with the British. In London, as shown above, the British, in anticipation of such talks, were preparing their positions carefully (and being as optimistic as possible about the strength of Singapore). On November 30, the prime minister's birthday, the British learned that the president had finally approved staff conversations in Washington. Eight days later Churchill sent Roosevelt a long letter that he subsequently described as one of the most significant documents of the war.[58] In the course of a frank and wide-ranging survey of Britain's prospects for 1941, the prime minister told the president that " . . . in the Far East . . . it seems clear that Japan is thrusting southward through Indo-China to Saigon and other naval and air bases, thus bringing them within a comparatively short distance of Singapore and the Dutch East Indies . . . . *We have today no forces in the Far East capable of dealing with this situation should it develop.*"[59] This was a much franker exposition than the one Churchill was to send a fortnight later to Menzies.[60] The prime minister made no specific proposals to Roosevelt about the Far East; but on December 15, when the Chiefs of Staff met with the British delegates to the staff talks, they emphasized the importance of holding Singapore as the key to the protection of Western interests in East Asia. They added that the movement of much of the United States Fleet from Hawaii to Singapore, where it would cover the Netherlands East Indies and block any southward thrust by Japan, was the most important contribution that America could make to security in the Far East. The Defence Committee subsequently approved these instructions, but added that in all matters concerning the Pacific, "deference" must be shown to American views. "We should not ask the Americans to come and defend Singapore, Australia and India, but rather offer them the use of Singapore if they require it."[61] The British delegation sailed early in January on the new battleship *King George V*, which also carried Lord Halifax, the new British ambassador to Washington. When they reached the United States, in civilian clothes and listed as technical advisors to the British Purchasing Commission, they plunged at once into intensive discussions with American staff officers. By the end of March these talks produced the agreement known as ABC-1, the "Germany first" policy that was the fundamental Anglo-American strategic document of the war.

There was little relief for Britain's Eastern concerns in ABC-1, but this was secondary to American agreement with British strategic priorities: Europe was the vital area and Germany and Italy must therefore be dealt with first. Then the Anglo-American alliance could settle with Japan, if that country meanwhile entered the war. Agreement on this fundamental proposition was more easily attained because, in the West, British and American perceptions of their respective vital interests coincided to a considerable degree. In his memorandum for the president, Admiral Stark had urged a concentration of effort in the West and the avoidance of war with Japan. Roosevelt himself, on January 16, 1941, told General George Marshall, the army chief of staff, that in the event of war the United States would make its main effort in the West while standing on the defensive against Japan. The bulk of the United States Fleet would remain at Pearl Harbor. Only the miniscule Asiatic Fleet, based on Manila, would be given the discretion to withdraw to Singapore.

ABC-1, therefore, contained nothing substantial about the Far East. It was agreed that Anglo-American strategy there would be defensive. The United States agreed to exchange liaison officers with Australia and New Zealand and to take part in a conference at Singapore on Far Eastern defense, to which the Dutch would also be invited. This was a poor substitute for the sight of American battleships dropping anchor in the Johore Straits, but it is hard to believe that the British were terribly surprised. The United States had added another to the series of "unneutral acts" that had begun in the summer of 1940, and that Churchill valued so highly. The fundamental British strategic concept for the prosecution of the war had been accepted by the Americans. For the moment that was enough.

The British had in any case been pressing their quest for a Far Eastern guarantee through different, and more exalted, channels. On January 9, 1941, Harry Hopkins arrived in London as Roosevelt's personal emissary. In his first meeting with Churchill, he was left in no doubt about the prime minister's priorities. "Britain will control the Mediterranean and the Suez against Germany . . . . it is clear Churchill intends to hold Africa . . .," he reported to the president.[62]   In a subsequent conversation, Eden asked Hopkins "repeatedly what our country would do if Japan attacked Singapore or the Dutch East Indies, saying it was essential to their policy to know."[63]   In a note about this conversation that he wrote later, Hopkins pointed out that "neither the President nor Hull could give an adequate answer to the British on that point because . . . the isolationists and, indeed, a great part of the American people, would not be interested in a war in the Far East merely because the Japanese attacked the Dutch."[64] This was clearly true, but it was certainly not the impression of likely American reactions that the British were passing on to the Australians. Nor did it offer them anything with which to solace Dutch fears.

When the "February crisis" suddenly erupted, Churchill seized the opportunity to press Roosevelt once again for some promise of assistance in the Far East. "I think I ought to let you know that the weight of the Japanese Navy, if thrown against us, would confront us with situations beyond the scope of our naval resources," he cabled the president on February 15, adding that "everything that you can do to inspire the Japanese with the fear of a double war may avert the danger. If, however, they come in against us and we are alone, the grave character of the consequences cannot easily be overstated."[65] Five days later, as the brief flurry of concern over Japanese intentions began to subside in London, Churchill sent another message to Roosevelt pointing out that his estimate of the consequences of a Japanese attack on the British would hold good for the foreseeable future.[66] Even though no assurances from Washington were forthcoming, the prime minister told the Japanese ambassador on February 24, that it would be unfortunate for Japan, with a war in China on its hands, if it also became embroiled with Britain and the United States.[67] On March 4, after a further talk with the ambassador, Churchill minuted that he doubted whether Japan would move until Britain's defeat seemed certain, and that he thought it unlikely that Japan would honor the Axis pact if the United States joined Britain in the war against Germany.[68] Yet a question mark remained: what if Japan confronted the United States with an ambiguous situation, and Britain with an agonizing choice, by attacking the Dutch? In his message to Roosevelt on February 15, Churchill had tried to draw the Americans on this point. "I do not myself think that the Japanese would be likely to send the large military expedition necessary to lay siege to Singapore. The Japanese would no doubt occupy whatever strategic points and oilfields in the Dutch East Indies and thereabouts they covet, and thus get into a far better position for a full-scale attack on Singapore later on."[69] The War Cabinet, prompted by the Admiralty, had repeatedly refused to give the Dutch any guarantee because of the uncertainty about American action. Roosevelt did not rise to Churchill's lure in February, and, in the ABC-1 agreement concluded the following month, the Americans agreed only "to support the defense of the Malay barrier [i.e., the arc from Malaya to Australia] by diverting Japanese strength away from Malaysia."[70] This still left open the question of an American response to an attack on the Dutch alone. When, on April 9, the Defence Committee again took up what was becoming the hardy perennial of a guarantee to the Dutch, Churchill therefore declared that "he was prepared to enter into any declaration or any commitment providing the Americans joined it," and, once again, no decision was taken.[71]

Despite the uncertainty about American policy in the event of an attack by Japan on the Dutch, or even on the British, Churchill sent a cable on April 2 to the Japanese foreign minister, Yosuke Matsuoka, who was visiting Berlin and Moscow, in which he implied a much closer understanding with the United States in the Far East than in fact existed.[72] The British knew that a Japanese attack on the Dutch would put them in an impossible situation, not least because of the pressure such an attack would produce from Australia and New Zealand for a British response. Yet, unable adequately to defend themselves in the Far East, they were reluctant to guarantee the Dutch without some assurances from the United States, and such assurances were not forthcoming. They could only bluff and hope. The Americans were drawing steadily closer, however, to open support in the Atlantic. And, in the last analysis, that was more important to the British.

How very much more important was about to be demonstrated. On April 29 Churchill had told the Defence Committee, and Menzies, that Japan would not attack the British and Dutch if it meant involvement with the United States, which, he said, it certainly would. That same day Colonel Frank Knox, Roosevelt's secretary of the navy, asked Rear Admiral V. H. Danckwerts of the British staff mission in Washington a very important question: What did the British think of the idea of moving the whole Pacific Fleet (as the United States Fleet had been renamed on February 1, 1941) to the Atlantic, leaving Hawaii to fend for itself? Conscious of the fact that the United States Pacific Fleet was supposed to defend a great deal more than Hawaii, the naval members of the staff mission discouraged the idea. The Defence Committee, meeting in London the following night, overruled both the staff mission and the Admiralty on political grounds. The movement of the Pacific Fleet into the Atlantic would be too important a symbol of the growing American commitment to Britain for it to be rejected. The Defence Committee added that they hoped enough would be left at Pearl Harbor to act as an "effective deterrent" to Japan. Menzies was not present at this meeting, and his subsequent protests that Australia and New Zealand ought to have been consulted forced the British government to delay for a week its answer to Washington. In the end the message sent welcomed the proposed transfer but, in deference to both dominion views and the representations of the British ambassador in Tokyo, expressed the hope that at least six capital ships and two carriers would be left in Hawaii. In the end only three battleships and a carrier were detached from the Pacific Fleet.[73] This episode occurred during the prolonged discussion of priorities in London that has already been described. During that argument Churchill had repeatedly pointed to America as the decisive factor in deterring Japan from a southward move that the British alone could not stop. The "American deterrent" was the United States Pacific Fleet, which the British had repeatedly, and vainly, tried to entice to Singapore. Yet, without consulting the dominions, Churchill was willing to see the Pacific Fleet steam through the Panama Canal, leaving the Pacific virtually denuded of Anglo-American sea power. A member of Churchill's staff reflected in his diary shortly after Pearl Harbor: "His policy during 1941 was to draw the Americans slowly but surely further across the Atlantic so that a clash with Germany would be inevitable sooner or later . . . ."[74] This accords with the maxim he had laid down in October 1940, that nothing compared in importance with American participation in the war. But it makes nonsense of his oft-stated premise that the presence of the American fleet in the Pacific would be a decisive factor in restraining Japan. British survival depended on what happened in the West. Therefore, no American gesture there could be ignored, particularly, as the same staff officer noted, since Churchill "did not believe the Japanese intended to come into the war, and therefore didn't see the point of keeping large forces in the Pacific."[75] What if that belief proved false? It is hard to avoid the conclusion that the prime minister had privately decided to take that chance, and, in effect, wrote off the Far East in April-May 1941 under the terrible pressures of the widening war in the West.

The exchanges over the possible transfer of the Pacific Fleet may have finally pushed the British toward making a gesture to the Dutch. On May 15 the Defence Committee approved ABC-1, in which the United States had at least committed itself to "supporting" the defense of the "Malay barrier." The defense of the Netherlands East Indies was a matter of intense concern to Australia and New Zealand, who had been given cause enough for concern lately. In any case, the Dutch had put the British in a rather embarrassing position. Their foreign minister, in a broadcast on May 6, had announced that any attack on the East Indies would be resisted, and he rather pointedly added that such an attack would concern the British as well. The Defence Committee, therefore, finally decided to go some way toward meeting the Dutch. They would use the hoary diplomatic ploy of a public statement along "parallel lines." In the event, various reasons — including a futile attempt to get the United States to agree that such a statement ought to be made — were found for delay, and the parallel declaration was never actually made.[76]

The discussion about the East Indies, however, did not distract the dominions from pressing for naval reinforcements for the Far East. On May 19 the Defence Committee took this up, and the first sea lord put the position, as seen from London: "Sir Dudley Pound said that it was impossible to get away from the fact that until the United States came into the war, we could get no relief for capital ship escorts for convoys and we had to maintain Force H at Gibraltar. It was from these two sources that any fleet destined for the Far East would have to come."[77] And there the matter stood. Britain could wring no assurances about the Far East, beyond the generalities of ABC-1, from the Americans. They would therefore give no binding assurances to the Dutch. They could afford no naval, or air, reinforcements for the Far East. They hoped that America would restrain Japan, but, in pursuit of survival in the West, they were willing to see much of the American fleet, on which so much of that hope reposed, leave the Pacific. In the face of this ruthless determination to concentrate on the war at hand, the dominions and the Dutch could do little.

One last attempt to change British priorities came two months later, and from a more powerful quarter. The Americans expressed doubts about the degree of British commitment in the Middle East and the effect it might have on their ability to defend both the British Isles themselves and Singapore, precisely the points Kennedy and Dill had raised in the late spring. Already, at the end of the Greek campaign, Churchill had received a message from the president that, although phrased with typical Rooseveltian ambiguity, nonetheless made American doubts about the Middle East clear enough. "I am satisfied," the president wrote, ". . . that even if you have to withdraw farther in the Eastern Mediterranean, you will not allow any great debâcle or surrender, and that in the last analysis the naval control of the Indian Ocean and the Atlantic

Ocean will in time win the war."[78]   This arrived as Churchill faced domestic pressure to consider alternatives to an all-out defense of the Middle East and his response was sharp.

> We must not be too sure that the consequences of the loss of Egypt and the Middle East would not be grave. It would seriously increase the hazards of the Atlantic and the Pacific, and could hardly fail to prolong the war, . . . remember that the attitude of Spain, Vichy, Turkey, and Japan may be finally determined by the outcome of the struggle in this theatre of war. I cannot take the view that the loss of Egypt and the Middle East would be a mere preliminary to the successful maintenance of a prolonged oceanic war . . . . We are determined to fight to the last inch and ounce for Egypt, . . . I adjure you, Mr. President, not to underrate the gravity of the consequences which may follow from a Middle Eastern collapse.[79]

Churchill defended his strategic priorities successfully against all comers in the spring; but in July Harry Hopkins, on his second visit to London, raised the issue again. On the night of the 24th, Hopkins, accompanied by Admiral Ghormley and Major General James Chaney, the two senior members of the unofficial American military mission, as well as by Brigadier General Raymond Lee, the American military attaché, met Churchill and the British Chiefs of Staff. Hopkins, as was his wont, put the matter bluntly. "Our Chiefs of Staff — the men who make the big decisions on all matters related to defense — believe that the British Empire is making too many sacrifices in trying to maintain an indefensible position in the Middle East." Chaney added that from the American point of view the defense of the British Isles and the Atlantic sea lanes came first, with Singapore second. Churchill replied at length. With reference to the Far East, he reiterated his conviction that Japan would not enter the war unless Britain was defeated, and that the Japanese had no desire to fight Britain and the United States together. Singapore, if attacked, could hold out, but the Japanese Navy could disrupt trade and communications in the Eastern seas, forcing a diversion of naval strength from the Mediterranean. This situation would, of course, be altered, the prime minister added, if America entered the war as a consequence of a Japanese attack on the British. Whatever happened, Churchill concluded, and despite American doubts, the Middle East would be held. The British Chiefs of Staff were then called on to explain how much more secure Britain was against invasion than it had been in the previous year. Churchill, perhaps with a touch of malicious humor, then asked Dill to discuss the Middle East. "Without expressing any opinion contrary to his paper of May, he gave a powerful exposition of some of the reasons which made it necessary for us to stay there," the prime minister later wrote. Dill spoke to a brief drawn up, ironically, by Kennedy, which made all the familiar points — strategic, political, and economic — in favor of retaining the Middle East, and added the enormous adverse effect in India and the Muslim world of a British collapse there.[80] Once again Churchill had underlined his determination to concentrate on the one war Britain was already fighting, and in which it was barely holding its own. The Middle East and the Atlantic were the crucial theaters in the war, and Churchill would allow no diversion of forces from them. He told Hopkins on the 24th that half of Britain's war production over the preceding eight months had gone to the Middle East. He counted on Japanese rationality and American power to protect Britain, the Dutch, and the dominions in the Far East; but under the intense pressures of the spring of 1941 he had wavered even on this, as shown above, when he saw a chance of America's commitment to Britain being deepened by the transfer of the bulk of its fleet to the Atlantic.[81] As a British planning paper put it in mid-June: "the active belligerency of the United States has become essential for a successful prosecution and conclusion of the war."[82]

This was underlined the day after Hopkins heard Churchill reiterate his determination to hold the Middle East. In retaliation for the Japanese move into southern Indochina, America froze Japan's assets and cut off her oil supplies. Faced with the depletion of her fuel reserves, Japan would have to give way — or fight. Australia's appeal to London to get an American guarantee quickly followed. On the 30th Eden told the War Cabinet that they could no longer avoid making a commitment to the Dutch, and, with Churchill's assent, he told the Dutch that the British would extend all possible aid in the event of a Japanese attack. The British he added, would remain the sole judges of what constituted such aid.[83] Churchill later recalled that, as he set off for the Atlantic conference, the growing danger from Japan preoccupied him.[84]

As the new battleship H.M.S. *Prince of Wales* carried Churchill westwards, the vice chief of the naval staff, Vice Admiral Sir Tom Phillips, told the Defence Committee that the entire Indian Ocean area was virtually defenseless. "Our strategy should be to avoid war with Japan, and give way as long as we could afford to, until America was ready and willing to support us."[85] Phillips was well behind events. The power to affect the timing of any war with Japan was no longer in British hands. What remained was to try to extract from the Americans a promise that a Japanese attack on the British and Dutch would bring America in as well.

iii

During the critical months leading up to the imposition of economic sanctions against Japan in July 1941, General Headquarters, Far East, under Brooke-Popham, struggled with only moderate success to organize and invigorate the defenses of the vast area for which it was responsible. It was in this struggle to make bricks without straw that the consequences of London's priorities became obvious. Brooke-Popham arrived in Singapore, after stops in Cairo, Delhi, and Rangoon, on November 14; and his headquarters opened four days later. Because of his dependence on the FECB for intelligence, he established it at the naval base, on the other side of the island from Malaya Command headquarters at Fort Canning. Air Headquarters was at yet another location on the island. The scattered nature of the service headquarters was an apt symbol of the compartmentalization in the Far East that Brooke-Popham's appointment was supposed to overcome, but did not. The limited powers, and limited staff, given to him were largely responsible. Flight Lieutenant T.C. Carter, arriving in Singapore a few months after Brooke-Popham, was told at Air Headquarters where the other services were located, but was cautioned that "we don't have much to do with them."[86] He later recalled that Brooke-Popham's existence did not seem to have much effect on interservice coordination. This was not for lack of effort on the commander in chief's part. He quickly recognized the need for a much larger staff. On the way out to Singapore he had discussed with Wavell in Cairo the causes of the enormous growth in the size of Middle East Command Headquarters. A prolonged argument with London finally resulted in a small increase being authorized in August 1941, but the war broke out before the augmentation took effect. In the meantime the burden of overwork began to wear down Brooke-Popham's original staff. Major General R.H. Dewing, his chief of staff, collapsed in April, and his post was vacant for nearly three months until the arrival of Major General I.S.O. Playfair in late

June. Numerous other members of the G.H.Q. staff became sick as well.[87]   Overwork also told lower down the scale. When Flight Lieutenant Carter reached Singapore he was told that more than two or three hours work a day in Singapore's climate could be fatal. The experience of the radar unit seemed to provide some confirmation for this piece of local folk wisdom. Its first commander had a nervous breakdown within two months. Carter took over and later wrote, "I was on the verge of one four months later. . . . "[88] It was not merely the newcomers from England, unacclimated to Malaya, and possessed by a greater sense of urgency, who were being worn down by overwork. In the RAF, for instance, tours in the Far East had been lengthened due to shipping shortages, and many officers had been there for years.[89]   Playfair later wrote:

> When I reached Singapore in June 1941, I was shocked to find so many tired people, longing for a change, working long hours, and out of touch with the war. I got the impression that some of them were already drawing on their reserves of moral and nervous energy, though there were, of course, a great many exceptions. A cable was sent to the War Office asking for a systematic change-over of personnel with fresh officers and men who had had first hand experience of modern war. Evidently this was not possible.[90]

This state of affairs was allowed to persist for the same reason that Malaya was denied anything in sufficient quantity. There were more urgent demands elsewhere. No organization ever has an unlimited supply of first-class talent, and there was an understandable reluctance in England to post good officers to the Far East when the need for them at home and in the Middle East was so pressing.[91]

It was not merely that the Far East did not get fresh officers in sufficient numbers. In some cases those that were sent were played out. In a memorandum he wrote for the chief of the air staff in March 1942, after his return from the Far East, Brooke-Popham wrote of "the feeling . . . that the RAF in the Far East were not getting their fair share of the best type of officer," and that "the Far East was regarded as a place to which tired officers could be sent."[92]   A decade later, in notes for the authors of the official history, he again reverted to "the 'forgotten' feeling. Were we given unwanted aircraft and officers?"[93]   What was true of the RAF seems also to have been the case with the army. A staff officer then with a unit in England later recalled that when drafts for the Far East were being made up, unit commanders chose

officers and men that they were happy to lose.[94]   Again there is
an element of inevitability here, and the disposition of commanders
at all levels to hang on to the best and rid themselves of the worst
in postings to the Far East could only have been countered by a
resolute policy coming from the top — the same sort of resolution
with which Churchill compelled a reluctant War Office to accept
the commandos. The impulse from the top was not there because
neither Churchill nor anybody else at the top concerned themselves,
except intermittently, with the needs of the Far East. Indeed, as
has been seen, in January 1941 Churchill exerted himself to see
that experienced RAF pilots were not posted there.

In the same way, the intelligence organization, which Brooke-
Popham immediately realized was inadequate, was never improved.[95]   The FECB, as noted above, was under naval control
and naturally gathered material of interest primarily to the Admiralty. RAF representation on it was very weak. Its estimates of the
Japanese army and the capabilities of Japanese airmen, like those
of the intelligence departments in London, were very wide of the
mark, and, as has often been pointed out, helped to mislead everyone, thus making the shock in December 1941 all the more severe.
But perhaps the intelligence agencies have been blamed for too
much. Even if they had been much more accurate in their estimate
of Japanese capacity, it still would not have changed London's
priorities. It was primarily the demands of the Middle East, not
optimistic intelligence, that kept Malaya's defenses so impover-
ished.

In the face of weaknesses of which he was all too aware, Brooke-
Popham had little choice but to put on a brave front and pretend
to a confidence that he certainly did not feel. "The main thing I
try to do is to convey an impression of confidence," he wrote to
Ismay in October 1941. A "most secret" document in his papers,
dated August 30, 1941, stresses the importance of giving the
Japanese "an exaggerated impression of our strength, and of our
confidence in our security."[96]   In April 1941 Colonel G. T. Wards,
the British military attaché in Tokyo, gave a frank and factual
account of the quality of the Japanese armed services to an audience
of army officers in Singapore. He also pointed out that the Japanese were fully aware of British weaknesses in the Far East. At
the conclusion of the lecture he was publicly contradicted by the
GOC, Lieutenant General Bond. When the astounded Ward spoke to
Bond privately afterward, he was told, "we must not discourage the
chaps and we must keep their spirits up."[97]   There is no doubt

that the Japanese were underestimated, but there can be little doubt now that much of the loudly expressed confidence was deliberate bluff. Unfortunately it missed its mark; indeed, it misfired badly. The Japanese were not fooled, and false confidence, encouraged by episodes like Bond's denigration of Ward's lecture, made the collapse all the more complete and traumatic when reality finally broke in. The public optimism of the commanders in the Far East also exposed them, after the event, to accusations of fatuousness that are not entirely fair.

If Brooke-Popham could do little about the number and quality of the officers posted to the Far East, or about the perceptiveness of his intelligence service, he did at least end the open quarreling between the services, although in a fashion that was far from even-handed. Very shortly after his arrival he began by taking on Vlieland, whom he savaged at a meeting of the Singapore War Committee while Sir Shenton Thomas sat quietly by. The next day Vlieland resigned from his position as defence secretary.[98] He subsequently resigned from the Malayan Civil Service as well and left for England, a deeply embittered man. Babington, who was as much to blame as Vlieland for the difficulties, remained until his tour came to an end in April, when he was replaced by Air Vice Marshal C. W. H. Pulford. It is interesting that it was Vlieland, the civilian, who alone fell victim to the injunction given Brooke-Popham before his departure: "our Far East position is so serious that you may feel that the risk of possible injustice to an individual should be accepted." Babington, who, at least in Admiral Layton's opinion, was most at fault, and who Brooke-Popham came to feel was not up to his job, went home to a promotion and two years as head of the RAF's Technical Training Command. Apparently Babington's refusal to cooperate with the army was not as grievous an offence as Vlieland's espousal of the strategy for the defense of Malaya whose adoption had brought Brooke-Popham to Singapore. In March Brooke-Popham asked the War Office to replace Bond, who he felt was "played out" — too deeply involved with past feuds, worn down by the climate, and burdened with a sick wife. Bond's tour was not yet over, and his replacement came as a shock to him. Trying to cushion it, the commander in chief put in a good word for him in a letter to Ismay, a courtesy Vlieland did not receive.[99] But Bond was lucky. His replacement would have to carry the burden of surrendering Singapore.

Acting Lieutenant General A. E. Percival, who assumed command on May 14, 1941, was returning to Malaya for the second time. In 1936-37, as a senior staff officer to General Dobbie, he had planned an attack on Malaya from the Japanese point of view, which proved to be a remarkably accurate forecast. A protégé of Sir John Dill's, his career had advanced steadily as his mentor rose. At the time that Dill selected him to succeed Bond, he was commanding a division in England. Since his promotion to colonel in 1932, however, he had spent nine years in staff appointments, most recently as an assistant CIGS under Dill. Although an extremely competent staff officer, he was given command of a force that by December 1941 would amount to an army without ever having commanded a formation larger than a battalion in action. He was not, moreover, a forceful or dynamic man — someone who knew him later recalled that he was a very pleasant man, highly intelligent, and unquestionably brave — but quiet, "not the man for a whirlwind."[100]   Percival had another, equally important, drawback. He was taking command of a force that would be largely composed of Indian Army units, but he had never had any contact with that service and shared the widespread British officers' prejudice against it. This was to exacerbate his relations with the senior Indian Army officer in Malaya, Lieutenant General Sir Lewis Heath, who had also been senior to Percival until the latter's sudden promotion. In a note written years later for the official historians, Percival made his attitude very clear.

> the greatest handicap from which Gen. Heath suffered was what might be called the "Indian Army complex." He had not been to any of the Staff Colleges and he had seldom, I think, come into contact with British troops. To him the Indian Army was everything and *his loyalty to it was probably far stronger than it was to the "Imperial Army" of Malaya.*[101]

It would, of course, be equally true to say that Percival shared the British service complex about the Indian Army. In any case, this was the origin of the tension between the two men that flared into the open at the conference on February 13, 1942. One observer, reflecting later on the relations between British and Indian Army officers in Singapore, remarked that the Indian Army thought of the British Army as amateurs while the British service thought of the Indian Army as "non-U." This professional rivalry, grounded in the differing social origins of the respective officer corps, was very old. The fact that no Indian Army officer reached the summit of the British military establishment between Lord Roberts, who retired in 1904, and Sir William Slim, who became CIGS in 1948 after the Indian Army had ceased to exist, did nothing to mitigate the strain. Once again London had made a decision affecting the defense of the Far East without apparently realizing that it might make an already difficult task harder. There is no evidence that anyone in Malaya was consulted about the appointment — or that any thought was given to naming an Indian Army officer.

Another matter vitally affecting the defense of the Far East was the incredibly convoluted manner in which military and civil lines of control cut across one another. Here again, nothing was done to simplify matters. First there was Burma, placed under Brooke-Popham's operational control, but with administrative responsibility for its defense forces retained by the War Office in London, and political control in the hands of the secretary of state for India and Burma, L. S. Amery, who was not a member of the War Cabinet. The Government of India had objected to this arrangement, since any reinforcements for Burma would have to come from India, and because of Burma's relationship to the defense of India's eastern frontiers. As usual, India was overruled. After his three day stopover in Rangoon on the way out, Brooke-Popham only got back to Burma twice, in June and September. In any case there was little that he could do for Burma, which suffered from an even lower priority than Malaya. It was in Malaya itself that the complexities of the military-civil relationship, and their attendant strains, were most marked. General Playfair later summed up the problem very well.

> The government was a complicated machine comprising no less than eleven separate administrations in Malaya and four more in British Borneo. There was a strong public agitation in 1940 for the creation of some central war administration, but the official view was that it would be a gross breach of faith to suspend or curtail the powers of the various State Governments. . . . . The holders of the principal government offices had been for 30 years or more in the enervating climate of Malaya, a country which was untouched by the 1914-1918 war. It was not easy for them to acquire a war mentality. The Governor may have had this in mind when, in 1938, he asked for powers to retire any officer over the age of 50 who showed himself to be unsuited to his responsibilities. This might not be thought to be a very drastic request at a time of crisis, but it was refused.[102]

The pattern of British administration in the Far East, built up over a century and a half of piecemeal imperial expansion, could only have been shaken up from the top. It was too much to expect an initiative in this respect from a tradition-bound and overworked civil administration, in any case hardpressed to increase tin and rubber output, while simultaneously coping with the influx of military units. It is odd that Brooke-Popham made no representations to Whitehall about this. He may have felt that in view of the priority given to Malaya's tin and rubber production nothing would be done. In any case, as will be shown, he had his hands full simply trying to wring reinforcements out of London. When Sir Archibald Clark-Kerr called London's attention to the problem of coordination in the Far East, the only result was the decision to send Duff Cooper to investigate the problem.

A related issue, one that has figured prominently in every account of the fall of Singapore, is the state of tension between the military and the civilians, whether the latter were administrators or businessmen. It is not hard to find substantiation for the low esteem in which many of the military held the civilians.[103] "Most of the British population of Malaya were there to make as much money out of the country as they could," Playfair later commented. "They counted the days to the time when they would leave. Their social and economic structures were highly artificial. They strongly opposed the introduction of an income tax in 1940. They had no natural patriotic feeling for Malaya and not enough was done to help them change their outlook . . ."[104] "The European population were possessed of a supreme confidence born of complete complacency," another officer recalled. "With a few notable exceptions their attitude to the war in general and the chances of its coming to Malaya was one of almost complete indifference. I have heard it said by civilians that it would be much better if the army were not in Malaya — they would attract the Japanese whereas without them it would be possible to make satisfactory terms with the Japanese! That was in the summer of 1941."[105] "They considered the soldier brutal and licentious and would have nothing to do with him," wrote Carter. "A man's worth was to them in direct proportion to his bank balance, . . . the war was something that happened in Europe and caused a grand boom in the Far East."[106] Years later Brooke-Popham recalled for the authors of the official history a conversation with a member of the Malayan Civil Service who, "in answer to some criticism of mine about air-raid precautions said, 'My dear Air Marshal, I'm convinced that the possibilities of war against Japan are at least 500 to

1 against.' " "I found that in Singapore itself the attitude of the British Merchants was that they disliked the presence of the fighting services and (wished?) to be left alone to make money as they did in the Kaiser's war," he added.[107]

All this — and it could easily be augumented by dozens of commentaries in the same vein — adds up to a damning picture of an English community out of a Somerset Maugham novel, or perhaps a genre film: stupid, arrogant, and smugly striding toward well-merited disaster. But, without denying that there was substance in some of the military strictures on the civilians, it is necessary to emphasize that there is another side to the story that has received far less attention. Military officers, many fresh from a grimly united England fighting with the consciousness that survival was at stake, found it difficult to adjust not only to the climate and the peacetime (in some respects pre-1914) atmosphere of Malaya, but to the complexities of an exotic pluralistic society over which British administrators and businessmen were the thinnest of crusts. One administrator later wrote:

> Co-operation was difficult. The Services and the civilians were working to conflicting directives, the first to get ready for war should it come; the second to maintain maximum production of tin and rubber and their swift despatch to Europe and America. This led to innumerable clashes of interest: priority for labour, for transport, for interference with normal business or damage to rubber estates or interruption of supplies, and so on. Added to this was some irritation to the civilians to be ordered about somewhat peremptorily on occasions and to find their clubs and cinemas over-run by hordes of newcomers who seemed to have far more spare time and money than we did! Don't forget that the civilian population was generally working extremely hard; full blast at peacetime production and all that went with it plus mounting war work, usually in the evenings and over week-ends.

He added that, as a corollary to the official policy of getting out as much tin and rubber as possible, "civil morale had to be maintained and confidence in the immediate future. Hence the Japanese threat was minimised and their ability to invade Malaya was be-littled."[108]   Another administrator noted something else that soldiers fresh from England often failed to understand: "The loyalties of the Malays were to their local chiefs and Sultans, the Chinese to their families, and the Indians basically to India . . . the army could not expect (though they seemed to do so) any mass support from the population at large as would have happened had they been fighting, for example, in defence of England."[109] What often seemed to soldiers and airmen, who were intent upon preparing defenses, to be obstructionism by administrators was simply a concern for the susceptibilities of the Asian population they governed or the rights of the Malay States, which were not British colonies but protected states with considerable internal autonomy.[110] Carter, for instance, found that it was difficult to work in some of the Malay states because the Malays did not want British troops near their *kampongs* (villages). It was a most inconvenient prejudice from a military point of view, but one with which the administrators had to contend.

Moreover, the emphasis, in many accounts, on the military's complaints has obscured the very considerable amount that was done by both administrators and civilians in Malaya. There were only some 9,000 British males in Malaya in 1939, and a very large number of them would have left for home to join the services at the outbreak of the war if the government had not refused exit permits except in special circumstances. Almost all these men were members of the local Volunteer Forces, or worked in one of the various civil defense organizations that proliferated after 1940, and in which very large numbers of Asians participated as well. Only 11 percent of Malaya's European male population was exempt from war service for reasons other than health, and these exemptions were invariably connected with the vital tin and rubber industries. For example, one mining company had 59 of its 88 European staff subject to mobilization, leaving 29 to run fifteen tin dredges, six hydraulic mines, and the head office. European women (a much criticized group) worked equally hard. "In one district there were 35 English women," Sir Shenton Thomas later wrote. "Of these 25 served in the Medical Auxiliary Service and many of them travelled 10 to 15 miles to attend training and practice." There is simply no evidence on which to convict Malaya's European population of not doing their best to ready Malaya for war. The "gin-soaked planter" is a colorful, but largely mythical, figure.[111] Similarly, the Malayan Civil Service has been accused of harboring "antimilitary" attitudes, an outlook that the author of the official history attributed to "the fact that very few of the senior Malayan civil servants of the time had taken any part in the 1914-18 war, ..." There is almost no substance to this "fact" either. On January 1, 1940, there were 224 officers in the M.C.S. Thirteen of these were Malays. Of the 211 Europeans, 118 were too young to have served in the 1914-18 war. That leaves 94 who were eligible, and 61 of them had served.[112] In fact, there seems to have been little genuine antimilitary feeling, but a very real difference in duties and perspective, which the military tended to interpret as obstruction and hostility.

It is, of course, true that a great deal of money was being made in Malaya, but it is equally true that Malaya was making very large financial contributions, on both government and private account, to the British war effort, over and above the massive contributions made by its rubber and tin exports. On top of the £ 15 million contributed for Imperial defense 1919-39 (mostly in connection with the building of the Singapore Base), Malaya gave £ 17 million for the same purpose 1939-42. This represented two-thirds of the amount contributed by the entire colonial empire (i.e., the empire outside the dominions and India) during the war. During the same period the Malayan Patriotic Fund raised some £ 385,000, much of it contributed by the Asian population, for use by the British Red Cross. When Sir Shenton Thomas later tabulated the private activities undertaken to provide amenities of various kinds for the growing number of soldiers and airmen in Malaya, the list covered two closely typed pages.[113] It is unfortunately true that Malaya's civilians did far less for Indian troops than for European, and Indian soldiers formed the bulk of Malaya's garrison.

The military, on their side, gave the civilians ample cause for any irritation they may have shown. Many of them, fresh from England, simply did not understand the complexity of Malayan society and administration, as has been pointed out. In particular, some had difficulty in grasping the implications of a multiracial society, in which much wealth was held by Asians, and both Asians and the 20,000 Eurasians played important roles in society and government. One small incident that occurred in 1940 illustrates the gap that separated the services from local society in this respect. During a dinner party at Government House in Singapore, at which several senior officers were present, a cipher telegram from London arrived for the governor. Sir Shenton summoned the Eurasian clerk in charge of his office to decode the cable. The next morning Mr. A. H. Dickinson, the inspector general of police and chief security officer, was told by one of the officers that "he was horrified by the fact of entrusting, in wartime especially, to a Eurasian subordinate the decoding of secret cipher messages." The military complained to London as well, and within twenty-four hours Sir Shenton received a telegram from the Colonial Office asking for explanations. Dickinson's Special Branch, as a matter of routine, already had a file on the clerk and was able to give the governor a satisfactory report with which to soothe London. However, Dickinson later recalled, "the feeling of suspicion and lack of confidence in the Governor to which the incident gave rise" on the part of the services was never completely erased. Another incident of the same sort occurred in 1941 when Brooke-Popham suggested to Ismay that London should press the Dutch government-in-exile to replace its commanding general in the East Indies, who, among his other faults in the commander in chief's eyes, "has native blood in his veins", a request that Ismay sensibly refused.[114]

The insistence of the services that their demands — for example, on the hard-pressed Public Works Department for various military construction projects — ought to have a priority that the civil government had no authority to concede was as annoying to the administrators as its refusal was to the services, while the army's hesitant approach to training in Malayan conditions struck many civilians as ridiculous.[115] Compounding all the other sources of friction was the strain on everyone's nerves that was produced by overwork in a climate as yet unmodified by air conditioning. "I had been in Malaya twice before," Playfair wrote, "and knew it to be a place where, for various reasons, the tempers of busy people become easily frayed; where it seemed more natural to take offence than to 'laugh it off'; and where criticism was more common than discretion. The lack of a change-of-air-station had something to do with this. The hill stations, (Fraser's Hill and Cameron Highlands), were so small as to be negligible. Splendid holiday resorts existed in Sumatra and Java, but these were expensive."[116] The cost of living was a particularly sore point with the military because British service personnel in Singapore paid income tax at the very high wartime rates that prevailed in Britain, while the local civilians did not.[117] Brooke-Popham later wrote that civil-military relations were better in up-country Malaya than in Singapore itself. It this was so, it may be due less to differing civilian attitudes than to the fact that in the up-country world of rubber estates and tin mines the soldiers bulked larger than they did in the bustling, wealthy, cosmopolitan city of Singapore. Because they were not as important in Singapore as in many other overseas stations, the services simply may not have felt very comfortable there.[118]

On the whole subject of civil-military relations, three things must be remembered. The first is that the mere fact of having to

explain a humiliating defeat made all the survivors prone to remember, and stress, the mistakes of institutions and services other
than their own. Second, the civilians in Malaya were expected to
do simultaneously two incompatible things: prepare for war and
maximize production of vital dollar-earning raw materials. The
latter, ordered by their superiors, they did very well. Tin and
rubber production rose steadily. Toward the former they made
considerable, although uneven, progress, much of it on their own
time. That there was stupidity, complacency, and arrogance is un-
doubted, but there were more admirable qualities on display as
well. In any case, these defects were by no means confined solely
to civilians. Finally, nothing the civilians in Malaya did, or failed
to do, was or could have been decisive. Playfair began his analysis
of the collapse with this succinct reminder.

1. Fundamental defects, which no improvement in other directions could have remedied
   (i) There were not enough forces.[119]

This was the consequence of a policy laid down (or at least enforced) from London, just as the concentration on "business as
usual," which struck the military as selfish and unrealistic, was the
consequence of a policy also laid down in Whitehall. The only
place where the two chains of command in Malaya met was in
London, a consequence of the decision made there to limit Brooke-
Popham's powers. Thus the only authority that could have elimi-
nated the confusion, cross purposes, and consequent friction in
the Far East was 12,000 miles from Singapore in bomb-battered
London, vested in men who, when they could spare time to think
about Malaya, devoutly hoped that nothing would happen there.
   Against this background, Brooke-Popham waged a continuous,
and largely futile, battle not only for reinforcements, but even for
information. The commander in chief had spent too many years in
Whitehall not to know how things worked there, and one of his first
steps was to try to open his own channel to the top by initiating a
correspondence with Ismay. He plied Churchill's chief of staff
with long letters that intermingled relatively trivial bits of gossip
with pleas for reinforcements and attempts to bring the realities in
the Far East to the attention of the prime minister and Chiefs of
Staff. Ismay's replies were infrequent, brief, bland, and not very
helpful. In the first of them he told Brooke-Popham, "I ought to
let you know at once that I took the liberty of sending copies pri-

vately to each of the Chiefs of Staff; and that they have been intensely interested, and have asked to receive copies of any future letters you may be kind enough to write." Intensely interested the Chiefs of Staff may well have been, but they were also unmoved, as Ismay revealed, perhaps unconsciously, later in the same letter — written incidentally during the February 1941 war scare, and only three days after the Chiefs of Staff had admitted that there was no available counter to Japan except diplomatic pressure. "Just at the moment trouble in your part of the world appears to be more imminent than many of us thought likely. *If it should unhappily materialise, I hope and believe that your requirements would be given a very high measure of priority.*"[120]   This, of course, because of the time lag that intervened between decisions in London and forces ready in Malaya, meant absolutely nothing.

It is impossible to say whether Churchill saw any of Brooke-Popham's self-styled "indiscreet letters" to Ismay. If he did, they made no difference whatsoever in his reactions to the commander in chief's official representations. In January Brooke-Popham, after a visit to Hong Kong, cabled London about reinforcements for the colony's defenses. Churchill flatly refused to consider the request.[121]   It was also in January, as shown above, that Churchill exerted himself to hold to a minimum the diversion of RAF resources to the Far East. In that same month, by which time the decision had been taken in London to equip the RAF in the Far East with Buffaloes and to send out only a handful of experienced pilots from the U.K., Brooke-Popham wrote an important letter to the permanent under-secretary at the Air Ministry: ". . . there is a peculiar undercurrent here which, if it were flowing through any organization other than the Royal Air Force, one might term inferiority complex. It is due to a variety of reasons . . . but one of the big contributory factors is that the RAF are flying aeroplanes of obsolete design and vintage and there are no reserves to keep them going if war should start."[122] This, like his other representations, had no effect. The Chiefs of Staff had rejected the figure of 582 aircraft that was put to them by the Singapore Defence Conference as the necessary minimum in the Far East. Brooke-Popham therefore concentrated on trying to persuade the Chiefs of Staff to provide at least the 336 aircraft that they deemed sufficient. The Air Ministry, on February 23, 1941, raised the requirement for reserves of all aircraft, except flying boats, to 100 percent.[123] This meant that by the end of 1941 there would have to be 663 aircraft in the Far East if London's own program was to be met. In

a long cable sent off at the beginning of March, Brooke-Popham
pointed out that, on the basis of currently scheduled deliveries,
"by the end of 1941 we can only reckon on . . . 64% (215) of the
numbers considered necessary by the Chiefs of Staff."

> I realise that our main enemy is GERMANY . . . . I realise the
> difficulty of making reliable forecasts at the present time and
> further that at any moment aircraft may have to be diverted
> to meet some sudden emergency. But I should be grateful
> for information as to what plans the Air Ministry have for the
> supply of aircraft to this Command up to the end of 1941 so
> as to meet the recommendations of the Chiefs of Staff.[124]

A few weeks later he cabled again about aircraft reinforcements,
this time pointedly referring to a recent boast by Lord Beaverbrook, the minister of aircraft production, about the strength of
the United Kingdom's aircraft reserves. Again he failed to pry
anything loose.

Nor was the pressure to send more up-to-date aircraft to the Far
East of any avail. Portal, as shown above, assured Menzies on
March 27 that the Buffalo was adequate to that area's needs. A
month later, at a Chiefs of Staff meeting, Sir Tom Phillips, the vice
chief of the naval staff, urged the dispatch of Hurricanes to the
Far East. Air Chief Marshal Sir Wilfred Freeman, the vice chief of
the air staff, assured him that Japanese aircraft were not of the most
modern type and that the Buffalo really was good enough.[125]
It was not only modern fighters that were lacking in the Far East.
The RAF was supposed to act as a striking force, but its obsolete
Blenheim, Vildebeeste, and Wirraway aircraft were completely inadequate for that role, as Brooke-Popham made plain to Ismay in
early July: "My principal worry at present is the repeated post-
ponement of our Glen Martin bombers and our Beauforts. Wasn't
it the elder Moltke who said that the art of war consists in the
practical adaption of the means in hand to the end in view? And I
wish I could see more clearly how to adapt Vildebeestes to attain
the object of sinking Japanese troopships if they're escorted by
cruisers and covered by fighters off carriers bearing in mind that
we've got to keep squadrons going for six months, so can ill afford
heavy casualties."[126]

The failure to supply modern aircraft was compounded by the
failure to send experienced pilots. Eight pilots left Great Britain
for the Far East early in January 1941. The rest came directly

from Flying Training Schools in Australia and New Zealand, and some of these had never flown anything but trainers. They had no experience of retractable undercarriages, variable pitch propellers, or flaps. To prepare these very raw pilots for combat, Brooke-Popham wanted to form an operational training unit (O.T.U.), which was a standard feature in other RAF commands. He was told by the Air Ministry that since neither planes or personnel could be spared to form an O.T.U. in the Far East, further training would have to be done by the squadrons themselves. Realizing that this would delay their operational readiness, Brooke-Popham arranged for the formation of a skeleton O.T.U. out of local resources. This, of course, stretched such experienced pilots as were available even thinner. Despite every effort, two squadrons had still not been passed as operationally fit when war came. Brooke-Popham later pointed out that even a single good squadron of Hurricanes or Spitfires would have provided a standard of comparison for pilots that was otherwise lacking in the Far East, and would have exposed the shortcomings of the Buffalo as well. It is not surprising that Carter later remembered Air Vice Marshal Pulford as having a perpetually worried look.[127] With unconcious irony, Ismay wrote cheerfully to Brooke-Popham in mid-June: "It must be a great comfort to you to have some effective . . . fighters which the Japs would simply loathe to meet."[128]

Admitting the pressure under which they were operating, it is still hard to avoid the conclusion that the Air Ministry could have done a great deal more for the Far East than they did. Having made it an "RAF theatre," they seem to have then nearly forgotten it. Why? During the months when Brooke-Popham was vainly pleading with London for reinforcements, Fighter Command was trying to mount its own offensive against the German air force in the West, carrying out sweeps over northern France known as *rhubarbs* or *circuses.* Bomber Command, the only weapon available with which the British could strike Germany itself, was struggling, not very successfully, to carry out the hope that Churchill had expressed in a minute to Beaverbrook the previous summer that a strategic bombing offensive against Germany would prove decisive.[129] The existence of two RAF offensives mounted from the U.K., in one of which at least Churchill was deeply interested, together with the demands of the Middle East and the Battle of the Atlantic, explains, but does not completely excuse, the Air Ministry's neglect of the Far East. These offensives became very important politically by mid-summer 1941 because they were all the

British had to show their new and demanding Soviet ally in the way of direct pressure on Germany. The circus operations were stepped up noticeably — 8,000 sorties between mid-June and the end of July, at a cost of 123 pilots. They were, however, a costly failure. Over the year as a whole, the Germans shot down two British fighters for every one they themselves lost over northern France, and even the RAF official history felt constrained to admit, "whether this was a wise allocation of resources at a time when there were only thirty-four fighter squadrons to sustain our cause in the whole of the Middle and Far East is, perhaps, an open question."[130]

What was true of planes was also true of radar, without which defending fighters could not be used to best advantage. In February 1941 Brooke-Popham and Babington established an order of priority for the development of radar coverage that put Singapore first, with emphasis on an attack coming in from the northeast, over the sea — that is, a carrier strike. Second came the extension of coverage up Malaya's east coast. When Pulford replaced Babington in April, he realized that Singapore needed cover against an attack coming in overland from the north as well. Progress in meeting these requirements was painfully slow. An order for valves for the radar sets, placed urgently on March 3, 1941, produced by December 10, only 25 percent of the quantity needed while the balance finally reached Ceylon on March 7, 1942. As radar cover was pushed north from Singapore, it became necessary to link the stations by land lines to the Filter Center in Singapore. This brought the Public Works Department as well as Posts and Telegraphs into the picture. They estimated that it would take at least eighteen months to get the necessary equipment from the U.K. to improve internal communications in Malaya. On one occasion Carter, who became command radio officer in May 1941, was told by the Post Office that one of his requests for additional land lines would require more material than there was in all of Malaya. "It was a marked characteristic of the Far East that the whole RAF program was consistently held up by the slowness of the Office of Works," he wrote in his subsequent report. "Works services which in the U.K. took no more than a few weeks . . . in the Far East took six months. Part of the reason for this slowness was undoubtedly the extreme peace-time financial control . . . ." He later recalled that the question "who will pay?" kept cropping up. Then there was the problem of getting clearances for work in the Malay states via the complicated chain that ran from Sir Shenton Thomas via the British resident to the ruler. In defense of the Public Works and Posts and Telegraphs departments, it must be remembered that the influx of troops, the construction of airfields, and the demands of the booming civilian economy were putting tremendous strains upon them; that they could not avoid the question of finance because no one had released them from peacetime accounting procedures; and that the delays in getting material from England were not their fault. Nevertheless, the nervous collapse of Carter's predecessor is understandable.

It was quickly discovered that the high frequency radio telephones used by ground controllers to direct fighters were so badly affected by Malaya's frequent electrical storms as to be virtually useless. Carter asked for VHF radio telephones in June 1941, only to be told by the Air Ministry that they could not be provided until June 1942. Some VHF equipment was improvised locally for internal communications between the radar units, but none was available for the fighter squadrons. Thus, effective control of fighters from the ground was limited to ten miles, and even that was liable to be interrupted by adverse weather. All things considered, the degree of air defense that Singapore enjoyed by December 1941 was a remarkable, if inevitably transient, achievement.[131]

Requests from the Far East for matériel were requests to divert important items from active theaters. It is much harder to account for the failure to supply, despite repeated requests, reminders, and protestations, up-to-date information. As seen above, Brooke-Popham told Ismay in February 1941, "Out here we suffer from lack of information regarding the lessons that have been learnt from operations in Europe and elsewhere, . . . the ignorance of modern war conditions out here does worry me . . . ," and went on to list some of the things he wanted information about: civil defense, techniques of ocean reconnaissance and attack on ships, as well as the latest information on ways of dealing with night bombing. Ismay's reply, some months later, was to point out that a great deal was being sent out through departmental channels.[132] After mid-summer 1941 the flow of information improved, but, commented Brooke-Popham in his dispatch, "we were always uncertain whether we were being kept up to date."

This feeling of being neglected was naturally intensified by the distance of London from Singapore, and the whole position in this respect would have been greatly improved if visits by

liaison officers from the War Office and Air Ministry had been
made from time to time. This was actually started in the case
of the War Office, and the first liaison officer arrived in Singapore in November, 1941. I believe it was intended to do the
same in the case of the Air Ministry. It would have been a great
help if this had been done twelve months earlier.[133]

The Middle East, and even more India and the Far East, were, in
fact, physically isolated from England by wartime dislocations of
shipping and cable traffic, as well as by the shortage of long-range
aircraft, to an extent that is hard to realize today. Nevertheless,
greater efforts should clearly have been made, for on two occasions
the failure to get information out to Malaya may have been an important factor in the speed of the subsequent defeat.

The first occasion is what Sir Arthur Conan Doyle might have
called "the strange case of the chief engineer's instructions." In
May 1941 Brigadier Ivan Simson was appointed chief engineer,
Malaya Command. In a verbal briefing at the War Office, Major
General W. Cave Browne, the director of fortifications and works,
told Simson that he was being sent out to "modernize" defenses
in Malaya "specifically against possible beach landings and against
tank and air attack." When Simson asked for written instructions
to this effect, he was refused. Cave Browne told him, however,
that Dill would be writing to Percival about the importance of
improving Malaya's defenses, and in that letter he would be mentioned by name as the officer best qualified to carry this out. The
letter was never written. Simson attributed his subsequent failure
to persuade Percival to sanction an extensive program of defenses
(including antitank defenses at every likely point on the west
coast road, defenses north of the Johore Strait to keep the Japanese artillery out of range of the naval base, and defenses on the
north shore of Singapore Island itself) to this lack of authoritative
backing from London. Simson's explanation for the lapse — "presumably the C.I.G.S. letter was overlooked in the pressure of the
more urgent business of waging war with Germany" — is probably
as close to the truth as we can now get.[134] Simson's belief that,
had the letter arrived, matters might have gone differently in
Malaya cannot, however, be accepted without qualification. The
defenses that Simson advocated might indeed have helped slow
down the Japanese, although they would hardly by themselves
have affected the final issue, but they remained unbuilt not solely
because Dill failed to write to Percival about Simson. There was in

the first place the rivalry between various other forms of military construction — airfields, radar stations, housing for troops, and so on — and defenses. Then there was competition between the construction of defenses and training in the allotment of the troops' time. It must be remembered that the troops reaching Malaya in 1941 were very raw and badly in need of additional training. What the episode does illustrate clearly is the casual way in which Far Eastern matters were being handled in London, as well as the lack of urgency in dealing with requests from Singapore. Simson wrote twice to Cave Browne by airmail, in September and October 1941, to urge that written confirmation of his instructions be sent, as promised. The letters were never answered. But in late November a telegram arrived instructing Malaya Command not to cable the War Office for decisions on requests from the Far East until at least three months had elapsed since the original request.[135]

The second failure was more serious, because it involved the basic assumption that Japanese aircraft were "not of the most modern type," and therefore the untested Buffalo could cope with them. The Japanese Zero that was to come as such an unpleasant surprise in December 1941 had been used in China as early as the spring of 1940. Some details of its performance had appeared in stories filed by American correspondents in Chungking. Then, in May 1941, a Zero had been shot down in China. Details of its armament and fuel capacity reached FECB in July and were passed on to both the Air Ministry and Pulford's headquarters on the 26th. The British air attache in Chungking sent FECB estimates of the Zero's performance (which turned out to be reasonably accurate), and on September 26 FECB dutifully forwarded this as well to London and Pulford. The RAF representation on FECB was not strong, and it is possible that the full significance of the information was not recognized there. Headquarters, Air Command, Far East was also undermanned, and, incredibly, its establishment did not include an intelligence staff. Critical information on the Zero therefore came to rest in a mass of unsorted intelligence data. Pulford, conscious of the weakness of air intelligence in the Far East, asked the Air Ministry in July for authority to form an intelligence section in his headquarters. In October he took matters into his own hands and set up a makeshift intelligence staff "in anticipation of approval" from London. It began to work through the accumulated files, but the data on the Zero had not been reached by the time war came.[136] In consequence, Pulford's pilots, many inadequately trained and nearly all lacking combat experience, went into action with assumptions that were immediately proved false, with unfortunate effects on their morale.

The Air Ministry knew by September 1941, at the latest, that its confidence in the Buffalo was unfounded, yet no warnings were passed to Singapore. The Air Ministry may have assumed that Pulford already knew but they also knew that his headquarters did not have an intelligence staff. Moreover, Pulford had to take the initiative in setting up a scratch intelligence section after vainly waiting several months for London to sanction one, just as the improvised O.T.U. had been the result of Brooke-Popham's initiative. The weakness in the collection of air intelligence in the Far East ought to have been corrected, at latest, when the defense of the area became primarily an RAF responsibility. That it was not may have been due to the same inattention that marked all of London's dealings with the Far East — compared to everything else that was happening, the Far East simply did not matter very much. It is also possible that, having decided that they had nothing modern to spare for the Far East, the Air Ministry was reluctant to lower morale there by calling attention to the inadequacy of the aircraft they had provided.

Despite all the shortcomings within his command and the discouraging feeling that London was not paying very much attention to its problems, Brooke-Popham did his best to work out effective defense plans for Malaya, and to coordinate arrangements within the vast area entrusted to him. The latter involved a tremendous amount of traveling. During his year as commander in chief, he visited Hong Kong, Burma and Australia twice, Manila three times, and the Netherlands East Indies five times, in addition to travel within Malaya, a country the size of England and Wales (or of Illinois). This involved not only lengthy and tiring journeys for a man of his age in the relatively primitive aircraft of the day, but considerable embarrassment as well, since he was frequently forced to borrow transport from the Americans or the Dutch. "The Dutch and Americans were very good about all this," Playfair recalled, "but found it difficult to understand why a British Air Chief Marshal should not possess the means of moving himself about in his own area."[137] This reflected not just the Far East's usual low priority for equipment, but the basic poverty of resources for global war that was making Britain increasingly dependent on the United States. The British built no transport aircraft at all in 1939 or the first half of 1940, and, following the inevitable decision in

May 1940 to concentrate on fighters and bombers, they agreed in October to buy transport planes from the United States. The British allocation of American production, itself just beginning in 1941, was 9 percent.[138] None of it trickled through to the Far East — little, in fact, reached Britain itself.

The most important of the potential allies for Britain in the Far East was the United States, a fact that was reflected in Brooke-Popham's three trips to Manila. There were, in addition, two conferences at Singapore, in February and April, at which American representatives were present. The second was a full-dress affair with representatives from Australia, New Zealand, India, and the Netherlands East Indies in attendance, and was held in consequence of the ABC-1 agreement. Although useful work in local coordination was accomplished by both those conferences and Brooke-Popham's shuttling, on two major points all the conferring and visiting was nugatory. In the first place, it proved impossible to tie the Americans down. The fate of the ADB (American-Dutch-British) agreement on combined operations in the event of war with Japan, drawn up at the second Singapore conference in April, illustrated how fragile and shot through with mutual reservations Anglo-American cooperation in the Far East was, even after ABC-1 had aligned the two closely in the West. When they cabled the agreement to London, Brooke-Popham and Layton pointed out that the defense of the Far East was ultimately dependent on offensive operations by the United States Pacific Fleet, even though this could not be put into the report. They also emphasized the importance of strengthening the defenses of the Philippine Islands. (Brooke-Popham was up-to-date enough to point out to the Americans that concentrating their air strength on a few fields near Manila, within striking distance of Japanese aircraft on Formosa, was unwise.) The British Chiefs of Staff, however, did not want the Philippines strengthened at the expense of the American effort in the Atlantic, and declined to press this point. Then the Americans reneged. Marshall and Stark were alarmed at the political implications of the agreement and feared that the U.S. Asiatic Fleet would be drawn into the defense of Singapore, which they did not see as a vital American interest, and about the success of which they were already doubtful. On July 3, 1941, they informed London that not only had they rejected the ADB agreement, but that the decision taken during the Washington staff talks to allow the Asiatic Fleet to operate under British control was canceled.[139]

Uncertainty about American intentions also frustrated the attempt made at both conferences to define certain Japanese moves (other than direct attack) that would call for immediate counteraction. A Japanese movement into southern or western Thailand, or the appearance of Japanese warships or an escorted convoy, "which from their positions and course were clearly directed upon the east coast of the Isthmus of Kra or the east coast of Malaya, or had crossed the parallel of 6° north between Malaya and the Philippines . . ," would so clearly presage an attack that any delay while reference was made to London might be disastrous. The British Chiefs of Staff in both cases ruled out the delegation of authority for automatic counteraction to the commander in chief, Far East. They knew that the Americans would not agree to be bound by a decision taken by a British commander in Singapore, and, that being the case, they would not sanction any automatic response, except to direct attack, "until such time as the United States made it clear what their attitude would be should war break out." [140] The cloud of ambiguity that hung over American intentions meant that London would not authorize Brooke-Popham to do anything that might involve Britain in unilateral hostilities against Japan. This made all the effort that was put into Far East Command's only offensive plan completely unavailing.

Operation Matador called for the preemptive seizure of the Kra Isthmus in southern Thailand, which was the obvious jumping off place for a Japanese drive down the west coast of Malaya, as well as a position from which the Japanese could easily cut the air reinforcement route from India. In the spring of 1940 Bond had pointed out that such an operation would require at least two divisions. Brooke-Popham took up the idea soon after his arrival in Singapore. Given the resources necessary, it was the obvious counter to an equally obvious Japanese move. It was, in fact, the only offensive operation open to the British, in the absence of either a fleet or an effective air striking force. A great deal of detailed planning was done, and on April 7, 1941, the Chiefs of Staff approved the idea, with the proviso that the final decision to launch Matador would be reserved to London. Even so, as shown above, the prime minister immediately weighed in with a minute indicating that he did not want forces locked up in Malaya waiting for the signal to seize the Kra Isthmus. The key point about Matador, recognized from the beginning in the Far East, was time. At least twenty-four hours' start *before the Japanese began to land* was necessary if the operation was to have a chance of success. But the reluctance to give Brooke-Popham a free hand, because of the uncertainty about American reaction, meant that the precious twenty-four hours might well be lost in references to London. Vlieland had opposed Matador on precisely these grounds when Bond first proposed it.[141]

The only moderately bright spot in the whole Far Eastern picture in the period under consideration was the increase in the number of troops in Malaya. Until the autumn of 1940 there were in Malaya, besides the prewar garrisons of the "fortresses" of Singapore and Penang Island (off Malaya's west coast), only the Twelfth Indian Infantry Brigade, which had arrived in August 1939, and the two British battalions that were withdrawn from China a year later. In October and November 1940 the Sixth and Eighth Indian Infantry Brigades arrived, with the headquarters of the Eleventh Indian Division. (These were the two brigades whose employment in Malaya instead of the Middle East so irritated the prime minister.) In March and April 1941 two more Indian brigades (the Fifteenth and Twenty-second) and a second divisional headquarters (the Ninth) reached Malaya. In May the Third Indian Corps headquarters under Lieutenant General Sir Lewis Heath was established in Kuala Lumpur to control the two divisions plus the garrison of Penang and the local Volunteer Forces. All this sounds impressive enough until looked at closely. Both Indian divisions were composed of units raised since the outbreak of the war. Prewar regulars were spread very thin by 1941. "In some cases the commanding officer and a grizzled subadar major would be the only representatives in a battalion" of the pre-1939 Indian Army. Most of the junior officers had only recently joined and lacked both the linguistic facility and understanding of Indian troops that made the regulars so effective. Many of the rank and file had less than twelve months training — and that oriented toward the Middle East. Both divisions lacked their third brigade, as well as their field artillery and signals units.[142] In the discussions in London on the expansion of the Indian Army, Churchill had minuted that Britain must get fighting units from India in return for the equipment sent there.[143] In August 1939 one division was projected as India's contribution to operations outside the subcontinent. By midsummer 1941 there were two divisions — the cream of the Indian Army — in North Africa, and seven infantry brigades, an armored brigade, and a machine gun battalion scattered over Syria, Iraq, and Persia. This was in addition to five brigades in Malaya, one in Burma, and the two battalions in Hong Kong. There were also

Indian Army units in Borneo and at Aden. In India itself still more units were being raised. Britain got very good value for money out of the Indian Army, something that Churchill, in a lapse from his usual generosity, never acknowledged.

In addition to Australian pilots, Brooke-Popham also got an Australian division. In December 1940, alarmed by the weaknesses revealed at the Singapore Defence Conference, Australia had offered a brigade from its Eighth Division, then forming. The offer was quickly accepted by London. The British Chiefs of Staff had looked to Australia as a source of reinforcements for Malaya since June 1940, although Churchill wanted to see the Eighth Division go on to join the Australian Corps in the Middle East in the spring of 1941, when another Indian division would be ready for Malaya. The Eighth Division's leading brigade arrived at Singapore in February 1941 aboard the Queen Mary.

As the Australians disembarked at Singapore, Brooke-Popham was meeting with the Australian War Cabinet and Chiefs of Staff. Sir Robert, who in one of his letters to Ismay had expressed the hope that the war would not mean the end of fox-hunting ("develops the best characteristics of the rising generation") found the Australians a bit hard to take.[144]   For their part, the Australians found his optimism the opposite of convincing, particularly after he pointed out that the minimum naval strength at Singapore was four or five battleships and ten or twelve cruisers, but admitted that only American participation in the war would free the Royal Navy to actually provide such a force. Brooke-Popham's feeble performance on this occasion not only undermined Australian confidence in Britain's ability to face the growing Japanese threat, but led directly to a decision to hold the entire Eighth Division for use in the Far East.[145]   The arrival of the Australians in Malaya brought, however, in addition to welcome reinforcements, further complications in the already unwieldy command structure. Australian units could not be used in the same way as British or Indian formations. Major General H. Gordon Bennett, their commander, received a directive from his own government that stressed that his division must retain its identity as an Australian force, that no part was to be detached without his consent, and that if imperative operational necessity compelled the splitting up of his division, he could comply — but he could at the same time, if he wished, protest and report the matter to Australian Army Headquarters in Melbourne.[146] Bennett was an ambitious man and made the most of his instructions. Brooke-Popham and Percival knew that there were delicate "political" considerations involved in the use of

Australian troops, and the disposition of the forces in Malaya in December would reflect the need to have a separate Australian sphere of responsibility.

When America froze Japan's assets, the picture in the Far East was dismal. The forces necessary to defend the area were simply not available. Those on the spot were ill-equipped and incompletely trained. Cooperation between civil and military authorities was not good and there were tensions as each tried to do what London had told it to, and fell foul of the other in the process. Australia was increasingly anxious. London was watching America, whose attitude remained uncertain. In April Churchill had accepted that it would be his responsibility to give three months notice if the assumptions on which he based Britain's Far Eastern strategy should change. When he boarded his train that August day, there were four months of peace left in the Far East.

Notes to Chapter 5

1. Brooke-Popham to Ismay, February 2, 1941, Brooke-Popham Papers (BPP) v/1/5, The Liddell Hart Centre for Military Archives, King's College, London.

2. Interview with Dr. T. C. Carter, November 27, 1973.

3. J.R.M. Butler, ed., *History of the Second World: United Kingdom Military Series*, "Grand Strategy" series, vol. 2, J.R.M. Butler, *Grand Strategy (September 1939-June 1941)* (London: H.M.S.O., 1957), pp. 372-74. In view of all that has been written about Churchill's personal preoccupation with Turkey and the Middle East, it ought to be noted that the Chiefs of Staff and their Joint Planners were, at this point, every bit as eager for Turkish belligerency as the prime minister: Sir J. Slessor, *The Central Blue* (London: Cassell & Co., 1956), pp. 231, 272-73. The November 1940 forecast of British strength in the Middle East by the summer of 1941 was approximately correct, although the buildup was slower after that.

4. Butler, *Grand Strategy II*, pp. 388-89.

5. Ibid., p. 492.

6. Ibid., pp. 492-93; E. L. Woodward, *British Foreign Policy in the Second World War*, 5 vols. (London: H.M.S.O., 1970-), 2:178. Ironically, the success of the British raid on Taranto was one of the tactical inspirations for the Pearl Harbor attack. Butler was chairman of the interdepartmental committee on the Far East set up by the War Cabinet in October to keep developments in the area under review.

7. Winston S. Churchill, *The Second World War*, vol. 2, *Their Finest Hour* (Boston: Houghton Mifflin, 1949), p. 699.

8. Ibid., pp. 704-5.

9. Butler, ed., *History of Second World War*, "Campaigns" series, S.W. Kirby et al., *The War Against Japan*, vol. 1, *The Loss of Singapore* (London: H.M.S.O., 1957), p. 55.

10. Chiefs of Staff to Prime Minister, January--, 1941, Public Record Office (PRO), PREM 3, 156/3.

11. Hollis to Prime Minister, January 27, 1941, Ibid.

12. Butler, *Grand Strategy II*, pp. 383-84.

13. Ibid., pp. 497-500; Woodward, *British Foreign Policy*, 2:178-79; Minute by First Sea Lord, February 15, 1941, PRO, ADM 205/10; COS (40) 74, February 6, 1941, PRO, PREM 3, 156/6. Indian State Forces were units from the princely states of India. They were not generally British-officered and their training and equipment were designed basically for internal security duties.

14. Butler, *Grand Strategy II*, p. 500.

15. M. Tsuji, *Singapore: The Japanese Version* (New York: St. Martin's Press, 1960), pp. 3-4.

16. Churchill, *Their Finest Hour*, pp. 718-22.

17. Butler, *Grand Strategy II*, p. 448.

18. Covering note by the Chiefs of Staff to Prime Minister on COS (41) 230, PRO, PREM 3, 156/4. Butler, *Grand Strategy II*, p. 500, discusses Menzies's memorandum, but does not mention his request for an answer to the question of what would happen if Japan entered the war and American remained neutral.

19. Prime Minister to Ismay for the Chiefs of Staff, April 10, 1941, PRO, PREM 3, 156/6.

20. Annex IV to COS (41) 230, PRO, PREM 3, 156/4.

21. J. Connell, *Wavell: Soldier and Scholar* (London: Collins, 1964), pp. 229-31, 421.

22. J. Kennedy, *The Business of War*, ed. B. Fergusson (New York: William Morrow & Co., 1958), pp. 104-7.

23. A. Bryant, ed., *The Turn of the Tide 1939-1943: A History of the War Years based on the Diaries of Field Marshal Lord Alanbrooke* (New York: Doubleday, 1957), pp. 202-3. Neither Churchill nor Ismay mention this episode in their memoirs.

24. Winston S. Churchill, *The Second World War* vol. 3, *the Grand Alliance*, (Boston: Houghton Mifflin, 1950), p. 761.

25. Kennedy, *The Business of War*, p. 108.

26. Butler, *Grand Strategy II*, pp. 577-78. The curious will find the sentence omitted rather squeamishly by Butler in Kennedy, *The Business of War*, p. 109: "Anyone who can kill a Hun or even an Italian has rendered good service."

27. Churchill, *The Grand Alliance*, p. 3.

28. Ibid., pp. 211-12; Butler, *Grand Strategy II*, p. 453.

29. Kennedy, *The Business of War*, pp. 110-11.

30. Butler, *Grand Strategy II*, pp. 501-2. See also Pound's memorandum to Menzies of April 26, 1941, PRO, ADM 205/10.

31. Churchill, *The Grand Alliance*, pp. 421-22.

32. Butler, *Grand Strategy II*, pp. 578-79.

33. Churchill, *The Grand Alliance*, pp. 422-23. Churchill did not say why Japanese raids on trade routes in the Indian Ocean were more to be feared than an attack on Singapore. But it is reasonable to assume that he feared not only the severance of the links with India and Australia but the cutting of the supply lines to the Middle East and the Persian Gulf oil fields.

34. Butler, *Grand Strategy II*, pp. 580-81.

35. Churchill, *The Grand Alliance*, p. 426.

36. Churchill, *Their Finest Hour*, pp. 690-91.

37. Ismay to John Connell, n.d., in R. Wingate, *Lord Ismay: A Biography* (London: Hutchinson & Co., 1970), p. 57.

38. Wingate, *Lord Ismay*, p. 57. Dill's wife, paralyzed by a stroke in 1940, was slowly

dying. Bryant, ed., *Turn of the Tide*, p. 204, fn. 47, reproduces Brooke's diary entry of November 22, 1940, and his postwar reflections on the relationship between Dill's somber home life and his declining effectiveness as CIGS. Dill left few papers behind when he died in 1944, and it is unlikely that an adequate biography will ever be written.

39. Churchill, *The Grand Alliance*, p. 343.

40. Ibid., pp. 344-5; Kennedy, *The Business of War*, p. 119.

41. Butler, *Grand Strategy II*, pp. 507, 549, italics mine; B. Bond, ed., *Chief of Staff: The Diaries of Lieutenant General Sir Henry Pownall*, 2 vols. (London: Leo Cooper Ltd., 1973-74), 2:22-27.

42. Butler, *Grand Strategy II*, p. 550.

43. J. Connell, *Auchinleck: A Critical Biography* (London: Cassell & Co., 1959), pp. 246-48; Kennedy, *The Business of War*, p. 134.

44. Churchill, *The Grand Alliance*, pp. 370-71.

45. Ibid., pp. 381-82.

46. Butler, ed., *History of the Second World War*, "Grand Strategy" series, vol. 3, J. M. A. Gwyer and J. R. M. Butler, *Grand Strategy (June 1941-August 1942)*, 2 pts. (London: H.M.S.O., 1964), pt. 1, p. 98.

47. Churchill, *The Grand Alliance*, p. 394.

48. Butler, *Grand Strategy II*, pp. 524-25; Gwyer and Butler, *Grand Strategy III*, pt. 1, p. 164.

49. Brooke-Popham to Ismay, July 3, 1941, BPP v/1/4.

50. Babington to Brooke-Popham, August 1, 1941, BPP v/11/1.

51. Churchill, *The Grand Alliance*, p. 587.

52. Gwyer and Butler, *Grand Strategy III*, pt. 1, p. 284.

53. Ibid., p. 278.

54. Trevor Wilson, *The First Summit* (Boston: Houghton Mifflin, 1969), p. 92.

55. Gwyer and Butler, *Grand Strategy III*, pt. 1, p. 275.

56. Ibid., p. 184.

57. Butler, *Grand Strategy II*, p. 418.

58. This letter is reprinted in full in Churchill, *Their Finest Hour*, pp. 558-67.

59. Ibid., p. 562. Italics mine.

60. See Churchill's long telegram to Australia of December 23, 1940, in Churchill, *Their Finest Hour*, pp. 704-5.

61. Butler, *Grand Strategy II*, pp. 424-25. Churchill followed the course of the Anglo-American staff talks very closely, and when it looked as if Admiral Bellairs was ignoring this particular instruction, Pound received a sharp "personal minute" from the prime minister. "You will remember that I asked particularly that our advocacy of a forward strategy in the Pacific should not be pressed upon the United States Naval Authorities unduly. The Americans were to have been left to put their own stamp upon the Pacific warfare with the feeling that they would find Hawaii too far away. We were to indicate our ideas but only for their consideration." Churchill to Pound, February 8, 1941, PRO ADM 205/10.

62. Robert E. Sherwood, *Roosevelt and Hopkins*, rev. ed. (New York: Harper & Bros., 1950), p. 239.

63. Ibid., p. 259.

64. Ibid.

65. Churchill, *The Grand Alliance*, pp. 178-79.

66. Ibid., p. 179.

67. Ibid., p. 180.

68. Ibid., pp. 180-81.

69. Ibid., p. 178.

70. Butler, *Grand Strategy II*, p. 504.

71. Ibid.

72. Churchill, *The Grand Alliance*, p. 190.

73. Butler, *Grand Strategy II*, pp. 502-3. Churchill does not mention this episode in his memoirs. The prime minister, who had clashed with Danckwerts (then the Admiralty's director of plans) when he was first lord in Chamberlain's War Cabinet, thereafter disliked him for not welcoming Knox's suggestion more warmly.

74. Diary of Sir Ian Jacob, of the Arcadia Conference, pp. 31-32.

75. Ibid.

76. Woodward, *British Foreign Policy*, 2:134-36, 179. The account of this episode in Butler, *Grand Strategy II*, p. 505, is so ambiguous as to be misleading.

77. PRO, CAB 69, D.O. (41) 31, May 19, 1941.

78. Churchill, *The Grand Alliance*, p. 235.

79. Ibid., pp. 235-36.

80. Ibid., pp. 424-25; Sherwood, *Roosevelt and Hopkins*, pp. 313-17; Kennedy, *The Business of War*, pp. 153-57.

81. By mid-June, when things had eased somewhat, the Defence Committee decided to urge the Americans not to move any more battleships to the Atlantic. Butler, *Grand Strategy II*, p. 507.

82. Ibid., p. 548.

83. Woodward, *British Foreign Policy*, 2:179.

84. Churchill, *The Grand Alliance*, p. 427.

85. PRO, CAB 69, D.O. (41) 56, August 8, 1941.

86. Interview with Dr. T.C. Carter, November 27, 1973.

87. Air Chief Marshal Sir Robert Brooke-Popham, "Operations in the Far East, from 17th October 1940 to 27th December 1941," *Supplement to the London Gazette*, January 22, 1948, par. 7 (cited hereafter as Brooke-Popham, *Dispatch*); BPP v/1/2, v/4/14, 17, 20, 28; Brooke-Popham, "Notes on the Far East," March 12, 1942, pp. 2-3, BPP v/9/5/2.

88. Carter to family, April 11, 1942, Carter Papers, TCC 3/3, Imperial War Museum, London.

89. Ibid. Interview with Dr. Carter, November 27, 1973.

90. Maj. Gen. I. S. O. Playfair, "Some Personal Reflections on the Malayan Campaign," n.d. [covering letter to Brooke-Popham dated May 10, 1943], p. 11, BPP v/9/28 (cited hereafter as Playfair, "Personal Reflections").

91. Interview with Lt. Gen. Sir Ian Jacob, G.B.E., January 14, 1971. It should, however, be emphasized that Brooke-Popham's successive chiefs of staff were both men of considerable ability. Dewing had been Kennedy's predecessor as director of military operations at the War Office, and was later to be a member of the British joint staff mission in Washington. Playfair had been director of plans at the War Office prior to his posting to the Far East to replace Dewing.

92. Brooke-Popham, "Notes on the Far East," p. 3, BPP v/9/5/2.

93. Brooke-Popham, "Comments on the draft of The War Against Japan, Volume I," April 16, 1953, BPP v/9/34.

94. Private information from an officer who was then a brigade major (chief of staff) to an infantry brigade in Great Britain.

95. Brooke-Popham to Ismay, December 5, 1940, January 6, 1941, BPP v/1/3, 4; Brooke-Popham, "Notes on the Far East," pp. 8-9; idem, v/9/5/2; Brooke-Popham *Dispatch*, par. 8.

96. Brooke-Popham to Ismay, October 29, 1941, BPP v/1/19; Brooke-Popham,

"Most Secret. Agressive Action Against Japan," August 30, 1941, BPP, v/4/29. Sir Andrew Gilmour, a former M.C.S. officer who was shipping controller in Singapore until November 1941, speculated in an article in the Singapore *New Nation*, May 3, 1971, that Dewing's breakdown was due to the strain of maintaining the bluff about the strength of Malaya's defenses. I am grateful to Mr. A. H. P. Humphrey, C.M.G. for drawing my attention to this article.

97. S. W. Kirby, *Singapore: The Chain of Disaster* (New York: Macmillan, 1971), pp. 74-75. Colonel Ward was later a member of the team that wrote the official history of the war against Japan.

98. Brooke-Popham's account of the critical meeting of the Singapore War Committee that led to Vlieland's resignation is in Brooke-Popham to Ismay, January 6, 1941, BPP v/1/4. See also Brooke-Popham's "Comments on the first draft of The War Against Japan, Volume I," April 16, 1953, BPP v/9/34. Vlieland's account, "Disaster in the Far East 1941-42," in the Liddell Hart Centre for Military Archives, King's College, London, differs in a number of important particulars from Brooke-Popham's. Kirby, *Singapore: The Chain of Disaster*, p. 73 gives an account that varies in some respects from both Brooke-Popham's and Vlieland's. The governor's silence is probably explained by the fact that he had come to believe that Vlieland had gone beyond the scope of his office by taking such an active part in the Bond-Babington quarrel. Sir Shenton Thomas, "Comments on the Draft History of the War Against Japan," October 1954, par. 55, Thomas Papers, Rhodes House Library, Oxford.

99. Brooke-Popham to Ismay, May 16, 1941, BPP v/1/12.

100. Interviews with Lt. Gen. Sir Ian Jacob, who knew Percival at the army staff college at Camberley, January 14, 1971 and June 9, 1975; Kirby, *Singapore: The Chain of Disaster*, p. 129. There is a sympathetic study of Percival, based on his papers, by Sir J. Smyth, V. C., *Percival and the Tragedy of Singapore* (London: Macdonald, 1971).

101. "Confidential Notes by Lieut-General A. E. Percival CB DSO OBE MC on certain Senior Commanders and other matters," n.d. Percival Papers, Box 5, Imperial War Museum, London. Italics mine. Heath, while not a staff college graduate, had served as an instructor at the Senior Officers School in India, and, as a divisional commander, had had more British formations under his command *in action* than Percival.

102. Playfair, "Personal Reflections," p. 8.

103. Brooke-Popham to Ismay, January 6, 1941, BPP v/1/4.

104. Playfair, "Personal Reflections," p. 8.

105. Lt. Col. B. H. Ashmore, O.B.E., "Some Personal Observations on the Malaya Campaign," July 27, 1942, Percival Papers, Box 5, p. 21.

106. T. C. Carter to family, April 11, 1942, Carter Papers, TCC 3/3. Carter was only invited into one civilian home in the year he spent in Singapore. Interview with Dr. Carter, November 27, 1973.

107. Brooke-Popham, "Comments on the first draft of The War Against Japan, Volume I," April 16, 1953, BPP v/9/34.

108. Sir William Goode, G.C.M.G., letter to the author, January 5, 1974. At the time Sir William was assistant secretary for civil defense in Singapore.

109. W. L. Blythe, C.M.G., letter to the author, January 1974.

110. This point was made by A. H. P. Humphrey in a letter to the author, January 22, 1974. Another former M.C.S. officer, Mr. H. P. Bryson, has made the point, however, that to most Malays Japan was just another foreign power, and that they might have been more enthusiastic about preparing for war if the government had "stressed over the preceding years that we were there to lead Malaya towards self-government — which was presumably our ultimate aim, but we never, or seldom, acted as if we believed that."

H. P. Bryson to A. H. Dickinson, November 15, 1968, Bryson Collection, Royal Commonwealth Society Library, London. In the same letter Mr. Bryson admits that this argument owes a great deal to hindsight, and there was no lack of enthusiastic Malay volunteers for the expansion of the Malay Regiment, four of whose Malay officers were later to be executed by the Japanese for refusing to remove their British rank badges.

111. Sir Shenton Thomas, "Comments on the Draft History of the War Against Japan," par. 59; Sir Shenton Thomas, "Malaya's War Effort," July 1947, Bryson Collection. Ultimately, Sir Shenton estimated, some 45,000 Europeans, Eurasians, and Asians were enrolled either in the local Volunteer Forces, or as air raid wardens, auxiliary police, fire service, and medical personnel, etc.

112. Kirby, *Singapore: The Chain of Disaster*, pp. 29-30 makes the accusation. I am grateful to Mr. A. H. P. Humphrey, who compiled the figures that refute it, for making them available to me. Mr. Humphrey commented that some men were recruited into the M.C.S. after 1918 on the basis of their excellent war records — and not all of them turned into good civil administrators. Interview with the author, June 1, 1975.

113. Sir Shenton Thomas, "Malaya's War Effort," pp. 23-24.

114. Memorandum by A. H. Dickinson, "Security in Government House, Singapore," enclosed in Dickinson to Bryson, April 21, 1970, Bryson Collection; Brooke-Popham to Ismay, February 28, July 15, 1941, BPP v/1/7, 15, Ismay to Brooke-Popham, September 16, 1941, BPP v/1/17.

115. See, for example, G. C. Madoc to A. H. Dickinson, January 27, 1970, Bryson Collection. A company of infantry, ordered on a jungle exercise, planned to take four days to cover what two M.C.S. officers had walked in eight hours. Then the exercise was canceled because the troops, in addition to their own equipment, could not manage the large quantity of medical supplies that the army doctors regarded as essential in the jungle.

116. Playfair, "Personal Reflections," p. 8.

117. Brooke-Popham to Ismay, December 5, 1940, BPP v/1/3. An example of the mood that this aroused can be found in Carter to family, April 11, 1942, Carter Papers, TCC 3/3. An added complication was that Indian Army officers were paid on a different scale from British service officers — and often their pay was higher.

118. Brooke-Popham, "Comments on the draft of The War Against Japan, Volume I," April 16, 1953, BPP v/9/34; Interview with Mr. A. H. P. Humphrey, June 1, 1975.

119. Playfair, "Personal Reflections," p. 1.

120. Ismay to Brooke-Popham, February 9, 1941, BPP v/1/6. Italics mine.

121. Churchill, *The Grand Alliance*, p. 177.

122. Brooke-Popham to Street, January 15, 1941, BPP v/1/2.

123. Brooke-Popham, *Dispatch*, App. J.

124. Secret. Easfar to Air Ministry, March 1, 1941, BPP v/4/11. The figure (215) refers to the initial establishment, not to the complete outfit, including reserves.

125. Kirby et al., *The Loss of Singapore*, p. 240, fn. 3.

126. Brooke-Popham to Ismay, July 3, 1941, BPP v/1/14. The Beaufort was a modern torpedo bomber, just coming into service, and the obsolete Vildebeeste was the only torpedo bomber currently available in the Far East. The ancient Wirraway was no longer considered an operational aircraft by the RAF. The Glen Martin was an American light bomber, used by the Dutch Army Air Service in the N.E.I. The reference to "six months" is interesting, as it indicates that Brooke-Popham believed that it would take twice as long to reinforce the Far East as London assumed.

127. Brooke-Popham, "Notes on the Far East," March 12, 1942, p. 11, BPP v/9/5/2; idem, "Comments on the draft of The War Against Japan, Volume I," April 16, 1953,

pp. 9-10, BPP v/9/34; idem, *Dispatch*, pars. 79-83; Interview with Dr. T. C. Carter, November 27, 1973.

128. Ismay to Brooke-Popham, June 15, 1941, BPP v/1/13.

129. Churchill, *Their Finest Hour*, p. 643.

130. D. Richards and H. St. G. Saunders, *The Royal Air Force 1939-1945*, 3 vols. (London: H.M.S.O., 1953-54), 1:383-87. Of course the bulk of these 34 squadrons were in the Middle East — 29, in fact. Even more important, the Middle East squadrons were flying modern aircraft, not Buffaloes.

131. Squadron Leader T. C. Carter, "History of R.D.F. Organisation in the Far East 1941-1942," n.d. [but written sometime in 1943], Carter Papers, TCC 2/1; T. C. Carter to family, April 11, 1942, Carter Papers, TCC 3/3; Interview with Dr. T. C. Carter, November 27, 1973; Brooke-Popham, *Dispatch*, par. 54; Air Vice Marshal Sir Paul Maltby, "Report on Air Operations During the Campaigns in Malaya and the Netherlands East Indies From 8th December 1941 to 12th March 1942," *Supplement to the London Gazette*, February 26, 1948, pars. 81-84 (cited hereafter as Maltby, *Dispatch*). The relevant volume of the RAF official history, D. Richards and H. St. G. Saunders, *The Royal Air Force 1939-1945*, vol. 2, *The Fight Avails* (London: H.M.S.O., 1954), does not discuss the Air Ministry's failure to supply VHF equipment and is generally somewhat unreliable about events in the Far East.

132. Brooke-Popham to Ismay, February 3, 1941, BPP v/1/5; Ismay's reply is in BPP v/1/11.

133. Brooke-Popham, *Dispatch*, par. 46; see also idem, "Notes on the Far East," March 12, 1942, p. 4, BPP v/9/5/2; idem, "Comments on the draft of The War Against Japan, Volume I," April 16, 1953, p. 13, BPP v/9/34.

134. I. Simson, *Singapore: Too Little, Too Late* (London: Leo Cooper Ltd. 1970). pp. 13-40.

135. Ibid., p. 52.

136. Kirby et al., *The Loss of Singapore*, p. 240, fn. 3. The account in Richards and Saunders, *The Royal Air Force 1939-1945*, 2:11, differs in some details; see also Brooke-Popham, *Dispatch*, par. 8; Maltby, *Dispatch*, pars. 67-68.

137. Playfair, "Personal Reflections," p. 13. Brooke-Popham's habit of napping during conferences, which is commented upon adversely by Kirby, *Singapore: The Chain of Disaster*, p. 56, and by Sir Andrew Gilmour in his article in the Singapore *New Nation*, May 3, 1971, may have had as much to do with his exhausting schedule as his waning physical strength.

138. Butler, *Grand Strategy II*, pp. 251-52, 259; Butler, ed., *History of the Second World War*, "Grand Strategy" series, vol. 5, J. Ehrman, *Grand Strategy (August 1943-September 1944)* (London: H.M.S.O., 1956), pp. 38-40.

139. Kirby et al., *The Loss of Singapore* pp. 61-63; Brooke-Popham, *Dispatch*, par. 45; Playfair, "Personal Reflections," p. 10; Samuel Eliot Morison, *History of United States Naval Operations in World War II*, 15 vols. (Boston: Atlantic Little, Brown, 1947-62), 3:53-56, 57, fn. 21; H. Feis, *The Road to Pearl Harbor* (Princeton, N.J: Princeton University Press, 1950), p. 170.

140. Kirby et al., *The Loss of Singapore*, pp. 55-56, 63; Brooke-Popham, *Dispatch* par. 44.

141. Vlieland, "Disaster in the Far East 1941-1942," pp. 76-77.

142. C. MacKenzie, *Eastern Epic, vol. 1, Defence* (London: Chatto E. Windus, 1951), pp. 224-25. A subadar major was the senior Indian officer in a unit, and roughly equivalent to a warrant officer in the U.S. Army.

143. Butler, *Grand Strategy II*, p. 349.

144. Brooke-Popham to Ismay, January 6, February 28, 1941, BPP v/1/4, 7.

145. Kirby, *Singapore: The Chain of Disaster*, pp. 73-74; *Australia in The War of 1939-45:* Series I (Army), vol. 4, L. Wigmore, *The Japanese Thrust* (Canberra: Australian War Memorial, 1957), pp. 58-59.

146. Wigmore, *The Japanese Thrust*, p. 65; Kirby, *Singapore: The Chain of Disaster*, pp. 105, 131-32. This "charter" was a normal feature of Commonwealth military relationships. Canadian commanders had similar rights, as did Australian, New Zealand, and South African commanders in the Middle East. One South African, Major-General D. Pienaar, often "interpreted" his orders in a manner that would have gotten a British divisional commander sacked.

6

COUNTDOWN:
July-December 1941

i

In her brief career, H.M.S. *Prince of Wales*, which carried Churchill to his first meeting with Roosevelt, had not been a lucky ship. Fresh from the builders, and with workmen still aboard, she and the elderly battle cruiser H.M.S. *Hood* had engaged the *Bismarck* and the *Prinz Eugen* on May 24, 1941. The *Hood* was lost and the *Prince of Wales* suffered severe damage. Captain John Leach was one of only three survivors of a direct hit on the *Prince of Wales's* bridge by one of *Bismarck's* 15-inch shells. The scars of that engagement were still visible on the ship when the prime minister boarded her some two months later. Finding his alloted quarters uncomfortable, Churchill took over the Admiral's quarters on the bridge. The prime minister, who was reading C. S. Forester for relaxation during the voyage, took a great liking to Captain Leach.[1] It would be Churchill's decision three months later that would send Leach and the *Prince of Wales* to their doom.

A meeting between Roosevelt and Churchill had been brewing since the spring and had become urgent by mid-summer, largely because of the growing menace from Japan, as Churchill later wrote in his memoirs.[2] But, for the prime minister, the conference was to be barren as far as the defense of the Far East was concerned, something he did not stress in his postwar account.

The urgency of securing some commitment about the Far East from the Americans had been underlined the day before Churchill left Chequers for Scapa Flow to board the *Prince of Wales*. The

139

Joint Intelligence Committee warned that Japan's next move might
be against the Isthmus of Kra.[3] This would pose a direct threat to
Malaya and the air reinforcement route from India to Singapore. A
Japanese move against the Kra Isthmus had been defined in the stillborn ADB agreement as an action requiring an immediate response.
On the 5th the Chiefs of Staff committee met to discuss Matador
with Vice Admiral Sir Tom Phillips and Lieutenant General Sir
Henry Pownall deputizing for Pound and Dill, who were with the
prime minister. The Chiefs of Staff felt that they ought to recommend mounting the operation but decided to ask the commander in
chief, Far East, for his views. At a meeting of the Defence Committee the same day, Eden cautioned the Chiefs of Staff that the
American reaction to Matador would have to be ascertained before
final approval could be given.[4] The following day London got
Brooke-Popham's reaction, which was very cautious. He was conscious of the fact that Bond had estimated that it would take five
divisions to hold Malaya *and* seize the Kra Isthmus, while he had
only the equivalent of two, and those incomplete in many respects.
He was also aware of a telegram sent four days earlier by Percival
to the War Office in which the GOC asked for the equivalent of
two more divisions plus two tank regiments over and above the
forces already allotted to Malaya. In his answer Brooke-Popham
therefore suggested that the United States, Britain, and the Dutch
should jointly warn Japan that they would treat any violation of
Thai territory as a *casus belli*. Meanwhile, he did not recommend
launching Matador unless it was clearly established that Japan had
assembled the forces necessary to occupy Thailand.[5] His caution
dampened the brief flicker of enthusiasm in London for Matador.
After digesting his reply, the Chiefs of Staff stipulated on August
7 that "until we are assured of the military support of the U.S.A.
in the event of war with Japan, we should take no action save in
defence of our vital interests, which is likely to precipitate war."
They went on to define Thailand, including the Isthmus of Kra, as
falling outside the category of vital interests.[6] This definition was
odd in view of the general agreement that control of the Kra Isthmus
was critical to the defense of Malaya. It makes sense only if it is remembered that the British were almost as worried about American
reaction as they were about Japanese action. At the Defence Committee meeting on August 8, Sir Tom Phillips remarked that "our
strategy should be to avoid war with Japan, and give way as long
as we could afford to, until America was ready and willing to
support us."[7] The same day Sir Henry Pownall confided to his

diary that Matador would be worth doing if the Americans agreed, but not otherwise, for unilateral action by Britain "wouldn't start a war with Japan, in all probability, but it would remove all chance, though that is little enough, of America coming to our aid over Siam . . . ."[8] The Kra Isthmus, Pownall reflected, while "important," was not "vital." Staying in step with the United States was, in fact, more important in London's eyes than Matador, even though the operation represented Brooke-Popham's one slim chance of denying the initiative to the Japanese.

The caution that had emerged in London was reflected in a telegram that the Defence Committee sent to the prime minister, who was still *en route*.

3. Blunt warning that we would regard further Japanese moves into Siam as *casus belli* might in itself be too challenging, and obviously goes beyond what United States Government could constitutionally say. Moreover we should not regard Japanese move into north or east Siam as constituting such a direct threat to our own interests as Japanese attempt to occupy Kra Isthmus.

4. Defence Committee are unanimous in view that situation would best be met by parallel warnings by United States privately to the Japanese Government through the diplomatic channel to the effect that any incursion by the Japanese forces into Siam would produce a situation in which we should be compelled to take counter measures likely to lead to war between our respective countries and Japan.[9]

Even Brooke-Popham's cautious recommendations had therefore been rejected. Everything now hinged on what the Americans could be brought to do, or at least agree to the British doing.

It is, therefore, not surprising that the British official historians described "the growing menace of Japan" as "the real crux" of the Atlantic meeting as far as Churchill was concerned. He had always counted on American pressure to deter Japan. If the Americans declined either to exert that pressure, or to guarantee their support to the British and Dutch against Japan, the prime minister's entire policy for the Far East was bankrupt. In his discussions with the president, and in parallel conversations that Sir Alexander Cadogan, the permanent under-secretary at the Foreign Office, held with under-secretary of state Sumner Welles, the British pressed hard for both an American warning to Japan and a guarantee for themselves and the Dutch. At the same time Pound, Dill, and Air

Chief Marshal Wilfred Freeman (deputizing for Portal, who remained in London) discussed the Far East with Marshall, Stark, and Lieutenant General H. H. Arnold, the chief of the Army Air Forces.

The military discussions on the Far East went nowhere. The British quickly discovered that the Americans had no plans at all for the area beyond building up a modest naval and air striking force based on the Philipines, which would not be complete until the spring of 1942. And, try as they might, the British simply could not interest the Americans in the future of Singapore. Contradicting what General Chaney had said in London the previous month about the high value that the Americans placed on Singapore, Admiral Stark suggested that perhaps Great Britain could dispense, if necessary, with the supplies she drew from the Far East. A member of the War Cabinet staff noted in his diary after this meeting: "Admiral Stark attaches very little importance to the Far East and imagines that we can afford to see it all 'go West' without bothering ourselves unduly." The Americans did, however, reiterate their view that the Middle East was a military liability that the British could well do without.[10] It is an interesting commentary on the amount of detailed attention London had hitherto paid to the Far East that in one of the private meetings of the British Chiefs of Staff to discuss that area, Dill suddenly asked "What kind of aeroplanes have the Japanese got?"[11] It was rather late in the day to ask that critical question. American reluctance to become involved in Singapore's defense may well have owed something to the feeling that the British themselves were not treating it very seriously.

The talks at the political level seemed at first more fruitful. Churchill put very heavy pressure on the president, telling Roosevelt that if Japan attacked the United States, Great Britain would immediately declare war on Japan.[12] Under Churchill's prodding, Roosevelt agreed to a joint warning to Japan, which, on America's part, would take the following form: "Any further encroachment by Japan in the South West Pacific would produce a situation in which the United States Government would be compelled to take counter measures even though these might lead to war between the United States and Japan."[13] Churchill jubilantly cabled Eden in London that, if Japan pushed on, the "conditions indicated . . . would come in play with great force."[14] He believed that he had finally succeeded in committing the Americans to a position that would either halt Japan's southward march or at least ensure that a Japanese attack on Malaya or the Netherlands East Indies would bring America into the war alongside Great Britain. If that happened the United States Pacific Fleet would be the major Japanese pre-occupation.

The prime minister's moment of triumph was brief. Before parting from Roosevelt, Churchill asked for a copy of the warning note that the president would hand to the Japanese ambassador when he returned to Washington. He was told that it had not yet been drafted. On August 17, the day before Churchill returned to London, Roosevelt saw Admiral Nomura and gave him a much weaker declaration. This was the result of pressure by Hull and the State Department, who found the language agreed upon between Roosevelt and Churchill much too vigorous. The prime minister was given no advance notice of this departure from what had been settled. On August 19 he wrote in his report of the Atlantic Conference: "I am confident that the President will not tone [the warning to Japan] down."[15] That same day the first doubts began to creep in with a message from Roosevelt that he had given the Japanese ambassador a warning "substantially similar" and "no less vigorous than" the one agreed upon at the Atlantic Conference. Halifax was immediately told to ask for a copy of the statement. Only when this arrived in London during the night of August 22-23 was the collapse of the agreement plain.[16] Churchill's response was to repeat in a broadcast on August 24 that Britain would stand beside the United States if it was involved in war with Japan. No reciprocal pledge echoed back across the Atlantic.

The collapse of the agreement with Roosevelt meant further disappointment for the increasingly anxious Pacific dominions. Churchill had cabled Menzies (Fraser was in London on a visit) when he left England: ". . . the whole field of future action can be explored . . . I hope you will approve of this action, which may be productive of important benefits."[17] The Australians, however, had their own ideas about how Japan ought to be warned off. "We now say and emphasize that an early despatch of capital ships east of Suez would itself be most powerful deterrent and first step," Menzies cabled Churchill on August 12, repeating his cable to the other dominions.[18] Churchill rather blandly replied three days later that the warning he had persuaded Roosevelt to deliver to the Japanese would keep them quiet temporarily, especially if Britain and the dominions associated themselves with it.[19] As August 1941 entered its last week, the prime minister faced the disappointment of his hopes for a firm American warning that would stop

Japan. Nor was there any American guarantee to come in if Japan struck Malaya or the East Indies, much less Thailand, while the oil embargo initiated by the United States increased the likelihood of a Japanese move south. One of Churchill's staff officers later recalled that it was his private nightmare in the months prior to Pearl Harbor that Japan would attack Britain or the Dutch, while leaving America alone, and that the United States would consequently stand aside.[20] Four months earlier Churchill had laid down as a fundamental premise of British strategy that Japan would not attack Britain if it meant drawing the United States in, which would certainly be the case. Now that this premise looked rather shaky, what could be done by London for the Far East?

ii

In the spring, after the conclusion of ABC-1, the Admiralty had reaffirmed its intention of sending a battle cruiser and a carrier to the Indian Ocean if war with Japan erupted. This had been their position since August 1940 when the *Renown* and the *Ark Royal* were designated as available — indeed, two capital ships had been the maximum that the Admiralty had been willing to consider sending since June 1939. After ABC-1 however, with the prospect of American naval assistance in the Atlantic and the virtual certainty that the Americans would not base the Pacific Fleet on Singapore, the Admiralty planned eventually to send five more battleships east.[21]   In August, at the time of the Atlantic Conference, the Joint Planning Staff submitted to the Chiefs of Staff a scheme for building up an Eastern Fleet. They suggested moving one battleship, either the *Barham* or the *Valiant*, from the Mediterranean into the Indian Ocean by mid-September. By the end of the year it would be joined by four more battleships of the "R" class. The *Valiant* and the *Barham*, launched in 1914, had been modernized, but the four "R's," launched in 1915-16, had not. They were, at best, obsolescent, and were currently being employed to protect important Atlantic convoys against German raiders. The Joint Planning Staff pointed out that no cruisers or fleet destroyers could be spared for the Eastern Fleet, but hoped that the aircraft carrier *Eagle* could join it early in 1942. H.M.S. *Eagle*, originally laid down as a battleship in 1913, had been converted to an aircraft carrier at the end of the First World War. She was old, slow, and carried only 21 aircraft. With the exception, therefore, of the one battleship to be drawn from the Mediterranean, the planned Eastern Fleet, conjured by the Joint Planners out of Britain's overstretched resources, was a floating maritime museum whose effectiveness would have been further impaired by the lack of cruisers and destroyers. The Joint Planners proposed to base it on Ceylon until March 1942 when, enlarged and strengthened by more capital ships, two cruisers, and twenty-four destroyers, it would move to Singapore.[22] There matters stood until after the Atlantic Conference.

On August 25, within forty-eight hours of discovering that Roosevelt had backed out of his promise to warn Japan off, and the day after he broadcast his pledge to stand with America if Japan struck, Churchill sent a very revealing minute to Pound.

It should be possible in the near future to place a deterrent squadron in the Indian Ocean. Such a force should consist of the smallest number of the best ships. We have only to remember all the preoccupations which are caused us by the *Tirpitz* — the only capital ship left to Germany against our fifteen or sixteen battleships and battle-cruisers — to see what an effect would be produced upon the Japanese Admiralty by the presence of a small but very powerful and fast force in Eastern waters . . . . This powerful force might show itself in the triangle Aden — Singapore — Simonstown. It would exert a paralyzing effect on Japanese naval action . . . . I do not like the idea of sending at this stage the old "R" class battleships to the East . . . the old ships are easy prey to modern Japanese vessels, and can neither fight nor run . . . I am however in principle in favour of placing a formidable, fast, high-class squadron in the aforesaid triangle by the end of October, and telling both the Americans and Australians that we will do so. It seems probable that the American negotiations with Japan will linger on for some time. The Americans talk now of ninety days,[23]

Churchill clearly sensed that time was running out in the Far East. At the Atlantic meeting, when he was thinking, temporarily at least, in terms of a stiff warning to Japan, Roosevelt had spoken to Churchill about gaining a month's respite, during which, the prime minister cabled home, British defenses in the Far East could be strengthened.[24] Presumably the "softer" approach adopted with Nomura led to a lengthening of the estimated time remaining before a crisis in the Far East — to the end of November, by which time Churchill hoped to have his "deterrent squadron" in position.

This minute to Pound was as close as Churchill ever came to giving the three-months warning on which the Chiefs of Staff had insisted in May. At that time Kennedy had expressed doubts as to whether such foresight was possible. Yet the ninety days that Churchill mentioned came very close to the mark, and the prime minister clearly wanted something done about the complete absence of naval power in the East.

Even this new determination was shot through with reservations and misconceptions, however. The most important of these was the idea of a small, powerful "deterrent squadron." Churchill had grown up in a world where the movement of British battleships was one of the most powerful of diplomatic counters, and he clearly overestimated the effect that the appearance of a few British battleships would have on Japanese decisions. Moreover, the whole analogy with the *Tirpitz* was misconceived. The Atlantic convoys were absolutely vital to Britain's survival. No interruption of the convoy cycle could be accepted. The mere threat of a raid into the Atlantic by Germany's few heavy ships was enough to tie down a disproportionate amount of British naval strength. The situation in the Far East was entirely different. A few modern British ships roaming the Indian Ocean would pose no threat to anything as crucial to Japan as the Atlantic convoys were to Britain. Any Japanese attack on Malaya or the East Indies would be so well covered by heavy surface ships and planes, both carrier borne and land based, that it would be impossible for a small squadron to interfere. Moreover, if the Japanese entered the Indian Ocean in force, the deterrent squadron could do little but get out of the way. In April 1942, when Admiral Chuichi Nagumo's carrier striking force made the only major Japanese incursion of the war into that area, the Eastern Fleet, although by that time comprising five battleships (four of them "R's" however), three carriers, seven cruisers, and fourteen destroyers, could do nothing except fall back from Ceylon to East Africa.

These considerations, if they presented themselves at all to Churchill, were the more easily set aside because strategic considerations were far from being the only ones in his mind when he composed the minute to Pound. There were the Australians, anxious about their security and clutching a sheaf of promissory notes that went back twenty years, who expected to see a British fleet. Events in the Middle East (which will be discussed below) were putting further strains upon Anglo-Australian relations and made a reassuring gesture very timely. Then there were the Americans.

Churchill's repeated public and private statements that Britain would immediately declare war on Japan if the latter attacked America indicated his belief that such action would be the best policy for Britain, but they were also aimed at embarrassing the Americans into some response. The deterrent squadron may have sprung, in part, from the same idea. Britain had declared its intention of standing by America, come what may. If this was followed up by the diversion of scarce naval resources to the Far East, perhaps the United States would be encouraged — or feel compelled — to make some reciprocal gesture. There is no hard evidence for this, and there may well never be unless the unpublished Churchill papers contain some, but, given the prime minister's previous policy, it is highly probable that America was as much in his mind as Japan when he dictated this minute.

The first sea lord's response, on August 28, was completely negative. He wanted to keep the three new battleships of the *King George V* class (*King George V, Duke of York,* and the *Prince of Wales*) in the Atlantic to deal with the *Tirpitz*. "The Atlantic is the vital area, as it is in that ocean and that alone in which we can lose the war at sea," he reminded Churchill. There was at present in the Indian Ocean the carrier *Hermes.* Launched in 1919, she was the first carrier built as such for the Royal Navy, and had been in semiretirement at the outbreak of the war. The battle cruiser *Repulse*, launched in 1916 and unmodernized, would escort a troop convoy bound for the Middle East and then go on to Ceylon, where she would arrive on October 7. "By sending a battle cruiser and aircraft-carrier to the Indian Ocean we hope to deter the Japanese from sending their eight-inch cruisers to attack our trade in this area," Pound explained. The next step would be to create the Eastern Fleet proper. Between the end of November and mid-January, the battleships *Nelson* and *Rodney*, reasonably modern ships launched in 1925 and carrying the only sixteen-inch guns in the Royal Navy, and the battle cruiser *Renown*, the *Repulse's* modernized sister ship, would arrive in the Indian Ocean, to be followed in April 1942 by the modern armored carrier *Ark Royal.* "*Nelson* and *Rodney* will form the most homogenous fleet we can provide as regards speed," Pound explained. He added that "depending on the situation at the time, and if war with Japan has not broken out, it may be found desirable to send *Nelson, Rodney, Renown* and the aircraft carrier to Singapore in the first instance, as they would thus form a greater deterrent. If war eventuated they would have to retire to Trincomalee." In addition to all this, from mid-September to early January, the four "R's" would be sent east. No longer needed in the Atlantic, where indeed their vulnerability to air and submarine attack made them liabilities, they would be used for convoy escort in the Indian Ocean. "Until we can form a fleet in the Far East which is capable of meeting a Japanese force of the strength they are likely to send south, it is necessary to deter Japanese action in the Indian Ocean. By sending capital ships to escort our convoys in the Indian Ocean we hope to deter the Japanese from sending any of their battleships to this area," Pound explained, adding, "their presence in the Indian Ocean, together with *Nelson, Rodney*, and *Renown*, will go some way to meet the wishes of Australia and New Zealand for the Far East to be reinforced."[25]

To cover the next three critical months, the first sea lord could offer only the obsolescent *Repulse* and *Hermes*. By January 1942 three fairly modern capital ships could be provided, barring accidents elsewhere, and three months after that a modern carrier would join them. Even then the Eastern Fleet could not hope to remain at Singapore once war broke out. In the meantime a stage army composed of the four "R's" would promenade the Indian Ocean, reassuring the dominions and trying to stay out of trouble.

Churchill reacted strongly to Pound's minute. "It is surely a faulty disposition to create in the Indian Ocean a fleet considerable in numbers, costly in maintenance and man-power, but consisting entirely of slow, obsolescent, or unmodernized ships which can neither fight a fleet action with the main Japanese force nor act as a deterrent upon his modern, fast, heavy ships, if used singly or in pairs as raiders," he replied the next day. "The "R's" in their present state would be floating coffins . . . . The potency of the dispositions I ventured to suggest in my minute is illustrated by the Admiralty's own extraordinary concern about the *Tirpitz. Tirpitz* is doing to us exactly what a *K.G.V.* in the Indian Ocean would do to the Japanese Navy. It exercises a vague general fear and menaces all points at once. It appears and disappears, causing immediate reaction and perturbation on the other side," he argued, revealing again a mental picture of Far Eastern naval realities as misleading as his view of Singapore's defenses. "I must add that I cannot feel that Japan will face the combination now forming against her," he concluded. "Nothing would increase her hesitation more than the appearance of the force I mentioned, and above all a *K.G.V.* This might indeed be a decisive deterrent."[26]

Obviously Churchill and Pound were not using "deterrent" in quite the same way. To the prime minister a deterrent squadron in the Indian Ocean meant not only naval security there, but the possibility of bluffing Japan, soothing Australia, and enticing America forward. The first sea lord obviously considered Singapore a write-off, at least for the foreseeable future, and concentrated on the maintenance of maritime control in the Indian Ocean, through which passed Britain's vital communications with the Middle East and the Persian Gulf oil fields. Pound wanted to build up a large balanced fleet to hold on to at least this. Churchill wanted to rush out a symbolic force in a gambler's throw to hold much more.

What is surprising about this exchange is that it ended with Churchill's reply to Pound. His pressure on the Admiralty abruptly ceased, and Pound had his way, at least temporarily. The *Repulse* set out on her fateful journey east. Why did Churchill, despite his sense of the urgency of the matter, allow Pound to gainsay him? Why was the first sea lord not hammered as Dill had been in the spring? The answer probably lies in Churchill's respect for Pound and confidence in his judgment, as well as in Pound's skill in dealing with the prime minister. Despite his reservations, Churchill, preoccupied with many problems, dropped his proposal for the time being.[27]

The same petering out is observable in every consideration of reinforcements for the Far East undertaken in London during the month following the Atlantic Conference. On August 12, galvanized by Roosevelt's remark to Churchill that diplomacy might gain thirty days in the Far East, the War Cabinet asked the Chiefs of Staff what reinforcements could be sent in that time. The possibilities discussed were oddly inconsequential: a medium bomber squadron, another Indian infantry brigade, two antiaircraft regiments, and some light tanks from the Middle East. In the end, this too came to nothing, for in thirty days nothing worthwhile could be done.

On September 14 Portal circulated a note to the other members of the Chiefs of Staff about RAF strength in the Far East. There was no hope, the Chief of the Air Staff admitted, of reaching the target figure of 336 first-line aircraft by the end of of 1941. In 1942 slow progress might be possible. He had tentatively alloted 590 aircraft to the Far East for that year (i.e., less than the 336 with their immediate reserves figured in), but even this depended on production figures. Since no accurate forecast of 1942 production could yet be made, Portal would make no firm promises.

"The Chiefs of Staff took note of this without comment . . . ."
Comment was in fact superfluous. The RAF was also writing off
the Far East for the foreseeable future.

Two days later it was the army's turn. The Joint Planning Staff
reported to the Chiefs of Staff on Percival's request for reinforcements that would nearly double the size of his command. "In
view . . . of our present weakness at sea and in the air, we consider
the proposed increase to be a reasonable target figure in present circumstances. Nevertheless, the reinforcement of the garrison to this
figure cannot be completed in the foreseeable future." The Joint
Planners added that by the time the units Percival wanted became
available, increased naval and air strength in the Far East would
make them unnecessary. Again, nothing more could be done for
the Far East.[28]

Despite what has already been said about his relations with
Pound, Churchill's acquiescence in this round robin of naysaying is
curious. He had approved the dispatch to the Middle East of an
armored brigade in the summer of 1940 at a time when invasion
was a real possibility and that brigade represented nearly half the
tank strength in the U.K. In April 1941 he had rushed tanks through
the Mediterranean to Wavell, despite grave doubts on the part of
the Chiefs of Staff about the feasibility of the operation. He had
repeatedly shown himself willing and able to impose priorities and
force compliance with them. Yet in the month following his return
from the Atlantic meeting, he tamely accepted the finding that
nothing could be done for the Far East, despite his knowledge that
time was running out there. No hectoring minutes with the famous
"Action this Day" label showered down on Pound, Portal, or even
Dill. No searching queries with the ominous beginning, "Pray explain," were directed at them. Why? In carefully neutral language,
the official historians of British strategy have concluded that "no
single or completely satisfactory explanation can be given."[29]
But a great many problems all simultaneously pressing for attention in London help to account for the ease with which the inability
to do anything for the Far East was accepted.

In the first place there were the massive demands of the Middle
East. Auchinleck was preparing an offensive, dubbed *Crusader*, in
which great hopes were invested — not least by the prime minister.
Between July and October the Middle East received 770 tanks,
34,000 trucks, 600 field guns, 240 antiaircraft guns, 200 antitank
guns, and 900 mortars. "Yet these consignments, large as they were,
were not large enough to replace all the losses and wastages that

had occurred and allow any reasonable reserves to be built up."[30]
The Middle East would, therefore, need even more once Auchinleck's offensive got rolling. The flow of divisions to the Middle
East also continued unabated: by December there would be three
armored and thirteen infantry divisions in Middle East Command
plus two more tank brigades and numerous brigades and battalions
not incorporated in divisional formations.[31] Churchill clearly intended to see that this flow continued. In order to provide Auchinleck with the reserve necessary to maintain the momentum of his
offensive, he concerned himself during August and September
with finding the shipping needed to have two divisions rounding
the Cape on the way to the Middle East by the end of the year.
To do this he had to borrow troopships from the Americans.
Roosevelt, seeing a chance to compensate for his failure to warn
Japan off, immediately agreed, blithely telling Churchill on September 6 that he welcomed the British decision to reinforce the
Middle East.[32] Once he had the necessary shipping, the prime
minister was adamant that it should be used to cram the maximum
reinforcement into the Middle East. To assure the proper administrative support for Auchinleck's forces, he ordered five battalions
destined for India to be delayed. The 4,000 passages saved would
be used to carry Royal Army Service Corps personnel out to Egypt.
Despite this, Churchill minuted on September 18 that India should
be instructed to continue its expansion program.[33] Less than a
month before, that program had set the prime minister to riding
one of his favorite hobbyhorses when he discovered that an Indian
Army division in Iraq did not have the customary three British
battalions. A minute to the Chiefs of Staff on August 24 ordered
three sent as rapidly as possible.[34] Only a week before the prime
minister, in his September 18 minute, postponed reinforcements
for India in the interest of the Middle East, Wavell, who was home
for consultations, had given the War Cabinet a "Note on Indian
Military Problems." India, the commander in chief pointed out,
was currently raising five divisions (four infantry and one armored) for the 1942 expansion program. With them India would
have raised fifteen divisions for overseas service, plus units for the
defense of the subcontinent. The Indian armed forces would shortly
number over a million men, an incredible expansion from the
183,000-man army of 1939. India desperately needed British
personnel: 6,500 officers and 76,000 "other ranks" to make up deficiencies and continue the expansion program. It also needed 4,000
vehicles for training purposes. And that was only the beginning.

There is not a single aircraft in India at present capable of taking the air against modern German or Japanese machines; India has not at present a single modern tank or armoured car; has only eighteen light and twelve heavy anti-aircraft guns (against requirements of 200 and 300 respectively); and only twenty 2-pdr. anti-tank guns. The 4th and 5th Indian Divisions, which have now been in the field two years and one year respectively, have not yet been equipped with anti-tank regiments. The same applies to the Indian divisions in Iraq and Malaya.

Wavell warned that there could be serious repercussions in India if a disaster befell Indian troops due to lack of modern equipment that British and dominion troops in the same theater enjoyed.[35] He need not have worried on this point. Everyone in Malaya was to be equally illequipped.

    In the air the picture of concentration on the Middle East was the same. On July 3 the Air Ministry raised its target figure for the Middle East to 62½ squadrons with 1,046 first-line aircraft, which explains Portal's *non possumus* about the Far East. By mid-October there were 52 squadrons in the Middle East, with 846 first-line aircraft, of which 780 were modern. These were backed up by a huge administrative establishment that included three O.T.U.'s. Between January and October 1941, 1,996 aircraft reached the Middle East, including 857 Hurricanes (even the Middle East did not get Spitfires).[36] The flow of aircraft into the Middle East had become so massive that, in the four weeks preceding the launching of Crusader on November 18, the increasing tempo of RAF activity could easily be supported by a steady supply of replacement aircraft for front line units — 232 in these four weeks alone.[37]

    Turkey also continued to affect London's calculations. At Chequers on August 2, Auchinleck had been told that Turkey was to be his principal concern, once Crusader had secured the desert flank. He was also told that, if Russia collapsed, as seemed likely in early August, a German threat to Turkey could develop as early as November 1. He was authorized to offer the Turks four divisions and an armored brigade, assistance in the air whose scale would depend on operations in the desert, and, as a special sweetener, 100 modern 3.7 inch AA guns, which would be made available immediately to cover the defenseless Turkish cities. When conversations opened in Ankara on August 15, it was quickly evident that the Turks feared the *Luftwaffe* more than the *Wehrmacht*, and the British offer was accordingly amended to include twenty squadrons of aircraft, of which four fighter squadrons would be made available to the Turks in November, "regardless of the situation elsewhere."[38]   This promise provided, as so many others had done since November 1940, an additional reason for reinforcing the Middle East heavily. At any moment heavy drafts might be made on it for Turkey, as its strength had been drawn upon for Greece in the spring. It is only with hindsight that the British concern about Turkey seems exaggerated. By August 1941 German armies had covered half the distance to Moscow in barely six weeks. There seemed no reason why they should not cover the remainder before winter. From the points of view of London and Cairo, a German attack on the Middle East via Turkey, in the wake of victory in Russia, seemed all too likely.

The need to do everything possible to prevent German domination of Turkey, and other undesirable things, from happening in the wake of a Russian defeat, was another distraction from the problems of the Far East. The need to sustain Russia had led to the diversion of 200 new fighters in July. The Arctic convoys began in August, and two squadrons of Hurricanes were sent to cover the terminal port of Murmansk. On the 12th Churchill and Roosevelt sent a cable to Stalin from the Atlantic meeting, proposing a conference in Moscow on supplies for Russia. The Russians promptly agreed. Without waiting for all this to be thrashed out, Churchill cabled Stalin offering 200 more Hurricanes. The reply was a demand for 400 aircraft and 500 tanks a months starting in October — and a second front. At a War Cabinet discussion on September 5, Lord Beaverbrook, the minister of supply and foremost advocate of all-out aid to Russia, persuaded the prime minister and his colleagues to offer half the Russian demand from British production and to hold out to the Soviets the hope that the United States might provide the balance.[39]

When the American delegation to the Moscow supply conference sat down in London for preliminary talks with the British on September 15, it transpired that the Americans would indeed make up the balance, but only in a way most unwelcome to the British. Supplies for Russia would come out of the total available for export from the United States over the next nine months — that is, out of supplies that the British believed had been firmly committed to them. In particular, the British lost 1,800 aircraft (divided equally between heavy and light bombers and fighters). At the ensuing Moscow conference the Russians were promised 400 aircraft a month — half, all fighters, from British production. The British also promised 250 tanks a month, as well as 500 antitank guns spread over the next nine months.[40]

Thus every fighter that could be spared from home defense and the Middle East was earmarked for Russia, leaving nothing for the Far East at all. For, despite Churchill's later assertions, there is not much evidence that the flow of aircraft to the Middle East was seriously affected by the Moscow agreements. In September, for example, 226 Hurricanes reached the Middle East.[41] In January 1942, by which time shipments to Russia and war with Japan were in full swing, the figure was still 186.[42] Even without aid to Russia the Far East might have fared badly in competition with the demands of the RAF at home and in the Middle East. Aid to Russia ensured that there was no elasticity left in British aircraft supply, particularly the supply of fighters. Hence the finality with which Portal wrote off the Far East in mid-September. Modern fighter aircraft were the critical need in the Far East. The RAF preferred, however, to meet the Russian demand for aircraft with British fighters rather than cut into the planned expansion of Bomber Command, the instrument of its own "independent" offensive against Germany.

It was not only on questions of supply that Russia made an impact. The demand for a second front had also to be weighed. The British could do nothing in the West, beyond air action, which was another argument for building up the RAF at home. Crusader had little direct relation to the situation on the Russian front. Churchill had urged the Chiefs of Staff in June and again in August to examine the feasibility of operations in northern Norway — the beginning of a strategic obsession that was to last for several years. In October he was toying with an attack on the port of Trondheim in central Norway.[43] The idea of using British troops based on the Caucasus to support Russia's southern flank — and, if Russia collapsed, to deny Germany the oil of the Caucasus — was under consideration in London from August on, and by October a plan was before the War Cabinet. A force of two or three divisions would be assembled at Baku supported by eight RAF squadrons. Both Cairo and Delhi had their doubts about this scheme, but the Chiefs of Staff ordered all the necessary preparations made by March 1942.[44] Since Russian forces were still fighting well west and north of the Caucasus in October 1941, the idea is a measure both of the pessimism in London about Russia's chances and of the desperate search for means of both propping up Soviet resistance and averting the worst consequences of a Russian defeat.

The interlocked problems of Russia, Turkey, the Middle East, and supply were by no means the total of British preoccupations in the late summer of 1941. In the Atlantic fifty-one ships were lost in September. A force of divisional strength was standing by in England to mount operation "Pilgrim," the preemptive seizure of the Spanish and Portuguese Atlantic Islands in case the Germans drove through Spain against Gibraltar.[45]   There were worries and distractions enough to drive the Far East out of mind, particularly since, in the face of other priorities, nothing could be done there in any case. And, as September wore on, it began to seem that perhaps nothing, after all, would happen.

The alarms of late July and August were succeeded by a deceptive calm. The much-feared move into Thailand did not occur. The thirty days of which Roosevelt had spoken passed, and the Japanese were still talking with the Americans. To have this anti-climax follow the fears expressed in August, and the subsequent discovery that nothing could be done for the Far East, produced a sudden, brief optimism (even, as will be seen, in Singapore). Churchill had always believed that Japan would not face the combined power of Britain and the United States. America, it is true, had not given Japan the unequivocal warning that the prime minister wanted, but the mere fact that the leaders of the two countries had met, and America's increasing support for Britain in the West, might well give the Japanese pause. This, too, made it easier to push the Far East, and its needs, into the background.

In fact, there was a great deal of discussion in London in the two months following the Atlantic meeting about a possible Japanese move north, to take advantage of Russia's preoccupations. In the late summer Japan reinforced her Manchurian army, which provided some grounds for what the official historians call "the all too welcome belief" that Japan's next objective might be Siberia.[46]   Yet oil was Japan's great need, and there was little of it in Siberia. It is hard to escape the conclusion that in London any sign that Japan would not move south was grasped with uncritical avidity. But even here, discussion came back to the great enigma. What would the United States do? On October 16, 1941, a possible Japanese move against Russia was discussed by the War Cabinet.

The Prime Minister said that if Japan declared war on Russia, the latter would certainly press us to declare war on Japan. We were of course already committed to go to war with Japan if

Japan was at war with the United States. But we ought not to
commit ourselves to any action which would involve war with
Japan unless the United States was also at war with that country . . . . We ought to regard the United States as having taken
charge in the Far East. It was for them to take the lead in this
area, and we would support them.[47]

Events in the Far East suddenly dispelled the comparative optimism in London. On October 15, Prince Konoye, the Japanese prime minister and a "moderate," resigned. Japanese-Amer-
ican negotiations in Washington were deadlocked. On the 16th
Eden sent Ismay a note, asking that the dispatch of capital ships to
the Far East be placed upon the agenda for the next Defence Committee meeting. The prime minister agreed, and on the following
day the matter was taken up. Churchill reverted to the idea of sending a modern capital ship, instead of waiting for the Admiralty's
plans to produce more slowly a larger force of vintage battleships.
He repeated his *Tirpitz* analogy. The *Repulse*, he pointed out, was
already in the Indian Ocean. The *Prince of Wales* should be sent out
immediately to join her. The foreign secretary strongly backed the
prime minister. "Mr. Eden said that from the point of view of deterring Japan from entering the war, the despatch of one modern
ship, such as the *Prince of Wales*, to the Far East would have a far
greater affect politically than the presence in those waters of a
number of the last war's battleships. If the *Prince of Wales* were to
call at Cape Town on her way to the Far East, news of her movements would quickly reach Japan and the deterrent affect would begin from that date." The only opposition came from the Admiralty
representatives. A. V. Alexander, the first lord, was opposed; but
he carried no weight at all on the Committee. Pound was absent,
but Phillips argued strongly against the proposal. Nevertheless,
Churchill persisted and ordered that all preparations should be made
to send the *Prince of Wales* east. In the face of the Admiralty's
opposition, he agreed to defer a final decision until the 20th, when
Pound could be present.[48]

The discussion three days later was a rather rambling affair.
The prime minister again stressed the deterrent value of a fast
modern capital ship in the Far East. Then, rather surprisingly, he
added that "the War Cabinet were quite prepared to face the loss
of shipping which might take place if the *Tirpitz* came out into the
Atlantic." Pound repeated the Admiralty argument that one battleship would simply not be enough; the situation required a balanced

fleet. Then he said, somewhat irrelevantly, "of course if the United States would base their fleet on Singapore, the situation would be greatly altered, but up to the present they had been quite adamant on retaining their Fleet at Hawaii." Churchill replied that "he did not foresee an attack in force on Malaya. He thought the main danger would be to our trade from Japanese battlecruisers." The foreign secretary again stressed the diplomatic advantages of the course that he and the prime minister were urging: "Mr. Eden said . . . . From the political point of view there was no doubt as to the value of our sending, at the present time, a really modern ship." The prime minister added that while "he did not believe that the Japanese would go to war with the United States and ourselves," nevertheless, "he would like to see the *Prince of Wales* sent . . . ." Pound then fell back on a strategy of delay. He proposed that the *Prince of Wales* sail for Cape Town. When she arrived there a further decision could be taken on her ultimate destination.[49] This was agreed, but the next day (ironically enough, it was Trafalgar Day) the Admiralty informed various naval commanders that the *Prince of Wales* would sail for Singapore.[50]

Although the final orders had not yet been formally given, it is clear that from October 20 on Singapore was the *Prince of Wales's* destination in Churchill's mind, and that Pound had accepted this. It is also clear that the primary reason for the decision was political.[51] The *Prince of Wales* and the *Repulse* were intended to warn Japan and to draw out the Americans. The U.S. Navy Department had expressed the belief that British weakness at sea in the Far East made planning for joint operations there irrelevant. The arrival of the *Prince of Wales* and the *Repulse* at Singapore might therefore alter American opinions. The concern in Australia, recently emphasized by the dispatch of a special envoy to London, would certainly be assuaged. All in all, it clearly seemed to the prime minister a gamble worth taking.

On October 25, 1941, H.M.S. *Prince of Wales* left England, flying the flag of acting Admiral Sir Tom Phillips, commander-designate of the Eastern Fleet. Phillips was going back to sea after a long spell in Whitehall, where he had been successively director of plans, deputy, and then vice chief of the Naval Staff. He was a very odd choice for command in a theater where air power was bound to play a major role. For Phillips, in Ismay's words, "refused to believe that properly armed and well-fought ships had anything to fear from air power." Ismay also recorded an argument, some years before, between Phillips and an RAF officer that

ended with the airman snapping, "one day Tom, you will be standing on . . . your bridge . . . and your ship will be smashed to pieces
by bombers and torpedo aircraft. As she sinks, your last words will
be, 'That was a . . . great mine.'"[52] Churchill, who admired
Phillips's spirit and abilities, had great confidence in him.[53] The
experience of the Norwegian campaign, and of the Mediterranean
fighting, had dented somewhat Phillips's skepticism about the air
threat to capital ships, and there is some evidence that he left
England with a strong premonition of impending doom.[54] But
Churchill's willingness to send the *Prince of Wales* and the *Repulse*
to Singapore may have stemmed in part from a feeling that the
ships, ably commanded, would be able to take care of themselves —
at least against the Japanese.

Originally, the two ships were intended to have the company of
the new fleet carrier *Indomitable*. Fate intervened, however. On
November 3, while "working up" her ship's company, *Indomitable*
went aground off Jamaica. Two days later Churchill, in a circular
telegram to the dominion prime ministers, announced that the
Prince of Wales and the *Repulse* were being sent to Singapore to
deter further Japanese aggression. The ultimate destination of the
two ships was never again considered by the War Cabinet, the Defence Committee, or the Chiefs of Staff. There is no trace in the
voluminous British records of exactly when and by whom the decision was taken that resulted in an Admiralty telegram sent on
November 11 (five days before the *Prince of Wales* reached Cape
Town), ordering Phillips to Ceylon and then, with the *Repulse*,
on to Singapore. Three men, however, played key roles: Churchill,
with Eden encouraging him, and Pound. Of these, Churchill was
clearly the key figure. A few weeks later he told Sir Henry Pownall
that he had had to beat down a great deal of Admiralty resistance
before he could get his way.[55] The prime minister's ability to
override the naval staff hinged on his relations with Pound. While
he respected the first sea lord, he also dominated him. Pound could,
as noted above, often manage to sidetrack ideas that he regarded
as unsound. He had done so in August. When the prime minister
was determined he very often got his way, and there is no doubt
that he was very determined to send the *Prince of Wales* to Singapore. The obverse of the prime minister's respect for his first sea
lord was Pound's deference to Churchill. Pound's health may have
been a factor in this. He was first sea lord only because of the untimely death of his predecessor, Admiral Sir Roger Backhouse,
shortly before the outbreak of the war. At that time Pound was

commander-in-chief in the Mediterranean. His health was already so bad that his Fleet Medical Officer feared he would not be equal to the strain of wartime command. The doctor could not bring himself to tell the Admiralty, however, and so Pound became first sea lord. His health, and his respect for the Prime Minister, kept him from engaging in the bruising encounters that were necessary to balk Churchillian determination — clashes of the sort that wore down Sir John Dill. Consciousness of his own failing health may have made Pound even more dependent on his relationship with the prime minister and less able to stop him when really set on a course of action. One thing is certain. Churchill, who had suffered political catastrophe once, in 1915, in a clash with a stubborn first sea lord, would never have ordered the *Prince of Wales* and the *Repulse* to Singapore if Pound had absolutely refused to agree. The first sea lord's acquiescence was crucial. Great events, as the nursery rhyme has it, often turn on small things — Pound's health may well have been one of them.[56] No attempt was made to provide another carrier to replace the damaged *Indomitable*. There were no carriers to spare. Of Britain's five modern fleet carriers, two were undergoing repairs for battle damage. To these the *Indomitable* had now to be added. One was with the Home Fleet and could not be detached. The fifth, H.M.S. *Ark Royal*, whose Swordfish torpedo planes had crippled the *Bismarck* in May, fell victim to a U-boat on November 14. Of the older carriers, the *Eagle* was standing by in home waters to provide air cover for Pilgrim while the *Furious* was ferrying aircraft to Takoradi in West Africa, whence they flew on to the Middle East. That left the *Hermes*, which was being refitted at Durban in South Africa. Nine days after the loss of the *Ark Royal*, the prime minister minuted to the first sea lord that he assumed one of the older carriers would be assigned to the Indian Ocean.[57] And the *Hermes* was the only carrier east of Suez when war came.

Churchill had cabled General Smuts about the *Prince of Wales's* impending arrival at the Cape, referring warmly to Phillips as "a great friend and one of our ablest Admirals," and asking Smuts to meet him. The *Prince of Wales* reached Cape Town on November 16, and Phillips flew up to Pretoria to meet the South African prime minister. Smuts was an old friend of Churchill's, one of the few men whose mind, according to the prime minister, worked like his own (the others, Churchill said, were Beaverbrook, Brendan Bracken, and Pound — a very oddly assorted trio). On his return to Cape Town, Phillips told his chief of staff, Rear Admiral A. F. E.

Palliser, that Smuts agreed with the policy of using the *Prince of Wales* and the *Repulse* as a deterrent to Japan. If this was an accurate account of Smuts's feelings, it is odd that the South African prime minister cabled Churchill on November 18 to voice his concern that two Allied fleets, based on Singapore and Hawaii, "each separately inferior to the Japanese," were an invitation to a "first class disaster."[59] But the decision had already been taken; the *Prince of Wales* would go to Singapore. And it would go, as Eden had suggested, in a blaze of publicity. On November 1, Churchill had sent a personal minute to Pound, enquiring "what steps can be taken to enable presence of P. of W. at Capetown [sic] to be reported to the enemy." He went on to suggest that a dummy battleship might join the *Prince of Wales* at sea off the Cape and sail eastwards with her, giving the illusion that two *King George V*-class battleships were in the Indian Ocean. Two days later the prime minister had another idea: "Also consider," he minuted to Pound, "publicity, i.e., Thanks of Australasia for the formation of an Eastern Battle Fleet." Neither of these ideas bore fruit, but they do underline the element of bluff in Churchill's decision to form the "deterrent squadron." Two days after the *Prince of Wales* arrived at Cape Town, Pound reported to Churchill on the arrangements for publicity. He added that the director of naval intelligence had taken steps to monitor the reports from the Japanese consul general at Cape Town to Tokyo.[59] Nothing was left to chance. The Japanese were not to be allowed to miss the eastward move of two British capital ships. The fact that no one questioned the wisdom of giving the potential enemy that much more time to prepare for them indicates that it was a diplomatic gesture, not a military operation, that was uppermost in London's mind.

The departure of the *Prince of Wales* was followed by the decision to replace Brooke-Popham. This change had been discussed in London since August. With the temperature rising in the Far East, it was found possible to spare someone from the small circle of senior officers of proven ability. On November 5 Churchill cabled Brooke-Popham informing him, rather brusquely, of the decision to replace him with "an army officer with up-to-date experience," and offering him a baronetcy. It is, incidentally, the only message from the prime minister in Brooke-Popham's papers. Since air power would not be available as a surrogate for the fleet, the army would have to hold the position; and an officer of that service as commander in chief therefore made sense. The next day the Air Ministry told Brooke-Popham that his replacement would be Lieutenant

General Sir Bernard Paget, one of the few officers to emerge from the disasterous Norwegian campaign of 1940 with an enhanced reputation.[60] But Churchill was prepared to accept a considerable delay in actually getting Paget out to Singapore, leaving Brooke-Popham a lame duck in the interim. The Air Ministry telegram to the commander in chief had warned him that Paget's arrival might be delayed by the necessity "to pay certain visits," visits that the prime minister was trying very hard to arrange. On the same day that Churchill informed Brooke-Popham of his coming supercession, he minuted to Ismay that he had become doubtful about the feasibility of putting a large British force into the Caucasus. RAF heavy bombers based in North Persia could support the Russians in the Caucasus, and, if they collapsed, bomb the Baku oil fields, the prime minister felt. That, he added, was all the British were currently able to do.[61] Anxious, in spite of this, to impress on Stalin the British desire to cooperate, he had cabled Moscow on the 4th:

> In order to clear things up and to plan for the future I am ready to send General Wavell, Commander-in-Chief in India, Persia, and Iraq, to meet you in Moscow, Kuibyshev, Tiflis, or wherever you will. Besides this, General Paget, our new Commander-in-Chief, secretly designated for the Far East, will come with General Wavell. General Paget has been in the center of things here, and will have with him the latest and best opinions of our High Command. These two officers will be able to tell you exactly how we stand, what is possible and what we think is wise.[62]

Even though Stalin's reply poured cold water on the proposed meeting, Paget still did not leave for the Far East, because a major shake-up in the high command of the British army took place. It had been pending at least since the row between Churchill and Dill in May. On Thursday November 13 the CIGS told General Sir Alan Brooke that his days in office were numbered, and that the succession lay between Brooke himself, Paget, and Major General Archibald Nye, the director of staff duties at the War Office. Nye, Churchill's personal favorite, was ruled out by lack of seniority. Brooke was summoned the following Sunday to Chequers where, after dinner, Churchill offered him the highest post in the British army. Other displacements followed. Paget succeeded Brooke as commander in chief, Home Forces. Nye was pushed up and made Vice CIGS, which involved getting rid of the incumbent, Lieutenant General Sir Henry Pownall. Pownall, therefore, became available to go to the Far East.[63] It was the beginning of December before Pownall got away from London. His departure was delayed by an argument that broke out when the decision was taken to replace Brooke-Popham by a soldier. The RAF, having lost control of the Far Eastern theater, attempted to dismantle what little there was of an integrated command structure there. The Air Ministry raised the issue by suggesting that the command in the Far East should be reconstituted along the lines of the system employed in the Middle East, where the three service commanders formed a trinity of equals. The idea had no appeal for Pownall, whose diary entry reflects the deep antagonism between the RAF and the older services, which had already done so much damage, not least in the Far East. "I didn't care for the idea. For one thing having got the RAF in *one* place in the world, in their proper place, I didn't like letting go of them — we should only encourage them in their 'independent' nonsense. If Brookham could command both Army and Air Force I don't see why I can't do the same."[64] In the end matters were left very much as they stood. Pownall's directive was almost a carbon copy of Brooke-Popham's, with all its limitations. The only major change was that Pownall was made jointly responsible with Phillips for the overall direction of operations.[65]   By the time Pownall's directive was settled, there were only five days of peace left in the Far East.

iii

For nearly three months after the Atlantic meeting, the British waited anxiously for some indication of what the Americans would do if the Japanese attacked Thailand, Malaya, or the Netherlands East Indies. The Dutch in turn waited for some indication of what the British would do if they were attacked. The Australians, anxious and irritable, their relations with London increasingly tense, waited as well.

Menzies's telegram of August 12 to Churchill had been one of the last he sent as Australian prime minister. Understandably, in view of London's dominant role in the Imperial war effort, Menzies decided to pay another visit to England. The opposition Labour Party seized upon this to attack Menzies. A political crisis ensued, which led to Menzies's resignation on August 28. His successor, A. W. Fadden, was to be less amenable to London's wishes. There was no party truce in Australia, as there was, to some extent, in England, and "the Australian government, weakened by the loss of its ablest figure, had a majority of only one, and were confronted in this grievous period by a party Opposition, thirsting for local power," Churchill later wrote censoriously. A month later Fadden's government also fell, and J. W. Curtin formed a Labour government, also with a one vote majority. "Our relations with Mr. Fadden's Government, and afterwards with Mr. Curtin's Labour Administration, were not as easy as they had been with their predecessors," Churchill recalled.[66] One reason for this deterioration was the British government's continued refusal to share control over the Empire's policy and strategy. When Fadden took office Churchill sent a congratulatory telegram, and followed it with a long cable explaining why the Australian desire for representation on the War Cabinet was impracticable. The cable argued against any variation in the existing arrangements whereby Australia was represented in London by its high commissioner (Stanley Bruce), whose normal channel of communication with the government was the secretary of state for the dominions, who, in turn, was not a member of the War Cabinet. The prime minister did extend an invitation to any dominion prime minister who wished to visit London to sit with the War Cabinet.[67] In Australia, where a prime minister had just been forced to resign on the issue of a second visit to London within six months, this offer may not have seemed either realistic or generous.

Almost immediately after Fadden took office a serious quarrel erupted between Britain and Australia. Since late April the backbone of the isolated and besieged Tobruk garrison had been the Ninth Australian Division, and the Australian government began to fear that its long spell there, in very trying conditions, was affecting the health of the troops and therefore their fighting qualities. In July the question of relieving them so that they could be rested, reequipped, and joined with the other two divisions in a single Australian Corps was officially raised by the Australian government. One brigade was brought out in August. On September 7 Fadden cabled London to insist on the relief of the two remaining brigades. The suggestion was considered very untimely. The Australians could only be pulled out by the Royal Navy during the moonless periods in September and October. This would put a great additional strain on Auchinleck's command, and particularly upon the navy, on the eve of Crusader. Appeals to Fadden proved vain, and in the September dark period another brigade was withdrawn. Churchill then asked Curtin, who had just replaced Fadden, to allow the last brigade to remain. The Australians were adamant, however, and in October nearly all the remaining troops of the Ninth Division came out of Tobruk. The relief of the Australians had cost the Royal Navy a fast minelayer, a type of warship invaluable for running stores and men in and out of besieged places like Tobruk and Malta. A cruiser, two destroyers, and two supply ships were damaged. In the end the operation caused no delay in Crusader but very considerable irritation in London. On the other hand, a long review of British strategy in the Middle East, which Churchill sent Fadden on September 7, could only have increased Australian frustration. In it Churchill listed everything that the Turks would be offered to encourage them to fight the Germans, oddly oblivious that the Australians might well compare it with the catalogue of deficiencies in the Far East.[68] The Australian government decided in September to send a representative to London to press their views on the importance of strengthening the Far East. Sir Earle Page, the minister of commerce, set off for England via Singapore and the United States.

The Dutch also presented problems. They had agreed, in the talks held at Singapore in February and April, to joint plans for the use of their naval and air forces. These plans were important because the Dutch, with 144 aircraft, including modern Glen Martin bombers, were still at least as strong in the air as the British in the Far East, and the three Dutch cruisers, seven destroyers, and thirteen submarines in the East Indies were a very important contribution to Allied naval strength in the area. In fact, prior to Phillips's arrival, the Dutch fleet was stronger than Layton's, and almost as strong as the United States Asiatic Fleet at Manila. On the eve of the Atlantic meeting, Eden had given the Dutch a verbal assurance of British support in the event of attack. On September 5 the British put this in writing. The same letter also formally approved the arrangements by which four squadrons of Dutch planes would reinforce Malaya, and Admiral Layton would exercise overall direction of naval operations. In early October Churchill told Eden that "he was in favour of some more definite assurance" to the Dutch. What exactly made the prime minister suddenly so forthcoming is unclear, unless, like the dispatch of the *Prince of Wales* and the *Repulse*, he saw this as a way of both warning Japan and pressuring the United States. The Foreign Office also felt that a formal defensive agreement with the Dutch was now desirable, and on October 31 Eden asked the War Cabinet to sanction such a pact.[69]

When the War Cabinet discussed Eden's request, they were conscious that troop concentrations in Indochina indicated that another Japanese move to the south was impending. Britain was as far as ever from any sort of agreement with the United States over the defense of the Far East. In late August the British had submitted a revised version of the ADB agreement to the Americans. The United States Navy rejected this paper (ADB-2) in October, largely because British naval weakness in the Far East seemed to the Americans to make joint planning irrelevant — a fact that, as seen above, may well have been very important in Churchill's decision to send the *Prince of Wales* and the *Repulse* to Singapore.[70] "We were prepared to support any action, however serious that the United States might decide to take," had been Eden's summation of British policy in mid-October.[71] The unwillingness of the Americans to indicate what action they would take — or even whether they would take any at all — was the decisive factor in the War Cabinet discussion on November 3. Churchill's brief enthusiasm for a "more definite assurance" to the Dutch had entirely vanished. "Our policy in the Far East should be to persuade the United States to cover our weak position in that area. We should not run the risk of finding ourselves at war with Japan without American support." Viscount Cranborne, the dominions secretary who was in attendance for the discussion, pointed out that "there would be a painful impression in Australia and New Zealand if we did not intervene in the event of the Netherlands East Indies being attacked." In the end it was decided that Eden would draft a telegram for the prime minister to send to the president, in which Roosevelt would be told that, while Britain would support the United States, "we could not take the lead."[72] Two days later the cable went off, emphasising once again that the British could not, by themselves, deter Japan, but would join in any action taken by the United States.[73]

The War Cabinet met to discuss the Far East again on November 5. Sir Earle Page, the Australian special envoy, was present and urged immediate air and naval reinforcements for the area. In particular, he pointed to the disparity between the 336 aircraft the Far East was supposed to have, and the 130 actually there. Churchill explained that the needs of home defense, aid to Russia, and the Middle East had priority. Modern bombers, he bluntly told Page, were best used bombing Germany and northern France. Whatever happened in the Middle East, he added, Australia itself would be saved from Japan. Secretary of State for Air Sir Archibald Sinclair, whose ministry had given up trying to reach the 1941 target figure for the Far East two months before, tried to reassure Page by pointing out that the aircraft total for the Far East would be 250 if those available at two weeks notice were figured in.[74] Since most of these would come from India's assortment of obsolete aircraft, Sinclair's statement was very misleading. In any case, a great deal could happen in two weeks. Although Page thus got little satisfaction, his presence, a visible reminder of Australian fears and expectations, was probably another factor in the decision to send the *Prince of Wales* onward to Singapore. On this same day, in Tokyo, Imperial General Headquarters approved the plans for the attack on the Philippines, Malaya, and the East Indies.

The War Cabinet went over the problem of the Netherlands East Indies again on the 11th — the day that the Admiralty ordered the *Prince of Wales* on to Singapore. Churchill continued to oppose any agreement with the Dutch until the uncertainty about America's intentions was dispelled.[75] The next day Page was back to press for further reinforcements for the Far East, and to make the point that the British policy of waiting for America to take the lead might be unsound. The Chiefs of Staff then explained to him at length why nothing more could be sent. Finally the prime minister reiterated the basis upon which he had established his Far Eastern strategy.

> Our correct strategy was to move our strength from theatre to theatre as the situation changed. At the present time the theatre in which forces could be most profitably employed was the Middle East. A policy of spreading our resources to guard against possible but unlikely dangers, might be fatal.
> What was the best deterrent to employ against the Japanese? In his view the answer was to maintain a stiff attitude towards her but not to become involved in war with her unless we had the assurance of United States participation.[76]

Five days before, the Japanese armed services had been warned that the war would begin on December 8.

At the War Cabinet meeting on the 12th Churchill and Eden had both stressed for Page's benefit the "rapid development of U.S. opinion."[77] But in fact the opposite was true. The entire month of November was taken up just in negotiating with the Americans the procedure that Phillips and Admiral Thomas Hart (commander in chief, Asiatic Fleet) would follow to develop the framework for the later elaboration of joint operational plans.[78] On November 19 Page and Stanley Bruce, the Australian high commissioner in London, told Portal that the British assumption that they would have a choice about going to war with Japan if the East Indies were attacked might well "break up the Empire."[79] The following day Churchill finished a letter that Clement Attlee, the ranking Labour member of the War Cabinet, would deliver to Roosevelt. In it the prime minister reiterated his pledge to declare war immediately if Japan attacked the United States.[80] There was no answer to this. Churchill claimed that he did not really expect one. But there can be no doubt about his hopes. "My deepest fear," he later wrote, "was that Japan would attack us or the Dutch, and that constitutional difficulties would prevent the United States from declaring war."[81]

On November 21 preliminary Japanese naval movements began. The Pearl Harbor attack force sailed five days later. On the 27th the Navy Department warned the Pacific Fleet that hostilities against Japan might be imminent. The next day London learned of this through Admiralty channels. Simultaneously a cable arrived from Brooke-Popham requesting authority to order Matador if escorted Japanese convoys approached the coast of Thailand. Clarification of American attitudes was now urgent. November 29, 1941, was an extremely busy day in London. The Chiefs of Staff told Brooke-Popham that the power to implement Matador would not be delegated to him unless there was a prior assurance of American support. The Foreign Office cabled Washington, instructing Halifax to tell Roosevelt and Hull about Matador. The ambassador was to stress that an attack on Thailand appeared likely, point out that Brooke-Popham wanted authorization for the operation, and ask for assurances of American support if it became necessary to launch Matador.[82] Simultaneously the Dominions Office sent a circular telegram asking the dominions for their views on Matador. The replies were quick in coming. New Zealand was ready to support any course of action that London took, while South Africa urged action on the assumption that American support would follow. Australia wanted Brooke-Popham given the authorization he sought. An invitation from the Thai government to enter their country would be nice, the Australians felt, but not essential. Neither, they clearly implied, was American approval. Indicative of the opposing forces acting on London, however, was the cable from Canadian prime minister Mackenzie King.

I cannot express too strongly my view that so long as there is any uncertainty about the degree and immediacy of United States support it would be a terrible mistake to permit any course of action which might result in war between Japan and the British Commonwealth of Nations . . . Britain I think should not intervene until the United States have declared themselves.[83]

When the War Cabinet met on December 1, the United States had still not "declared themselves." Churchill, therefore, told his colleagues that "in his view we should not resist or attempt to forestall a Japanese attack on the Kra Isthmus unless we had a satisfactory assurance from the United States that they would join us should our action cause us to become involved in war with Japan."[84]

The next day, while half a world away the *Prince of Wales* and the *Repulse* steamed slowly up Johore Strait to the Singapore Naval Base, the prime minister sent Eden a minute. "Our settled policy is not to take action in advance of the United States . . . . If they move we will move immediately in support." It therefore followed that "we should not take forestalling action without a definite guarantee of United States support." If Japan attacked the Dutch, Britain would wait to see what American reaction would be. If the United States did nothing Britain would then go to the support of the Dutch anyway.[85] Here Churchill doubtless had Page's warning in mind. Even as Churchill dictated however, a cable from Washington that had reached London at 7:20 A.M., was being decoded. The sphinx had finally spoken.

On December 1 Halifax had a long conversation with Roosevelt. "At one point he threw in an aside that in the case of any direct attack on ourselves or the Dutch we should obviously all be together." In the apparently lighthearted way that he often made major policy decisions, the president had given the guarantee for which the British had waited so long. On the question of Matador however, he was not so forthcoming, although he agreed that Britain had to do what strategic necessity dictated in the Kra Isthmus.[86] Upon receipt of this Eden immediately wrote a minute for the War Cabinet urging the conclusion of a formal agreement with the Dutch.[87]

Nevertheless, when the Defence Committee met at 5:30 P.M. on December 3, caution was still the ruling emotion. Churchill did not want to go beyond the policy he had enunciated in his minute to Eden, which meant no authorization for Matador, but, he admitted, "we were now bound to go a bit further with the Dutch than we had done up to the present." He still argued for a short interval between a Japanese attack on the Dutch and a British declaration of war — presumably to make sure that the Americans would carry out Roosevelt's promise. He had, after all, been burned once, in August. "All he wanted to avoid," the prime minister declared, "was being landed in an automatic declaration of war and he also did not wish to give the anti-British party cause for saying that the United States were again being dragged into a British war." Pound expressed his long-standing concern about having to aid the Dutch without American support. Churchill summed up by saying that "he was prepared to take any action that might be necessary, provided he was quite sure of American support." The Defence Committee decided to send a cable to Roosevelt, to nail down the American guarantee as firmly as possible. Eden was authorized to speak to the Dutch along the not very cheery lines of the prime minister's December 2 minute.[88]

The whole discussion was an odd reaction to the news from Washington. The British had their guarantee, insofar as Roosevelt could give one. They had already committed themselves to an automatic declaration of war if Japan attacked the United States. The hedging about the Dutch reflects a lingering uncertainty about American reactions, the product of eighteen months of frustration. If Roosevelt could not make good his promise, Britain would find itself facing Japan alone. Churchill's sudden concern over giving a handle to American Anglophobes was also strange. If Roosevelt made good his promise in the event of a Japanese strike against the British and Dutch, such an imputation would obviously be made. It was, in any case, too late to worry about it.

At 8:55 P.M. London time, a cable went off to Halifax. "We note particularly President's statement that in case of any direct attack on ourselves or the Dutch we should obviously all be together. We fully endorse this statement." The cable went on to state that the British government assumed that the support the president indicated for Matador was armed support. In that case they were prepared to order it. Washington's answer was received at 11:00 A.M. the next day (December 4). The president had assented to Matador, even if the Japanese only moved into northern Thailand, and promised that American support would be armed support. At the last minute Roosevelt had promised more than, constitutionally, he had any right to. The ambassador concluded, "I have no doubt in this case you can count on armed support of the United States."[89]

At 6:00 P.M. that evening the War Cabinet assembled. After hearing an account of the Halifax-Roosevelt conversations, they authorized both the conclusion of a defense agreement with the Dutch, and a cable to Brooke-Popham giving him the authority to launch Matador. Eden pointed out that the agreement with the Dutch would have to be announced to the Americans very carefully, since they doubtless assumed that the British had concluded such a pact long ago.[90]

On December 1, 1941, Imperial General Headquarters in Tokyo had told all Japanese forces that the final decision for war had been made. The next day December 8 was confirmed as the date when hostilities would begin. The opening action would be a landing at Kota Bharu in Malaya at 15 minutes past midnight, December 8, 1941.

iv

As the weeks slipped by after the American decision to freeze Japan's assets and cut off her oil supplies, the mood of the British high command in the Far East paralleled that in London. Concern over strengthening the area's defenses was followed by a brief burst of optimism, and then mounting anxiety as Japan resumed its southward march.

On August 14, as London anxiously pondered what could be done in the next thirty days, Brooke-Popham sent a long cable to the Air Ministry, pointing out that the current total aircraft deficiency in the Far East was 368. "It would be helpful if I knew what is the Air Ministry policy for meeting this deficiency," the commander in chief commented mildly. "I feel the time factor may not be fully appreciated in England. From the time when the order is given for aircraft to be sent to this country from the U.K. until these aircraft are ready for issue to squadrons out here is between 4 and 5 months. Similarly to form a new squadron out here with pilots trained only up to the F.T.S. [Flying Training School] stage is a matter of some three months from the time when the pilots arrive in this country assuming aircraft are ready for them."[91] This delay of seven to eight months before a decision in London took shape as an operationally fit squadron in Malaya made nonsense of the Chiefs' of Staff insistence in May that they needed ninety days to reinforce Malaya, and even greater nonsense of the attempt to find something to do in the next thirty days. It may be one of the reasons that the effort to do so guttered out. But it is odd that this time lag had never been properly appreciated in London. Just as no estimate of what it would take to hold all of Malaya had been made before Bond did it in the spring of 1940, the exact consequences of the decision to rely on planes shipped from the United States and pilots drawn straight from basic flying schools only became apparent when someone in the Far East pointed it out.

At the end of August Brooke-Popham cabled London an estimate drawn up by Playfair of probable Japanese moves in the event of war, that was a reasonably accurate forecast of what would happen in December.[92] In the face of London's silence on reinforcements, Brooke-Popham could only continue his attempts to keep up confidence and deceive the Japanese. In a "Most Secret" paper dated August 30, GHQ, Far East, stressed the need "to give the Japanese an exaggerated impression of our strength in the Far East, and of our confidence in our security." This, it was hoped, would bluff them into slowing down.[93]

If the commander in chief hoped that the July-August "scare" would shake loose any reinforcements for him, he was disabused by a cable from the Chiefs of Staff in mid-September. In it they pointed out to Brooke-Popham that production difficulties and the requirements of the Middle East made any firm program of aircraft reinforcements impossible. The 1941 target, they told him, would not be met, something that could not have come as much of a surprise. The tentative 1942 target of 590 aircraft was mentioned, but whether it was met would depend on production in America and Australia, as well as on the "strategic situation as a whole." "For the time being Mideast must take priority for shipping and air resources for which there are competing claims."[94]

The reference to Australian production was to a plan to build Beaufort torpedo bombers in Australia. This type of aircraft was desperately needed in the Far East.[95] Australia was supposed to produce 180 Beauforts in 1941, half to go to Brooke-Popham's command. Aircraft manufacture in Australia was in its infancy, however. Much of the material, and some of the parts for the Beaufort had to come from America or Britain. Delays mounted up, in spite of urgent appeals from Australia. Finally, in early August, Menzies sent Bruce a special cable about it. But, despite every effort in Australia, the program never got off the ground. A few days before the Japanese struck, six Beauforts, the first fruits of Australian production, reached Singapore. The aircraft were not yet fully operational and their crews entirely untrained. Brooke-Popham and Pulford sent all but one, which they hoped to use for photoreconnaissance, back to Australia out of harm's way.[96]

The whole subject of photographic reconnaissance was another area where the Far East's representations were unavailing. Due to the failure to get information out to him, Brooke-Popham, who had retired in 1937, was not aware of the great strides that had been made in this area until a specialist officer visited Singapore in August. Immediately the commander in chief asked for a photo-reconnaissance Spitfire. None was available. In November 1941 he formed his own PRU (Photographic Reconnaissance Unit), drawing four Buffaloes from his already inadequate reserves and training personnel locally.[97]

Duff Cooper reached Singapore on September 9, having taken some seven weeks to make his way out from London. Three weeks later he held a full-dress conference. Shenton Thomas, Brooke-Popham, and Layton attended, as well as Clark-Kerr from Chung-king, Sir Josiah Crosby, the British minister to Thailand, and Sir Earle Page, passing through Singapore on the first leg of his journey to London. The discussion was tinged by the same optimism that was simultaneously affecting Whitehall. Japan had not moved any further south. The reinforcement of the Manchurian army might mean that the next Japanese move would be against Russia. The conference felt that, in the absence of a fleet, the propaganda value of even one or two capital ships would be immense, and that a public statement that a coordinated plan existed for the defense of American, British, and Dutch territory in the Far East would be a useful warning to Japan. It also came to the conclusion that a Japanese attack on Malaya's east coast during the northeast monsoon (which begins in October/November and lasts five months) was very unlikely and that the danger of war had therefore receded for several months to come.[98]

The optimism of the conference has been described as "almost unbelievable."[99] While it was certainly excessive, it corresponded very closely with the contemporary mood in London. Both hinged on the same things: intelligence that seemed to point to a Japanese move north, and the relief that followed when nothing happened in August and September. The desire for a symbolic force of British capital ships at Singapore, and the belief that their arrival would actually mean something, was matched by Churchill's and Eden's. A public announcement by the ABD powers would have been very welcome in London as well as Singapore, but that, as shown above, was impossible because of American reluctance. The statement that landings were impossible during the northeast monsoon, however, is a different matter.

In October 1937, Major General Dobbie (whose chief staff officert was the then Colonel A. E. Percival) reported to the War Office the result of exercises he had held during the preceding northeast monsoon period. They established that landings were not only possible but probable, since bad visibility would hamper both air reconnaissance and air strikes against an invader.[100] Nonetheless, the belief that the monsoon was a shield persisted. In a "Secret" office memo of September 4, GHQ Far East picked late February 1942 — that is, the end of the monsoon period — as the most probable date for the outbreak of war.[101] Brigadier Simson, when he discovered this, told Percival that while he was serving at the War Office some eighteen months before, he had seen photographs taken from a British ship in 1938 that showed "Japanese troops landing on the Chinese coast in rough seas during the height of the N.E. Monsoon."[102] Percival should have needed no reminding on this point. Whether he discussed the matter with Brooke-Popham is unknown, but the commander in chief certainly made no effort at the conference on the 29th to counteract the belief that the monsoon meant a respite of several months. Of course Brooke-Popham might simply have been unwilling to dampen the morale of the civilians present. In that case, however, it is odd that two months later his chief of staff, Playfair, in a lecture to staff officers, repeated that landings during the monsoon were impossible. Simson, who had been refused permission by Percival to attend the lecture, sought Playfair out and repeated the story he had told the GOC in September. He also retailed it to Air Vice Marshal Pulford.[103] In his reflections on the campaign written in 1943, Playfair pointed out that the east coast of Malaya and the Kra Isthmus were sheltered from the full force of the northeast monsoon by the projecting southern bulge of French Indochina — an oblique admission, perhaps, of the onetime belief that the monsoon brought security temporarily.[104] It is yet another riddle in the story of Singapore's fall that may never be finally resolved, but there is no doubt that such a belief existed, and was widely held by soldiers and civilians alike.[105] The Japanese opened their assault in December by doing something widely believed to be impossible, and the jolt to morale was correspondingly sharp.

Following the conference on September 29, Duff Cooper spent a month drawing up his report. "British Administration in the Far

East," dated October 29, was sent home by the hand of W. J. Keswick of Duff Cooper's staff, who was briefed to answer any additional questions the War Cabinet might have about the Far East. When Keswick got to London on November 24, no questions were asked. The report he brought was printed and circulated, but no action was taken on it prior to the outbreak of the war. "Those who are responsible for carrying out British policy in Asia are less closely in touch than they have been for a long time with those who are responsible for framing that policy in London," Duff Cooper pointed out. He recommended the appointment of a commissioner general to act as a general reference point and coordinator for the area. In the event of war, the commissioner general would become chairman of a Far Eastern War Council. It was a suggestion that was at least a year too late. Such an appointment, made at the same time as Brooke-Popham's, could have been very useful. By the time Keswick reached London it was beside the point.[106]

As the sands ran out in the autumn of 1941, more reinforcements for Percival's command reached Singapore. A second brigade joined the Eighth Australian Division in August, but the division never got its third brigade. The Australian divisional artillery was reequipped with modern 25-pounder field guns only in November. Another Indian brigade, the Twenty-eighth, reached Malaya in September. The following month the two Indian divisions finally got their field artillery. Just before the war began the Third Cavalry Regiment arrived from India to act as the reconnaissance unit of III Indian Corps. It should have been "mounted" in armored cars, but in fact had light trucks. Only recently mechanized, its training was so incomplete that drivers for some of the trucks had to be borrowed from infantry units.[107]

The attempt to provide some armored support for the troops in Malaya illustrated the tremendous handicaps under which the Far East labored in preparing itself for war. As far back as the spring of 1940, Bond had asked for two tank battalions. Percival, in August 1941, repeated the request. On August 14 the War Office offered GHQ, Far East, forty light tanks that were currently being used in the Middle East to defend airfields, because they were obsolescent and unfit to face German, or even Italian, tanks. This offer was conditional, however, on the Far East agreeing to employ the tanks in an operational role, and manning them from local resources. This last condition presented a problem, since Malaya Command was short of truck drivers and had no armored personnel. The Australians stepped in with an offer to provide the necessary men, train them in Australia, and have them ready by January 1, 1942. No sooner had this obstacle been surmounted than Middle East Command, on November 12, decided that it could not spare the tanks after all, a decision London complacently accepted.[108]

The same story of delay and frustration characterized the attempt to get armored cars for Malaya. One model, mounted on an American chassis, was borrowed from the Dutch, and six copies were made at the naval base in Singapore. Production then had to stop because there was no more boiler plate for armoring the vehicles. Eighty-four armored cars had been ordered from South Africa. These were Marmon-Herringtons built there using Ford engines and components from the United Sates. They were obsolescent in design and carried only a single machine gun, but would have been better than nothing. Sixteen reached Singapore early in December — fresh from the factory, not broken in, and lacking spare parts, tools, and, incredibly, their machine gun fittings. Turned over to the inexperienced drivers of the Third Cavalry and their equally raw mechanics, thirteen were ditched or otherwise rendered unserviceable on the journey from Singapore to the front.[109]

Not all of Malaya's difficulties with armor were beyond its control, however. Lacking any tanks of its own, training in antitank tactics for the infantry took on added importance in Malaya Command. This was particularly the case with the Indian units, many of whom had never even seen a tank, for, as Wavell had pointed out to the War Cabinet in September, there was not a single modern tank or armored car in the entire subcontinent. In this case the War Office had done the logical thing and sent out pamphlets on antitank defense. In late November Brigadier Simson (again!) discovered them lying, in unopened bundles, in a closet at Fort Canning. He immediately took up the matter with Percival, who agreed that Simson ought to condense the information into a single illustrated booklet. Driving his office staff overtime, Simson had a forty-page illustrated manual, compiled with the needs of the Indian troops particularly in mind, ready on December 6. Then Percival's Chief of Staff, Brigadier K.S. Torrance, refused to sign the covering letter that would accompany it. Simson saw Percival about this on the morning of December 8, by which time war had begun. Percival also refused to sign the letter, thereby depriving the pamphlet of much authority. Simson nevertheless personally delivered it to brigade and divisional commanders. But it was far too late. Few now had time to read it, much less initiate

antitank training in their units.[110] Japanese tanks played a crucial
role in the first calamitous defeat inflicted on the Eleventh Indian
Division at Jitra in northern Malaya (December 9-12). Why Percival
and Torrance acted as they did is unknown, although Simson's
relations with Malaya Command headquarters could not have
been good. The real mistake, however, had been made earlier and
at a lower level, by whoever filed the War Office pamphlet away.
Malaya Command headquarters was considerably understaffed and
overworked. "After the outbreak of war with Germany," Percival
later wrote, "the filling of vacancies on the staff became more and
more difficult as the supply of trained staff officers in the Far East
became exhausted . . . . The supply of trained staff officers from
Home was naturally limited by nonavailability and by the difficulties of transportation. At the same time, . . . the work at
Headquarters Malaya Command was particularly heavy, including . . . the functions of a local War Office and those of a Headquarters of a Field Force."[111] Still it is hard to avoid the conclusion
that in this instance a serious error was committed, and that, however overworked they were, the urgency of antitank training should
have been grasped by someone at Malaya Command. Percival, after
all, had been an assistant chief of the Imperial General Staff during
the German conquest of France and the Low Countries and should
have known how devastating armor could be to troops unprepared
to deal with it, and inadequately supported from the air, a situation
all too likely to prevail in Malaya.

On the eve of the war Percival had approximately the number
of troops that the Chiefs of Staff had estimated in August 1940
were necessary to hold Malaya while the RAF was brought up to
strength. But his command had not reached the strength Bond had
recommended, much less the even higher estimate Percival himself
had made in August 1941, and which the Joint Planning Staff in
London had accepted as reasonable. The principal deficiencies on
the latter estimate were seventeen infantry battalions (nearly two
divisions), four light AA regiments, and two tank regiments. It is
strange that while these deficiencies existed in Malaya, the Chiefs
of Staff decided in September to send more troops to Hong Kong,
on the incredible grounds that the defenses of Malaya were in
better shape than they had been. Even stranger, Churchill, who in
January 1941 had refused to increase the Hong Kong garrison on
the grounds that it was an indefensible outpost, agreed on September 19. Strangest of all is the fact that Brooke-Popham, in whose
command Hong Kong lay, was not informed about the decision

until the two ill-fated Canadian battalions were already on their
way. The Canadian government agreed to send them under the
impression that the policy of treating Hong Kong as an expendable
outpost had been abandoned. But when Brooke-Popham, startled
by the announcement that Canadian troops were being sent to
Hong Kong, wrote to ask whether there had been a change of policy,
the Chiefs of Staff told him there had not: the colony was still an
outpost. Whatever lay behind this particular episode — and it may
have been still another attempt to bluff the Japanese — there is
little doubt that the two Canadian battalions would have been of
more use in Malaya, or nearly anywhere else.[112]

The list of deficiencies in Malaya on the eve of war is nearly
endless. Infantry units were short of antitank rifles, as well as
skill and practice in their use. There was even a shortage of rifles,
and the reserve of small arms ammunition was over a third below
what it should have been. For an army that would be short of air
cover, the antiaircraft situation was particularly grim. The authorized strength in Malaya was 176 heavy and 100 light AA guns,
while the estimated need was 212 and 124 respectively. Moreover,
144 more light AA guns were needed to provide adequate cover
for troops in the field. But only seventy heavy and seventy-eight
light guns were available. The missing four light AA regiments
meant that there was virtually no cover for the troops at all.[113]

Malaya's weaknesses were not only material. Many of the troops
were poorly trained. A great deal has already been said about the
difficulties under which the Indian Army suffered, difficulties
that became more acute as the expansion program went on. The
three Gurkha battalions of the Twenty-eighth Brigade, for example,
came from famous regiments, but had been recently raised. They
had then been "milked" very heavily to provide cadre for more
new units. Many of Percival's British units had been in the Far East
on garrison duty for years before the war and were far from fresh.
Wavell, who saw one British battalion in northern Malaya on
October 31, thought that the men looked slovenly and depressed.
The Australians, although not "milked" like the Indian units, or
jaded like some of the British, were nevertheless new and untried in
combat. Training had suffered from the late arrival of equipment
(like the field artillery of the Indian divisions), from mistakes
(like the "lost" antitank pamphlets), and because training schedules
were constantly interrupted for the construction of defenses. This
in turn was due to London's refusal to authorize the payment of
daily rates high enough to enable Malaya Command to raise labor

companies in a market where labor, because of the boom in rubber
and tin, was expensive and scarce. A request for labor companies
from India was turned down on the grounds that all such companies
were needed in the Middle East.[114]

The climate of Malaya certainly encouraged relaxation, and the
troops were obviously affected by the belief that nothing could
happen during the northeast monsoon. Wavell made a quick visit
to Singapore in early November. He later wrote disapprovingly
that "the whole atmosphere in Singapore was completely unwar-
like." But at the time, he was sufficiently optimistic about Malaya's
defenses to write to Auchinleck on November 8: "From the very
little I saw and what I heard of the lay-out, I should think the Jap
has a very poor chance of successfully attacking Malaya and I
don't think myself, that there is much prospect of his trying."[115]
In fact, Malaya's garrison, underequipped, partially trained, and psy-
chologically unready, was about to be hit by an enemy who would
enjoy command of the air and sea, and whose spearhead would be
two crack divisions, battle hardened in China and accompanied by
tanks. And to their many deficiencies the defenders of the British
Empire in the Far East had to add, at the last minute, a lame duck
commander in chief.

Early in November, as we have seen, Brooke-Popham was informed by Churchill of his pending replacement. In his reply the
commander in chief accepted the baronetcy that the prime minister
offered, and asked for another job. He also telegraphed his congratulations to his successor, but warned Paget: "Before you leave
ascertain policy regarding . . . programs for despatch of aeroplanes
to Far East."[116] Then came the long delay due to the complicated
switching of jobs that was going on in London and the concurrent
argument there over whether to retain the existing command system
in the Far East. On November 22 Brooke-Popham, on behalf of
himself, Layton, Percival, and Pulford, cabled London arguing for
the maintenance of the existing system.[117] Immediately following this he sent another cable arguing that the commander in chief
ought to remain an airman, and he suggested Air Chief Marshal Sir
Arthur Longmore, until recently air officer commanding in the
Middle East.[118] On November 29 Brooke-Popham was told that
the existing command system would continue, but his replacement
would now be Sir Henry Pownall, with Air Vice Marshal Paul
Maltby as his chief of staff. The commander in chief promptly
sent Pownall the same telegram of congratulations and warning he

had sent Paget. Meanwhile Australia had complained that there had been no advance consultation about Brooke-Popham's removal.[119] In London Pownall noted mordantly in his diary, "Australia and New Zealand, who were told Paget was coming and that he was a cat's whisker, were suddenly faced with the public announcement that he is going to Home Forces. So *they* wanted to know what the game was too. No doubt a number of flowery adjectives are being used to them about me to allay their fears and suspicions."[120] The knowledge that Brooke-Popham had been replaced was widespread in Malaya by the end of November. He had to face the next critical weeks aware that he was on borrowed time, while the services and civilians in Malaya knew that the commander in chief had, for whatever reasons, been found wanting.[121] As in so many other instances where the Far East was concerned, London had contrived to do something in the worst possible way.

On November 28 Brooke-Popham and Layton complained to London that the only information they were getting about the negotiations in Washington was from press reports.[122] The next day Brooke-Popham got not only the name of his successor, but the information that American forces had been alerted to expect hostilities with Japan.[123] On December 1 Phillips arrived in Singapore. The *Prince of Wales* had joined the *Repulse* at Colombo in Ceylon on November 28, and Phillips had been ordered to fly on to Singapore ahead of his ships. From there he was to go on to Manila for conferences with Hart. The Admiralty signaled him at Singapore the day he arrived, suggesting that he get the *Prince of Wales* and the *Repulse* away from the naval base. Phillips's staff were, in fact, already working on a scheme to use Port Darwin on Australia's north coast — isolated, undeveloped, and undefended, but at least out of range of Japanese aircraft.[124] The next day the "Eastern Fleet" finally arrived at Singapore. "On 2 December 1941 all the high officials were gathered at the Naval Base to see these ships steam up the Johore Straits," Playfair recalled. "Somebody remarked that with their arrival the whole strategical situation changed. Somebody else remarked that he hoped that a couple of lucky bombs would not change it back again."[125] Brooke-Popham later told the official historians that, "like the Foreign Office we in Singapore expected the political effect of the arrival of the ships to be greater than it actually was.[126] In fact, the Japanese decision for war, taken while Phillips was on his way east, was completely unaffected by the existence of the "deterrent squadron."

December 8 was confirmed by Imperial General Headquarters in Tokyo as the opening day of hostilities on the day the Eastern Fleet reached Singapore.

The day after the ships arrived the Admiralty signaled Phillips again, suggesting that in his talks with Hart he try to get some American destroyers sent to Singapore to augment his own scanty antisubmarine screen. Phillips had brought four fairly modern destroyers out with him, while Layton had four elderly ones available. The Admiralty also repeated their recommendation that he get his ships away from Singapore, eastwards into the island-studded waters of the Malay archipelago. The prime minister had seen this message before it was dispatched and commented that the sooner the ships vanished, the better. Phillips replied the same day that the *Repulse* and two destroyers would soon leave Singapore on a visit to Port Darwin.[127] Before a shot had been fired, London and Singapore were agreed that the great naval base was so insecure that the Eastern Fleet's only chance of safety lay in making itself scarce. The Admiralty, of course, had never wanted the ships to go on to Singapore. Churchill's *volte-face* seems surprising at first sight. By December 3, however, the prime minister knew that war was imminent and, more importantly, that the United States would stand with Britain against Japan. The ships were no longer needed at Singapore as counters in an elaborate game of bluff and enticement. Therefore they had better get out of the way.

Phillips left for Manila and talks with Hart and General Douglas MacArthur on December 4. The only record of the Manila discussions is in the report that Hart telegraphed to Washington. They had agreed on a tentative operational plan, which was doomed to be quickly rendered irrelevant by the march of events. In addition, Phillips signaled Pound that both he and Hart felt that Singapore was not secure enough to be a suitable base for the Eastern Fleet. Therefore he would move to Manila as soon as air defenses there were improved, probably by April 1, 1942. Hart, who was very impressed by Phillips, agreed to send four of his destroyers to Singapore on the outbreak of war. As the two Admirals talked, news reached them that a large, escorted convoy had weighed anchor from Camranh Bay in southern Indochina and was heading into the Gulf of Siam. Phillips immediately left for Singapore.[128]

The Japanese convoy movements brought the Matador problem to a head for Brooke-Popham. By this time there was no doubt at GHQ, Far East, that the Kra Isthmus was a prime Japanese objective. Parties of British officers in plain clothes sent in August and

September to reconnoiter the area had encountered parties of un-disguised Japanese officers doing the same thing.[129] Japanese planes from bases near Saigon had begun overflying southern Thailand and Malaya on reconnaissance missions in mid-October. They flew too high and too fast for Pulford's Buffaloes to get positive identification, but no one had any doubt what the planes were, and what their presence meant.[130] As the expectation of a hostile move by Japan grew, the commander in chief kept after the Chiefs of Staff about Matador. On November 21 he pointed out that the ability to get to Singora, the principal Thai port on the Kra Isthmus, before the Japanese was the essence of the oper-ation, and he asked if London could indicate what circumstances would warrant launching Matador without further reference home. This authority, for which Brooke-Popham had been pressing since February, was again denied him by the Chiefs of Staff on the 25th. Sir Robert was told that he would get the War Cabinet's decision on Matador within thirty-six hours of the receipt in London of news that the Japanese were on the move. Next to this someone at GHQ, Far East, wrote, "Too slow." Singora was only thirty-three hours' sailing time from Saigon. At the bottom of the cable Brooke-Popham wrote: "No good arguing further."[131] But, in fact, he did. On the 28th he again cabled London, as shown above, arguing for authorization to launch Matador, only to be again turned down.

He had, meanwhile, done what he could to be ready to launch Matador if consent could be extracted in time from London. Per-cival was warned on the 22nd to be ready for the operation. On the 28th, in consequence of an intelligence report from Saigon that Japan would strike at the Kra Isthmus on December 1, GHQ, Far East, ordered Pulford to fly daily reconnaissance over the Gulf of Siam. The following day III Corps was placed at twenty-four hours notice for Matador. Heath in turn put the two brigades of Major General D.M. Murray-Lyon's Eleventh Indian Division, the forma-tion earmarked for Matador, at six hours notice.[132] The minimum estimate of the forces required for the operation was three brigades. Nevertheless, Eleventh Division had been training and preparing for its offensive role for some months, was confident, and keyed up to go.

On December 1 Brooke-Popham was told by London that an assurance of American support, on which hinged the delegation to him of authority for Matador, had been sought from Washington. Then, after four days of tense silence, a cable reached Singapore at quarter to two in the afternoon of December 5: the Americans had agreed, and Brooke-Popham could launch Matador without further reference to London. Playfair handed the cable to the commander in chief with the damping comment, "They've now made you responsible for declaring war."[133] The repeated warnings from London about the dangers of involving Britain in war had left an unfortunate legacy of caution at GHQ, Far East. Now that he was free to move, the necessity actually to take the fateful decision began to paralyze Brooke-Popham.

London's release had come at literally the last minute. At two o'clock the next afternoon, December 6, 1941, a Hudson aircraft of No. 1 Squadron, Royal Australian Air Force, flying from Kota Bharu in northeast Malaya, sighted three Japanese convoys eighty-some miles off the southern point of Indochina, steering west. The reported composition of the convoys (a battleship, eight cruisers, seventeen destroyers, and forty-five merchant ships) left no doubt that the Japanese were about to strike. All forces in Malaya were brought to the highest degree of readiness. Percival phoned Heath about 3:15 and told him that the Eleventh Division must be ready to move at short notice. The division's six battalions stood to beside their trucks and trains and waited in the drenching, incessant monsoon rains that were to have made a Japanese move impossible.[134]

Notes to Chapter 6

1. Winston S. Churchill, *The Second World War*, vol. 3, *The Grand Alliance* (Boston: Houghton Mifflin, 1950), p. 429.

2. Ibid., p. 427.

3. Public Record Office (PRO), PREM 3, 156/6, note by Ismay, August 8, 1941.

4. Ibid., CAB 69, D.O. (41) 54, August 5, 1941.

5. S. W. Kirby, *Singapore: The Chain of Disaster* (New York: Macmillan, 1971), p. 105; J.R.M. Butler ed., *History of the Second World War: United Kingdom Military Series,* "Grand Strategy" series, vol. 3, J. M. A. Gwyer and J. R. M. Butler, *Grand Strategy (June 1941-August 1942),* 2 pts. (London: H.M.S.O., 1964), pt. 1, p. 132; Commander-in-Chief, Far East, to War Office, August 6, 1941, PRO, PREM 3, 156/6.

6. PRO, PREM 3, 156/6, COS (41) 479, August 7, 1941.

7. PRO, CAB 69, D.O. (41) 56, August 8, 1941.

8. B. Bond, ed., *Chief of Staff: The Diaries of Lieutenant General Sir Henry Pownall,* 2 vols. (London: Leo Cooper Ltd., 1973-74) 2:36.

9. Gwyer and Butler, *Grand Strategy III,* pt. 1, p. 133.

10. Colonel E.I.C. Jacob, Diary of the Atlantic Meeting, p. 19, Jacob Papers, in the possession of Lt. Gen. Sir Ian Jacob, G.B.E. Sir Ian's diary captures the hectic atmos-

phere of the first Anglo-American "summit" very well (refered to hereafter as Jacob, "Diary"). See also Gwyer and Butler, *Grand Stategy III*, pt. 1, pp. 125-29.

11. Jacob, "Diary," p. 11.

12. Churchill to Stalin, September 21, 1941, Churchill, *The Grand Alliance*, p. 467. Curiously, Churchill does not refer to this pledge in his account of the conference itself (ibid., pp. 427-50), nor do the official historians (Butler and Gwyer, *Grand Strategy III*, pt. 1, pp. 111-38). In any case, it had been the prime minister's position for some time — see, e.g., his minute to Eden of October 4, 1940, in Winston S. Churchill, *The Second World War*, vol. 2, *Their Finest Hour* (Boston: Houghton Mifflin, 1949), p. 675. Churchill publicly repeated his pledge twice in the months between the Atlantic meeting and Pearl Harbor. The first occasion was in a broadcast on August 24, and the second, during his address to the annual Lord Mayor's Banquet on November 10, 1941. The prime minister's remarks on the latter occasion are in idem, *The Grand Alliance*, p. 594.

13. Gwyer and Butler, *Grand Strategy III*, pt. 1, p. 134.

14. Ibid., p. 136. The full cable is in Churchill, *The Grand Alliance*, pp. 439-40. Sir Alexander Cadogan was also optimistic about the results of the conversations, recording in his diary for August 11, ". . . the Joint Declaration . . . will give the Japanese a jar . . . Quite a satisfactory day, . . ." in D. Dilks, ed., *The Diaries of Sir Alexander Cadogan, O.M., 1938-1945* (London: Cassell & Co., 1971), p. 399.

15. Gwyer and Butler, *Grand Strategy III*, pt. 1, p. 137. In his memoirs Churchill does not mention the way in which Roosevelt reneged on his agreement about the warning to Japan.

16. E. L. Woodward, *British Foreign Policy in the Second World War*, 5 vols. (London: H.M.S.O., 1970-), 2:147-48.

17. Gwyer and Butler, *Grand Strategy III*, pt. 1, pp. 118-19.

18. The cable is in PRO, PREM 3, 156/6. It is not mentioned by either Churchill or the official historians.

19. Churchill, *The Grand Alliance*, pp. 448-49.

20. Interview with Lt. Gen. Sir Ian Jacob, January 14, 1971.

21. Butler, ed., *History of the Second World War*, "Grand Strategy" series, vol. 2, J. R. M. Butler, *Grand Strategy (September 1939-June 1941)* (London: H.M.S.O., (1957), p. 507. As early as February 15, 1941, Pound wrote a minute in which he envisioned an Eastern Fleet composed of five battleships and a battle cruiser, PRO, ADM 205/10.

22. Gwyer and Butler, *Grand Stragegy III*, pt. 1, p. 268.

23. The entire minute was reprinted by Churchill in *The Grand Alliance*, pp. 854-55.

24. Ibid., p. 439.

25. Ibid., pp. 855-58.

26. Ibid., 858-59.

27. Arthur J. Marder, *Winston Is Back: Churchill at the Admiralty 1939-1940* (London: Longman, 1972), pp. 4-5, discusses Churchill's relationship with Pound. Marder's views have been challenged by S. W. Roskill, "Marder, Churchill and the Admiralty 1939-1942." *Journal of the Royal United Services Institute for Defence Studies* 117 (December 1972): 49-53. Marder has replied to Roskill in his *From the Dardanelles to Oran: Studies of the Royal Navy in War and Peace 1915-1940* (London: Oxford University Press, 1974), pp. 173-78. Captain Roskill's judgement must command respect, but, in this case at least, Marder's analysis seems to be borne out by the results. On the troopship *Orontes* in convoy W.S. 11, which H.M.S. *Repulse* escorted as far as the Cape, was a young British Army signals officer, W. J. Reader, whose mother had told

him just before he sailed: "I hope you go to Singapore. It's about as far from any fighting as you could possible be" (information from Dr. W.J. Reader).

28. Gwyer and Butler, *Grand Strategy III,* pt. 1, pp. 279-80.

29. Ibid., p. 280.

30. Butler, ed., *History of the Second World War,* "Campaigns" series I. S. O. Playfair et al., *The Mediterranean and Middle East,* 6 vols. (H.M.S.O., 1954-), 3:4.

31. Ibid., p. 412.

32. Churchill, *The Grand Alliance,* pp. 490-93.

33. Ibid., p. 495.

34. Ibid., p. 480.

35. PRO, CAB 69, D.O. (41) 19, September 11, 1941; J. Connell, *Wavell: The Supreme Commander 1941-1943* (London: Collins, 1969), pp. 29-31, gives the deficiencies as 10,000 officers and 50,000 British other ranks.

36. Playfair et al., *The Mediterranean and Middle East,* 2:288-90, 361. On May 10, 1941, Churchill, in an "Action this Day" minute to Portal, had declared that aircraft were more important than tanks in the struggle to hold Egypt, in Churchill, *The Grand Alliance,* pp. 763-64.

37. Playfair et al., *The Mediterranean and Middle East,* 3:13.

38. Gwyer and Butler, *Grand Strategy III,* pt. 1, pp. 183-84.

39. Ibid., pp. 146-48.

40. Ibid., pp. 148-61.

41. Playfair et al., *The Mediterranean and Middle East,* 2:362.

42. Ibid., 3:458.

43. Gwyer and Butler, *Grand Strategy III,* pt. 1, pp. 95, 204-6.

44. Ibid., pp. 206-11, 214-16.

45. Ibid., p. 8.

46. Ibid., p. 281.

47. PRO, CAB 65, WM (41) 103, October 16, 1941.

48. PRO, CAB 69, D.O. (41) 65, October 17, 1941. See also the letter from Phillips to Pound about this meeting, quoted in S. W. Roskill, *Hankey: Man of Secrets,* 3 vols. (London: Collins, 1970-1974), 3:539.

49. The record of this discussion is in PRO, CAB 69/8, D.O. (41) 66, October 20, 1941. CAB 69/8 is the "Secretary's Standard File," the bland euphemism for those items too important — or too sensitive — to be included in the regular series of Defence Committee minutes. It is curious that Churchill's remark about Japanese battlecruisers went uncorrected, since in fact the Japanese had none. In view of his remark about the willingness of the War Cabinet to accept the consequences of a breakout by the *Tirpitz,* it is also interesting that in a cable to the Australian prime minister on October 24, 1941, Churchill declared: "I must make it clear that movements of *Prince of Wales* must be reviewed when she is at Cape Town because of danger of Tirpitz breaking out and other operational possibilities," in PRO, ADM 205/10.

50. Butler, ed., *History of the Second World War,* "Campaigns" series, S. W. Roskill, *The War at Sea,* 3 vols. (London: H.M.S.O., 1954-1961), 1:557.

51. Eden, in the relevant volume of his memoirs, *The Memoirs of Anthony Eden, Earl of Avon: The Reckoning* (Boston: Houghton Mifflin, 1965), pp. 364-65, minimizes his own role, making it appear that all the pressure for the dispatch of the *Prince of Wales* and the *Repulse* came from Churchill.

52. H.L. Ismay, *The Memoirs of General Lord Ismay* (New York: Viking Press, 1960), p. 240.

53. Marder, *Winston is Back,* p. 55. S. W. Roskill claims that during his last months

in England Phillips had become estranged from Churchill due to differences over strategy, in Roskill, *Hankey*, 3:512, fn. 4.

54. Interview with Lt. Gen. Sir Ian Jacob, January 14, 1971.

55. Roskill, *The War at Sea*, 1:557-58; Gwyer and Butler, *Grand Strategy III*, pt. 1, p. 274; Bond, ed., *Chief of Staff*, 2:65.

56. The works referred to in n26 above provide most of the material on which this judgement of Pound is based. L. Kennedy, *Pursuit: The Chase and Sinking of the Battleship Bismarck* (New York: Viking Press, 1974), p. 107, tells the story of the fleet medical officer's doubts. It would be interesting to have Pound's side of the story. Although he died in 1943, no study of him has yet been done, and his private papers, if any, have not yet come to light.

57. Churchill, *The Grand Alliance*, p. 836.

58. Churchill to Smuts, November 2, 1941, PRO, ADM 199/1934; Roskill, *The War at Sea*, 1:558. In his memoirs Churchill makes no mention of this message from Smuts. What, if any, answer it elicited is also unknown. The relevant volume of Smuts's biography, W. K. Hancock, *Smuts*, vol. 2, *The Fields of Force 1919-1950* (Cambridge: Cambridge University Press, 1968), makes no mention of it either.

59. Churchill to Pound, November 1, 3, 1941; Pound to Churchill, November 18, 1941, ADM 205/10.

60. Churchill to Brooke-Popham, November 5, 1941, Brooke-Popham Papers (BPP) v/5/1, The Liddell Hart Centre for Military Archives, King's College, London; Air Ministry to Brooke-Popham, November 6, 1941, BPP v/5/2. Paget was at the time GOC, Southeastern Command, which covered that part of England most exposed to invasion.

61. Churchill, *The Grand Alliance*, p. 526.

62. Ibid., p. 527.

63. On these changes see A. Bryant, ed., *The Turn of the Tide: 1939-1943: A History of the War Years based on the Diaries of Field Marshal Lord Alanbrooke* (New York: Doubleday, 1957), pp. 211-12; Bond, ed., *Chief of Staff*, 2:53-54.

64. Bond, ed., *Chief of Staff*, 2:55.

65. Butler, ed., *History of the Second World War*, "Campaigns" series, S. W. Kirby, et al., *The War Against Japan*, vol. 1, *The Loss of Singapore*, pp. 484-87, prints Brooke-Popham's directive, and Pownall's. Kirby's account of Pownall's appointment in *Singapore: The Chain of Disaster*, pp. 119-20, is incorrect.

66. Churchill, *The Grand Alliance*, p. 410-11.

67. Ibid., pp. 844-46.

68. Ibid., pp. 411-18; Playfair et al., *The Mediterranean and Middle East*, 3: 23-25; J. Connell, *Auchinleck: A Critical Biography* (London: Cassell & Co., 1959), pp. 276-83; Gwyer and Butler, *Grand Strategy III*, pt. 1, pp. 224-26. In an interview with the author, January 14, 1971, Lt. Gen. Sir Ian Jacob confirmed the degree of irritation that the Australian decision caused in Whitehall. In a message to Curtin on November 27, 1941, dealing with Australian criticism of the British failure to declare war on Germany's Finnish, Hungarian, and Rumanian allies, Churchill pointedly mentioned that the argument over the withdrawal of the Australian division from Tobruk had never been allowed to become a matter of public knowledge in Great Britain and added, "we should try so far as possible to understand each other's difficulties . . . ." PRO, ADM 205/10. The Australian side of the argument is very well put in *Australia in the War of 1939-1945* (Series IV: Civil), vol. 1, P. Hasluck, *The Government and the People 1939-1941* (Canberra: Australian War Memorial, 1952), pp. 616-24.

69. Woodward, *British Foreign Policy*, 2:179-80; Air Chief Marshal Sir Robert Brooke-Popham, "Operations in The Far East, From 17th October 1940 to 27th Dec-

ember 1941," *Supplement to the London Gazette,* January 22, 1948, par. 45 (cited hereafter as Brooke-Popham, *Dispatch).*

70. Kirby et al., *The Loss of Singapore,* pp. 76, 86.

71. PRO, CAB 65, WM (41) 104, October 20, 1941.

72. Ibid., WM (41) 108, November 3, 1941.

73. Churchill, *The Grand Alliance,* pp. 592-93.

74. PRO, CAB 65, WM (41) 109, November 5, 1941.

75. Ibid., WM (41) 111, November 11, 1941.

76. Ibid., WM (41) 112, November 12, 1941.

77. Ibid.

78. Kirby et al., *The Loss of Singapore,* p. 86.

79. There is a note on this conversation in PRO, PREM 3, 156/6.

80. Churchill, *The Grand Alliance,* p. 548.

81. Ibid., pp. 600, 646.

82. The cable is in PRO, PREM 3, 156/5.

83. The Dominions Office cable and the replies it elicited are in PRO, PREM 3, 156/5.

84. PRO, CAB 65, WM (41) 122, December 1, 1941.

85. Churchill's minute is in PRO, PREM 3, 156/5.

86. A copy of Halifax's cable is in PRO, PREM 3, 156/5.

87. WP (41) 296 in PRO, PREM 3, 156/5.

88. D.O. (41) 71, December 3, 1941, in PRO, PREM 3, 156/5.

89. This exchange of cables is in PREM 3, 156/5.

90. PRO, CAB 65, WM (41) 124, December 4, 1941.

91. Brooke-Popham and Layton to Air Ministry, August 14, 1941, BPP v/4/25.

92. Brooke-Popham to Chiefs of Staff, August 20, 1941, BPP v/4/26.

93. This paper is in BPP v/4/29.

94. Chiefs of Staff to Brooke-Popham, September 17, 1941, BPP v/4/33.

95. See, for example, Brooke-Popham to Ismay, July 3, 1941, BPP v/1/14; Brooke-Popham, *Dispatch,* par. 80.

96. Brooke-Popham, *Dispatch,* pars. 79-86; *Australia in the War of 1939-45* (Series I: Army), vol. 4, L. Wigmore, *The Japanese Thrust* (Canberra: Australian War Memorial, 1957), p. 45.

97. Brooke-Popham, *Dispatch,* pars. 87; Air Vice Marshal Sir Paul Maltby, "Report on The Air Operations During the Campaigns In Malaya And Netherlands East Indies From 8th December 1941 to 12th March 1942," *Supplement to the London Gazette,* February 26, 1948, par. 91 (cited hereafter as Maltby, *Dispatch);* Brooke-Popham, "Comments on the draft of the War Against Japan, Volume I," April 16, 1953, BPP v/9/34.

98. Kirby et al., *The Loss of Singapore,* p. 79; Brooke-Popham, *Dispatch,* par. 61.

99. By Kirby in *Singapore: The Chain of Disaster,* p. 118.

100. Kirby et al., *The Loss of Singapore,* p. 15; Kirby, *Singapore: The Chain of Disaster,* p. 31.

101. This memo is in BPP v/4/30.

102. Ivan Simson, *Singapore: Too Little, Too Late* (London: Leo Cooper Ltd., 1970), pp. 48-49.

103. Ibid., p. 49.

104. Maj. Gen. I. S. O. Playfair, "Some Personal Reflections on the Malayan Campaign," n.d. [covering letter to Brooke-Popham dated May 10, 1943], p. 10, BPP v/9/28 (cited hereafter as Playfair, "Personal Reflections").

105. This belief is referred to in a letter from H. P. Bryson to the author, February 3, 1974.

106. The report is in PRO, CAB 66, WP (41) 286; it is paraphrased in Gwyer and Butler, *Grand Strategy III*, pt. 1, pp. 285-89.

107. Wigmore, *The Japanese Thrust*, p. 84; C. MacKenzie, *Eastern Epic*, vol. 1, *Defence* (London: Chatto & Windus, 1951), p. 229; Playfair, "Personal Reflections," p. 7.

108. Brooke-Popham, *Dispatch*, par. 92.

109. Ibid.; Kirby et al., *The Loss of Singapore*, p. 217 fn.; R. M. Ogorkiewicz, *Armor: A History of Mechanized Forces* (New York: Praeger, 1960), p. 436.

110. Simson, *Singapore: Too Little, Too Late*, pp. 54-57.

111. Lieut. Gen. A. E. Percival, "Operations of Malaya Command, From 8th December 1941 to 15th February 1942," *Supplement to the London Gazette*, February 26, 1948, par. 15 (cited herafter as Percival, *Dispach*).

112. Kirby et al., *The Loss of Singapore*, pp. 80-82; Brook-Popham, "Comments on the draft of the war against Japan, Volume I," April 16, 1953, BPP v/9/34.

113. Percival, *Dispatch*, pars. 23-24, 47; Brooke-Popham, *Dispatch*, par. 92, Appendices E, F; Playfair, "Personal Reflections," p. 7.

114. Kirby, *Singapore: The Chain of Disaster*, pp. 97-99.

115. Connell, *Wavell: The Supreme Commander*, p. 41. In Brooke-Popham's papers there is a letter from Wavell, dated November 13, 1941, which includes this sentence: "I should be most doubtful if the Japs ever tried to make an attack on Malaya, and I am sure they will get it in the neck if they do," in BPP v/5/13.

116. Brooke-Popham to Churchill, November 7, 1941, BPP v/5/3; Brooke-Popham to Paget, November 7, 1941, BPP v/5/4.

117. Brooke-Popham to Chiefs of Staff, November 22, 1941, BPP v/5/14.

118. Brooke-Popham to Portal, November 7, 1941, BPP v/5/15; see also Brooke-Popham to Portal, November 7, 1941, BPP v/5/5.

119. The cable of November 22, 1941, from Australia to the Dominions Office is in PRO, CAB 66, WP (42) 37, January 25, 1942.

120. Bond, ed., *Chief of Staff*, 2: 54-55.

121. Brooke-Popham, *Dispatch*, par. 130; idem, "Comments on the draft of the War Against Japan, Volume I," BPP v/9/34.

122. Brooke-Popham to Chiefs of Staff, November 28, 1941, BPP v/4/40.

123. Brooke-Popham, *Dispatch*, par. 95.

124. Roskill, *The War at Sea*, 1: 559.

125. Playfair, "Personal Reflections," p. 9.

126. "Comments on the draft of the War Against Japan, Volume I," BPP v/9/34.

127. Roskill, *The War at Sea*, 1: 559; Gwyer and Butler, *Grand Strategy III*, pt. 1, p. 308.

128. Roskill, *The War at Sea*, 1: 561-62; Gwyer and Butler, *Grand Strategy III*, pt. 1, pp. 273-74; Samuel Eliot Morison, *History of United States Naval Operations in World War II*, 15 vols. (Boston: Atlantic Little, Brown, 1947-62), 3: 156-57. Phillips's plane stopped to refuel at Labuan Island on its way to Manila, and the Admiral spent the night of December 4 as the guest of the British resident, Mr. A. H. P. Humphrey. In response to a question from Humphrey, Phillips gave it as his opinion that the war with Japan was unlikely (information from Mr. Humphrey). It would be interesting to know whether Phillips really believed this, or whether he too was engaged in boosting local morale.

129. Kirby, *Singapore: The Chain of Disaster*, p. 110.

130. Brooke-Popham, *Dispatch*, par. 95; M. Tsuji, *Singapore: The Japanese Version* (New York: St. Martin's Press, 1960), pp. 45-52, gives an interesting account of one reconnaissance flight in late October on which he was a passenger.

131. Kirby et al., *The Loss of Singapore*, p. 173; Chiefs of Staff to Brooke-Popham, November 25, 1941, BPP v/4/39.

132. Kirby et al., *The Loss of Singapore*, pp. 173-74; Maltby, *Dispatch*, par 144.

133. Chiefs of Staff to Brooke-Popham, December 5, 1941, BPP v/4/41; Brooke-Popham, "Comments on the draft of the War Against Japan, Volume I," April 16, 1953, BPP v/9/34.

134. Kirby et al., *The Loss of Singapore*, p. 180-81; D. Richards and H. St. G. Saunders, *The Royal Air Force 1939-1945*, 3 vols. (London: H.M.S.O., 1953-54), 2: 15. The Hudson was an American built aircraft, generally used by the British for reconnaissance, although able to double as a light bomber.

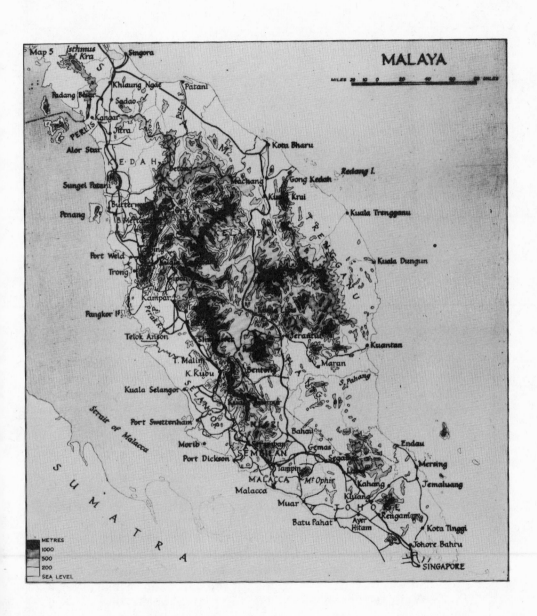

7
CATASTROPHE:
December 6-15, 1941

i

The sightings on December 6 put Brooke-Popham in a quandry. He had been given the power to launch Matador barely twenty-four hours before, but the Eleventh Indian Division was ready to go. He had, however, been warned on the 2nd by FECB that the Japanese might try to bluff the British into violating Thai territory first. Perhaps the convoys were such a bluff. Even though he now had authority for Matador, the repeated warnings about putting Britain in the wrong with American opinion by making the first move were having their effect. Brooke-Popham conferred with Layton and Rear Admiral Arthur Palliser, Phillips's chief of staff, during the afternoon and decided not to order Matador. It was still not clear where the convoys were bound — Bangkok, Singora on the Kra Isthmus, or the east coast of Malaya. If it was a bluff, they might not be bound anywhere.[1] So the commander in chief waited for further information, and the Eleventh Division waited in the rain for the starter's whistle.

The delay was a fateful mistake. Matador was predicated upon beating the Japanese to the Kra Isthmus. This was particularly important since the Eleventh Division had only two brigades, one fewer than was considered desirable for the operation (which Bond had originally estimated as calling for two complete divisions). The authorization received from London covered the situation in which Brooke-Popham found himself. As he had correctly pointed out sometime before, Saigon was only thirty-three hours steaming

190

from the Kra Isthmus. Matador needed at least twenty-four hours head start to forestall the Japanese. By the time he was certain of the Japanese destination, it might be, in fact probably would be, too late. Moreover, even if the Eleventh Indian Division was ordered to drop Matador and take up defensive positions, a column would cross the Thai frontier to seize a key position known as "the Ledge," which blocked access, via a secondary road, to Malaya's west-coast trunk road. Thai territory was going to be violated whatever happened.

Why did Brooke-Popham dither at this last critical minute, and lose the only chance to forestall the Japanese? Fear of American reaction, which lingered in Singapore even after it was dispelled in London, was certainly a factor. But it is also true that Brooke-Popham was by now a tired man. A year in Malaya's enervating climate, punctuated by long tiring journeys, and the uphill struggle to prepare for war had taken their toll of the sixty-three year old commander in chief. He also knew that he no longer enjoyed London's confidence and that his subordinates knew this. Brooke-Popham was tired and hesitant when he was called upon to make his most important decision.[2]

After the meeting with Layton and Palliser, Brooke-Popham told Pulford not to lose touch with the convoys. This was easier to order than to do. The monsoon weather over the Gulf of Siam was very poor. The Hudson that made the original sightings did so at the extreme limit of its range, and had been unable to maintain contact. Two Catalina flying boats from Seletar on Singapore Island, whose range was about twice that of the Hudson, were sent out to track the convoys during the night. One failed to make contact. The other succeeded but was shot down before it could signal its base. Percival, arriving back in Singapore from a visit to Heath, was surprised to discover that Matador had not already been ordered, but apparently he made no protest to Brooke-Popham. H.M.S. *Repulse* and two destroyers, which had left the preceding day for Australia, were recalled.

At dawn on December 7 three Hudsons from Kota Bharu went out to relieve the Catalinas. Bad weather also plagued them, and two had to turn back. The third carried on, but found nothing. The hours ticked by. Brooke-Popham ruled that B.O.A.C. flights through Bangkok should continue until the last possible moment. Phillips arrived back from Manila. The one Beaufort in Pulford's command, which had been converted to a photoreconnaissance role, was sent off shortly after noon to reconnoiter anchorages on the west coast of Cambodia. Two and a half hours later it returned, also baffled by bad weather. During the afternoon there were two inconclusive sightings, each of a single merchantman. Finally, at ten minutes to six, a Hudson found an escorted merchantman steaming toward Singora. The warship promptly fired on the plane. An hour later four more Japanese warships were sighted, sixty miles north of Patani on the Kra Isthmus, steering south.[3]

About nine o'clock Brooke-Popham had all this information. But he also had a telegram from Crosby, the British minister in Bangkok, pleading that British forces should not violate Thai territory first. The commander in chief and Percival went to the naval base to confer with Phillips, and, for the second time, the decision on Matador was postponed. There was still no certainty that the ships sighted were part of an expedition bound for the Kra Isthmus. If they were, the opportunity for Matador was already gone. But they might only be the bluff that Brooke-Popham feared. The one positive decision taken that evening was to order another reconnaissance of the Singora area at first light, on the results of which a decision on Matador would finally be given. B.O.A.C. was now warned to avoid Bangkok, and Heath was told (at 11:20 P.M.) to be prepared to put Matador into operation at dawn on the 8th. The Eleventh Indian Division settled down to a second dreary night in the rain.[4] Less than an hour later the fog of uncertainty began to lift. Shortly before midnight ships were reported off the Malayan coast at Kota Bharu.

In extreme northeastern Malaya, Kota Bharu was the capital of the largely undeveloped state of Kelantan. It was linked to the rest of the country only by a single-track rail line. There were, however, three airfields in the area. One was at Kota Bharu itself, where the reconnaissance squadron of Hudsons and a section (two aircraft) of Buffaloes were based. Thirty miles down the coast at Gong Kedah was another airfield, and a squadron of ancient Vildebeeste torpedo bombers. At Machang, nearly twenty miles inland along the winding Kelantan River, was the third airfield, uncompleted and unoccupied. This area of nearly six hundred square miles, with three scattered airfields and more than thirty miles of beaches to watch, was the responsibility of Brigadier B. W. Key's Eighth Indian Infantry Brigade. Key had been given an extra battalion to supplement his three. He also had the light guns of an Indian mountain battery, and the eight 25-pounders of a British field artillery battery. Nevertheless, the defenders were spread very thin, particularly on the beaches where two battalions held over thirty miles. The rain, which had been steady for several days, now ceased, and the weather perversely cleared at about the time the Japanese arrived. The wind fell calm, and there was a bright moon, making landings much easier. By 12:30 A.M. the first troops of the assaulting Japanese regiment were ashore. About the same time the RAF station commander, Wing Commander C. H. Noble, rang up Pulford to report that ships had been seen off the coast. A half hour later Noble rang back confirming the presence of the ships and reporting artillery fire. Pulford told him to send out a Hudson to find out what was happening. Before Noble had a chance to do this, a report reached Singapore from Key's headquarters that landings were taking place. Pulford thereupon ordered Noble to get his seven Hudsons airborne immediately. The Vildebeestes were to follow at first light. Struggling off their waterlogged airfield, the Hudsons hit all three Japanese transports, one of which sank the following day. But a third of the squadron was lost. On the beaches the 3/17th Dogra Regiment fought savagely, several of its defense posts resisting to the last man, but by 4 A.M. the Japanese had a firm beachhead. At the same hour they began unopposed landings at Singora and Patani.[5]

Almost simultaneously, Singapore abruptly discovered that it was at war. Shortly after 3:00 A.M. the radar stations picked up approaching Japanese planes, about fifty-five minutes' flying-time away. The Japanese bombers arrived over Singapore about 4:00 A.M. The city's lights were still blazing. No alarms had been sounded, and the civil defense services had not been alerted. In his report on the radar units in Malaya, Squadron Leader Carter described this remarkable episode.

> It was later stated by W/Cdr CAVE, who was that night in the filter room, that the Governor of the Straits Settlements had given instructions that the air raid alarms were not to be sounded without his permission for fear of alarming the civilian population, and that when 35 minutes after the first plot had been passed, he gave permission for them to be sounded, the arrangement for sounding them went astray in that the civilian air raid officer responsible could not be found.[6]

The incredible fact was that the civil Air Raid Precautions H.Q. was not manned. (It was, after all, the weekend.) As Carter put it in a private letter, "it took 30 minutes of the precious 55 minutes for [Sir Shenton Thomas] to make up his mind, the remaining 25 were spent trying to find the Civil A.R.P. man who had the keys which unlocked the box which contained the alarm. The Jap got there first, . . ."[7] Thus Singapore went to war. Since there was a full moon that night, the fact that Singapore was not blacked out was less important than it might otherwise have been. But it shows how unreal the threat of war seemed in the Far East, as well as the importance the civil administration placed on not disturbing civilian morale in the fragile, and economically vital, multiracial society over which it presided.

Early on the 8th Phillips relieved Layton, whose command merged with the Eastern Fleet. Brooke-Popham issued an "Order of the Day" at 6:30 A.M. It had been drawn up the previous May, to allow time for its translation and distribution. Brooke-Popham later admitted that it was "bombastic," but, with the condescension that marked the dealings of so many British officers with the Indian Army, he claimed that "the main object I had in view when preparing it was to make an effective appeal to the Indian troops, as I considered it would be necessary to stimulate them rather than the British." "We are ready," it trumpeted. "We have had plenty of warning and our preparations are made and tested . . . . We are confident. Our defences are strong and our weapons efficient." Coming a few hours after the air raid episode, the Order of the Day was rather unfortunate.[8]

Percival's H.Q. telephoned Brooke-Popham's shortly after 8:00 A.M. to ask about Matador, only to be told to wait for the results of the dawn reconnaissance over Singora. An hour and fifteen minutes later the badly damaged photoreconnaissance Beaufort staggered into Kota Bharu. Its pilot brought word that large scale Japanese landings were taking place at Singora and Patani. By 9:45 Brooke-Popham had this information and could, finally, make his decision. Matador was off. The Eleventh Division would assume its alternate role, manning a defensive position on the west-coast trunk road at Jitra, and seizing the Ledge inside Thailand. Then further delays occurred, largely because no one in Singapore was yet gripped by a sense of urgency. Percival was away from his H.Q. attending a previously scheduled meeting of the Straits Settlements Legislative Council, and it was 11:00 A.M. before he learned of Brooke-Popham's decision. Meanwhile Heath's H.Q. had been ringing up Malaya Command repeatedly in search of a ruling on Matador. Even after Percival gave his orders at 11:30 there were more delays in passing them on to Heath, and not until 1:30 P.M. was the long-suffering Eleventh Division told to scrub Matador, and take up defensive positions. The Japanese had been given a ten-hour head start. In a halting, muddled fashion Far East Command had gone to war.[9]

The prime minister was spending the weekend at Chequers. With him were Averell Harriman, Roosevelt's special representative in London, and John Winant, the American ambassador. Nine years later Churchill was able to recall the evening vividly.

> I turned on my small wireless set shortly after the nine o'clock news started.... at the end a few sentences were spoken regarding an attack by the Japanese on American shipping at Hawaii,. . . I did not personally sustain any direct impression, but Averell said there was something about the Japanese attacking the Americans, and, in spite of being tired and resting, we all sat up. By now the butler, Sawyers, who had heard what had passed, came into the room, saying, "It's quite true. We heard it ourselves outside. The Japanese have attacked the Americans.". . . I got up from the table and walked through the hall to the office which was always at work. I asked for a call to the President. . . . In two or three minutes Mr. Roosevelt came through. "Mr. President, what's this about Japan?" "It's quite true," he replied. "They have attacked us at Pearl Harbor. We are all in the same boat now."[10]

Churchill's reaction was one of overwhelming relief: "So we had won after all!" There is little doubt that he had at that moment no real conception of the disaster that impended in the Far East, despite his retrospective comment that he expected heavy initial defeats there. America had not deterred Japan; much of the United States Pacific Fleet, upon which Churchill had counted so much, was settling into the mud at Pearl Harbor. Malaya, starved in the interests of home defense, the Middle East, and Russia, was about to be hit by a military avalanche. Churchill expected the defeats in the Far East to be temporary setbacks. American entry, he believed, meant ultimate victory. And so it did. But the nature of the defeat in the Far East, and of the wartime partnership with America, also meant the end of Britain as a world power. That, however, lay in the future. Meanwhile, the prime minister "went to bed and slept the sleep of the saved and the thankful."[11]

ii

Churchill's slumbers might have been less restful if he had known what was happening to Malaya's first line of defense. On the eve-

ning of December 7, 1941, Air Vice Marshal Pulford's command
consisted of fourteen squadrons of aircraft. Only five were fighters,
and one of these was made up of obsolescent Blenheim bombers
converted to night fighters. There were four bomber squadrons,
one just arrived from Burma to do bombing practice, and none
with modern aircraft. There were two squadrons of Hudsons, intended for reconnaissance but able to double as bombers, two of
ancient Vildebeeste torpedo bombers, and one of Catalina flying
boats. Instead of the 336 modern first-line aircraft prescribed by
the Chiefs of Staff, there were 158 largely obsolete aircraft in
Malaya. Instead of the 100 percent reserves to back them up, as
prescribed by the Air Ministry in February, there were a grand
total of 88. Fifty-two Buffalo fighters were in reserve, but 21 of
them were unusable because new engines that were being fitted to
them had developed valve trouble. This force faced 580 operational
Japanese aircraft. The 180 Japanese fighters, half of them Zeros,
were nearly double Pulford's total force of Buffalo and Blenheim
fighters.[12] Most of the RAF's strength was concentrated in northern
Malaya. At Kota Bharu and at Kuantan, further down the east
coast, were Hudsons and Vildebeestes for reconnaissance and anti-
shipping strikes; on the west side of the peninsula Blenheims and
Buffaloes stood ready to support III Corps in Matador. Of the 158
available aircraft, 110 were in the north by dawn on December 8.
There was no radar cover in northern Malaya. A station had been
built at Kota Bharu, but its equipment had not yet been installed.
There was therefore no warning system, and no coordinated
defense of the forward airfields. Antiaircraft defenses were slight
due to the shortage of light AA weapons.

The Japanese hit Pulford's exposed squadrons quickly, and very
hard. British aircraft were often caught on the ground, refueling and
rearming, giving rise to ugly (but largely groundless) rumors of
treachery and fifth column activity. At Alor Star in northwest
Malaya a Blenheim squadron caught on the ground was reduced to
two planes; at Sungei Patani, south of Alor Star, two fighter squadrons (one of them Blenheim night fighters) were similarly caught.
Only four in each squadron remained serviceable, and the guns of
the four usable Buffaloes were defective. The remaining aircraft
withdrew from Sungei Patani to nearby Butterworth, and the RAF
ground staff hastily evacuated the station, leaving between 100,000
and 200,000 gallons of aviation fuel, as well as the bomb stores
and the runways intact, despite the fact that no Japanese troops
were anywere near. At the end of the day only 50 operational air-

craft were left in the north. Brooke-Popham and Phillips were telegraphing London that everything hinged on air superiority, and appealing urgently for two squadrons of heavy bombers and two of night fighters. But the full extent of the day's catastrophic losses was not yet known in Singapore. In fact, the Japanese had already won control of the air in the north.[13]

They had also won an airfield at Kota Bharu. Key's brigade, not one of whose four battalions was British, fought stubbornly throughout the day. But the three airfields were made untenable by continual bombing and strafing. The Japanese used antipersonnel and fragmentation bombs, rather than damage fields they would soon use themselves. At 4 P.M. Pulford ordered the remaining aircraft to withdraw to Kuantan. Simultaneously, the rumor spread that the Japanese had broken through the defenses. Whatever contempt was expressed by senior officers for Japanese fighting qualities, there is no doubt they had considerable "bogey man" value as far as most of the British in Malaya were concerned. Stories of their ferocity in China had, after all, been given widespread publicity for years. In a panic, the RAF station staff, mechanics and administrative personnel — all untrained in ground combat — set fire to the buildings and decamped. The fuel stores, runways, and some 550 tons of bombs were left intact. That night Key's brigade fell back from the beaches and took up a position covering the remaining two empty airfields. As it withdrew, the Eighth Indian Infantry Brigade set fire to the fuel stores abandoned by the RAF.[14]

The second day of the war was worse. Three squadrons of Dutch Glen Martin bombers and a squadron of their Buffaloes arrived at Singapore. But these reinforcements were more than offset by further disaster. Early that day Pulford decided to thin out the concentration of aircraft at Kuantan. The Japanese, who averaged about 120 sorties a day for the first three days of the war, got there first, destroying seven aircraft on the ground. Pulford promptly pulled all the remaining aircraft back to Singapore. Attempts to strike back at the Japanese led to further losses. Six Blenheims left Singapore that morning to strike the Singora area. Fighters were to join them over northern Malaya, but the only two left there already had their hands full trying to protect their airfield and fly tactical reconnaissance for the army. Pressing on unescorted, the Blenheims encountered heavy flak and thirty enemy fighters. They lost half their number. A second strike was nevertheless planned, but as the remnants of the force from Singapore and the remain-

ing Blenheims in northern Malaya were about to take off from
Butterworth, they were hit by the Japanese, who destroyed all but
one. The lone Blenheim went on to deliver a heroic single attack.
Its wounded pilot, Squadron Leader A. S. K. Scarf, then brought
his damaged plane back to Alor Star where he crash landed without
injury to his crew. That evening he died in hospital. He was subsequently awarded a posthumous Victoria Cross. Despite the
gallantry shown by the British pilots, the Japanese suffered no
serious losses. By the time the disastrous 9th of December had run
its course, Alor Star had joined Sungei Patani on the list of airfields
abandoned, and all that was left of the British air strength in
northern Malaya, ten planes, was concentrated at Butterworth.
The Japanese were by this time operating about 150 aircraft from
airstrips in the Singora-Patani area. Pulford came to the inevitable
conclusion that daylight bombing operations over northern Malaya
were impossible. Since the three Dutch bomber squadrons were
only trained for daylight work, they had to be sent back to the
East Indies to retrain.[15] There was another disorderly withdrawal
of ground staff, this time from Kuantan, on the 10th. On the same
day Pulford decided to evacuate Butterworth and concentrate his
remaining fighter aircraft on the defense of Singapore itself,
through which alone reinforcements could arrive. The withdrawal
of the shaken personnel of the squadrons at Butterworth was
chaotic. Local "followers," who had been hired as drivers, cooks,
casual laborers, and so forth, had vanished. Railway labor was
deserting, and one trainload of equipment had to be driven by an
RAF Flight Lieutenant. A lone photoreconnaissance Buffalo
remained at Butterworth. Otherwise, the skies over the battle area
belonged to the Japanese. At Kota Bharu, on the east coast, Key's
brigade finally abandoned the two remaining airfields on the night
of the 10th/11th, destroying much that had been abandoned by
the RAF. Unfortunately it was not possible for them to destroy the
runways. These were grass, and the RAF had positioned dumps of
material for filling in bomb craters close at hand. Since there was
no way to destroy or disperse this, blowing holes in the runways
was useless.[16]

By the evening of December 10 British airpower in Malaya had
been virtually wiped out. Before the battle for the west-coast trunk
road had even begun, the troops that were to fight it had been
deprived of air cover, and further depressed by the sight of RAF
dumps and stores being set ablaze by hastily withdrawing ground
parties.

iii

No sooner had Phillips assumed command of the Eastern Fleet on the morning of the 8th than he faced a crucial decision. What to do with the *Prince of Wales* and the *Repulse*? Even before the outbreak of war, the Admiralty, with Churchill's approval, had urged him to get the ships away from Singapore. Phillips himself told Hart that Singapore was not a secure base. Yet could he steam away to safety, leaving the army and what there was of an air force to fight on alone? The traditions of his service, and his own personality, all said no. Phillips discussed the situation with his staff on board the *Prince of Wales* during the morning of the 8th, and the decision to strike at the Japanese shipping off Singora was unanimous. Phillips then asked Pulford for reconnaissance to the north of his intended course, and fighter cover over the Singora area from first light on the 10th. Pulford apparently warned the Admiral at this point that he was doubtful whether he could provide air cover over Singora. Nevertheless, leaving Palliser behind as his link with Pulford and Brooke-Popham, Phillips sailed at 5:35 P.M., accompanied by four destroyers.

By that time the RAF in northern Malaya had been crippled. Shortly after midnight, December 8th/9th, Palliser signaled Phillips, who was maintaining wireless silence, that air cover definitely would not be available, although reconnaissance could probably be provided. He also passed on reports that Japanese battleships were covering their landings, as well as information on Japanese air strength in southern Indochina. Phillips decided to press on, provided he was not sighted by Japanese aircraft during the ensuing day.

In fact, the Japanese were more than ready for Force Z, as Phillips's squadron was called. The departure of the *Prince of Wales* for the East had been intended as a public gesture, and no pains had been spared to broadcast to the world the arrival of she and the *Repulse* at Singapore. Japanese naval aircraft of the Twenty-first and Twenty-second Air Flotillas were standing by on airfields near Saigon. Manned by the pick of the naval air arm, they were specially trained in attacks on shipping. The Japanese convoys themselves were heavily escorted, and covered by the Vice Admiral Takeo Kurita's four heavy cruisers and a strong force of destroyers. Off southern Indochina, giving distant cover to the whole operation, was Vice Admiral Nobutake Kondo with two battleships, two more heavy cruisers, and ten destroyers. A screen of twelve submarines lay off the east coast of Malaya. One of them reported Force Z early in the afternoon of the 9th. Surprise, Phillips's one remaining ally, was gone, although he did not realize this until three aircraft were sighted from the flagship that evening. Reluctantly, Force Z reversed course for Singapore.

Meanwhile, the sighting report from the submarine had reached Admiral Kondo. He ordered Kurita's cruisers to fly off their spotting aircraft to locate and shadow the British ships. It was these planes that were sighted from the *Prince of Wales* that evening. Kurita was also ordered to join Kondo's flag. The naval aircraft based near Saigon were bombed up for a raid on Singapore. They hastily switched their bombs for torpedoes and took off for a night attack on Force Z.

During the evening more signals from Palliser reached Phillips. He learned that the northern airfields were all untenable and that the remaining aircraft were being concentrated on the defense of Singapore. Then, at 10 P.M., Malaya Command received reports that a landing was taking place at Kuantan, whose airfields had been abandoned during the day. Pulford ordered a force of Vildebeestes and Hudsons to strike the Japanese there before dawn. About midnight Palliser passed this information on to Phillips. The Admiral now faced a very difficult decision. From Kuantan one of the two east-west lateral roads in the peninsula traversed Malaya. A Japanese force pushing west along it would cut into the west-coast trunk road well behind III Corps. Phillips knew that the Japanese had sighted him steering north at dusk. They would not expect him off Kuantan at dawn. Kuantan was not far off his return course to Singapore, and it was 400 miles from the Japanese airfields in Indochina. It was also within range of fighter cover from Singapore. At 12:52 A.M., December 10, Force Z altered course to close Kuantan. One of Phillips's staff later explained that the Admiral expected Palliser to divine his intention and arrange air cover at dawn off Kuantan. Phillips therefore did not risk losing the chance of surprise by breaking radio silence to warn Singapore of his change of plan. It was a large assumption and a serious error.

Shortly before Force Z altered course, the Japanese air striking force, baffled in its search, returned to its bases. At 2:30 A.M. Kurita made his rendevous with Kondo, and the combined force shaped a course to intercept Force Z during the day. Then another report came in from one of the submarines. The British were steaming south. Kondo immediately realized that he now had no chance of bringing them to action. He turned north and ordered the Twenty-second Air Flotilla to attack at dawn. While it was still dark a dozen reconnaissance planes flew off to find Force Z, followed at first light by a striking force of 85 planes.

Pulford's Vildebeestes reached Kuantan at 4 A.M. and found nothing. Neither did the Hudsons, arriving shortly after. By dawn it was obvious that the "attack" was a false alarm. But no signal to this effect was made to Force Z. No one in Singapore knew that it was heading for Kuantan.

It was still December 9 in London. At 10 P.M. the prime minister ended a very busy day by convening a staff conference, largely made up of Admiralty personnel, in the Cabinet War Room. The discussion centered on Phillips's squadron. "They had been sent to these waters to exercise that kind of vague menace which capital ships of the highest quality whose whereabouts is unknown can impose upon all hostile naval calculations," the prime minister later recalled. "How should we use them now? Obviously they must go to sea and vanish among the innumerable islands. There was general agreement on that." But apparently not on their destination. Churchill wanted them to cross the Pacific and join what was left of the American Pacific Fleet. He thought it would be a gesture appreciated by the Americans. Rather oddly, he also felt that it would be the best protection for Australia. There was some feeling, however, that the ships should go directly to Australia. In the end, a decision was deferred until the next morning.

It was now daylight off Malaya. Force Z reached Kuantan and found nothing. Phillips decided to search the area to be sure. He still made no signal to Singapore. At 6:35 P.M. the previous evening he had detached one of his destroyers, H.M.S. *Tenedos,* which was low on fuel, to make for Singapore. The *Tenedos* was ordered to signal Singapore at 8:00 A.M. on the 10th, giving Phillips's anticipated position *at dawn on the 11th,* but no indication of his current whereabouts. At 10:30 A.M. Force Z picked up reports from the *Tenedos* that she was being bombed 140 miles to the southeast. Twenty minutes later a shadower found Phillips. The *Repulse's* radar soon picked up approaching aircraft, and at 11:00 A.M. the Japanese were sighted. Force Z opened fire thirteen minutes later. Still no signal passed to Singapore, where eleven Buffaloes were standing by to fly air cover for Phillips. At 11:30 A.M. the *Prince of Wales's* spotter aircraft, which had been flown off early in the morning, landed at Penang Island off the west coast of the Malay peninsula. The pilot's report, telephoned through to

Singapore, was the first news that Force Z was off Kuantan. Shortly before noon the *Prince of Wales* was crippled by two torpedoes. At 11:50 Captain W. G. Tennant of the *Repulse* took matters into his own hands and made an emergency signal to Singapore: "enemy aircraft bombing." Even this, however, did not give the squadron's position. It was handed to Pulford's operations room at 12:19 P.M.; seven minutes later fighters were airborne and heading for Kuantan. It was too late. Hit by five torpedoes, the *Repulse* sank at 12.33 P.M. The Buffaloes arrived in time to see the *Prince of Wales* go down at 1:20 P.M. The majority of the nearly three thousand men on the two ships were picked up by the destroyers, but Phillips and his flag captain, John Leach, were not among them.

The Japanese lost three planes. They had sunk two capital ships at sea, a feat never before accomplished by aircraft. Within forty-eight hours Japanese naval airmen had smashed Anglo-American sea power, and won undisputed control of the Pacific. Brooke-Popham asked Duff Cooper to broadcast on the night of the 10th, and Duff Cooper did his best. The sinking of the two ships, he declared, must lead to a determination to fight harder and avenge their loss. But the chilling fact, apparent to even the slowest mind in Malaya, was that the despised Japanese had won control of the skies over the peninsula, and the seas around it, in two days.

News of the disaster off Kuantan reached London on the morning of the 10th (by which time it was mid-afternoon in Singapore). "I was opening my boxes," Churchill later wrote, "when the telephone at my bedside rang. It was the First Sea Lord. His voice sounded odd. He gave a sort of cough and a gulp, and at first I could not hear quite clearly. 'Prime Minister, I have to report to you that the *Prince of Wales* and *Repulse* have both been sunk — and we think by aircraft. Tom Phillips is drowned.' 'Are you sure it's true?' 'There is no doubt at all.' So I put the telephone down. I was thankful to be alone. In all the war I never received a more direct shock. . . . As I turned over and twisted in bed the full horror of the news sank in upon me." Sir Charles Wilson, Churchill's doctor, saw him shortly afterwards. "I found him with his head in his hands. After a time he looked up; he seemed dazed. 'You know what has happened?' the prime minister asked." Churchill was not the only person shaken to the core. Harold Nicolson recorded in his diary that evening: ". . . as I cross Oxford Circus, I see a poster, '*Prince of Wales* and *Repulse* sunk!' The whole circus revolves in the air and I lose my breath. I feel sick." He ruminated about "the depressing feeling that seapower is at the mercy of air power."

Even more than Singapore itself, the ships were a symbol of British power, and a symbol as well of the prestige on which the Empire lived. Their destruction by the Japanese was a portent, as Churchill and Nicolson both realized. The memory of that horrible morning never left Churchill. In 1953, after a major stroke, he told his doctor that he had dreamed about the loss of the ships. Then he became too agitated to continue, and the doctor feared he would have another seizure. Churchill liked Phillips and knew Leach. He had traveled in the *Prince of Wales*. His was the paramount, although not exclusive, responsibility for ordering the ships to Singapore. He had a deep feeling for the Royal Navy. But most important, perhaps, was Churchill's appreciation of the symbolism of power. The *Prince of Wales* and the *Repulse* had been sent east to represent British might. There loss made manifest British impotence. There was no remedying this.

On the following day the Admiralty ordered Layton, who had already embarked on a liner for passage home, to rehoist his flag as commander in chief, Eastern Fleet. His first recommendation, promptly approved by London, was to get his handful of old cruisers and destroyers away to the safety of Ceylon. Before the war was a week old, the Royal Navy had abandoned Singapore.[17]

iv

Disaster in the sky and on the airfields; disaster at sea; and the main battle on land had yet to be joined. But on the day that Force Z was destroyed, the first brushes occurred between Japanese and British forces on the west-coast trunk road, foreseen as the axis of a Japanese overland thrust at Singapore as far back as 1925. Within forty-eight hours the numerically inferior Japanese had not only mauled their opponents and forced them into retreat, but had won the initiative, tactical and psychological, which they never surrendered until they hoisted their flag in Singapore seventy days later.

On December 7 Heath's III Corps headquarters in Kuala Lumpur, some two hundred miles north of Singapore and 250 from the Thai frontier, controlled two Indian divisions, Major General A. E. Barstow's Ninth and Major General D. M. Murray-Lyons's Eleventh. Barstow's headquarters were near Heath's at Kuala Lumpur. His two brigades, however, were hundreds of miles away. The Twenty-second was at Kuantan on the east coast, some two hundred miles away at the other end of the east-west lateral road, and the Eighth was at Kota Bharu, 250 miles to the northwest at the end of a single-track railway. The location of these two brigades was determined primarily by the existence of airfields, as well as by the need to cover the lateral road from Kuantan. Murray-Lyon's Eleventh Division had its two brigades (Sixth and Fifteenth) close up to the frontier, north of Alor Star, ready for Matador. Heath's reserve brigade, the newly arrived Twenty-eighth, was at Ipoh, roughly halfway from Kuala Lumpur to the frontier. Percival himself retained control of three formations. There was the "Singapore Fortress" garrison commanded by Major General F. Keith Simmons, made up of the troops that manned the fixed and antiaircraft defenses, and two newly raised Malay infantry brigades. On the mainland, in the southernmost Malay state of Johore, was Major General H. Gordon Bennett's Eighth Australian Division. Its two brigades were positioned to meet a possible Japanese landing at Mersing on the east coast, from whence two vital roads radiated: an east-west lateral joining the trunk road, and one running direct to Singapore. At Port Dickinson on the west coast, about fifty miles south of Kuala Lumpur, was Brigadier A. C. M. Paris's Twelfth Indian Brigade, Percival's "command reserve," and the best formation in Malaya — an unmilked prewar Indian Army brigade that had arrived in Malaya in August 1939. One of its three battalions was the Second Argyll and Sutherland Highlanders, whose commanding officer, Lieutenant Colonel Ian MacArthur Stewart, had gotten a local reputation for eccentricity by driving his men very hard in rigorous jungle training. His influence permeated the whole brigade, which was probably the best prepared in Malaya to meet the Japanese. Unfortunately, the Twelfth Brigade was never to be used as a unit.

Percival thus had a force equivalent in size to the three divisions of the Japanese Twenty-fifth Army. But it was scattered over a huge area to cover the RAF's east-coast airfields as well as exposed points, like Kuantan and Mersing, that gave access to lateral roads across the peninsula. These scattered forces were linked by communications that were extremely vulnerable once the Japanese had won control of the air, and by a signals net that was deficient in personnel and equipment. Heavy use was consequently made of the insecure and inadequate civil telephone system, leading to further delay and confusion.

Percival's dispositions have been sharply criticized. In particular it has been argued that he should not have wasted Barstow's two brigades on the defense of the east-coast airfields. He should have arranged for the demolition of those airfields the minute a Japanese landing seemed imminent, and concentrated his forces for the crucial battle on the trunk road. Furthermore, this argument goes, he should have taken his stand well back from the Thai frontier, in a good defensive position, even though this meant writing off the airfields at Alor Star and Sungei Patani. These dispositions might well have slowed the Japanese down, and they look attractive in retrospect. But, since August 1940, the first line of defense in the Far East had been the RAF. The army's duty was to hold all of Malaya in order both to secure the airfields the RAF needed, and to keep the Japanese air force as far away from Singapore as possible. That directive had never been altered, even when it became apparent in the late summer of 1941 that RAF strength would be inadequate in the foreseeable future. Brooke-Popham never asked London to reconsider the basis of Far Eastern defense policy, and Whitehall never showed any disposition to initiate a reconsideration on its own. Percival never pressed for a change in the policy that sprawled his force across the face of Malaya. The GOC, although very capable, was not a forceful man. He had been given a problem, and, like the competent staff officer he was, he produced the only possible solution given the forces provided and the task set. Like every other senior officer in Malaya, Percival was very conscious of the need to sustain morale. Writing off a large part of the country beforehand would not have been very helpful in this respect. The widespread belief that the Japanese would not attack until after the monsoon, by which time further reinforcements might well reach Malaya, was doubtless another important factor. It is on this last point that Percival seems most open to criticism. If anyone in Malaya should have known that the monsoon was no protection, that person was the GOC. His failure to make this point understood, and his reactions to Simson's attempt to do so, are simply inexplicable.

Percival's dispositions meant that in northern Malaya, astride the trunk road, stood only two brigades, less than one-fifth of his total force. Furthermore, the Eleventh Division was given two roles, one offensive, the other defensive. In an ideal situation it would have been ready to move into either of them, but Malaya in 1941 was far from an ideal world militarily. The bulk of the divisions's time and effort had been concentrated on Matador. When the troops were alerted on the afternoon of December 6, morale was high, the division keen to be off. Then followed forty-eight hours of anticlimax in the pouring rain. The edge of eagerness had been well blunted by the morning of the 8th. The orders to assume the defensive and man the Jitra position lowered spirits still further. This was a more serious matter with these raw troops than it would have been with a veteran formation. The Jitra position did not help matters. It was not a good defensive site, merely the best that could be found far enough forward to cover Alor Star and Sungei Patani. The defenses were not complete because priority had been given to training for Matador. When the Eleventh Division moved in to occupy them on the 8th, they were waterlogged from the recent rains and had to be pumped out. Because the division was organized for a rapid move forward, the stores necessary for a defensive position were not with the units but held in the rear. Barbed wire, antitank mines, and field telephone cable all had to be brought forward and installed by troops already wet, tired, and dispirited. The only bright spot was that Heath released his reserve brigade to reinforce Murray-Lyon for his defensive battle.

A further complication, in a situation that scarcely needed it, was the existence of a secondary road from Patani in Thailand that crossed the Malayan frontier near Kroh and joined the trunk road well south of the Eleventh Division. To block this was the task of *Krohcol*, a force of some two battalions, which was to cross the frontier and push some thirty miles into Thailand to seize the Ledge. Murray-Lyon was put in charge of Krohcol, even though he could exercise no effective control over a force operating one hundred miles away. Krohcol was a distraction from the defense of the Jitra position and ought to have come directly under III Corps.

The disaster on land began with Krohcol. It was not completely concentrated when ordered forward at 1:30 P.M. on the 8th. An hour and a half later it entered Thailand, only to encounter opposition from frontier guards who slowed Krohcol down so much that by nightfall it was only three miles inside Thailand. Meanwhile a regiment of the Japanese Fifth Division, accompanied by a battery of guns and two tank companies, began to race forward from Patani. Seventy-five miles separated them from the Ledge. Krohcol made slow progress against the Thais on the morning of the 9th. In mid-afternoon, however, opposition abruptly ceased, and by evening Krohcol's leading battalion reached Betong, the first major town across the border. At six the next morning it set out for the Ledge in trucks driven by Australian reservists, all veterans of World War I. Seven and a half hours later the infantry "debussed" six miles from their objective — a long walk, but the last point on the road at which the trucks could turn around. Moving ahead, they encountered tank-supported Japanese infantry. The Fifth Division, covering seventy-five miles in sixty hours, had won the race. Despite heroic efforts, by nightfall the 3/16th Punjab Regiment had lost half its strength and was catching its breath behind a makeshift antitank obstacle. The Japanese were in a position to threaten the Eleventh Division's line of communications even before the battle for the Jitra position opened.

The rest of the Fifth Division (two infantry regiments and a battalion each of tanks and field artillery) had begun to push south on the road that led to Jitra — and Singapore. The Eleventh Division was still struggling to prepare its defenses, surrounded by all the demoralizing signs of disaster. On the 8th, Sungei Patani airfield behind them was hastily abandoned by the RAF. By the morning of the 10th, when the Japanese crossed the frontier and made contact with Murray-Lyon's outpost battalion, British air power in northern Malaya had been broken and the ground staff at Alor Star airfield, just behind the Jitra position, had begun to fire the petrol dumps and bomb stores there, adding to the jumpiness and despondency among the troops. To gain more time to prepare his defenses, Murray-Lyon sent a second battalion forward, ordering the outpost units to hold the Japanese north of Jitra until dawn on the 12th. By the evening of the 10th the loss of the *Prince of Wales* and the *Repulse* became known, adding to the feeling of isolation.

On the 11th the Japanese advanced guard, a mechanized column spearheaded by tanks, drove down the trunk road. About 4:30 P.M. it caught the outpost battalion, the 1/14th Punjab Regiment, retiring to its next position. The Indian troops, who had never seen a tank before, were dumbfounded. The Japanese drove right through the marching column, rushed the bridge in front of the position held by the second outpost battalion (2/1st Gurkhas) before it could be blown, and went on to scatter that battalion as well. Murray-Lyon had lost two of his nine battalions. Worse followed. A subsidiary road from the northwest joined the trunk road at Jitra. The covering troops on it were ordered back on the afternoon of the 11th. As the column of vehicles and guns approached the main position after dark, a jittery officer, mindful of the afternoon's disaster on the trunk road, blew up the only bridge leading to it. Since no engineer material was available to repair it, the column's guns and transport had to be abandoned. Under these depressing auspices the battle for the main Jitra position began.

All through the night of December 11/12, the infantry of the Japanese advance guard probed at Murray-Lyon's right flank, while several frontal attacks, supported by tanks, were launched down the trunk road. The attacks were held, but early on the 12th Murray-Lyon, conscious that his troops, the only ones available to defend the trunk road, were tired and dispirited, and aware of the threat to his communications posed by the Japanese on the Kroh road, asked III Corps for permission to fall back thirty miles to the next defensive position. Heath was in Singapore, and the request was passed on to Malaya Command. Percival feared the effect on morale of such an early and lengthy withdrawal, and ordered Murray-Lyon to hang on.

Further Japanese pressure during the day led Murray-Lyon to renew his request that evening. He feared that his troops might well be destroyed by enemy armor the next day. This time he was authorized to withdraw. The retreat was as calamitous for Murray-Lyon's raw and disorganized troops as defeat in the field. Communications within the division were poor. Orders to withdraw failed to get through, and some units had to make their own way back the next day, abandoning most of their equipment. Guns and trucks bogged down in the mud and were left behind. Some troops, hoping to avoid the congestion on the trunk road, struck out cross-country; others retired down the railway, or headed for the coast in the hope of finding boats. After forty-eight hours in action, the Eleventh Indian Division was, at least temporarily, no longer a coherent force. The Fifteenth Brigade was down to a quarter of its strength, the Sixth Brigade was little better off, and the Twenty-eighth Brigade had lost an entire battalion, while the other two had suffered heavy casualties. The loss of equipment was very heavy, and none of this could be made good.

The Japanese advance guard, two battalions, with about ten tanks and some guns and engineers attached, had done all this damage with trifling casualties to themselves. The Japanese main body was never involved. What had happened? The Japanese had the initiative from the beginning. The dithering over Matador depressed morale, and cost time. That meant failure for Krohcol and the loss of two battalions that were trying to hold the enemy away from Jitra while the sodden defenses were put into shape by equally sodden troops. Then Indian troops were attacked by tanks, which they had never seen and were not trained to meet. Many of the troops and their officers were raw, and by the critical night of December

11/12 no one's nerves were good. Murray-Lyon was doubtless right to insist on a withdrawal, but his shaken division, encumbered with a scale of transport more appropriate to the Middle East than Malaya, was no longer able to stage an organized retreat. Tough, determined, well-led veteran troops pushed and bluffed tired, raw, dispirited, often clumsily-led troops into retreat.

The significance of the defeat at Jitra was profound. It gave the Japanese a decisive psychological edge over their opponents. The British lost control of the pace and timing of the withdrawal to Singapore. The Japanese would henceforth push steadily down the trunk road, while Percival fed units piecemeal into the battered Eleventh Division, trying to buy enough time for reinforcements to arrive. It has often been remarked that Percival's force was as large as the Japanese force that defeated it. So it was. But Percival's force never fought as a whole. It was defeated piecemeal on the west-coast trunk road. There was no way to overcome the consequences of the original dispositions, or the result of the initial disaster.[18]

v

London was very busy during the four days that it took for disaster to envelop Malaya. Eden was *en route* to Russia, and Churchill had added the Foreign Office to his own duties. As acting foreign secretary, he drafted on the 8th the British declaration of war against Japan. It was an ornate document, perhaps the last of its kind. When he spoke to the Commons that afternoon, he warned that the war against Japan would begin with heavy defeats. But the center of his attention in these opening days of the Japanese onslaught was not really the Far East, but, as had so often been the case, Washington.

As soon as he awoke on the 8th, Churchill decided to visit the United States to confer with Roosevelt. American entry into the war, so long sought and so devoutly welcomed, nonetheless brought problems. Under the impact of Pearl Harbor, American opinion might veer towards a war effort centered in the Pacific. Britain would then face stalemate in the war against Germany. Supply was another problem. On the day of Pearl Harbor a complete embargo was placed on the export of war material from the United States. Much of the affected material was destined for Britain, and British planning was contingent on its arrival. Even though in its

complete form the embargo lasted only a few days, the whole
question of British allocations from American production would
obviously require urgent review. Churchill quickly got the approval
of both the Cabinet and the King for his trip, and during the 9th
and 10th signals flashed back and forth across the Atlantic as the
prime minister forced himself upon the reluctant president, who
obviously felt the need to adjust to the new state of affairs before
facing Churchill. On the 11th Roosevelt finally agreed, although
he stressed the dangers of the journey for the prime minister. He
evidently had not yet fully grasped how deep the strains of determination and pugnacity ran in Winston Churchill.

In the midst of all this, decisions had to be taken about command in the Far East, and reinforcements for the area. Pownall,
who had reached Cairo when war broke out, was ordered by the
War Office to stand fast there. He was left kicking his heels for
nearly a week before he was told to continue on to Singapore.
When Pownall cabled Brooke-Popham on the 11th to say that he
was still in Cairo awaiting orders, Playfair commented tartly: "In
my view nothing could be worse than this wavering. There is quite
enough to think about without always having to be bothered by
the extent to which you are committing your successor." Nevertheless several more days passed before London released Pownall,
who did not, in the end, reach Singapore until the 23rd. The delay
was almost certainly the result of second thoughts about the wisdom of changing commanders in the Far East at a critical moment,
as well as the preoccupation of everyone in London with other
things. Brooke was just taking over from Dill, and the prime minister was preparing to leave for the United States. The consequence,
however, was further unsettlement in Singapore, where it was
scarcely needed.

Churchill cabled Duff Cooper on the 9th, informing him of his
appointment as resident minister for Far Eastern Affairs. He was
to form a War Council and "to assist the successful conduct of
operations in the Far East (a) by relieving the Commanders-in-
Chief of those extraneous responsibilities with which they have
hitherto been burdened; and (b) by giving them broad political
guidance." It would have been an extremely useful appointment
for a year, or even six months, before, when "a local clearing-house
for prompt settlement of minor routine matters which would otherwise have to be referred to separate departments" in London
would have been highly desireable. Direct access to the War Cabinet would also have been very helpful earlier. Duff Cooper's

appointment was too late, however, to affect the course of events in the Far East. In the short time before his position was made redundant by the decisions taken by Roosevelt and Churchill at the Arcadia Conference, Duff Cooper made little impact, and that little was not all gain.

Sometime during the 9th the plan to establish RAF squadrons in North Persia or the Caucusus was canceled, but no measures to reinforce the Far East were taken. The day ended with the staff conference, already described, about the future of Phillip's squadron. The next day brought the news of the loss of the *Prince of Wales* and the *Repulse*, which Churchill announced at 11 A.M. to a hushed House of Commons. The rest of that day, and most of the next, were taken up with persuading Roosevelt to agree to a conference and making arrangements for the prime minister's departure. Only on the evening of the 11th, less than twenty-four hours before he left London, did Churchill preside over a staff conference at 10 Downing Street to discuss reinforcements for the Far East.

The pressure of Middle Eastern needs and commitments made themselves felt immediately. Auchinleck's offensive had been launched on November 18. After several weeks of confused fighting, Rommel began to fall back on December 7, and Tobruk was finally relieved on the following day. The long-sought victory in the desert seemed at hand, and Churchill's mind was already leaping far ahead of Auchinleck's advancing army. On October 28, before Crusader began, he had minuted to the Chiefs of Staff that an operation, *Gymnast*, ought to be prepared to take advantage of a victory in the impending offensive. He had in mind entry into French North Africa, either by French invitation or as a consequence of a German descent on the area. In the same minute he remarked that the Americans were interested in Morocco and that Knox had mentioned to Halifax that the United States might land 150,000 troops there. Now his mind was engaged, as it would be until he brought it off, with an American landing in Morocco, complementing a British drive westward from Egypt. With the prime minister in this frame of mind, it is not surprising that the staff conference on the evening of the 11th decided that any major diversion of British strength from other theaters to the Far East would be unsound. The Eighteenth Division, on its way to the Middle East in American transports, was diverted to Bombay, together with four RAF fighter squadrons that had been *en route* to the Caspian-Caucusus area. The Seventeenth Indian Division, brand

new and only partially trained, was the only formation immediately
available in India. It was earmarked for the Middle East, but
Wavell was ordered to hold it. Middle East Command was told to
send a squadron of light bombers to Malaya via the India-Burma
air reinforcement route. A signal was sent to Layton informing
him that the Eastern Fleet would be rebuilt by the end of March,
but the only major unit he could expect in the near future was the
carrier *Indomitable*, now repaired after her grounding in Jamaica
and due at Cape Town on New Year's Day. Burma was removed
from Brooke-Popham's command and, at the last minute, with
Japanese troops already across its frontiers, thrust on India.

Churchill signaled these decisions to Wavell on the 12th. "You
must now look east. Burma is placed under your command. You
must resist the Japanese advance toward Burma and India and try
to cut their communications down the Malay peninsula." It was
a very tall order. India and Singapore were further informed
during the day that they now had priority for reinforcements, but
that nothing would be pulled out of the Middle East. At some point
during these two days, Churchill told Ismay that the Eighteenth
Division ought to go to Rangoon, and from there operate against
Japanese communications in the Kra Isthmus. It was an utterly
wild idea, but it was the first step in a series of decisions that
would pull the luckless Eighteenth Division into Singapore.

In the four days following the Japanese attack, London's reactions amounted to very little. Burma, even less well prepared
than Malaya, passed from Far East Command to India, which had
repeatedly asked in vain for it. Wavell was allowed to keep one raw
division, whose only training had been for the Middle East, and
was told that he would get a British division, similarly trained and
out of condition after weeks at sea. Four squadrons of fighters
were certainly an improvement over no modern fighters at all, but
it was very little in view of the task Wavell had been given. At sea
little was, or could be, done. British sea power was stretched to
the breaking point. The *Ark Royal* had fallen victim to a U-boat in
mid-November. Another U-boat sank the battleship *Barham* on the
25th. Now the *Prince of Wales* and the *Repulse* were gone, and the
Tirpitz, like a magnet, held most of Britain's remaining capital
ships in the North Atlantic. In the whole area east of Suez there
was virtually nothing. The old "R" class battleship *Revenge* was at
Ceylon, and the *Hermes*, recently refitted in South Africa, was
available, but the rest of Layton's command was made up of old
cruisers and destroyers, earmarked to cover reinforcement convoys

into Singapore, something they could continue to do only so long as the Japanese did not interfere. The arrival of the *Indomitable* would make no difference to the brute fact of Japanese maritime control in the waters around Malaya. Little was done to reinforce the Far East because little could now be done beyond gestures. The Far East had been starved before December 8 on the gamble that war would not come. After December 8 Churchill still bent his energies to winning the war in the West. He had, at this point, no real choice. In the Far East he sought merely to limit British losses and retain positions from which, after the defeat of Germany, a counteroffensive could be launched against Japan.

On the 12th, before leaving London, Churchill addressed a silent and reserved House of Commons, warning them once again of the likelihood of serious reverses in the Far East, but assuring them that American entry into the war made final victory a certainty. Shortly after this address, he boarded the train that would take him north to the Clyde, where the new battleship H.M.S. *Duke of York*, sister ship of the ill-fated *Prince of Wales,* waited to carry him to America.

Two parting signals, made as he left England, sum up the priorities that the prime minister intended to maintain. The Chiefs of Staff were told to reinforce India, especially with armor, as soon as Auchinleck's offensive was successfully concluded. Sir Reginald Dorman-Smith, the Governor of Burma, was informed that four to six squadrons of desperately needed aircraft would be transfered to him from the Middle East — but, again, not until after Crusader. There was no mention in either signal of Malaya. As if to underline its isolation from aid, on this same December 13, Victoria Point, whose airfield was a critical link in the air reinforcement route to Singapore, was abandoned. Located at the extreme southern tip of the tail of Burmese territory, known as the Tenasserim, that straggles down the west side of the Isthmus of Kra, it was indefensible, and the platoon of armed police stationed there withdrew as the Japanese approached. On the 15th, as the *Duke of York* plowed westwards through heavy seas, Japanese infantry entered Victoria Point, and the air route to Singapore, on which so many RAF plans had depended, was cut.[19]

Notes to Chapter 7

1. J.R.M. Butler, ed., *History of the Second World War: United Kingdom's Military Series,* "Campaigns" series, S. W. Kirby et al., *The War Against Japan,* vol 1. *The Loss of Singapore* (London: H.M.S.O., 1957), pp. 174-75, 180-81.

2. Public Record Office (PRO), PREM 3, 161/1, Duff Cooper to Churchill, December 18, 1941, and B. Bond, ed., *Chief of Staff: The Diaries of Lieutenant General Sir Henry Pownall,* 2 vols. (London: Leo Cooper Ltd., 1973-74), 2: 67, contain observations on Brook-Popham's fatigue and indecisiveness. But it must be remembered that both were written after several weeks of disaster, and, especially in Duff Cooper's case, were far from disinterested.

3. Air Vice Marshal Sir Paul Maltby, "Report On The Air Operations During The Campaigns In Malaya And Netherlands East Indies From 8th December 1941 to 12th March 1942," *Supplement to the London Gazette,* February 26, 1948, pars. 157-65 (cited hereafter as Maltby, *Dispatch).* D. Richards and H. St. G. Saunders, *The Royal Air Force 1939-1945,* 3 vols. (London: H.M.S.O., 1953-54), 2: 16-17. One of the curiosities of the last day of peace in Singapore is a note from the Japanese Consul General to Sir Shenton Thomas, accepting an invitation to lunch at Government House on the 8th! The note is in the Thomas Papers in the possession of Professor Hugh Thomas.

4. Kirby et al., *The Loss of Singapore,* pp. 181-82.

5. Ibid., pp. 182-83, 188; Maltby, *Dispatch,* pars. 170-76.

6. Squadron Leader T. C. Carter, "History of R.D.F. Organization in the Far East 1941-1942," n.d. [but written in 1943], Carter Papers, TCC 2/1, Imperial War Museum, London.

7. Carter to family, April 11, 1942, Carter Papers, TCC 3/3. In defense of the civil administration, Sir Shenton Thomas later pointed out that the "first degree of war readiness," ordered at three thirty in the afternoon of December 6, did not include provisions for either "brownout" (dimming of lights) or blackout, and that neither of these precautions were subsequently ordered. Sir Shenton Thomas, "Comments on the Draft History of the War Against Japan," October 1954, pars. 95-96, Thomas Papers, Rhodes House Library, Oxford. It is odd, however, that these serious omissions in the air-raid precautions scheme had never been noted before the outbreak of hostilities. It is even stranger that with the first degree of war readiness in effect, A.R.P. headquarters was allowed to shut down.

8. Sir Robert Brooke-Popham, "Comments on the draft of the War Against Japan, Volume One," April 16, 1953, Brooke-Popham Papers (BPP) v/9/34, Liddell Hart Centre for Military Archives, King's College, London; Air Chief Marshal Sir Robert Brooke-Popham, "Operations In The Far East, From 17th October 1940 to 27th December 1941," *Supplement to the London Gazette,* January 22, 1948, par. 97, Appendix M (cited hereafter as Brooke-Popham, *Dispatch);* Kirby et al., *The Loss of Singapore,* pp. 183-84.

9. Kirby et al., *The Loss of Singapore,* pp. 185-86.

10. Winston S. Churchill, *The Second World War,* vol. 3, *The Grand Alliance* (Boston: Houghton Mifflin, 1950), pp. 604-5.

11. Ibid., p. 608.

12. Kirby et al., *The Loss of Sinapore,* pp. 511-24; Brooke-Popham, *Dispatch,* Appendix J.

13. Kirby et al., *The Loss of Singapore*, pp. 191-92, 238 fn. 2; Richards and Saunders, *The Royal Air Force 1939-1945*, 2: 22. Playfair, Brooke-Popham's chief of staff, later scouted rumors of treachery and fifth-column activity (Maj. Gen. I.S.O. Playfair, "Some Personal Reflections on the Malayan Campaign," n. d. [covering letter to Brooke-Popham dated May 10, 1943], p. 12, BPP v/9/28). Maltby, *Dispatch*, par. 183, and Richard and Saunders, *The Royal Air Force 1939-1945*, 2: 22, mention them, the latter treating them as fact. In fact, there was no significant fifth-column activity at all in Malaya, as clearly established by a file in the Bryson Collection, Royal Commonwealth Society Library, London: "Detection and Frustration of Organized Fifth Column in Malaya." The most important items in this file are four undated memoranda by A. H. Dickinson, and one by R. B. Corridon of the Malayan Security Service, dated June 23, 1946. The widespread belief that a fifth column was active did, unfortunately, lead to several cases in which Asians were maltreated or killed by frightened troops. The late Guy Wint, in P. Calvacoressi and G. Wint, *Total War* (New York: Pantheon Books, 1972), p. 724, tells this story, without citing any source: "An officer in the RAF, a citizen of southern Ireland, was pursuing his country's feud of twenty years back with the British government, and was detected signalling to the Japanese. This affair was kept secret. It had accounted for an unfortunate part of the air losses in the early stages of the campaign." This story circulated widely in Malaya at the time. There seems to be no doubt that, early in the campaign, an officer was arrested in northern Malaya and sent back to Singapore, charged with being in radio contact with the Japanese in Thailand. I have not been able to discover any further details, or, indeed, the fate of the officer. This incident is clearly the origin of the story that Wint printed. In any case, it is important to stress that the episode, despite Wint's statement to the contrary, did not play any significant role in the development of the campaign. The numerically and qualitatively superior Japanese, after all, hardly needed any assistance to blitz Pulford's weak, obsolescent force on its exposed and poorly defended airfields in northern Malaya.

14. Maltby, *Dispatch*, par. 190, is silent about the circumstances in which Kota Bharu was abandoned, while the account in Richards and Saunders, *The Royal Air Force 1939-1945*, 2: 21-22, is positively misleading. Kirby et al., *The Loss of Singapore*, pp. 180-81, 201, give a fair account. See also Kirby's *Singapore: The Chain of Disaster* (New York: Macmillan, 1971), p. 135. Ironically, on May 29, 1941, Churchill had sent a minute to Portal and Sinclair, urging that RAF ground staff ought to be trained and organized for the local defense of their airfields (Churchill, *The Grand Alliance*, pp. 776-77). It was, unfortunately, an idea without much appeal to senior RAF officers. See, e.g., Sir J. Slessor, *The Central Blue* (London: Cassell & Co., 1956), pp. 381-82.

15. Kirby et al., *The Loss of Singapore*, pp. 191-92, 201; Richards and Saunders, *The Royal Air Force 1939-1945*, 2: 22-23; Maltby, *Dispatch*, pars. 193-98.

16. Kirby et al., *The Loss of Singapore*, pp. 190, 201; Maltby, *Dispatch*, pars. 30, 204, 220-24.

17. This section is based on Churchill, *The Grand Alliance*, pp. 615-16, 620; Butler, ed., *History of the Second World War*, "Campaigns" series, S.W. Roskill, *The War at Sea*, 3 vols. (London: H.M.S.O., 1954-61), 1:563-69; Kirby et al., *The Loss of Singapore*, pp. 193-99; Butler, ed., History of the Second World War, "Grand Strategy" series, vol. 2., J. M. A. Gwyer and J. R. M. Butler, *Grand Strategy (June 1941-August 1942)*, 2 pts. (London: H. M.S.O., 1964), pt. 1, p. 316; Vice-Admiral Sir Geoffrey Layton, "Loss of H.M. Ships Prince of Wales and Repulse," *Supplement to the London Gazette*, February 26, 1948, passim; Charles, Lord Moran, *Churchill: The Struggle for Survival 1940-1965* (Boston: Houghton Mifflin, 1966), pp. 107-8; N. Nicolson, ed., *The Diaries and Letters of Harold Nicolson: The War Years 1939-1945* (New York: Atheneum, 1967), p. 196.

The statement, in Richards and Saunders, *The Royal Air Force 1939-1945,* 2: 25, that fighter aircraft were held back at Singapore instead of being sent to cover Phillips's squadron because of representations by Sir Shenton Thomas is incorrect. There is an interesting contemporary account of the impact in Singapore of the loss of the *Prince of Wales* and the *Repulse* in the anonymous "Singapore Diary," in the Bryson Collection: ". . . what began as a busy and interesting day has just been shattered by the devastating rumor, which spread like lightening *(sic)* this evening that "Repulse" and "Prince of Wales" have been sunk. No one believed it until it was confirmed by a special broadcast and later by Duff Cooper, an account by him which was literally a funeral oration. We are all stunned at the most astounding and disconcerting news I ever remember" (p. 10).

18. This section is based primarily on Kirby et al., *The Loss of Singapore,* pp. 186-88, 203-10. See Kirby's *Singapore: The Chain of Disaster,* pp. 113-16, for a detailed criticism of Percival's dispositions, and pp. 141-51 for a good analysis of the Jitra disaster.

19. This section is based primarily on Churchill, *The Grand Alliance,* pp. 552, 608-23, 635-36; Bond, ed., *Chief of Staff,* 2: 61-66; BPP v/5/36, 37; Gwyer and Butler, *Grand Strategy III,* pt. 1, pp. 317, 398 and pt. 2, pp. 404-5; A. Bryant, ed., *The Turn of the Tide 1939-1943: A History of the War Years based on the Diaries of Field-Marshal Lord Alanbrooke* (New York: Doubleday, 1957), p. 229.

8
AFTERMATH
AND BEGINNINGS:
December 1941-February 1942

i

The Pacific war was not very old when the defense of Burma became a major British concern, complicating further their position in the Far East. Burma was the eastern outpost of India, and, more important, it was America's link with China. The Burma road, opened in 1938, was China's only door to the West by 1941. By sea to Rangoon, by rail to Lashio in northern Burma, and then by truck over a fair weather road into Yunnan, supplies from the United States reached the country that aroused more intense American passion than did Britain itself. In April 1941 the Chinese agreed to the formation of several fighter squadrons manned by highly paid American volunteers. Officially called the American Volunteer Group (A.V.G.), imaginative publicists soon turned it into the more romantic "Flying Tigers." Rangoon was the port of entry for the A.V.G., and it began to assemble in June. By November there were three A.V.G. squadrons at Toungoo, north of Rangoon. They were flying Tomahawks (P-40's), a better fighter than anything the British (or Dutch) had in the Far East. In August the A.V.G. was given permission to do operational training in Burma, an "unneutral act" on the part of the British. Churchill, alert as always to anything that might affect American opinion, sent an "Action this Day" minute to Portal and the other Chiefs of Staff in early November calling their attention to the importance of adding British pilots and aircraft to the A.V.G.[1]

217

An American administrative staff established itself at Rangoon to handle Lend-Lease supplies for China. Chiang Kai-shek also had a representative there. Burma had thus become a Sino-American preoccupation well before the outbreak of the war, and eventually getting American supplies to China via Burma would dominate all other strategic considerations in the Far East.

Churchill signaled Chiang on the first day of the war. "The British Empire and the United States have been attacked by Japan. Always we have been friends: now we face a common enemy."[2] Chiang had agreed before the war broke out that an A.V.G. squadron could remain in Burma to bolster the air defenses of Rangoon. Accordingly, on December 12, one of Chennault's squadrons moved to Mingaladon airfield, near the city. The other two had gone on to Kunming in Yunnan, the Chinese terminus of the Burma Road. The Generalissimo asked Major General L. E. Dennys, the Indian Army officer who headed the British military mission in Chungking, to tell London that he was eager to send troops to assist in the defense of Burma, if the British authorities there could feed them.[3] When Burma was transferred to India Command on the 12th, the delicate problem of relations with Chiang, and his American supporters, became yet another of Wavell's many preoccupations.

When Wavell replied on the 13th to the cable informing him that Burma was now his responsibility, he pointed out how often India had asked in vain for control of Burma's defenses. He also reitertated how desperately India needed modern aircraft and AA guns. Then, with great foresight, he cabled Rangoon suggesting that the Government of Burma begin work on a road link between upper Burma and Assam in India, so that Burma would not be completely isolated if Rangoon was lost. The following day the Chiefs of Staff cabled Chiang, welcoming his offer of assistance. They also told Wavell to make contact with the Generalissimo, since Roosevelt was pushing the idea of an interallied conference, under Chiang's chairmanship, at Chungking. At the same time, Wavell got a cable from Lieutenant General D. K. McLeod, the GOC Burma, asking for just about everything India could provide: a divisional headquarters, two infantry brigades, a regiment of artillery, as well as three bomber and two fighter squadrons. Wavell decided that he would go to Chungking himself, stopping over at Rangoon. The Chiefs of Staff agreed, and expressed the hope that he could somehow persuade the Chinese to commit the entire A.V.G. to the defense of Rangoon.[4]

On December 19 Wavell flew down from Delhi to Calcutta. He conferred the next day with Pownall, who had finally been released from Cairo and was on his way through to Singapore. Afterwards, Pownall confided to his diary: "Singapore has *got* to be held, for to lose it may well mean losing Australia, if not N. Zealand. I don't mean losing them to the Japanese but to the Empire, for they will think themselves let down by H.M.G. at home."[5] The desperate need to reinforce Malaya had already begun to pull against the defense of Burma. By the time Wavell met Pownall, many of the reinforcements that were promised to India by Churchill on the 12th had already been nibbled away to meet Malaya's clamant needs. The Fifty-third Brigade of the Eighteenth Division had been diverted to Singapore, and the Seventeenth Indian Division's Forty-fifth Brigade was under orders for the same destination. Wavell had been warned that a second brigade (the Forty-fourth) from the Seventeenth Division would probably be needed in Malaya as well, and he was combing the training establishments to find replacements for the heavy casualties already sustained by the Indian divisions in Malaya. When he flew on from Calcutta to Rangoon on December 21, he knew that India could not find anything like the reinforcements Burma needed.[6]

His stopover in Rangoon was brief and bleak. Burma had hitherto rated even lower than Malaya and needed everything. Wavell had already ordered some twenty staff officers from India to Burma to make good the lack of numbers and ability at army headquarters there. The air defense of Rangoon was critical, but his only immediate hope of modern fighters lay in persuading Chiang to leave the A.V.G. squadron there. Burma needed a divisional headquarters and two brigades. Only the Seventeenth Indian Division could fulfill this need — if it was not diverted to Singapore. Rangoon needed AA cover. Wavell had already ordered the only seven mobile AA guns in India to Burma. The replacements he had expected had then been diverted to Singapore with the Fifty-third Brigade. He sent a long cable home describing Burma's manifold shortages and urging special attention to the provision of critically needed aircraft.[7] He also sacked McLeod and ordered his chief of staff, Lieutenant General Thomas Hutton, from India to replace him.

Wavell flew on to Chungking on the 22nd, in an American-piloted Chinese plane. Like Brooke-Popham, he did not have his own transport. With him went Major General G. H. Brett, U.S.A.A.F., who had arrived in Rangoon, via Singapore, on the 16th. He had been on his way to China to study the feasibility of basing American heavy bombers there, and now found himself the American representative at a very ad hoc interallied conference on December 22-23. The differing motives of the participants, and the haste with which the meeting was assembled and did its business, made for confusion. The personalities involved did not help, either. Wavell was by nature taciturn and reserved; Brett was garrulous. Neither Wavell nor Brett spoke Chinese, while Chiang spoke no English. Madame Chiang was perhaps not the most reliable interpreter. American and British accounts of what was said do not completely agree. Wavell, preoccupied with the problem of defending Burma, needed decisions on two points. He wanted the A.V.G. squadron left at Rangoon, and reinforced if possible. He also wanted some of the Chinese Lend-Lease supplies that had accumulated at Rangoon. There was far more there than the existing communications could carry to China, and many items would be invaluable to the defenders of Burma. These were both issues on which Dennys had been trying to get a decision out of Chiang since the war began. Chiang, however, wanted to discuss global strategy, which Wavell and Brett were neither authorized nor prepared to do, and he wanted to get Chinese troops into Burma. This point had been raised, in vague terms, by a Chinese military mission that had visited Burma and Singapore in April 1941. Chiang had offered troops again at the outbreak of the war, and on the 15th-16th Dennys was told that the Chinese were thinking of two armies as their contribution. This was a good deal less than it might seem. A Chinese "army," even at full strength — which it seldom was — was little bigger than a British division. Chinese formations were almost entirely without administrative services of their own. Even their infantry did not all have rifles. Chiang, moreover, made it a condition of their use in Burma that they could not be mixed with other troops, but had to have a separate line of communications and an operational area of their own. Burma would have to provide administrative support and victual them as well. Wavell, therefore, had to weigh the problematic military utility of the Chinese against the difficulties of using them. There were as well a number of political factors involved in accepting Chiang's offer. The Government of Burma, which answered not to Wavell but to Whitehall, was reluctant to have Chinese forces in the country. Burmese opinion was hostile to the Chinese, and the British administrators could not ignore this, particularly since the constitutional evolution of Burma had reached the point where Burmese ministers formed much of the government. But an even greater consideration in Wavell's mind than the views of the Governor of Burma and his ministers was the need to maintain British prestige. As commander-in-chief in India, Wavell, like every other British official in the East, knew that the life and soul of their empire was prestige. That invaluable commodity had taken a considerable beating lately. The *Prince of Wales* and the *Repulse* had been lost; Hong Kong was on the verge of surrender, while in Malaya there was a steady retreat. Wavell knew that this tale of disaster would certainly grow. It did not seem to him the opportune moment to accept the aid of a foreign and unfriendly power in the defense of British territory. He later wrote that he wanted British territory to be defended by British, or at least imperial, forces. There were still two brigades of the Eighteenth Division bound for India; he hoped to retain at least one, and possibly two brigades of the Seventeenth Indian Division. A request, made in November, for African troops, had finally been agreed to by London on December 16, and Wavell was told that he could have two brigades. With all this in mind, he accepted only two divisions of the Chinese VI Army for use in Burma, and asked that the Vth Army be held in reserve near Kunming. Chiang felt slighted. He refused to give any definite answer to Wavell's requests about the A.V G. squadron and the use of the Lend-Lease supplies at Rangoon. The Generalissimo's pique was soon made known in Washington, where Chinese desires, focused by the Americans, produced pressure on the British that Chiang himself could never have managed.[8]

Simultaneously, a second source of friction with the Chinese arose in Rangoon. To enable an ammunition ship to be unloaded on December 20, the governor of Burma, Sir Reginald Dorman-Smith, borrowed the drivers of some Lend-Lease trucks. Chiang's representative, General Yu Fei-peng, who was also the Generalissimo's cousin, thereupon wired Chungking that the British had seized Chinese Lend-Lease supplies. Three days later Rangoon suffered its first air raid. There were no AA guns — only the A.V.G. squadron and another of RAF Buffaloes. Some 2,000 people were killed. Refugees began to stream out of the city, and, as labor vanished, the working of the port began to break down. Wavell landed at Mingaladon airfield on Christmas Day, just as the second major Japanese raid came in. Five thousand more people died, and the exodus from the battered city increased. Brett cabled Washington, "Only six men working in motor transport assembly shop where 600 were working six days ago. Impossible to load ships or to handle

cargoes. Shops closed. Hotels closed. Food shortage imminent."
Wavell promptly borrowed Lend-Lease AA guns and light machine
guns to provide some cover for Rangoon, informing Chiang that he
had done so. Meanwhile, a ship loaded with Lend-Lease supplies
for China was ordered back to Calcutta because the state of Rangoon made it impossible to unload it. Another was unloaded, and
its cargo promptly moved away from the docks. Both actions were
represented to Chungking as further British seizures of Chinese
supplies. Shortly after Christmas Chiang informed Dennys that he
was releasing another A.V.G. squadron for Rangoon, which was
his lifeline to the West. He also ratified what had already taken
place by agreeing to release to the British certain items of equipment from the accumulated Lend-Lease stores. But his irritation
about the British "seizures" of Chinese supplies persisted, and this,
too, got back to Washington.[9]

By the time Churchill reached Washington for the Arcadia Conference, Burma was shaping up as a major problem, not only militarily, but, even more important for the prime minister, in terms
of alliance politics. The defense of Malaya was henceforth paralleled by growing British concern for Burma. As the one reached its
inevitable, tragic conclusion, the other emerged as the major British problem in the East.

ii

When Churchill left for Washington, he took Pound and Portal
with him. Brooke, the new CIGS, was left behind with Ismay to
"mind the shop." Brooke had persuaded Churchill to take with
him Sir John Dill, recently deposed as CIGS and promoted field
marshal. Churchill had originally planned to make him governor of
Bombay. As in the case of Wavell six months earlier, the prime
minister did not want Dill at loose ends in London. Brooke's intervention with Churchill was fortunate, for Dill was to become the
head of the British staff mission in Washington, where the close
friendship he developed with George Marshall became invaluable
to the Anglo-American alliance. As the *Duke of York* plowed westwards, battened down against heavy seas, Churchill spent most of
his time composing two remarkable papers on the future of the
European war. A third paper, on the Pacific, was completed only
after he reached Washington. His partial isolation, and preoccu-

pation with the future, diminished the prime minister's usual output of messages. But on December 15, after consultation with Dill, he signaled London: "Beware lest troops required for ultimate defense Singapore Island and fortress are not used up and cut off in Malay Peninsula. *Nothing compares in importance, with the fortress.*"[10] Four days later he signaled again to the same effect. In both signals he treated the Australian troops in the Middle East as a freely disposable reserve for the entire area east of Suez, suggesting the movement of one Australian division from Palestine to Singapore, and of another to India.[11]

Inevitably the burden of trying to cope with the disastrous situation in the Far East fell on the rump Chiefs of Staff Committee in London: Brooke and the naval and air vice chiefs, Vice Admiral H. R. Moore and Air Chief Marshal Sir Wilfred Freeman. They improvised the best response they could until the whole shape of Far Eastern strategy was altered by the Arcadia decisions. Brooke had had a number of conversations with Dill in which the departing CIGS had left his successor in no doubt about how poorly defended the Far East really was. "He had told me frankly that he had done practically nothing to meet this threat. He said that we were already so weak on all fronts that it was impossible to denude them any further."[12] If Brooke's postwar recollection of this conversation is correct, Dill was being very generous, for he alone among the Chiefs of Staff had tried to persuade the prime minister to reinforce Malaya. Lack of sea and air power were the worst deficiencies in the Far East, and while it was possible to divert the Eighteenth Division from the Middle East, finding planes and ships was another matter.

A squadron of Blenheims had been pulled out of the Middle East, and four squadrons of fighters had been ordered on to India when the plan to aid the Russians in the Caucasus was scrubbed. But the Japanese occupation of Victoria Point on December 15 meant that single-engine aircraft could no longer be flown direct to Singapore. Bombers, using Sabang in northern Sumatra as a staging point, could still make the trip, but only with difficulty. Of the eighteen Blenheims that set out from the Middle East, only seven made it to Singapore by Christmas. The others either crashed or made forced landings on the way. Arrangements were being made to fly forty-four Hudsons out from Great Britain, but even in peaceful times it had been a two- or three-week trip, and the first of them would not, in the event, even get started until four days after Christmas. There was now another claimant for aircraft reinforcements as well. Burma had been promised medium bombers. Wavell cabled London on the 17th, asking when they would arrive and pointing out that unless they did so quickly it might well be too late.[13]

On that day the Chiefs of Staff made the first attempt to get modern fighters, even more desperately needed than bombers, moving toward Singapore. A convoy then at the Cape carried fifty-one crated Hurricanes, twenty-four pilots, a wing head-quarters, and the ground staff for four squadrons. This was the force that had originally been intended for the Caucasus, then diverted to India. Now the Chiefs of Staff changed its orders again. The crated Hurricanes, pilots, and ground staff for one squadron would be transshipped and sent on to Singapore, while the re-mainder continued to Bombay. This would put a Hurricane squad-ron into Singapore about January 8, but the planes would still have to be uncrated, erected and tested, and modifications for climate made to the engines as well before they could be used. The pilots had passed out of O.T.U.'s but had never actually been in combat, which would also reduce the squadron's impact. (After taking this decision, Brooke noted despondently in his diary that it was probably too late to save Singapore, and that all efforts should, therefore, be concentrated on Burma.[14]) No heavy bombers were sent to India, Burma, or the Far East. Those available in the Middle East were all being used to support Auchinleck, and the Air Staff jealously guarded the integrity of Bomber Command.

The problem of naval reinforcements was even more intractable. Layton had been told to expect the *Indomitable* early in January, and on December 14, the vice chief of the Naval Staff gave the De-fence Committee a paper on naval power in the Indian Ocean. Commerce there ranked second in importance only to that in the Atlantic, Admiral Moore noted. The Admiralty therefore proposed to concentrate 75 percent of Britain's capital ships there. If Auchin-leck took Benghazi, and enough shore-based aircraft were available to hold the Italian fleet in check, interdict Rommel's supply lines, and cover convoys to Malta — a great many "ifs" — the battle fleet in the eastern Mediterranean might then pass through the canal to the Indian Ocean. To effect this concentration to the east, American help in the Atlantic would be essential, but the Admiralty assumed that it would now certainly be available: "it is in the Atlantic area alone that the vital interests of ourselves and the U.S. are identical." In the Far East, however, "there is no one base at which our own and American forces equal or superior to the Japanese can be assembled which would be acceptable to both powers as affording sufficient protection to their interests."[15] There, in brief, was the fatal flaw in Churchill's previous reasoning: the divergence of British and American interests in the Far East.

The Admiralty paper was based on a recognition of the importance of the Indian Ocean for communications with the armies and oil fields of the Middle East, as well as with Australia and New Zealand. But it was also based on assumptions about the availability of ships that were rapidly falsified. The Admiralty had asked Admirals Cunningham and Somerville on the 10th about the consequences of pulling the capital ships out of the Mediterranean Fleet or Force H at Gibraltar, or both. Cunningham had stressed that the only possible compensation for being stripped of his heavy ships was the seizure of the Benghazi area and the establishment there of an air force strong enough to dominate the central Mediterranean, and Moore's paper reflected this. Then the navy in the Mediterranean was suddenly crippled. Just after midnight on December 14-15, a cruiser was torpedoed and lost. In the early hours of December 19, Force K, the striking force based on Malta, was wiped out. A minefield near Tripoli sank a cruiser and a destroyer and damaged two other destroyers, one seriously. That same day, in one of the most daring operations of the war, Italian frogmen penetrated the Mediterranean Fleet's lair at Alexandria and fastened limpet mines to the keels of the battleships *Queen Elizabeth* and *Valiant*. Both ships were heavily damaged and would be out of action for months. Between mid-November and mid-December, the Royal Navy had lost two battleships, a battle cruiser, and a fleet carrier, while two more battleships had been heavily damaged. Losses and damage to cruisers and destroyers were also very heavy. Another battleship and two more fleet carriers were under repair for battle damage received earlier. Cumulatively it was far worse than Pearl Harbor. American losses would soon be made good by massive naval construction programs that were just getting into their stride. British shipyards were, however, choked with work on vital escorts and merchant shipping. Only two battleships and two fleet carriers were coming along for the Royal Navy. Still lurking in the background was the *Tirpitz*, tying down most of Britain's remaining modern capital ships. Hope of quickly moving anything worthwhile to the Indian Ocean vanished.

Against this background of unrelieved disaster, the Defence Committee met on December 19 to consider reinforcements for Malaya. The vice chief of the air staff "reminded the Committee that air forces were not strategically mobile and could not operate without spares, ground staff and ground equipment." This, of course, cut across many claims the Air Ministry had previously made, although no one was unkind enough to point it out. It also was another way of saying that nothing significant could be done by the RAF. Brooke reported that the size of the bridges in Malaya meant that only light tanks could be used there. (The Japanese, however, managed to use 15-ton medium tanks successfully.) The Committee also considered and approved a Chiefs of Staff paper, requested by Churchill before he left for the United States, that laid down a strategy of delay in Malaya: "We must contrive to fight the best possible delaying action in Malaya, the southern part of which is vital to the security of Singapore Island."[16] Percival's method of doing this would be to stand as long as possible on each successive position down the peninsula to gain time for the arrival of reinforcements — a policy that led to the piecemeal destruction of his formations. The next day Brooke wrote a glum and revealing note in his diary: "The more I look at the situation, the more I dislike it. My hopes of carrying on with the conquest and reclamation of North Africa are beginning to look more and more impossible every day. The Far East will make ever-increasing inroads on our resources."[17]

By the 23rd the Chiefs of Staff felt that Malaya's needs were so great that Wavell was ordered to release the Forty-fourth Brigade of the Seventeenth Division. His immediately available formations were now reduced to a divisional headquarters and one brigade, and his plans for reinforcing Burma were dislocated. That same day the timing of the Fifty-third Brigade's arrival at Singapore had to be settled. It was sailing in an American transport, U.S.S. *Mount Vernon*. The *Mount Vernon* could leave her convoy and refuel at Mombasa in Kenya. She could then join another convoy sailing on Christmas Eve from Durban for Singapore and carrying antiaircraft and antitank regiments. This would bring the Fifty-third Brigade to Singapore about January 10; but it would arrive without either its artillery or vehicles, which were in other ships — without, indeed, anything beyond a minimum of equipment. The men would be badly out of shape after two cramped months at sea. But with Heath's battered forces falling back rapidly in northern Malaya, there seemed to be no choice, and the *Mount Vernon* was ordered to Singapore by the most direct route.[18]

By Christmas the situation in Malaya was so bad that the prime minister, now in Washington, did something he had hitherto resisted. On Christmas Eve Auchinleck signaled Churchill the welcome news that Benghazi had fallen, but German resistance was now stiffening. The disasters to British sea power in the Mediterranean had removed the pressure on Rommel's maritime lifeline. Replacements and supplies were again reaching him. German air power was being switched from snowbound Russia to the Mediterranean. Yet at this moment, Churchill had to replay with Auchinleck the scenario enacted a year before with Wavell. Forces had to be diverted to meet a more pressing need. On Boxing Day (December 26) Churchill cabled Auchinleck both congratulations and a "hard request." "Only air power at Singapore and Johore will keep the door open, and if the door is shut the fortress will fall and this would take the bloom off our Libyan successes . . . . Naturally you must not divest yourself of anything that would prevent 'Acrobat' [an advance westwards towards Tripoli] but I am sure you will feel that all our successes in West would be nullified by fall of Singapore."[19]   The prime minister wanted four squadrons of Hurricanes and a hundred of Auchinleck's American-made light tanks. Auchinleck, an Indian Army officer and former commander-in-chief in India, replied the next day, offering far more than Churchill had asked. The four Hurricane squadrons were immediately made available. The *Indomitable* would pick up the planes, and their veteran pilots, at Port Sudan in the Red Sea. Escorted by three Australian destroyers from the Mediterranean, she would sail east and fly the Hurricanes off to Sumatra or Java, whence they could go on to Singapore. Fifty light tanks were made available, plus the Seventh Armoured Brigade, a veteran desert unit whose two armored regiments were equipped with American light tanks. The brigade would go as a self-contained unit, complete with headquarters, field and antitank batteries, signals, workshops, and recovery sections. Auchinleck also provided a quantity of small arms and antitank rifles, and offered to release an Australian infantry brigade if it could be replaced by April.[20]

Despite Auchinleck's helpfulness, there were limits to what could be pulled out of the Middle East. British forces were still pushing west beyond Benghazi, and neither Brooke nor the prime minister wanted either current prospects, or future possibilities like Acrobat and Gymnast, imperiled by diversions to the Far East. Turkey still remained an important consideration as well. Commitments had been made to the Turks in August, and, despite the

outbreak of war in the Far East, the Turks were assured early in
January that four brigade groups and twenty-six RAF squadrons
could still be made available.[21]

The fundamental factor in British strategy remained the war in
the West. On the same day that Auchinleck offered the Seventh
Armoured Brigade for the Far East, Brooke told the Defence Committee that Singapore and the Indian Ocean were second in importance only to the United Kingdom itself, *but* Germany remained
the principal enemy —" consequently for the present we should
not divert more of our resources than are necessary to hold the
Japanese."[22]

This, while not entirely convincing as logic, reflected the rapidly
growing anxiety of the Australian government about their country's
safety, which made it prudent to stress Singapore's theoretical
priority. Nevertheless, shortly after Christmas, Australian anger
was to erupt in a public clash between the two governments. By
the 27th, moreover, the prime minister had been in the United
States nearly a week, and pressure from Britain's powerful ally was
pushing him in new and somewhat unexpected directions. American determination to maintain their link with the Chinese via
Burma was about to impose a new shape on the British effort to
stem the Japanese tide in the Far East.

iii

In the early days of the fighting, the Australian government had
been prompt with both reinforcements for Malaya and pointed
questions to London. Australian air crews flew from Singapore to
Darwin to collect Hudsons to be ferried back to Malaya. Gordon
Bennett telegraphed twice to army headquarters in Melbourne to
say that if the situation in Malaya was to be held, an Australian
division from the Middle East would have to get there as quickly
as possible. On December 23, the day that the second of these
telegrams was received, the Australian government decided to send
a machine-gun battalion, exactly half the force still available for
overseas service, to Malaya. They also hastily collected 1,900 reinforcements and shipped them to Gordon Bennett. Since many of
these men were rushed literally from the recruiter to the troopship,
they were even greener than the Indian replacements that Wavell
was scraping up, and of correspondingly little value. In London,
Page and Bruce kept after the War Cabinet and Defence Committee,

both chaired in Churchill's absence by Attlee. Brooke growled in his diary on Christmas Eve that Duff Cooper was "inspiring the Australians to ask for more and more for the Far East."[23] In fact, the Australians needed no prompting. They had only to look north. On Boxing Day Brooke recorded, "in afternoon rung up by Attlee to find out whether we were ready for a Defence Committee to keep Australians quiet as they were fretting about reinforcements for Singapore . . . Later Mr. Bruce asked to see me and I had to explain to him what we were doing for the Far East. He went away satisfied," the CIGS complacently noted.[24] But if Bruce was satisfied, his government was not. On Christmas Day the Australian War Cabinet received from their representative in Singapore, V. G. Bowden, a blunt and accurate statement of the situation.

> deterioration of our position in Malaya . . . . is assuming land-slide proportions . . . . Present measures for reinforcing Singapore defences can from a practical viewpoint be regarded as little more than gestures. In my belief only thing that might save Singapore would be immediate despatch from Middle East by air of powerful reinforcements, large numbers of latest fighter aircraft with ample operational personnel. Reinforcements of troops should not be in brigades but in divisions and to be of use they must arrive urgently. Anything that is not powerful, modern and immediate is futile. As things stand at present fall of Singapore is to my mind only a matter of weeks.[25]

Curtin's reaction was to send a cable on the same day to both the president and the prime minister: "Reinforcements earmarked by United Kingdom Government for Singapore seem to us to be utterly inadequate in relation to aircraft particularly fighters . . . . It is in your power to meet situation. Should United States desire we would gladly accept United States command in Pacific Ocean area." R. G. Casey, the Australian minister in Washington, was told: "Please understand stage of suggestion has passed . . . ."[26] Curtin was trying to pressure Churchill by threatening in effect to secede from London's orbit to Washington's. His cable crossed one from Churchill in which the prime minister described the diversion of the Eighteenth Division to India and the decision to send its leading brigade directly to Singapore. "We cancelled the move of Seventeenth Indian Division from India to Persia, and this division is now going to Malaya," Churchill wrote, somewhat inaccurately.

We do not share the view expressed in your telegram . . . that
there is the danger of early reduction of Singapore fortress . .
. . You have been told of the air support which is already on
the way. It would not be wise to loose our grip on Rommel
and Libya by taking away forces from General Auchinleck
against his judgment just when victory is within our grasp.
We have instructed Commander-in-Chief Middle East to con-
cert a plan for sending fighters and tanks to Singapore immediately the situation in Libya permits . . . . You may count
on my doing everything possible to strengthen the whole
front from Rangoon to Port Darwin.[27]

Despite this optimistic cable, Churchill ordered tanks and planes
from the Middle East the next day. But that gesture came too late
to avoid an explosion in Australia. On December 27, the Melbourne
Herald carried an article signed by Curtin.

We refuse to accept the dictum that the Pacific struggle must
be treated as a subordinate aspect of the general conflict . . . .
The Australian Government, therefore, regards the Pacific struggle as primarily one in which the United States and Australia
must have the fullest say in the direction of the democracies'
fighting plan. Without any inhibitions of any kind, I make it
quite clear that Australia looks to America, free of any pangs
as to our traditional links or kinship with the United Kingdom.
We know the problems that the United Kingdom faces . . . . But
we know, too, that Australia can go and Britain can still hold on.
We are, therefore, determined that Australia shall not go.[28]

This bombshell exploded in the midst of a very complex series
of negotiations in Washington that were affecting the fundamental
shape of the war and the machinery for its direction. Churchill had
prepared for this during the voyage by drafting his papers dealing
with the European campaigns of 1942 and 1943. He began to com-
pose a third paper, "Notes on the Pacific", which he completed
after his arrival in the United States. The order in which the papers
were written is significant. The only thing that could be done in
the Far East, the prime minister felt, was to slow the Japanese down
by a stubborn defense. This would burn up Japanese resources,
and Churchill hoped that Anglo-American command of the Pacific
would be restored by May 1942. Thereafter a counteroffensive
could begin. The prime minister correctly foresaw the immense
importance that aircraft carriers would play in the vast reaches of
the Pacific. But the overall impression left by his note on the war

against Japan is of a grasp of the problem and its details infinitely less sure than that shown in his papers on Europe. A member of his staff commented: "Winston always seemed to me very vague on anything east of India."[29]   In fact, the final paragraph indicated that his chief concern was to prevent the Japanese war from interfering with the development of the struggle against Germany.[30]

In his account of the voyage to the United States, Churchill's doctor describes him as talking at large, in the best of spirits, about everything but the war in the East. "He is a different man since America came into the war. The Winston I knew in London frightened me . . . . I could see that he was carrying the weight of the world, and wondered how long he could go on like that and what could be done about it. And now — in a night, it seems — a younger man has taken his place. All day he keeps to his cabin, dictating for the President a memorandum on the conduct of the war. But the tired, dull look has gone from his eye; his face lights up as you enter the cabin . . . . at night he is gay and voluble, sometimes even playful."[31]   The prime minister now saw how victory in the West could be won. Compared to this, the Far East was relatively unimportant.

While Churchill worked on his papers, the Joint Planning Staff were producing their own blueprint of the future. "With the Japanese in control of the Netherlands East Indies oil and able to threaten the Indian Ocean, the retention of the Middle East has become of even greater moment than before," they wrote. They held out little hope for the Far East. The Japanese completely dominated the area, and all they could suggest was trying "to limit the advantages that Japan has gained by her recent successes . . . ." To this end, Singapore and the Dutch East Indies had to be held, together with Rangoon and Ceylon. The Joint Planners apparently did not notice the contradiction between their assumption that Japan would control the oil of the East Indies, and their recommendation to hold the area. Their paper offered the same prescription for the Far East as Churchill's — stubborn defense. Neither seemed really imbued with the belief that such a defense would be very successful. Churchill looked forward to resuming the offensive against Japan within months. The planners, more pessimistic or more prudent, emphasized the importance of retaining the Middle East. This meant safeguarding the maritime communications in the western Indian Ocean that led from the Cape to Suez, the Persian Gulf, and Bombay. Ceylon was essential for this. So was Madagascar. The planners pointed out that it might be necessary to occupy the latter to prevent the Vichy authorities there from giving facilities to either the Germans or the Japanese. Eventually the British would mount a major amphibious operation, *Ironclad*, followed by a lengthy campaign (April-November 1942) to preempt that possibility. The British seizure of Madagascar has excited the derision of some American commentators, but the British had, after all, seen the Vichy government give facilities to the Germans in Syria, and to the Japanese in Indochina. The concern about Madagascar indicates that, within a fortnight of Pearl Harbor, some British planners were already thinking in terms of what would have to be done to prevent collapse in the Far East from imperiling the Middle East as well.[32]

On the 17th the Chiefs of Staff who were accompanying the prime minister discussed the Joint Planners' paper, and the next day they met with Churchill and Beaverbrook. More meetings on the 19th produced the final version of the strategic prospectus that the British would present to the Americans. The prime minister stressed the importance of regaining control of the Pacific, but Pound was dubious about the practicality of a counteroffensive without a long preliminary process of attrition against the Japanese, during which an Anglo-American fleet reestablished itself at Singapore. In the event, the final version of the British position paper was very cautious about the Far East, committing itself to "maintaining only such positions in the Eastern theatre as will safeguard vital interests while we are concentrating on the defeat of Germany." These vital interests were defined as "the security of Australia, New Zealand and India" and "the continuation of Chinese resistance." "Secondly, points of vantage from which an offensive against Japan can eventually be developed must be secured." Under this heading came the retention of Singapore. But all of this was subordinate to the principal consideration, set out at the beginning: "Much has happened since February last, but, notwithstanding the entry of Japan into the war, our view remains that Germany is still the prime enemy and her defeat is the key to victory. Once Germany is defeated, the collapse of Italy and Japan must speedily follow."[33]

The British were thus well organized and had an agreed-upon position when the *Duke of York* steamed into Hampton Roads on December 22. Fretting with impatience, Churchill flew on to Washington with Portal, Harriman, and his doctor, leaving the rest of his party to follow by train. Unscarred, its lights shining brightly,

Washington struck many members of the British party as infinitely remote from the war.[34] Roosevelt met the prime minister's plane, and the two men held their first informal discussion that evening at the White House. Significantly, the subject was North Africa, where both had an interest in mounting Gymnast. At the first plenary session the following day, the president stressed the importance of Singapore — and China — while the prime minister said little about the Far East. The British Chiefs of Staff put their paper before the American service chiefs on Christmas Eve. With few amendments it was quickly accepted by the Americans, christened "W.W.I," and became the strategic basis of the alliance. The British had gotten the Americans to reaffirm "Germany first." But there was a price.

On Christmas Day Marshall proposed to Churchill a unified command in the Far East. Churchill was unenthusiastic; but Marshall persisted, and by the next day had won the support of the president and Hopkins. On the evening of the 26th the prime minister held a staff conference at the British embassy. He indicated that he felt that unified direction of the Pacific war from Washington was the price the British would have to pay for "Germany first," and the acceptance of British strategic concepts for Europe. The Chiefs of Staff thought that a unified command, whatever its drawbacks, might at least tie the United States more closely to the defense of Singapore and the East Indies. As it was, American forces in the Far East were concerned primarily with the defense of the Philippine Islands, a position the British regarded as simply an outpost of the Malay barrier.[35]

Late that night the stresses and tensions of the past eighteen months finally caught up with Winston Churchill. It was a typically humid Washington night, and the air conditioning in his White House bedroom failed. Straining to open a window, he suddenly felt chest pains that spread rapidly to his left arm. The next morning he mentioned it to Sir Charles Wilson, who privately diagnosed it as a mild heart attack, although he told the prime minister only that he had been working too hard. Curtin's bombshell thus could not have come at a worse moment.[36]

Churchill's reaction was sharp. The prime minister was extremely angry at being embarassed in front of the Americans and the Canadians. He cabled Attlee: "I hope there will be no pandering to this while at the same time we do all in human power to come to their aid . . . ." He also made it clear that he was unrepentant on the main issue: "If the Malay peninsula has been

starved for the sake of Libya and Russia, no one is more responsible than I, and I would do exactly the same again. Should any
questions be asked in Parliament I should be glad if it could be
stated that I particularly desire to answer them myself on my
return."[37]   It was not only Churchill himself who was intensely
angered by Curtin's action. One of his staff, with memories of the
argument over the relief of the Australians in Tobruk fresh in his
mind, reflected in his diary: "The Australian Government have
throughout the war taken a narrow, selfish, and at times a craven
view of events; in contrast to New Zealand who, though at times
naturally critical of failures, has throughout been a tower of
strength." He added, however, a very perceptive commentary and
prediction:

> I fear that the Prime Minister's treatment of Mr. Menzies is
> somewhat to blame. He has never really understood the Far
> East problem and has deliberately starved Singapore in favor
> of home and the Middle East, without paying enough atten-
> tion to the feelings of Australia. His policy was undoubtedly
> right, but he should have taken great pains to make Australia
> understand what was being done, and give them the impression
> that he was really taking them into his confidence. I am afraid
> we will have a lot of bother with Australia as a result.[38]

The prime minister in the first flush of his anger even considered
the idea of a broadcast to Australia. Wisely, he decided in the end
not to appeal to the Australian public over the head of its government. Perhaps he remembered Woodrow Wilson's experience in
1919. The prime minister simply could not understand why the
Australians did not behave more like the British: "It will always be
deemed remarkable that in this deadly crisis, when as it seemed to
them and their professional advisors, destruction was at the very
throat of the Australian Commonwealth, they did not all join together in a common effort. But such was their party phlegm and
rigidity that local politics ruled unshaken. The Labour Government,
with its majority of two, monopolized the whole executive power,
and conscription even for home defense was banned."[39]   Sir
Charles Wilson, observing Churchill a few days later with Canadian
Prime Minister Mackenzie King, noted that Churchill did not really
seem interested in his host: "He takes him for granted." The same
feeling lay at the root of Churchill's problems with Australia. As
another member of his staff observed years later, "Winston never
really understood the Australians."[40]

The prime minister did realize, however, that something had to be done to soothe Australia, and this may have made him more receptive to the idea of a unified command in the Far East. During the 27th the Chiefs of Staff came to the conclusion that they could accept Marshall's proposal, but were stunned when Churchill told them that evening that the Americans wanted Wavell as the Allied supreme commander. The prime minister himself had been taken somewhat aback when Hopkins broached the idea to him, fearing that the compliment was a rather empty one, since Wavell's new command was bound to be overrun quickly by the Japanese.[41] The Chiefs of Staff were more blunt. The Americans, they felt, were trying to shift the responsibility for the impending defeat onto British shoulders. Dill wrote to Brooke the following day. "It would, I think, be fatal to have a British commander responsible for the disasters that are coming to the Americans as well as ourselves . . . ."[42] The pressures of the moment swept doubts aside however. The Americans wanted a unified command, and such an arrangement might give the Australians the feeling that "their" war was getting its due share of attention. By the 28th Churchill and Roosevelt had agreed on the creation of the American-British-Dutch-Australian (ABDA) command, covering an immense area from Burma to Australia, and Wavell had been selected as Allied supreme commander. His orders would come "from an appropriate joint body, who will be responsible to me as Minister of Defence and to the President of the United States who is also Commander-in-Chief of all United States forces," the prime minister reported to the War Cabinet.[43]

Wavell learned of his new appointment two days later. After a rare day off, he rode back into Delhi on the evening of December 30. A long telegram from Churchill awaited him. "The President and his military and naval advisors have impressed upon me the urgent need for unified command in the South-West Pacific and it is urgently desired, pressed particularly by the President and General Marshall, that you should become supreme commander of Allied forces by land air and sea assigned to that theatre."[44] Wavell cabled back the same evening accepting the appointment. Privately, however, he wrote to Dill that he "had been handed not just a baby but quadruplets."[45] Churchill later wrote that only the highest sense of duty could have moved Wavell when he agreed to become Allied supreme commander.[46]

Despite Wavell's courageous acceptance of the worst prospect handed to a British senior officer in the course of the war, a number of problems still remained. The War Cabinet, in accepting the ABDA arrangements, raised the pertinent question of the composition of the "appropriate joint body" that would give Wavell his orders. It was decided to entrust this function to the British and American Chiefs of Staff, sitting together as the Combined Chiefs of Staff. When the British and American service chiefs were not together, the link between them would be the British staff mission in Washington, which Dill would now head. Thus there came into being the most important instrument of Anglo-American military cooperation.

Burma presented another difficulty. To the Americans Burma was their link with China. Chiang was already unhappy. Wavell and Brett, as Churchill put it in a message to Attlee, had made a rather poor impression.[47]   The Generalissimo was also unhappy over the alleged loss of his Lend-Lease supplies. For all these reasons the Americans wanted Burma included in "ABDACOM" (the Washington passion for acronyms already making itself felt). Sir Reginald Dorman-Smith protested vigorously about this, pointing out that since India assumed responsibility, something was finally being done for Burma: "I do not want to relapse into being nobody's child."[48]   Burma nonetheless went to ABDA, although administrative responsibility remained with India, a clumsy arrangement, and the fourth to which Burma had been subjected in little over a year. Roosevelt and Marshall were simultaneously making other arrangements that were to lead to endless complications in Burma. Chiang had been offered the command of all Allied forces in the China theater, which Roosevelt airily defined as including Thailand and Indochina, at the same time that ABDA was set up. When Chiang accepted, he asked for a senior American officer as his chief of staff. Eventually, on January 23, Marshall chose Lieutenant General Joseph W. Stilwell, who was also named commanding general of U.S. Army Forces in the China-Burma-India theater, Lend-Lease administrator for the area, and U.S. member of any Allied war council that might come into being in the Far East. This multiplicity of appointments was an administrative nightmare, a curious lapse for Marshall, whose military reputation rests largely on his administrative skill. No one, even with the ability, tact, and patience of an Eisenhower, could have done all the jobs Stilwell was given. But Stilwell's personality made matters far worse. One of those curious individuals whose egalitarian sentiments take the form of despising anyone different from themselves, he suffered as well from the delusion that rudeness and toughness were synonymous. He disliked Chiang, and in him all the traditional American suspicions of Britain were intensified to almost pathological dimensions. His appointment is a good indication of how terribly thin the veneer of Anglo-American cooperation really was in the Far East.[49]

The complications to arise out of Stilwell's appointment would only become apparent in the future, however. Meanwhile, before ABDA could be launched, Australia, New Zealand, and the Dutch all had to be squared. The Australians had expected to be members of the "joint body" that would give Wavell his orders. Even New Zealand protested its exclusion: "We feel we must be informed. We feel we must have an eye, an ear and a voice whenever decisions affecting New Zealand are to be made, and we are by no means happy with the arrangements, so far as we know them, for the conduct of the war against Japan."[50] The Dutch were equally unhappy, and Roosevelt had to fend off the Dutch prime minister, who wanted to visit Washington for discussions. Churchill beat off all challenges, even though the War Cabinet was clearly sympathetic to the criticisms leveled at the Arcadia arrangements. The prime minister assured his colleagues that arrangements would be made for Dutch and dominion opinion to be focused in London and transmitted to Washington. There, temporarily, the matter stood. Wavell's directive was cabled to him on January 3. The same day Churchill sent Curtin a long message in which he tried to soothe Australian anger over the course of the war and their own exclusion from the inner councils of the alliance. But he could not refrain from underlining his conviction that his policy had been the correct one. "It would have been folly to spoil Auchinleck's battle by diverting aircraft, tanks, etc. to the Malay peninsula at a time when there was no certainty Japan would enter the war."[51]

On New Year's Day the Chiefs of Staff in London had cabled Cairo and Singapore, emphasizing that while the security of Singapore and Indian Ocean communications ranked second to the safety of the British Isles, Germany's defeat came first, and only enough force to hold the Japanese would be diverted east. Crusader was to be exploited to the utmost subject to the dispatch of essential reinforcements for the Far East. The Chiefs of Staff then tabulated the reinforcements they planned to send: Malaya would receive a British division, an Indian division, and an armored brigade, while Burma would get two divisions, Indian or African. Two more divisions would go to the Netherlands East Indies.[52]

On the same day that Churchill sent his message to Curtin, the Australian government received a cable from London asking it to release the Sixth and Seventh Divisions from the Middle East for the East Indies. On January 6 the Australian cabinet agreed that the two divisions, with corps headquarters, corps troops, and administrative units, should be pulled out of the Middle East immediately.[53] They made no commitment, however, about their ultimate destination.

Nearly all this was an exercise in building sand castles. The ABDA area was a huge, unwieldy command, hastily put together for political reasons. Throughout its area the initiative lay with Japan. The New Year's Day cable from London about reinforcements was a pious hope. There were, in reality, only two divisions actually available for the ABDA area — the Eighteenth British and Seventeenth Indian — plus the armored brigade that Auchinleck had provided. There was no hope of sending them to Malaya *and* at the same time sending two divisions to Burma. The Australians could only move out of the Middle East slowly, and would reach the East Indies only if the Japanese gave them time. Nor could air reinforcements arrive quickly. There was no hope of establishing an Anglo-American battle fleet at Singapore, or anywhere else in the Pacific or ABDA area for that matter. Churchill may still have cherished hopes of Singapore's prolonged resistance, but the belief that disaster could be averted in the Far East must have been rapidly ebbing among his military advisers. Their reaction to Roosevelt's desire to name Wavell Allied supreme commander certainly points in this direction. The Australian government, seeing themselves in the path of the avalanche, and with Bowden's hardheaded reports coming in, were right to be very worried, even if their expressions of concern, as the British official historians subsequently complained, were not as decorous as those of New Zealand.

On January 6 Churchill flew from Washington to Florida to get some badly needed rest at a Palm Beach villa that had been placed at his disposal. But the prime minister could never relax completely. He studied reports of the damage to the *Queen Elizabeth* and the *Valiant*, and signaled Ismay that the precarious Mediterranean naval situation required the diversion of aircraft, especially torpedo bombers, from Bomber and Coastal Commands at home. He began preparing a fourth major paper on future strategy, which he completed on the train carrying him back to Washington on the 10th. In the European theater, he looked forward to the steady attrition of German air power, and to an Anglo-American occupation of French North Africa. About the Japanese war, there was a note of unwonted pessimism. Churchill recognized that the Japanese had the initiative throughout the ABDA area and would soon mop it all up, except, possibly, Singapore. How he expected it to resist in the face of Japanese sea and air power he did not say. Even his unflagging offensive spirit could find nothing more to recommend than large-scale commando raids against the Japanese. The whole section on the Pacific had a distinct "whistling in the dark" air, or, as the British official history put it, "Mr. Churchill's strategic flair was at its weakest when he lacked first-hand acquaintance with the theatre of operations."[54]   The prime minister arrived back in Washington to meet another blast from Curtin: "It is naturally disturbing to learn that the Japanese have been able to overrun so easily the whole of Malaya except Johore . . . . It is observed that the Eighth Australian Division is to be given the task of fighting the decisive battle . . . . I urge on you that nothing be left undone to reinforce Malaya . . . . I am particularly concerned in regard to air strength, as a repetition of the Greece and Crete campaigns would evoke a violent public reaction, . . ."[55] There was no real answer to any of this, and the prime minister's reply was both pugnacious and weak.

> I do not see how any one could expect Malaya to be defended once the Japanese obtained command of the sea and while we are fighting for our lives against Germany and Italy. The only vital point is Singapore Fortress and its essential hinterland . . . . I do not accept any censure about Crete and Greece. We are doing out utmost in the Mother Country to meet living perils and onslaughts. We have sunk all party differences and have imposed universal compulsory service, not only upon men, but women. We have suffered the agonising loss of two of our finest ships which we sent to sustain the Far Eastern war . . . . I hope therefore you will be considerate in the judgment which you pass upon those to whom Australian lives and fortunes are so dear.[56]

Much of this was true. That was the agony of Britain's, and Churchill's, position. There were not enough resources; choices had to be made. The Australians might well have retorted that all the hard choices were being made at their expense.

Shortly after sending his answer to Curtin, Churchill flew from Washington to Bermuda, on the first leg of his journey home. On the other side of the world, the Japanese entered Kuala Lumpur, halfway down the Malay peninsula, on the 11th — three days ahead of schedule.

iv

Churchill was away from London for a month. During that time the situation in Malaya steadily deteriorated. The initial series of disasters had been quickly followed by another one: the loss of the island of Penang. Situated only a few miles off the west coast of Malaya, Penang was the original British foothold in the area, occupied in 1784. It was also a "fortress" — that is, a naval anchorage with fixed defenses. Prewar plans had called for a two-battalion garrison if British forces had to withdraw from northern Malaya, a small enough force for an island of some two hundred square miles. In fact, the sole regular battalion there left at the outbreak of the war to join Krohcol. Only the troops manning the fixed defenses, the local Volunteer unit and two infantry companies, remained. The Japanese air blitz hit Georgetown, the island's principal town and port, on December 11 and 12. There was neither fighter defense nor antiaircraft cover. Half the town and much of the port was wrecked. Civilian casualties were very heavy, particularly during the first raid when the population turned out in the streets to watch. Most of the police force deserted, and nearly all the dock labor vanished, but about half the civil-defense and first-aid workers remained on the job. On the 12th the "Fortress Commander," Brigadier C. A. Lyon, and the senior civil administrator, Mr. Leslie Forbes, the resident counsellor, decided to evacuate European women and children, together with the patients at the military hospital, to the mainland. Some air cover was provided on the 13th, when Pulford ordered a Buffalo squadron up from Singapore to reoccupy the airfield at Butterworth. While it lasted, it provided a brief respite from absolute Japanese dominance of the skies. But it did not last very long, and by the 19th the squadron had been pushed back to airfields around Kuala Lumpur. Percival referred the future of Penang to Duff Cooper's War Council, which decided on the 14th that the island could not be held if III Corps fell back, and gave Heath the authority to evacuate the garrison and whatever stores could be removed, if he had to abandon northern Malaya. The Eleventh Indian Division was then occupying a position at Gurun, some fifteen miles south of Jitra. At 1:30 A.M. the next morning (December 15) the Japanese overran the headquarters of Murray-Lyon's Sixth Brigade. Only the brigadier, who was away at the time, survived. A battalion headquarters was also wiped out. The Japanese were only halted two miles behind the original front line. Murray-Lyon promptly ordered a seven-mile withdrawal. He planned to fall back still farther after dark on the 15th, putting another ten miles and a river between his troops and the enemy. Heath thereupon ordered Penang evacuated by the night of the 16th-17th, and Brigadier Lyon was ordered to put the "denial scheme" into effect. He had few troops, little time, and was working in a chaotic and panic-stricken atmosphere. Three thousand tons of tin ingots and alloys, admittedly rather difficult items to destroy, were left intact. The radio station was untouched, and the Japanese soon put it to good use. Twenty-four self-propelled craft and large numbers of junks and barges were left afloat in the harbor. This was the worst, and least understandable, mistake, for the Japanese were thereby presented with the means to mount improvised seaborne assaults against III Corps' long exposed flank down the west coast. British prestige was another major casualty, for it was the way in which the evacuation of the island was carried out, rather than the failure of the denial scheme, that gave rise to the most bitter recriminations.

The Far East War Council had discussed the near collapse of Penang's civil administration on December 13, and agreed that European women and children should be advised to leave and that others who wished to go should be allowed to do so, although Sir Shenton Thomas telegraphed Forbes that men should not be encouraged to leave. (Forbes and Lyon had, of course, anticipated most of this directive.) On the 15th, as the Eleventh Indian Division fell back, Percival urged the War Council to consider the great value of all European personnel, civil and military, to the war effort, and the governor agreed to inform the resident counsellor that as many Europeans as possible should be gotten away. Up to this point the discussion had apparently concerned those Europeans stationed on the island, and there had been general agreement on policy, although events on the spot were outstripping the deliberations in Singapore. Now the discussion shifted to the question of what ought to be done about the residents of Penang, both Asian and European. Immediately a breach opened between Duff Cooper and the military on the one hand, and the governor and his M.C.S. advisers on the other. According to his diary, the governor told the War Council that in any evacuation "we could not stand for racial discrimination, and anything of the sort might well lose us Malaya. Duff Cooper said he personally would give preference to Europeans over Asiatics though he would not say so publicly." Later in the discussion Sir Shenton remarked, "If we are going to win this war we must win it decently." The next day the argument continued. In his diary Sir Shenton noted that the War Council had been "rather heated," but in the end a telegram was sent to Forbes instructing him that "In any evacuation preference should be given to those who are essential to the war effort without racial discrimination." Duff Cooper was unhappy with the last three words but gave way. On December 17, according to the War Council minutes, Duff Cooper and Layton returned to the issue, demanding "that every effort should be made to evacuate white women and children in view of the bestiality and brutality of the Japanese," while the governor maintained his position: "no discrimination of races." Whatever might be said in Singapore however, had little influence on events in Penang. On the night of December 17-18, when the last of the four small ships that made up the evacuation fleet left the island, only the troops and the European civilians had been removed. Few knew of the argument in the War Council over evacuation policy, or that Brigadier Lyon had exceeded his instructions in pulling out the European residents (only three of whom chose to remain). The governor's anger over the resident counsellor's feeble performance was likewise not widely known. What was glaringly apparent was that, after 150 years of British rule, the Asian population of Penang was abandoned to its fate by European rulers who prided themselves on their disinterested guardianship over those they governed. The scuttle from Penang struck at the roots of the British claim to the loyalty of their subjects.

There can be no doubt that the evacuation of Penang was a psychological disaster of the first magnitude. It set an example that some Europeans were only too happy to follow, an example whose effect was never completely overcome. Years later Sir Shenton Thomas wrote that "Penang was a very discreditable affair and had a shocking effect on morale throughout Malaya." It was doubtless recognition of this fact that kept the argument about Penang rumbling on in the War Council even after the issue had become academic. At the meeting of December 20 Duff Cooper "stressed the grave danger of women and children being left behind — anyone who does not evacuate European women and children in time will carry a grave responsibility." Two days later Secretary for Defence Christopher Dawson of the M.C.S. read the Council a memorandum on the evacuation question, which stressed that the abandonment of the local population by the Europeans would have a catastrophic effect on both Asian morale and British prestige. Duff Cooper, replying, "considered that this view was profoundly wrong. The future of Malaya was infinitely small compared with winning the war. Our task was to defeat the enemy. People did not run away from Penang to save their skins; they came back in order to be of more use to their country in the war effort." That evening Duff Cooper announced in a broadcast that the population of Penang had been successfully evacuated before its fall. Sir Shenton noted despondently in his diary: "Everyone horrified . . . he was obviously thinking in terms of Europeans only. Very bad Asiatic reaction." The next morning the governor confronted Duff Cooper with this fact, but the resident minister was unrepentant. During the day a telegram arrived from the Colonial Office supporting the governor's stand against racial discrimination in any evacuations. Although he noted in his diary that he was "tickled to death" by London's support, it was really too late — the damage had already been done.[57]

There is another side of the picture, however, to set against the Penang disaster. There had been no prewar planning for the evacuation of British-ruled territories. Such an event must then have seemed unthinkable. No instructions had ever been issued to administrators about their responsibilities in such a situation, and certainly those at Penang were overwhelmed by events. Many accounts of the panic-stricken flight of Europeans from up-country Malaya are in fact based on what happened at Penang. Elsewhere evacuations seem to have been much more orderly, with many administrators and police officers leaving their posts only reluctantly or being overrun by the Japanese. Most European men had been mobilized into the Volunteer forces, and their local knowledge was invaluable throughout the campaign.[58] Undeniably fear of the Japanese was very strong among all Europeans, military and civilian alike, particularly after their initial successes. The conviction that European women must be saved at all costs from falling into Japanese hands was intense, especially in the resident minister and among the soldiers. But it should not be forgotten that it was through M.C.S. channels that the order was issued on the 16th that there ought to be no racial discrimination in any further evacuations from Penang. That the order was not obeyed was, in the circumstances, less significant than that it was given.

The rest of December, the rest of the campaign in fact, was a story of Japanese thrust followed by British withdrawal. Percival was never able to bring more than a fraction of his forces to bear against the main Japanese attack down the trunk road. Murray-Lyon's three brigades were worn down a little more in each successive battle and retreat. Malaya Command's best single unit, the Twelfth Brigade, had been broken up the minute fighting began. One battalion was railed to Kota Bharu to provide a reserve for Key's depleted Eighth Brigade, and the rest of the brigade was used to protect Eleventh Division's line of communications. By the time the Twelfth Brigade came under Murray-Lyon's command on the 17th, it only sufficed to make good some of his losses. The exhausted Sixth and Fifteenth Brigades were then withdrawn to rest, thus reducing the Eleventh Division temporarily to two under-strength brigades. The two brigades of Barstow's Ninth Division were still sprawled over eastern Malaya, hundreds of miles from divisional headquarters, each other, and the decisive battle. By the time the Eighth Brigade withdrew from Kota Bharu, and the Twenty-second from Kuantan, to concentrate in central Malaya, it was early January. Barstow's brigades had by that time suffered heavy losses in men and equipment. Then the Eleventh Division suffered yet another disaster on the west-coast road. By now Murray-Lyon had been replaced by Brigadier A.C.M. Paris of the Twelfth Brigade, and all the original brigadiers in the Eleventh Division had become casualties. On January 7 a Japanese armored column swept down the road and shattered the division again in what the official historians christened the "Slim River disaster." The immediate consequence was the loss of Kuala Lumpur, its airfields, and extensive supply dumps that could not be removed quickly enough. Percival's forces fell back to Johore, the last defensive position north of Singapore Island. Curtin had noted sarcastically that the defense of Johore had fallen to the Australians, but Gordon Bennett's two brigades were the only fresh formations available. In III Corps, the Eleventh Division had been virtually destroyed, and the Ninth seriously weakened. Before the first reinforcements reached Singapore, Malaya Command's losses in strength, cohesion, and morale were far greater than could be repaired by the arrival of one untried British and two very raw Indian brigades.

The strategy that had led to dispersion and piecemeal defeat has already been discussed. But a number of factors besides Percival's initial dispositions contributed to the devastating speed of the Japanese advance. After the first disasters in the north, Heath had suggested a long withdrawal back to Johore, buying time with space. Then the British could turn and meet the Japanese with their forces concentrated and within supporting distance of Singapore's airfields. Percival refused even to consider this because it would mean yielding airfields in central Malaya from which the Japanese could strike with great effect at the reinforcement convoys upon which all hope of restoring the situation rested. Heath's proposal was sound in the circumstances and would have fulfilled the Chiefs' of Staff desire for the "best possible delaying action." Instead the suggestion led Percival, dubious in any case about the Indian Army, to lose what confidence he had in III Corps. The Eleventh Division was committed to a slow withdrawal that led to speedy disaster. Churchill's instinct, expressed in his signal of December 15 to the Chiefs of Staff, was sounder here. Moreover, Heath's troops fought without air cover because Percival and Pulford decided to husband the remaining fighter squadrons to cover incoming convoys. Except for reconnaissance flights, the RAF abandoned the skies over the battlefield. Percival's failure to pull the two brigades of the Ninth Division out of eastern Malaya quickly so that the vital battle for the west-coast road could be fought by a united III Corps also contributed to the speed of the defeat. He seems to have been magnetized by the ill-sited airfields. In the event, Japanese got Kuantan, which the RAF had long abandoned, as soon as they were ready to take it, and the Twenty-second Brigade lost a third of its strength trying to hold it.

The governor noted in his diary on January 6, 1942: "We . . . have gone in for mechanized transport to the nth degree. It is a fearfully cumbersome method. We have pinned our faith to the few roads but the enemy uses the tracks and paths, and gets round to our rear very much as he likes."[59]   He had shrewdly identified one of the key factors in the destruction of III Corps, for the way the British were organized contributed to their defeat. Lavishly equipped with mechanical transport, they were completely road-bound. Tables of organization drawn up with Europe or the Middle East in mind lumbered units in Malaya with long columns of vehicles. These were ideal targets for Japanese aircraft, and the consequent stringing out of formations along roads also made them tactically sluggish and vulnerable to the standard Japanese tactic of pressing around an opponent and blocking his retreat. Time and again in Malaya, and later in Burma, having cut a road behind the British, the Japanese then forced them to abandon their vehicles and guns and to fight their way out. The loss of equipment and

supporting arms caused as much disorganization and demoral-
ization as the casualties that were sustained.

The Japanese divisions used in Malaya were not, as instant legend
had it, hardened jungle fighters. For one thing, the Japanese army
had never before done any jungle fighting. Two of the three divisions used in Malaya had, however, served in China, and all trained
hard for their Malayan venture, on Formosa, on Hainan Island off
the south China coast, and in Indochina. That they were not jungle
veterans was not very important because there was little true jungle
along the west-coast trunk road. Much of the land on either side of
the road was under intense cultivation — oil palm, rice, pineapple,
and, above all, rubber estates. Thus there was a network of estate
roads that were often used by the Japanese to bypass British positions on the trunk road. Nor was cross-country movement very
difficult, except for troops dependent on wheeled vehicles. The
Japanese advantages lay in other areas. They used veteran troops —
physically tough, confident, well trained, and aggressively led.
They had much greater tactical mobility and fewer administrative
units — and the latter could and did double as infantry. The Japanese had more bicycles and pack animals and fewer trucks than
their opponents. They had as well command of the air and sea,
the initiative, and the impetus that came from the knowledge that
they were winning. The Japanese were prepared for warfare in close
country — the British were not. All this was much more important
than any "fanaticism" on the part of the Japanese soldier. That
much-commented-upon quality helped to further unnerve raw
opponents, but by itself it could not produce victory, any more
than it could later avert defeat.

The eyes of the British army had been focused for decades on
western Europe, on the Northwest Frontier of India, and, latterly,
on the Middle East. "Bush warfare" was not much studied. The
only recent campaign of this type had been fought in East Africa
during the First World War. It had engaged few British or even
Indian units, and so hard was it to make sense of afterwards, the
official history of it was never completed. There were no training
establishments in Malaya, as there were in the Middle East, to produce and inculcate the tactical variations best suited to the country. Neither time nor staff were available. As a result, there were
no readily available counters to Japanese moves. Even if someone
had thought of the answer later discovered in Burma, it would not
have worked in Malaya, for that solution was heavily dependent
on the lavish provision of transport aircraft. It is also true that

many senior officers in Malaya had exaggerated notions of the in-
penetrability of the country off the main roads. This was doubtless because troops organized and trained like the British, Indian,
and Australian units in Malaya would have found such country
very difficult indeed. The Japanese were organized very differently, and the implications of this were not recognized until it was
too late.

For the first month of the war, the fighting was done by six
new and incompletely trained Indian Army brigades. The special
nature of the Indian Army must therefore be kept in mind. Unlike
the British or Australian soldier, the Indian soldiers' loyalty was
not to a nation state, or its ideology, and only in a shadowy sense
to the remote figure of the King-Emperor. Their allegiance was to
their unit, its traditions, and its officers. In this sense the Indian
Army was not modern at all. Everything depended on the ability
and character of the regimental officers. Many Indian units in
Malaya came, like the three Gurkha battalions of the Twenty-
eighth Brigade, from famous regiments, but they were newly
raised and prewar regulars were spread very thin. As these men
became casualties, unit cohesion and efficiency began to sag. It
was unfortunate that the burden of slowing the Japanese down
fell unremittingly on these raw Indian formations. A senior officer
with more knowledge of the Indian Army than Percival had,
and more respect for it, might have used his troops somewhat
differently. As it was, Heath's troops conducted a fighting retreat
averaging about ten miles a day for nearly two months, repeatedly
pulling themselves together after disaster, and the survivors remained capable of fighting to the very end on Singapore Island. If,
as the elder Moltke once said, a fighting retreat is the hardest test
any troops can face, the Indian soldiers who fought in Malaya,
and the officers who led them, deserve far more recognition than
they have ever received.[60]

While III Corps was slowly being destroyed, a series of command
changes took place in Singapore that did nothing to improve the
situation. Brooke-Popham was under sentence of dismissal when
the campaign began, and London then forgot him. He later commented, "I received no information from England regarding the
appointment of Mr. Duff Cooper or of the formation of the War
Council until I asked for it, and up to the time I left, no clear instructions had been issued as to what were intended to be the functions
of the War Council."[61] The War Council consisted of Duff Cooper,
the commander in chief, Sir Shenton Thomas, Percival, Pulford,

Layton, and Bowden. Gordon Bennett had the right to attend whenever he could make it: a reminder of special position of the Eighth Australian Division and its commander. The War Council might have been useful earlier; by the time it was put together it was too late to become more than another cog in an already clumsy machine. It consumed the time of terribly busy men and produced additional friction in an already bad situation. At the first meeting of the War Council, on December 10, there was a sharp clash over its powers between Duff Cooper and Brooke-Popham, in which the governor supported the commander in chief. Thenceforth both were in the resident minister's bad books. Then Sir Shenton and Duff Cooper clashed again over the evacuation of Penang. Relations between the resident minister on the one hand, and Brooke-Popham and Thomas on the other were very distant after these two episodes. Sir Shenton later wrote that he rarely saw Duff Cooper except at War Council meetings. Nor did the resident minister maintain close touch with Christopher Dawson, the secretary for defence. The governor could later recall only one request from Duff Cooper for government files. What Duff Cooper did do was regale dinner parties with imitations of the governor, the commander in chief, and the GOC, and canvas the opinions of the governor's subordinates about the desirability of replacing him. Sir Shenton Thomas later wrote that the difficulties he experienced with Duff Cooper "stemmed from his endeavours to magnify the responsibilities entrusted to him by the Prime Minister." A more detached observer reflected that "Duff Cooper . . . was a failed politician, exiled to Singapore with great responsibilities of the vaguest kind, no precise terms of reference and no authority. He quarreled with Brooke-Popham, and indeed took a dislike to most people in authority . . . because he found it irksome and frustrating to be sitting around with no special powers to do anything, and from the point of view of the others he was simply a nuisance, a fifth wheel." The responsibility for this state of affairs rested ultimately with London.

Duff Cooper's inability to understand the complexities of Malayan society made matters worse, as in the case of Penang, while the mood of frustration into which he rapidly drifted made him a ready listener to all complaints against the civil and military authorities (some dating from as far back as Sir Shenton Thomas's long leave). These he had the ability to bring to the attention of the prime minister himself.[62]   In cables to London, the governor claimed that Duff Cooper took many of his opinions on local matters from the *Straits Times*, and from F. D. Bisseker, leader of the "unofficial" members in the Legislative Council and a friend of Brigadier Simson's. Both were critics of the governor's administration.[63] Wherever he got them, the resident minister's opinions were almost universally condemnatory of everyone and everything in Malaya. "I feel bound to tell you," he cabled the Colonial Office early in January, "that in my opinion the Malayan Civil Service has failed lamentably in making adequate preparation for war." Of the governor his opinion was equally low: "he appears to have lost his grip on the situation."[64] By the hand of Captain Tennant of H.M.S. *Repulse* he sent home a long letter to the prime minister that is a fine sample of easy literary style applied to character assassination.

> Sir Robert Brooke-Popham is a very much older man than his years warrant and sometimes seems on the verge of nervous collapse. I fear also that knowledge of his own failing powers renders him jealous of any encroachment on his sphere of influence . . . . The Governor, Sir Shenton Thomas is one of those people who find it impossible to adjust their minds to war conditions. He is also the mouthpiece of the last person he speaks to . . . much influenced by his Colonial Secretary, a sinister figure called Stanley Jones who is universally detested in the Colony, where he is accused of having been defeatist since the beginning of the war . . . . General Percival is a nice, good man who began life as a schoolmaster. I am sometimes tempted to wish he had remained one. He is a good soldier, too — calm, clear-headed and even clever. But he is not a leader, he cannot take a large view; it is all a field day at Aldershot to him. He knows the rules so well and follows them so closely and is always waiting for the umpire's whistle to cease fire and hopes that when that moment comes his military dispositions will be such as to receive approval.[65]

When Churchill saw all this he minuted, "This is a shocking tale," but also shrewdly noted that Duff Cooper's prewar reports had contained no indication of such massive deficiencies.[66] By early January the press in the United Kingdom were savagely attacking the military and civil authorities in the Far East, without any serious contradiction from the government.[67] Such attacks may even have been welcome, since they distracted attention from Whitehall's role in the debacle. Many of these very partial views subsequently became enshrined in popular accounts of Singapore's fall.

At noon on December 23 Pownall finally reached Singapore and assumed command. He noted in his diary that Brooke-Popham was "pretty tired and quite out of business from dinner time onwards . . . he doesn't want it to look as if he had cleared off just when the war started." [68] This is less elegant but fairer than Duff Cooper's innuendos. Pownall spent Christmas and Boxing Day touring forward areas, while Brooke-Popham wound up his affairs. On Christmas Eve the departing commander in chief gave Pulford an order for distribution to all RAF units: "there appear to have been instances where aerodromes appear to have been abandoned in a state approaching panic . . . . This is utterly opposed to all the traditions of the air force formed over a period of 30 years." [69] He sent the Chiefs of Staff a Christmas reminder of where the responsibility for the disaster really lay: "The publicity given in the past to the flow of men and equipment to Malaya tends to obscure what was lacking . . . . Fully realize difficulties of many competing demands but desire that no one should assume local Commanders had all they wanted." [70] Brooke-Popham already realized that he was slated to be one of the chief scapegoats, along with Percival and Thomas. Duff Cooper's letter to Churchill was the opening shot. The Australian government sent Brooke-Popham a pleasant farewell telegram, but when Churchill asked, a few weeks later, if he could quote it in the Commons "in view of the violent and unjustified attacks which have been made upon him," the Australians refused. The message was "purely personal and valedictory." [71] They were not letting London off that easily. Brooke-Popham had to suffer in silence. About all that his papers contain in the way of official sympathy is a letter from Sir Archibald Clark-Kerr, the ambassador in Chungking: "It is all wrong that the people who try to carry out faithfully and patiently a policy, laid down from home, which they know (and say to those concerned) must lead to failure, should have to submit in silence to personal attacks." [72]

Pownall got back to Singapore on the 27th and promptly signaled Brooke, "Commanding Officer class has done well . . . Junior leaders raw . . . Heath is all right but not exciting . . . . Am much struck with distances here. When considering problems on small scale map, recommend having similar map of England alongside." To his diary he committed a more candid assessment. "They are immature troops and I suppose nobody below C.O.'s had ever before heard a bullet fired in anger . . . Heath is, I think, all right. He has aged a lot since I knew him in India, but that's ten years ago. He's not 'full of fire' but he does know what needs to be done to pull the troops around." Pownall had quickly spotted the tactical key to Japanese success: ". . . none of this country need stop good lightly equipped infantry."[74]

While Pownall was up-country, Simson had had another barren discussion with Percival. Arriving back in Singapore from Heath's headquarters late on the night of the 26th, he had gone to the GOC's residence and caught Percival just about to retire. Simson pressed Percival to give Heath's tired men the help of prepared field and especially antitank defenses as they fell back. To do this it was necessary to begin work immediately. Simson also pointed out to the GOC that time was running out for the construction of defenses on the north shore of Singapore Island itself. Percival refused to consider any of this. Defenses, he told his horrified chief engineer, were bad for the morale of soldiers and civilians alike. Therefore no defenses would be built on the north shore of the island, and none behind the battered III Corps. The argument between the two weary men became very heated. Then, after a long pause, Percival told Simson he could take up the matter of north shore defenses with Keith Simmons, the fortress commander. Simson immediately took advantage of this slight concession to press for prepared defenses in Johore into which Heath could retire. Percival still refused, and a weary and discouraged Simson left. Early the following morning he rang up Keith Simmons, who invited him to breakfast. Over the meal Simson tried to convince the fortress commander to sanction defenses on the north shore of the island. He pointed out that on the seaward front the defenses, already formidable, were being further strengthened by the erection of tubular scaffolding to prevent amphibious landings. On the north shore, more immediately threatened and completely undefended, nothing was being done. Keith Simmons was adamant: no landward defenses. Under prodding from Simson the fortress commander produced the same rationale as Percival. Defenses were bad for morale. "I finally left the Fortress Commander's house convinced that Singapore was as good as lost," Simson later wrote. The strangest part of this story is that on December 29 Percival wrote to Gordon Bennett and Heath suggesting that defenses should be built up-country, but by the civilian Public Works Department, which had no experience whatsoever in this sort of work, as well as a great many other things to do. The GOC did not inform his Chief Engineer of this curious reversal; Simson only discovered it when the official history was published, sixteen years later.

It is hard to make sense of all this. The safest assumption is that
Percival really believed that defenses were bad for morale and that
Keith Simmons was echoing his views. Simson was consistently un-
lucky in his relations with his superiors, who may have found his
personality and determination irritating. But Percival's orders on
the 29th, entrusting the Malayan PWD with the construction of
defenses, is very hard to fathom. Later on, as Percival and Simson
paced together in a Japanese prison camp, Percival admitted that
he had been wrong.[75]

On New Year's Eve Brooke-Popham left Singapore. In the War
Council Duff Cooper rammed through a measure making Simson
director general of Civil Defence with plenary powers. A subsequent attempt by Sir Shenton Thomas to curtail these had little
practical effect, and Simson was left to do the best he could, far
too late to make any real difference.[76] Pownall reflected in his
diary, "there wasn't a war here till recently and they obviously
took a chance on it — and lost the gamble." He also noted that
"something very akin to combined command of air and land forces
of all the allies (including Australia) is badly wanted. That cannot
be exercised from here, . . . It must be close to the center of the
arc, I think Java."[77]

Unknown to Pownall, such a rearrangement was taking shape
even as he wrote. Wavell had accepted his appointment as ABDA
supreme commander that day. The following day he cabled London that India had suffered greatly "from lack of regular and
rapid intercommunication" with Great Britain and expressed the
hope that this would now change.[78] He followed this rap on the
collective knuckles of the prime minister and Chiefs of Staff with
a further message on January 2, pointing out that he had received
no further instructions, no appreciation of the situation, and
no indication of the forces available. He added that he doubted
whether anything beyond the line Port Darwin — Timor — Java —
southern Sumatra — Singapore could now be held. But Wavell,
whose offensive spirit was as unflagging as Churchill's, was already
thinking about a counterstroke against the Japanese. The margin
of shipping available to support their operations was believed to be
small, he noted. Air and submarine attacks could erode this, while
other air strikes could cost Japan irreplaceable planes: "Understand
Japanese aeroplane industry not highly developed and that they
may have difficulty in replacing wastage."[79] Wavell's comparative
optimism would get a rude jolt within days. On January 3 the new
supreme commander finally got his directive, while the prime min-

ister cabled Pownall informing him of the creation of ABDA and the consequent winding up of Far East Command. After barely ten days as commander in chief, Pownall was now told he would be Wavell's chief of staff. Churchill also told Pownall to inform Duff Cooper, Percival, Pulford, and Layton about the new arrangements.[80]

The first convoy of reinforcements reached Singapore on January 3, covered by Pulford's attenuated squadrons. It carried Brigadier H. C. Duncan's Forty-fifth Brigade from the Seventeenth Indian Division. The brigade had been formed at Poona in western India in the summer of 1941, where it was trained exclusively for the Middle East. The "ancillary units" (transport, guns, etc.) had all been raised from scratch in the autumn of 1941. Brigade signals were not complete until just before it sailed. Bad as this was, it was worsened by the extensive milking that the brigade underwent in the summer and autumn of 1941 to provide cadre for further expansion. Nearly half of each battalion was consequently made up of raw recruits, many under eighteen and with only four or five months' training. The battalions had been bled of experienced Indian warrant officers and N.C.O.'s, and of potential N.C.O.'s as well. There were about three regular Indian Army officers per battalion, the balance being fresh from England with little knowledge of Indian troops. The divisional commander, Major General J. G. Smyth, V.C., had asked Brigadier D. T. Cowan, the director of military training at GHQ, India, to come up to Poona and look at his brigades. Cowan promptly agreed that in their current shape they were unfit to meet anything but a second-class enemy, and promised that when they reached Iraq they would have six weeks of intensive training. Then came the Japanese attack. Duncan's brigade went to Malaya, followed by Brigadier G. C. Ballentine's equally raw Forty-fourth Brigade. Less than three weeks after reaching Singapore, the Forty-fifth Brigade was to be annihilated by the Japanese.[81]

Churchill cabled Duff Cooper on the 6th informing him that the creation of ABDACOM brought his appointment to an end and ordering him home. At dawn on January 7 Wavell reached Singapore. He found Pownall waiting for him, and a reply from the Chiefs of Staff in London to his signal of the 2nd. Despite the list of divisions they had produced on New Year's Day, they could not tell Wavell what forces would be available to him, and therefore could not give him the appreciation for which he had asked. They felt, though, that the Japanese shipping position was not as tight

as Wavell believed. Then they added that he ought to be able to
hold all of Sumatra. After this auspicious beginning, Wavell spent
a day in Singapore, and then flew up to visit III Corps, where he
arrived the day after the Slim River disaster. "I have never seen
men look so tired," his A.D.C. wrote after meeting two Eleventh
Division brigadiers. When he returned to Singapore that evening,
he signaled London that III Corps was on its last legs. He also summoned Percival, kept him waiting for some time in an anteroom,
then called him in and handed him an operational instruction that
he had written out. He did not discuss it with the GOC, but made
it clear that it was to be put into effect forthwith. Briefly, the
Eighth Australian Division, the only fresh formation available,
would be put in charge of the defensive stand in northern Johore.
Gordon Bennett would take under command the newly arrived
Forty-fifth Brigade and the Ninth Division, which would be brought
up to strength with the few remaining combat-worthy units of the
Eleventh Division. Heath would withdraw III Corps and the
shattered Eleventh Division to southern Johore to rest and reor-
ganize. Wavell's plan has been criticized, but at least it took the
pressure off III Corps, which he correctly realized was on the
verge of collapse.[82]   Why Wavell treated Percival so brusquely is
not clear, but one clue may be found in Pownall's diary entry for
January 8: "[Percival] is an uninspiring leader and rather gloomy
(as he was in France when BGS to I Corps)."[83] Wavell had probably absorbed his chief of staff's negative view of Percival. The
supreme commander was, in any case, as determined an exponent
of "positive thinking" as the prime minister. Wavell then flew on
to Java to grapple with the next set of intractable problems in
his impossible command. But what he had seen in Singapore had
clearly shaken him, for on the 13th he flew back. That same day,
aided by low cloud and rain, the second reinforcement convoy
arrived safely. It brought in the Eighteenth Division's Fifty-third
Brigade, two antiaircraft regiments, an antitank regiment, and,
most important of all, the fifty-one Hurricanes.[84] But the Hurricanes had still to be unpacked, erected, and tested, and a week
would elapse before they were ready. The pilots also had to adjust to the new conditions in which they found themselves.
Wavell motored to the front and on his return cabled London,
"Battle for Singapore will be a close run thing . . . ." He was also
engaged in a lengthy telegraphic exchange with London about replacing Shenton Thomas with a military governor. In the end the
Colonial Office successfully defended Thomas, who remained, but

Jones, who had become a bête noire to the military, was sacked on the 16th in a telegram from the Colonial Office conveying Churchill's orders for his compulsory retirement.[85]

On the 14th Wavell returned to Java. There he received a personal signal from the prime minister.

> Please let me know your idea of what would happen in the event of your being forced to withdraw into Singapore Island . . . . What are defences and obstructions on landward side? Are you sure that you can dominate with fortress cannon any attempt to plant siege batteries . . . . It has always seemed to me that vital need is to prolong defence of island to last possible minute, but of course I hope it will not come to this.[86]

Back went an answer that Churchill read "with pained surprise."

> Until quite recently all plans based on repulsing seaborne attack on island and holding land attack in Johore or further north, and little or nothing was done to construct defences on north side of island to prevent crossing Johore Strait, . . . Fortress cannon of heaviest nature have all-round traverse but their flat trajectory makes them unsuitable for counterbattery work. Could certainly not guarantee to dominate enemy siege batteries with them. Supply situation unsatisfactory.[87]

This finally pricked the bubble. There was no "Singapore Fortress."

v

The prime minister returned from America to meet a storm of criticism. He faced the only sustained political challenge of the war during the first half of 1942, the inevitable consequence of the succession of hammerblows inflicted on British arms in every theater from December 1941 until Alamein eleven long months later.[88] In the face of military defeat, press criticism, and parliamentary challenge, Churchill struggled persistently, and in the end successfully, to bend the Anglo-American strategy into the shape he wanted for 1942 — the descent on French North Africa, Gymnast, later renamed *Torch*. It was one of his most remarkable and impressive performances. But it left little time or patience for anything else.

Meanwhile the Japanese ground inexorably onwards. Smyth and the headquarters of the Seventeenth Indian Division arrived in Rangoon on January 9. On the 15th, as Churchill made a hazardous flight back across the Atlantic, the first of the Hurricanes that had arrived, crated, at Singapore only forty-eight hours before took to the air. The following day Smyth's only brigade, the Forty-sixth, reached Rangoon. Now even India had nothing left. Curtin marked the prime minister's return to London with another sharpish cable on the 18th. For years Malaya's defenses had been neglected because London had been unduly complacent about the Far East, he told Churchill. The prime minister angrily replied the next day that he bore no responsibility for the policy of prewar British governments, and then repeated what was by now his standard defense.

> I deemed the Middle East a more urgent theatre than the newly created A.B.D.A. area. We also had to keep our promises to Russia of munitions deliveries. No one could tell what Japan would do, but I was sure if she attacked us and you the United States would enter the war and that the safety of Australia and ultimate victory would be assured . . . . I am sure it would have been wrong to send forces needed to beat Rommel to reinforce the Malay peninsula while Japan was still at peace. To try and be safe everywhere is to be strong nowhere . . . . No one could foresee the series of major naval disasters which befell us and the United States around the turn of the year 1941-42.

Only now, as a "deadly secret," did Churchill tell the Australians about the loss of the *Barham* and the damage to the *Queen Elizabeth* and the *Valiant*.[89]

On the day he sent this, Churchill had awakened to face Wavell's signal of the 16th. It ranked with Reynaud's early morning call and Pound's announcement of the loss of Phillips's ships for shock value. Even as he digested its unwelcome contents, another message was on its way from the supreme commander warning the prime minister that, once Johore was lost, Singapore could not hold out for long.[90] The prime minister reacted to the news that Singapore was "a battleship . . . without a bottom" in a very sharp minute to the Chiefs of Staff: "I must confess to being staggered by Wavell's telegram of the 16th . . . . It never occurred to me for a moment, nor to Sir John Dill, . . . that . . . Singapore . . . was not entirely fortified against an attack from northward . . . . What is the use of having an island for a fortress if it is not to be made into a citadel? . . . How is it that not one of you pointed this out to me at any time when these matters have been under discussion? More especially should this have been done because in my various minutes extending over the last two years I have repeatedly shown that I relied upon this defence of Singapore Island against a formal siege . . . . I warn you this will be one of the greatest scandals that could possibly be exposed. Let a plan be made at once to do the best possible . . . ."[91] He told the War Cabinet that same day that "he was prepared to take upon himself the full responsibility for the political decisions which had governed the size of our forces in Malaya at the outbreak of war with Japan. There were however certain matters connected with the defence of Malaya that called for enquiry."[92] That same day in Singapore, the governor wrote in his diary: "Police view is Chinese will not panic under [air] raids but 90 percent think Singapore will fall."[93]

The following day, January 20, the Chiefs of Staff cabled instructions to Wavell that Singapore was to be held as long as possible, and Churchill reinforced these by unequivocal orders of his own. In his minute to the Chiefs of Staff he had already indicated that the Singapore garrison must fight to the end. Now he told Wavell that there could be no question of a surrender until after Singapore's defenders had made a desperate stand amid the city's ruins.[94] In Singapore on that same day, 232 Squadron RAF, with eighteen Hurricanes, was ready for action, and none too soon, for the Japanese were now raiding the city continually. But the Hurricanes, from which so much was hoped, proved a disappointment. The Hurricane Mark II was slower and less maneuverable than the Zero below 20,000 feet, and the newly arrived pilots were not yet accustomed to Far Eastern conditions. They were also terribly outnumbered. On the day of the squadron's debut, three of its planes were lost. Wavell paid a flying visit to Singapore on that day, and gave Percival authorization for a withdrawal from Johore to the island, as well as orders for Singapore's defense. He correctly guessed that the island's northwestern shore was the danger spot. So had Brigadier Simson. Percival believed, however, that the northeast was a more likely site for a Japanese landing, and he disposed his troops accordingly.[95]

Even as orders went out for a last-ditch stand on Singapore Island, there were crosscurrents in London. Churchill had come back from the United States deeply impressed by the importance of China in American eyes and the necessity of deferring to his allies' obsession on the subject. He minuted to Ismay on the 20th that keeping the

Burma Road open was more important than holding Singapore.[96]
The next day he asked the Chiefs of Staff whether "we should not
at once blow the docks and batteries and workshops to pieces and
concentrate everything on the defence of Burma and keeping open
the Burma Road . . . ." Not only would this preserve the link to
China, the prime minister argued, but success in Burma would offset the shock to Indian opinion of Singapore's fall, which he now
clearly expected. The same day he took the matter up with the
Defence Committee. "It was now apparent that we could not consider Singapore as a fortress . . . it was possible that a prolonged
defence of Singapore Island could not be made." He then emphasized the importance of Burma. The Eighteenth Division, minus
the brigade already in Malaya, was still on its way from Bombay
to Singapore, in consequence of orders given by the Chiefs of Staff
at the beginning of the month. It was not too late to divert it to
Rangoon. But to do so would be, said Churchill, "an ugly decision." Neither the Chiefs of Staff nor the Defence Committee
were quite ready to face it that day.[97] In Malaya the RAF began
to evacuate its last airfields on the mainland during the 21st, and
in the skies over Singapore 232 Squadron lost two more Hurricanes. Brigadier Duncan died trying to lead the shattered remnants
of his Forty-fifth Brigade out of a Japanese encirclement, and, in
North Africa, Rommel opened a counteroffensive against Auchinleck.

Churchill's instinct about Burma was probably sound, as it had
been about the dangers of a slow withdrawal down the Malay
peninsula. There was enough on its way east — the balance of the
Eighteenth Division, the Hurricanes in H.M.S. *Indomitable*, and
the Seventh Armoured Brigade — to make the chances of holding
Burma much better if it had all been diverted to Rangoon at this
point. And success in Burma would at least have offset to some
extent the blows already inflicted on British prestige in Asia. There
can be no certainty, of course, that Burma would have been saved.
But it is hard to believe that a concentration of everything available on saving Burma would have produced in the end a worse
military result. The issue, however, was not to be decided by military considerations.

Sir Earle Page, the Australian special envoy in London, did not
attend Chiefs of Staff meetings, and Churchill had carefully not
invited him to the Defence Committee's meeting on the 21st, but
he nevertheless discovered what had been discussed. Page cabled
his government that the British were considering the evacuation of

Singapore. This was not completely accurate, but it led to an immediate emergency meeting of the Australian War Cabinet. On the 22nd Auchinleck's troops began to retreat, while in Malaya the third reinforcement convoy arrived. It brought in Ballentine's Forty-fourth Brigade and seven thousand green Indian replacements. Flying cover for it, 232 Squadron lost five more Hurricanes. Four Buffaloes were lost as well.[98]

January 23 brought a very stiff telegram from Curtin.

> Page has reported that the Defence Committee has been considering evacuation of Malaya and Singapore. After all the assurances we have been given, the evacuation of Singapore would be regarded here and elsewhere as an inexcusable betrayal . . . . the Australian people, having volunteered for service overseas in large numbers, find it difficult to understand why they must wait so long for an improvement in the situation when irreparable damage may have been done to their power to resist, the prestige of Empire and the solidarity of the Allied cause.[99]

Simultaneously, as if to underline that there was nothing left for Burma but the Eighteenth Division, a signal arrived in London from General Sir Alan Hartley, Wavell's successor as commander in chief in India. It pointed out that the Indian Army had finally reached the bottom of the barrel. No new formations would be ready for overseas service until mid-summer, and then only if Britain provided equipment. Nevertheless, as a desperation measure, one brigade of the brand-new Nineteenth Indian Division was preparing for Burma.[100]

"It is not true to say that Mr. Curtin's message decided the issue," Churchill later wrote. But in fact it did. Neither the War Cabinet nor the Defence Committee discussed the destination of the Eighteenth Division again. Opinion in London swung against appearing to abandon the struggle for Singapore. Not only had Australian views to be considered, but, Churchill felt, the reaction in the United States to "a British 'scuttle' while the Americans fought on so stubbornly at Corregidor was terrible to imagine."[101] Yet Churchill did not give up without one last try. "There is no doubt what a purely military decision should have been," he wrote. He sent Wavell a cable on the 23rd about the defense of Burma and the Burma Road. "I must enlighten you upon the American view," the prime minister told him, "China bulks as large in the minds of many of them as Great Britain . . . . If I can epitomize in one word the lesson I learned in the United States, it was 'China' "[102] This attempt to push Wavell into doing what no one in London dared to — if that is what it was — failed. Wavell, after all, had been told only three days before to defend Singapore to the bitter end. He was trying to cobble together a defense against Japan along an arc from Rangoon to Timor, and every minute that Singapore held out bought time. And Wavell knew as well as anyone about Australian views. "Wavell said when he was first appointed that the Australians would be the most 'difficult' of our allies," Pownall noted on the 25th. Wavell allowed the convoys carrying the Eighteenth Division to steam on.[103]

On January 24, as Rommel drove ahead and preliminary measures were taken for the evacuation of Benghazi, the fourth reinforcement convoy, carrying an Australian machine-gun battalion and 1,900 completely untrained reinforcements, reached Singapore. The following day the prime minister had to turn to the political crisis, which was coming to a head. He entertained Sir Stafford Cripps, until recently British ambassador in Moscow, and the favorite of the Labour left wing, to lunch at Chequers and offered him the position of minister of supply. On the 27th the Commons opened a three-day debate on the conduct of the war. Churchill knew that his safest course was to challenge his ill-assorted opponents to open combat. In a two-hour speech he ranged over the entire war. About the Far East he demonstrated an attitude that can best be summed up in one of his own phrases: "responsible but unrepentant."

> While facing Germany and Italy here and in the Nile Valley, we have never had any power to provide effectively for the defence of the Far East . . . . There never has been, there never could have been a moment, when Great Britain or the British Empire, single handed, could fight Germany and Italy, . . . and at the same time stand thoroughly prepared in Burma, the Malay Peninsula, and generally in the Far East . . . . The decision was taken to make our contribution to Russia, to try to beat Rommel, and to form a stronger front from the Levant to the Caspian . . . . For this decision in its broad strategic aspect . . . . I take the fullest personal responsibility.[104]

This, of course, like many of the prime minister's statements on the Far East, glossed over a number of questions, but it worked. The House, Churchill wrote, accepted his arguments unenthusiastically. That evening there was a War Cabinet meeting. Page was present, and the prime minister clearly showed his anger at the unabashed Australian for what he had done.[105] Two days later Churchill's political strategy was vindicated. He won a vote of confidence in the House, 464 to 1. Temporarily strengthened, he could then receive with relative equanimity Cripp's refusal to join the government without a seat in the War Cabinet.

On the day of the prime minister's parliamentary triumph, the main body of the Eighteenth Division reached Singapore, too late for the fighting on the mainland. Trained for the Middle East, it had been sent east on the assumption that it would have time for further training in Egypt before being committed to battle. Wavell paid another visit to Percival on the 30th. He approved plans for the final withdrawal to the Island, and ordered the evacuation of the naval base and the removal to Sumatra of all aircraft except eight Hurricanes and six Buffaloes. The Hurricanes on their way from the Middle East in H.M.S. *Indomitable* would now be diverted to Java.[106] The supreme commander then returned to his headquarters in Java. On the night of January 30-31, the last troops filed over the causeway that linked the Island to the mainland. The fighting in Johore had destroyed two Indian brigades, and another had lost all its transport and guns. Two Australian battalions had been savaged, and the newly arrived Fifty-third Brigade had been reduced in strength as well. The last unit to cross was the Argylls, marching as if on parade with their two remaining pipers playing them over. Then the causeway was blown. It was typical of everything that had happened in the Far East that the breach was not quite complete.

Auchinleck's withdrawal in North Africa continued with heavy losses. Malta was under renewed attack. Despite his victory on the 29th, Churchill knew that he would soon have to reshuffle his government. The Japanese invasion of Burma, which had begun in earnest on the 20th, was making alarming progress. Singapore the prime minister had written off, probably the moment he got Wavell's cable of the 16th. Maximum resistance, as much for its political value as for its military utility, was his aim now. He also wanted to insure that the Japanese inherited a wasteland. On February 2 he minuted to the Chiefs of Staff that the naval base should be so thoroughly wrecked that it would be useless for at least eighteen months. He also expressed concern at the consequences in India of the massive defeats that the Raj was sustaining, telling Ismay on the same day that it was urgent to reinforce India: "It will be necessary to have an additional number of British troops in India. These need not be fully formed divisions, as they are for internal security against revolt."[107] Churchill's basic distrust of the Indian Army (which was unmoved by the revolt when it came in August 1942) was seldom so clearly shown. The prime minister also demanded figures on "British and other" casualties sustained in Malaya, for it had become politically important to show the *British* contribution in the Far East.[108]

Wavell had been called to Burma on February 4 by the rapidly worsening situation there. After visiting Smyth's headquarters and examining the terrain, he made a crucial decision. The Seventh Armoured Brigade was still on its way to Malaya from the Middle East. Wavell now diverted it to Rangoon. It would prove to be the salvation of the British forces in Burma during their long retreat.[109] While Wavell was in Burma, the convoy carrying the last of the Eighteenth Division reached Singapore on February 5. Of all the reinforcement convoys, only this one, incredibly, sustained any loss. The S.S. *Empress of Asia*, lagging behind because part of its civilian crew was on the verge of mutiny, was caught by Japanese bombers and sunk. Most of the troops were rescued, but the antitank guns and equipment that the liner carried were lost. At ABDA headquarters in Java, Pownall noted, "if the Island were really defensible from the North we should be able to hold it for a long time. But my very private opinion is that it is not so defensible . . . . The urge to defend the island from the north only started some three weeks ago."[110] The next day his tireless chief returned from Burma. The following night (February 8-9) the Japanese assault on Singapore opened, on the northwest shore of the island, as Wavell, and Simson, had guessed it would. Wavell prepared for another journey.

On February 10, the day he sent Wavell the savage order (already quoted) for Singapore's garrison to go down fighting[111] the prime minister presided over the opening session of the Pacific War Council. Put together partly to soothe the sore feelings of Australia, New Zealand, and the Dutch at their exclusion from the Combined Chiefs of Staff, and partly at the insistence of the King (who was far more alarmed than his prime minister by dominion anger), it met four times each in February and March and then dribbled away into its intended insignificance.[112] In Singapore the last fighter departed for Sumatra. The naval base, hastily evacuated but not wrecked by the navy, was being looted, while at the same time the Eleventh Division's engineers and parties of Volunteers worked to demolish as much as possible.[113] That evening Wavell paid a farewell call on the governor. "He sat in our sitting room," Sir Shenton noted in his diary, "thumping his knees with his fists and saying 'It shouldn't have happened' over and over again." Lady Thomas, who was ill, declined Wavell's offer to take her with him to Java, and the supreme commander left shortly after midnight February 10-11, 1942. Forty-eight hours after Wavell returned from his last visit to Singapore, his chief of staff noted: "13 February (and a Friday). Singapore is on its last legs."[114] That afternoon Percival met his senior commanders for their penultimate conference at Fort Canning.

Notes to Chapter 8

1. Winston S. Churchill, *The Second World War*, vol. 3, *The Grand Alliance* (Boston: Houghton Mifflin, 1950), p. 832. Tests carried out in Burma during the autumn of 1941 showed how inferior the Buffalo was to the Tomahawk, the plane the A.V.G. planned to match against the Zero. Air Chief Marshal Sir Robert Brooke-Popham, "Operations In The Far East From 17th October 1940 to 27th December 1941," *Supplement to the London Gazette*, January 22, 1948, par. 26 (cited hereafter as Brooke-Popham, *Dispatch*).

2. Churchill, *The Grand Alliance*, p. 606.

3. J. R. M. Butler, ed., *History of the Second World War: United Kingdom Military Series*, "Campaigns" series, S. W. Kirby et al., *The War Against Japan*, vol. 2, *India's Most Dangerous Hour* (London: H.M.S.O., 1958), p. 16.

4. J. Connell, *Wavell: The Supreme Commander 1941-1943* (London: Collins, 1969), pp. 52-57.

5. B. Bond, ed., *Chief of Staff: The Diaries of Lieutenant-General Sir Henry Pownall*, 2 vols. (London: Leo Cooper Ltd., 1973-74), 2: 67.

6. S. W. Kirby et al., *The War Against Japan*, vol. 1, *The Loss of Singapore* (London: H.M.S.O., 1957), pp. 255-56; idem, *India's Most Dangerous Hour*, p. 15.

7. Connell, *Wavell: The Supreme Commander*, pp. 60-61.

8. Ibid., pp. 61-64; Kirby et al., *India's Most Dangerous Hour*, pp. 17-19. The account of the December 22-23 Chungking meeting in Barbara Tuchman's widely read *Stilwell and the American Experience in China 1911-1945* (New York: Macmillan, 1971), pp. 236-37, must, like all of Tuchman's descriptions of British actions and motivations, be treated with extreme caution. See also Butler, ed., *History of the Second World War*, "Grand Strategy" series, vol. 3, J. M. A. Gwyer and J. R. M. Butler, *Grand Strategy (June 1941-August 1942)*, 2 pts. (London: H.M.S.O., 1964), pt. 2, pp. 411-12.

9. Kirby et al., *India's Most Dangerous Hour*, pp. 19-20. Connell, *Wavell: The Supreme Commander*, does not discuss the question of Wavell's actions in connection with the Chinese supplies in Rangoon.

10. Churchill, *The Grand Alliance*, pp. 637-38. Italics mine.

11. Ibid., p. 638.

12. A. Bryant, ed., *The Turn of the Tide 1939-1943: A History of the War Years based on the Diaries of Field-Marshal Lord Alanbrooke* (New York: Doubleday, 1957),

p. 222. Bryant is here quoting from Brooke's postwar "Notes on my Life." The Alanbrooke Papers are in the Liddell Hart Centre for Military Archives at King's College, London, but are not yet open.

13. Kirby et al., *The Loss of Singapore*, pp. 253 fn., 254, 257; Connell, *Wavell: The Supreme Commander*, p. 57.

14. Kirby et al., *The Loss of Singapore*, pp. 254, 257; Bond, ed., *Chief of Staff*, 2: 97. Bryant, ed., *Turn of the Tide*, p. 236.

15. Public Record Office (PRO), CAB 69, D.O. (41) 40, memo by VCNS, December 14, 1941.

16. PRO, CAB 69, D.O. (41) 72, December 19, 1941; the COS paper is in ibid., D.O. (41) 40.

17. Bryant, ed., *Turn of the Tide*, p. 229.

18. Kirby et al., *The Loss of Singapore*, p. 256.

19. PRO, PREM 3, 169/2, Churchill to Auchinleck, December 26, 1941.

20. Ibid., Auchinleck to Churchill, December 29, 1941; Kirby et al.,*The Loss of Singapore*, p. 257; Butler, ed., *History of the Second World War*, "Campaigns" series, I. S. O. Playfair et al., *The Mediterranean and Middle East*, 6 vols. (London: H.M.S.O., 1954-), 3: 125.

21. Gwyer and Butler, *Grand Strategy III*, pt. 2, p. 456.

22. PRO, CAB 69, D.O. (41) 75, December 27, 1941.

23. Bryant, ed., *The Turn of the Tide*, p. 229.

24. Ibid., p. 230.

25. *Australia in the War of 1939-45:* (Series I (Army), vol. 4, L. Wigmore, *The Japanese Thrust* (Canberra: Australian War Memorial, 1957), p. 183.

26. Ibid.

27. Churchill, *The Grand Alliance*, pp. 668-69.

28. Wigmore, *The Japanese Thrust*, p. 183.

29. Lt. Gen. Sir Ian Jacob, G.B.E., in conversation with the author, December 12, 1973.

30. Churchill, *The Grand Alliance*, pp. 652-55; "Notes on the Pacifie" are also reproduced in full in Gwyer and Butler, *Grand Strategy III*, pt. 1, pp. 329-34.

31. Charles, Lord Moran, *Churchill: The Struggle for Survival 1940-1965* (Boston: Houghton Mifflin, 1966), pp. 9-10.

32. Gwyer and Butler, *Grand Strategy III*, pt. 2, pp. 340-44. For an American criticism of Ironclad, see Samuel Eliot Morison, *Strategy and Compromise* (Boston: Atlantic Little, Brown, 1958), p. 25, where Morison characterizes the operation as "extraneous and unnecessary."

33. Gwyer and Butler, *Grand Strategy III*, pt. 1, pp. 344-48.

34. Moran, *Churchill: The Struggle for Survival*, p. 11. Sir Ian Jacob, who was the prime minister's party, said much the same thing to the author.

35. Gwyer and Butler, *Grand Strategy III*, pt. 1, p. 369.

36. Moran, *Churchill: The Stuggle for Survival*, pp. 17-18. Churchill describes the incident (*The Grand Alliance*, p. 691) but puts it on January 5 — after the main business of the conference was over.

37. Winston S. Churchill, *The Second World War*, vol. 4, *The Hinge of Fate* (Boston: Houghton Mifflin, 1950), p. 9.

38. Sir Ian Jacob's diary of the Arcadia conference, p. 22.

39. Churchill, *The Hinge of Fate*, pp. 4-5. In fact, there was conscription for home defense.

40. Moran, *Churchill: The Struggle for Survival*, pp. 20-21; Interview with Lt. Gen. Sir Ian Jacob, June 7, 1975.

41. Churchill, *The Grand Alliance*, p. 673.

42. Bryant, ed., *The Turn of the Tide*, p. 235.

43. Gwyer and Butler, *Grand Strategy III*, pt. 1, pp. 370-71; Churchill, *The Grand Alliance*, pp. 675-76.

44. Connell, *Wavell: The Supreme Commander*, p. 69.

45. Connell, *Wavell: The Supreme Commander*, p. 71.

46. Churchill, *The Grand Alliance*, p. 677.

47. Churchill, *The Grand Alliance*, p. 686.

48. Connell, *Wavell: The Supreme Commander*, p. 78.

49. Gwyer and Butler, *Grand Strategy III*, pt. 1, pp. 376-77; Tuchman, *Stilwell*, pp. 240-46.

50. Gwyer and Butler, *Grand Strategy III*, pt. 1, p. 373.

51. Churchill, *The Hinge of Fate*, pp. 9-10.

52. Gwyer and Butler, *Grand Strategy III*, pt. 2, p. 407; Kirby et. al., *The Loss of Singapore*, pp. 259-60.

53. *Australia in the War of 1939-45:* Series I (Army), vol. 2, G. Long, *Greece, Crete and Syria* (Canberra: Australian War Memorial, 1953), pp. 549-50.

54. Churchill, *The Grand Alliance*, pp. 700-704; Gwyer and Butler, *Grand Strategy III*, pt. 2, p. 413.

55. Churchill, *The Hinge of Fate*, p. 10.

56. Ibid., pp. 11-12.

57. The fall of Penang is discussed in Kirby et al., *The Loss of Singapore*, pp. 218-19, and in S. W. Kirby, *Singapore: The Chain of Disaster* (New York: Macmillan, 1971), pp. 155-57. In unraveling this obscure episode I have also used Sir Shenton Thomas, Outline Diary, December 19, 23, 1941, "Comments on the Draft History of the War Against Japan," October 1954, pars. 102-4, Thomas Papers, Rhodes House Library, Oxford; idem, Diary, December 13-16, 22, 23, 1941, Far East War Council Minutes, December 13-22, 1941, Thomas Papers, in the possession of Professor Hugh Thomas. Interviews with Mr. A. H. P. Humphrey, C.M.G., June 1, 1975 and Mr. H. P. Bryson, June 12, 1975, were also of great help.

58. Sir W. Goode, G.C.M.G., letter to the author, January 5, 1974, and Mr. A. H. P. Humphrey, letter to the author, February 3, 1974, made observations of great value about the general attitude of European administrators and civilians during the campaign.

59. Sir Shenton Thomas, Diary, January 6, 1942, Thomas Papers, in the possession of Professor Hugh Thomas.

60. Kirby et al., *The Loss of Singapore*, pp. 229-49, 269-89, 301-46, covers the withdrawal down the penisula. See also Kirby, *Singapore: The Chain of Disaster*, pp. 152-87, 197-212, and I. Simson, *Singapore: Too Little, Too Late* (London: Leo Cooper Ltd., 1970), p. 66. Sir William Slim has some typically perceptive observations on the Japanese success of 1941-42, in *Defeat Into Victory*, 3rd ed. (London: Cassell & Co. Ltd., 1972), pp. 29, 119-120.

61. Brooke-Popham, "Notes on the Far East," March 12, 1942, Brooke-Popham Papers (BPP), v/9/5/2, Liddell Hart Centre for Military Archives, Kings College, London.

62. This description of the Singapore War Council's problems and personalities is based on the following: A. H. P. Humphrey, letter to the author, February 3, 1974; author interview with Mr. Humphrey, June 1, 1975; Sir R. Scott to A. H. Dickinson, August 20, 1967, Mrs. H. C. Reilly [one time cypher officer to both Duff Cooper and Shenton Thomas] to A. H. Dickinson, November 22, 1968, Bryson Collection, Royal Commonwealth Society Library, London; author interview with Mr. H. P. Bryson, June 12, 1975; Sir Shenton Thomas, "Comments on the Draft History of the War Against Japan," par. 124, Thomas Papers, Rhodes House Library; Sir Shenton Thomas,

Diary entry, December 10, 1941, undated (but postwar) note for Mr. F. S. V. Donnison (author of the official history of *British Military Administration in the Far East 1943-1946* [London: H.M.S.O., 1956]), Far East War Council Minutes, passim., Thomas Papers, in possession of Professor Hugh Thomas; article by Sir Robert Scott, *Daily Telegraph*, February 15, 1972. See also Kirby, *Singapore: The Chain of Disaster*, pp. 188-89.

63. PRO, PREM 3, 161/1, Shenton Thomas to the Colonial Office, January 3, 22, 1942. "Unofficial" members were private citizens, usually businessmen. The official members were M.C.S. officers, and, of course, unlikely to criticize much.

64. Ibid., Duff Cooper to Secretary for Colonies, January 3, 1942.

65. Ibid., Tennant to Prime Minister, January 6, 1942, enclosing letters from Duff Cooper to the Prime Minister of December 18, 20 1941. Percival, in fact, had never been a schoolmaster − he went from his public school, Rugby, into a firm of London iron-ore merchants, and then enlisted in the army in 1914, receiving a commission shortly afterwards. Stanley Jones, on the other hand, was doubtless a controversial figure. Some well-placed observers felt that his selection as colonial secretary was Sir Shenton Thomas's worst mistake. He was a dour man, described by one who knew him as "lugubrious" (a trait that may have struck others as defeatist). Capable, but blunt and plain spoken, he neither suffered fools gladly nor readily admitted errors. Much of the animosity that surrounded him dated from his time as O.A.G. during the governor's leave. There is no doubt that much of the animus with which he was regarded had more to do with personality clashes than substantive issues (information on Jones from H.P. Bryson, "Notes on Simson's Failure in Malaya 1941-42," January 10, 1969, A. H. Dickinson to H. Fairbairn, June 8, 1967, Bryson Collection; Interviews with H. P. Bryson, June 12, 1975, and A. H. P. Humphrey, June 1, 1975; Sir Shenton Thomas, Diary, January 16, 1942, Thomas Papers, in the possession of Professor Hugh Thomas). It is interesting to note that on the day after he wrote his letter to the prime minister condemning the Malayan administration, Duff Cooper signed a War Council subcommittee report, approving the arrangements for civil defense in Singapore, arrangements in which Jones played a major role: Sir Shenton Thomas, "Comments on the Draft History of the War Against Japan," October 1954, par. 108, Thomas Papers, Rhodes House Library, Oxford.

66. PRO, PREM 3, 161/2, Prime Minister to Colonial Office, January 12, 1942.

67. For a good example of this see M. Panter-Downes, *London War Notes* (New York: Farrar, Strauss and Giroux, 1971), pp. 185-210. This is a collection of columns that Miss Panter-Downes wrote throughout the war for the *New Yorker* magazine.

68. Bond, ed., *Chief of Staff*, 2: 67.

69. The order is in BPP v/5/49.

70. Brooke-Popham to Chiefs of Staff, December 25, 1941, BPP v/5/51.

71. PRO, CAB 66, WP (42) 35, 37, January 23, 25, 1942.

72. Clark-Kerr to Brooke-Popham, April 28, 1942, BPP v/5/68. Brooke-Popham's papers do, however, contain numerous private letters of sympathy from friends and colleagues.

73. PRO, PREM 3, 169/2, Pownall to Brooke, December 27, 1941.

74. Bond, ed., *Chief of Staff*, 2: 70-71.

75. Simson, *Singapore: Too Little, Too Late*, pp. 68-72.

76. Kirby, *Singapore: The Chain of Disaster*, pp. 192-95.

77. Bond, ed., *Chief of Staff*, 2: 72, 74.

78. PRO, PREM 3, 169/2, Wavell to the Chiefs of Staff, January 1, 1942.

79. Connell, *Wavell: The Supreme Commander*, pp. 90-91.

80. Ibid., pp. 72-73.

81. Kirby et al., *The Loss of Singapore*, pp. 249, 528; Sir J. G. Smyth, V.C., *Percival*

and the Tragedy of Singapore (London: Macdonald, 1971), p. 156. There can be no doubt that, by the summer of 1941, the milking of Indian Army units, in the interest of further expansion, bordered on the reckless. For example, the brigade signals officer of the Nowshera Brigade on the north-west frontier of India was suddenly stripped of his entire trained strength to make up a unit going overseas, and had to make do with partially trained men hastily drafted from infantry units (Interview with Colonel J. F. Worth, O.B.E., June 9, 1975).

82. Connell, *Wavell: The Supreme Commander*, pp. 78-79, 84-88; Kirby, *Singapore: The Chain of Disaster*, p. 185.

83. Bond, ed., *Chief of Staff*, 2: 76. Pownall had been chief of staff of the B.E.F., in which Percival had been chief of staff to Dill's I Corps, September 1939-February 1940.

84. Kirby et al., *The Loss of Singapore*, p. 287.

85. Connell, *Wavell: The Supreme Commander*, pp. 94-99. In a letter to the author (January 1974) Mr. W. L. Blythe, C.M.G., pointed out that Jones, just prior to his relief, had resisted a demand from the miltary to use camps prepared for refugees on the outskirts of Singapore, to accomodate arriving troops. Knowing the attitude of Duff Cooper toward him, the governor expected, when he received the telegram, that it contained orders for his own recall (Interview with A. H. P. Humphrey, June 1, 1975). Sir Shenton Thomas later wrote a lengthy defense of Jones in his "Comments on the Draft History of the War Against Japan," pars. 107-21, Thomas Papers, Rhodes House Library, Oxford.

86. PRO, PREM 3, 169/2, Prime Minister to Wavell, January 15, 1942, printed in Connell, *Wavell: The Supreme Commander*, p. 102.

87. PRO, PREM 3, 169/2, Wavell to Prime Minister, January 16, 1942, printed in Connell, *Wavell: The Supreme Commander*, p. 105. Wavell's signal, incidentally, should have prevented the legend that Singapore's guns "pointed the wrong way" from gaining currency. It is an instructive example of the power of myth that it is the one thing most people now remember about the fall of Singapore.

88. For the details of this, which Churchill minimized in his memoirs, see G. M. Thompson, *Vote of Censure* (New York: Stein and Day, 1968); B. Gardner, *Churchill in Power* (Boston: Houghton Mifflin, 1970), pp. 141-95; A. J. P. Taylor, *Beaverbrook* (London: Hamish Hamilton, 1972), pp. 506-40.

89. Churchill, *The Hinge of Fate*, pp. 15-16; Gwyer and Butler, *Grand Strategy III*, pt. 2, pp. 409-10.

90. Churchill, *The Hinge of Fate*, p. 54.

91. Ibid., pp. 49, 50-51.

92. PRO, CAB 65, WM (42) 9, January 19, 1942.

93. Sir Shenton Thomas, Diary, January 19, 1942, Thomas Papers, in the possession of Professor Hugh Thomas.

94. Churchill, *The Hinge of Fate*, pp. 51-53.

95. Kirby, *Singapore: The Chain of Disaster*, p. 212; Connell, *Wavell: The Supreme Commander*, pp. 111-13.

96. Churchill, *The Hinge of Fate*, p. 53.

97. PRO, PREM 3, 168/1, Churchill to Ismay for Chiefs of Staff, January 21, 1942, minutes of Defence Committee meeting, January 21, 1942; Churchill, *The Hinge of Fate*, p. 57, reprints the minute to Ismay.

98. Kirby, *Singapore: The Chain of Disaster*, p. 212; Churchill, *The Hinge of Fate*, p. 57; Wigmore, *The Japanese Thrust*, pp. 285-86.

99. Churchill, *The Hinge of Fate*, pp. 57-58.

100, PRO, PREM 3, 169/2, Hartley to War Office, January 23, 1942. This brigade, the 48th, went to Burma in January, arriving at Rangoon on the 31st.

101. Churchill, *The Hinge of Fate,* pp. 58-59. In an interview with the author on January 14, 1971, Sir Ian Jacob also stressed the military doctrine of throwing the last reserve in to hold a critical position. While Sir Ian's opinion must command very great respect, it seems to this writer that there is strong evidence that the decision to let the Eighteenth Division go on to Singapore was not taken primarily for military reasons.

102. Ibid., pp. 133-34.

103. Bond, ed., *Chief of Staff,* 2: 80. Kirby, *Singapore: The Chain of Disaster,* pp. 213-17, has an important analysis and criticism of the decision to allow the Eighteenth Division to go on to Singapore.

104. Churchill, *The Hinge of Fate,* pp. 68-69.

105. PRO, CAB 65, WM (42) 11, January 27, 1942.

106. D. Richards and H. St. G. Saunders, *The Royal Air Force 1939-1945,* 3 vols. (London: H.M.S.O., 1953-54), 2: 39; Connell, *Wavell: The Supreme Commander,* pp. 131-32.

107. Churchill, *The Hing of Fate,* pp. 95, 97. Did Churchill's desire to render the naval base useless until the autumn of 1943 indicate a new, and more pessimistic, estimate of the time it would take to rebuild British seapower in the Indian Ocean?

108. PRO, PREM 3, 169/3, Ismay to Wavell, February 2, 1942.

109. Connell, *Wavell: The Supreme Commander,* p. 146; Kirby et al., *India's Most Dangerous Hour,* p. 39.

110. Bond, ed., *Chief of Staff,* 2: 84; Kirby, *Singapore: The Chain of Disaster,* p. 227.

111. See chap. 1 above.

112. Gwyer and Butler, *Grand Strategy III,* pt. 2, pp. 434-37; Churchill, *The Hinge of Fate,* pp. 18-19. There were eventually Pacific War Councils in both London and Washington. The London body was wound up in August 1943.

113. Sir W. Goode, G.C.M.G., letter to the author, January 5, 1974; Kirby, *Singapore: The Chain of Disaster,* p. 227 fn. There is no doubt that the Naval Base was abandoned in a precipitate fashion by its staff: " . . . the whole place looks as if the staff had left for lunch and never returned," the governor was told on the 5th. The previous day he had noted a telephone call in his diary: "did we know that if you want anything out of the Naval Base you have only to go and get it? Apparently since Navy evacuated it a few days ago it has been at the mercy of anyone in uniform . . . . Things that are desperately needed here left under no sort of control." Sir Shenton Thomas, Diary, February 4, 5, 1942. Thomas Papers, in the possession of Professor Hugh Thomas. On the other hand it should be noted that Percival had specifically asked Rear Admiral E. J. Spooner *not* to fire the oil reserves at the Naval Base because the sight would depress morale. Connell, *Wavell: The Supreme Commander,* p. 157.

114. Bond, ed., *Chief of Staff,* 2: 85; Sir Shenton Thomas, Diary, February 10, 1942, Thomas Papers, in the possession of Professor Hugh Thomas.

EPILOGUE

The fall of Singapore did not come as quite such a shock in Great Britain as might have been expected. The loss of the *Prince of Wales* and the *Repulse* had certainly jolted public opinion; after that, disaster piled on disaster with such rapidity that the final catastrophe in the Far East was no great surprise. It was also blanketed to some extent by other war news. First the swaying fortunes of Crusader, then the Russian counteroffensive, and finally Rommel's sharp riposte at the end of January that quickly erased Auchinleck's gains, all provided a perhaps welcome distraction from the collapse in Malaya. On February 11-12, 1942, just as the drama of Singapore was reaching its tragic climax, events in the English Channel temporarily blotted out everything else. The German battlecruisers *Scharnhorst* and *Gneisenau* had been at Brest since March 1941. They were joined in June by the heavy cruiser *Prince Eugen*. Although repeatedly bombed by the RAF, this powerful squadron remained a standing menace to the Atlantic convoys. Hitler, who feared a British invasion of Norway almost as much as Churchill's advisers, decided toward the end of 1941 to bring the Brest squadron back to Germany, where it would be available to counter any British attack in the north. Hitler also decided that the ships would return by the most direct route, up the English Channel. After intensive preparations, the squadron left Brest late at night on February 11. All the next day they steamed up the Channel, beating off British air and naval attacks that were gallant in the extreme, but hastily mounted and illcoordinated. The British had been taken completely by surprise, and early on the 13th the German squadron reached its home waters. It was a humiliating episode. It was also a fortunate distraction.[1]

In the days and weeks following Singapore's fall, a trickle of escapers tried to make their way to the temporary safety of the

East Indies. It is a subject in itself worthy of a book.[2]   Here can
be noted the fate of only a few. Air Vice Marshal Pulford left
with the last "official" departures on the night of February 13.
His parting words to Percival were, "I suppose you and I will be
held responsible for this, but God knows we did our best with
what we had been given."[3]   The launch carrying Pulford was
attacked by Japanese aircraft, damaged, and forced ashore on a deserted and malarial island. There the Air Vice Marshal and seventeen
others died before the Japanese found the survivors. Bowden, the
Australian representative in Singapore, left on the 15th in a small
vessel called the *Mary Rose*. On the 17th it was captured by the
Japanese. When Bowden asked for an interview with a Japanese
officer in order to make his diplomatic status known, an altercation
with a guard resulted. Shortly thereafter Bowden was taken out,
kicked to an execution site, made to dig his own grave, and shot.[4]
Gordon Bennett, luckier than his civilian colleague, made good his
escape to Australia, where he found that his action in leaving his men
made him a highly controversial figure.[5]   The rest of the civil and
military high command in Malaya went into captivity. Beckwith-
Smith of the Eighteenth Division died of diptheria in November
1942, but most survived. Lower down the scale, the incidence of
death was much higher. Some 130,000 of Malaya's defenders became prisoners of war. During their three and a half years in Japanese hands, about 24,000 of them died. Those who survived all
too often did so with permanently damaged health.[6]   Malaya's
civilians fared no better. For the Malays and Chinese there was
maltreatment and massacre; for the European civilians, years of
internment and privation — and for them 1945 was not the end, as it
was for the soldiers. For they, and the administrators, emerged
from Japanese prisons to face the problems of reconstruction, rising
Malay nationalism, and the long Communist insurgency (1948-
60).[7]

Postmortems on the great disaster began immediately. Wavell
signaled London on February 15 that the Japanese had been badly
underestimated.[8]   His chief of staff mused, "we were frankly out-
generalled, outwitted and outfought [*sic*] ." Ten days after the surrender Pownall added, "There's no doubt we've underestimated
the Jap."

But suppose we'd made a better shot and got the Jap at his
true worth, would it have made any real difference? I very
much doubt it. Our policy was to avoid war with Japan as

long as we could (or to make America cause it, if it was to happen) and we gambled on that policy succeeding (or if it didn't succeed on America bearing the brunt). With all our other commitments I don't believe that however highly we had rated the Japs as fighters we would have been caused thereby to improve the condition of our services in the Far East. We just hoped it wouldn't happen. And it did.[9]

From his very different perspective, Squadron Leader Carter came to the same conclusion. After a successful escape from Singapore, he wrote home in April 1941, "Basically the fault lies in Whitehall . . . ."[10] The dominant figure there never regretted what he had done. In September 1943 Churchill wrote a minute to Eden about the final dispatch tendered by Sir Robert Craigie, who had been British Ambassador in Tokyo from 1937. "He writes of the breach with Japan as if it were an unmitigated disaster . . . . It was however a blessing that Japan attacked the United States and thus brought America wholeheartedly into the war. Greater good fortune has rarely happened to the British Empire than this event which . . . may lead, through the merciless crushing of Japan, to a new relationship of immense benefit to the English-speaking countries and to the whole world."[11] What it led to was the demise of Britain as a world power, and her reduction to an American satellite.

The basic fact was that Britain after 1918 was no longer able, and perhaps no longer willing, to defend her world position built up in the Victorian era. Churchill could not alter this. He did not, contrary to many assertions, create the Mediterranean commitment, although he certainly made it very much his own. What he did was to see clearly that Britain could fight one war — or lose two. Britain's essential interests were more immediately threatened in Europe than in Asia. Britain could preserve her independence and position as a great European power, but not simultaneously the Asian empire that made her a world power. From this everything else flowed. Troops from Australia and New Zealand were needed in the Middle East. Their governments' fears had, therefore, to be assuaged. Every man possible had to be gotten out of India, for as little investment in British personnel and equipment — and, on the part of the prime minister, gratitude — as possible. The Indian Army could simply be ordered where needed. The Pacific dominions had to be persuaded, and therefore matters of vital concern to them could not be ignored. But, in the Far East,

bluff and the display of some goods in the shop window, under-
pinned by hope in America and comforting misconceptions about
the Japanese, constituted the only policy London had. The British were never really frank with the Australians. In the circumstances they did not dare to be, and that is the best explanation
that can be given of their conduct. To the British and their indomitable leader, survival, nothing less, was at stake. Next to this,
nothing else mattered. The Australians, for their part, continued
to rely on British protection, despite mounting evidence that it
would be unavailing, because if they were not shielded by Britain,
they feared that they were not shielded at all.

It is easy to point out specific errors. The Air Ministry, having
made itself responsible for the Far East, then neglected it. Pownall believed that it was because of their obsession with the strategic bombing offensive against Germany, and he was probably
right. Here it is fair to fault Churchill. Even within the framework of his strategic priorities he could have done much more to
see that Malaya got some modern aircraft. He glossed over this
failure at the time and later in his memoirs. On the other hand,
the failure of the Chiefs of Staff to correct Churchill's erroneous
belief in a "Singapore Fortress" is inexplicable except upon the
damning assumption that they shared it. The muddled creation of
Far East Command, the failure to ensure the coordination of civil
and military activities in Malaya, the belief that battleships were
still potent talismans, the refusal to save the Eighteenth Division,
the shuttlecock treatment of Burma, Duff Cooper's appointment
— all these were also mistakes made in London. It is ironic that on
both the occasions when his instincts were correct — about the
speed of the withdrawal in Malaya in December and about the
need to concentrate on saving Burma in January — Churchill
found himself unable to translate them into action. Next to the
errors made in London, those made on the spot, however blame-
worthy in themselves, were far less significant. Brooke-Popham
should not have dithered over Matador. Percival should have lis-
tened to both Heath and Simson. The civil administration, while
not flawless, has been very unfairly criticized, and soldiers and
civilians could certainly have been more understanding of each
others problems. But all this affected at very most the speed, not
the fact, of defeat. *That* was as foreordained as anything ever can
be. One well-placed observer said years later: "If we had had our
best general out there, it would have made no difference."[1] [2]

Churchill, of course, did not think that the disaster in the Far

East was final. He always intended to win it all back with American help, thereby revealing the basic misreading of the United States' attitude toward Britain as a world power that was probably his greatest single mistake. Conscious of what was to him the perversely high value that the Americans placed on China, he cabled the governor of Burma on the day after Singapore fell that maintaining contact with China through Burma was the dominant feature of the war in the East.[13] The following day he minuted to Ismay that the leading brigade of the Australian Corps returning from the Middle East might be diverted to save Rangoon.[14] But, on the same day, a cable from the Australian government made it clear that they wanted their troops home. Churchill did not realize what the collapse in the Far East had done to the bonds of the British Empire, or to the prestige on which it lived. Nor did he yet grasp that his American allies would impose on him a strategy for the Far East shaped to meet their needs, and that the restoration of the British position there was not among them. Burma would become the focus of British strategy in the East for the remainder of the war, largely because the Americans wished it so. Reconquest of Burma would reopen for the United States a land link with China. Struggle as he might, Churchill could not alter what poverty of resources, and consequent dependence on America, entailed. The Americans thus did to the British what they had done earlier, to the Australians: imposed on an alliance a strategy that served primarily their own ends. No *British* victory would recover what the Empire had lost in the calamitous seventy days that ended on February 15, 1942. It would all be returned, but only after Japan was beaten by the Americans. No wonder the complex, ultimately brilliant, but politically barren Burma campaigns of 1943-45 scarcely find a place in Churchill's spacious war memoirs. They led nowhere. And the British, like the Dutch and the French, found that there could be no true restoration of their power in the East after 1945. The Indian National Army, recruited by the Japanese from among the dispirited and bewildered Indian soldiers taken prisoner in Malaya and Burma, was militarily useless to its masters, and even of little immediate propaganda value, but was a portent. The sun was beginning to set for the British Raj. It was setting as well for the other European powers in Asia. The French had been forced to bow to the Japanese in 1940-41. The United States, with an army of some 140,000 men in the Philippines (30,000 of whom were Americans), was beaten by a smaller Japanese army than the one used in Malaya. On March 8 the Japanese entered Rangoon, and on the same day in Java Lieutenant General H. ter Poorten surrendered the 98,000-man Royal Netherlands East Indian Army and some 8,000 British, Australian, and American troops as well. By May 1942 the Japanese stood on the frontiers of India. In six incredible months they had humiliated the Western powers militarily and in the eyes of their Asian subjects, and erased their centuries-old presence in East and Southeast Asia. Even the subsequent defeat of Japan could not undo the consequences. The European powers, weakened by the war, their prestige gone, came back in 1945 only to make preparations for a final departure, reasonably decorous in the case of the British, bitter for the Dutch, bloody and protracted for the French. In this collapse of the Western *imperium* in Asia, one of the central historical facts of our time, the fall of Singapore will always stand out — the most spectacular event of the chain that brought to an end Asia's dominance by the West.

Notes to Epilogue

1. J.R.M. Butler, ed., *History of the Second World War: United Kingdom Military Series*, "Campaigns" series, S. W. Roskill, *The War At Sea*, 3 vols. (London: H.M.S.O., 1954-1960), 2:149-61. In fact, the *Gneisenau* was so badly damaged during the breakout that she never went to sea again.

2. One good example of the "escape from Singapore" literature is Ian Skidmore, *Escape from the Rising Sun* (New York: Charles Scribners Sons, 1974). There are two good unpublished accounts in the Imperial War Museum, London: Lt. Col. B. H. Ashmore, O.B.E., "Singapore to Colombo: 1942," Percival Papers, Box 49; J. O. Dyke to T. C. Carter, July 2, 1945, Carter Papers, TCC 3/6.

3. Sir John Smythe, V.C., *Percival and the Tragedy of Singapore* (London: Macdonald, 1971), p. 287.

4. *Australia in the War of 1939-45*: Series I (Army) vol. 4, L. Wigmore, *The Japanese Thrust* (Canberra: Australian War Memorial, 1957), pp. 383-89 contains a number of escape stories.

5. Wigmore, *The Japanese Thrust*, pp. 383-85. Bennett, however, did eventually receive further employment as commander of III Australian Corps, 1942-44.

6. This, too, is a subject by itself. There is a great deal of "prison camp" literature. There is no overall treatment, but A. J. Sweeting's "Prisoners of the Japanese" in Wigmore, *The Japanese Thrust*, pp. 511-642, is very good. The best known account of a Japanese prison camp is, of course, P. Boulle's novel, *The Bridge on the River Kwai*. Smyth, *Percival and Tragedy of Singapore*, pp. 281-97, gives an account of the postwar struggle of the Far East Prisoners of War Federation, which Percival headed, to wring from the British government some recognition and compensation for the survivors of

Japanese captivity, an account that does scant credit to successive British governments.

7. The roots of the emergency are in the shattering experience of the British collapse in Malaya, and, more particularly, in the role of the Malayan Communist Party (MCP) in the resistance to the Japanese 1941-45. As early as December 18, 1941, contacts were made between British officers and the secretary general of the MCP in order to recruit local Chinese Communists to be trained as "stay behind parties," the nucleus of future guerrilla bands, and some 200 were trained prior to the fall of Singapore. On February 6, 1941, Sir Shenton Thomas met a group of MCP leaders, many until recently in jail, in connection with this project. Present at this meeting was Innes Tremlett, who later, as a lieutenant colonel, headed the Malayan section of Force 136, as the Special Operations Executive's Far East section was known. R. Clutterbuck, *Riot and Revolution in Singapore and Malaya 1945-1963* (London: Faber & Faber Ltd., 1973), p. 37; Sir Shenton Thomas, Diary, February 6, 1942, Thomas Papers, in the possession of Professor Hugh Thomas; B. Swett-Escott, *Baker Street Irregular* (London: Methuen & Co., Ltd., 1965), pp. 242, 264 fn. The classic account of the resistance to the Japanese in Malaya is Colonel F. Spencer Chapman's, *The Jungle is Neutral* (London: Chatto & Windus, 1949). The oft-remarked communist capacity to take long views is attested by the fact that on the evening of Singapore's surrender an attempt was made on the life of A. H. Dickinson, the inspector general of police and chief security officer (private information from a former officer of the Malayan Civil Service).

8. Public Record Office (PRO), PREM 3, 169/3, Wavell to War Office, February 15, 1942.

9. B. Bond, ed., *Chief of Staff: The Diaries of Lieutenant General Sir Henry Pownall*, 2 vols. (London: Leo Cooper Ltd., 1973-74), 2:92.

10. Carter to Family, April 11, 1942, Carter Papers, TCC 3/3.

11. PRO, PREM 3, 158/4, Churchill to Eden, September 19, 1943.

12. Lt. Gen. Sir Ian Jacob, G.B.E., interview with the author, January 14, 1971.

13. Winston S. Churchill, *The Second World War*, vol. 4, *The Hinge of Fate* (Boston: Houghton Mifflin, 1950), p. 153.

14. Ibid., p. 141.

BIBLIOGRAPHY

Unpublished Papers

London. Public Record Office:
  PREM 3 Papers of the prime minister's office.
  CAB 2/3 Committee of Imperial Defence Minutes.
  CAB 65 War Cabinet Minutes.
  CAB 66 War Cabinet Papers and Memoranda.
  CAB 69/4 Defence Committee Minutes and Memoranda.
  CAB 69/8 Secretary's Standard File.
  ADM 205/10 First Sea Lord's Records, 1939-45.
  ADM 199/1934 First Lord's Personal Records, 1939-45.

London. Imperial War Museum, Department of Documents:
  Percival Papers. A large but uncatalogued collection containing a great deal of information, although Percival was naturally unable to preserve very much in captivity so that there is relatively little on 1941-42. Access to this collection is by permission of Percival's son, Major A. J. Mac G. Percival.
  Carter Papers. A small but very interesting collection dealing mainly with the RAF radar units in the Far East.

London. King's College. The Liddell Hart Centre for Military Archives:
  Ismay Papers. A vast and well-indexed collection with, revealingly, very little on the Far East.
  Brooke-Popham Papers. This collection covers all of Brooke-Popham's career. The section on the Far East is large, and the whole collection is well indexed.
  Vlieland, C. A. "Disaster in the Far East 1941-42." This 77-page typescript is interesting, and in places revealing, but Mr. Vlieland's understandable bitterness at his treatment has produced a general interpretation that is somewhat eccentric.

London. The Royal Commonwealth Society Library:
Bryson Collection. This is an extremely valuable body of material, well indexed, and shedding a great deal of light on the civil side of the Malayan campaign and its background.

Oxford. Rhodes House Library:
Thomas Papers (MSS. Ind. Oc. S.). This collection, access to which is by permission of Professor Hugh Thomas, covers all of Sir Shenton's career and includes a small but valuable body of material on Malaya, especially the governor's outline diary for 1941-45 and his postwar comments on the draft of General Kirby's official history.

Professor Hugh Thomas:
Thomas Papers. A mass of papers from Sir Shenton's Malayan years, including a complete set of the minutes of the Far East War Council, December 10, 1941-February 9, 1942, and the governor's diary for December 8, 1941-February 10, 1942.

Lieutenant General Sir Ian Jacob, G.B.E.:
Jacob Diaries; Sir Ian's diaries of the Atlantic conference and Arcadia are very good for the atmosphere of those meetings, as well as for providing revealing insights into how matters appeared at the time to someone in the center of affairs. Sir Ian also kindly allowed me to read his unfinished memoirs.

Official Publications

Dispatches:
Brook-Popham, Air Chief Marshal Robert. "Operations In The Far East, From 17th October 1940 to 27th December 1941." *Supplement to the London Gazette,* January 22, 1948.

Layton, Vice Admiral Sir Geoffrey. "Loss of H. M. Ships Prince of Wales and Repulse." *Supplement to the London Gazette,* February 26, 1948.

Maltby, Air Vice Marshal Sir Paul. "Report On The Air Operations During The Campaigns In Malaya And Netherlands East Indies From 8th December 1941 to 12th March 1942." *Supplement to the London Gazette,* February 26, 1948.

Percival. Lieutenant General A. E. "Operations Of Malaya Command, From 8th December 1941 to 15th February 1942." *Supplement to the London Gazette,* February 26, 1948.

Histories:
  Australian:
    Australian in the War of 1939-45: Series I (Army).
        I. Long, G. *To Benghazi.* Canberra: Australian War Memorial, 1952.
        II. Long, G. *Greece, Crete and Syria.* Canberra: Australian War Memorial, 1953.
        IV. Wigmore, L. *The Japanese Thrust.* Canberra: Australian War Memorial, 1957.
    Series IV (Civil)
        I. Hasluck, P. *The Government and the People 1939-41.* Canberra: Australian War Memorial, 1952.
    These volumes, produced under the auspices of the Australian War Memorial, are very well done.
  British:
    Butler, J. R. M., ed. *History of the Second World War; United Kingdom Military Series.*
    A. "Grand Strategy" series:
        II. Butler, J. R. M. *Grand Strategy (September 1939-June 1941).* London: Her Majesty's Stationery Office, 1957.
        III. Butler, J. R. M., and Gwyer, J. M. A. *Grand Strategy (June 1941-August 1942).* London: H.M.S.O., 1964.
        IV. Howard, M. *Grand Strategy (August 1942-September 1943).* London: H.M.S.O., 1970.
        V. Ehrman, J. *Grand Strategy (August 1943-September 1944).* London: H.M.S.O., 1956.
        VI. ——— *Grand Strategy (October 1944-August 1945).* London: H.M.S.O., 1956.
    The quality of the volumes in this series varies considerably. Volumes 2 and 3 are unfortunately rather bland, unlike the remainder, which are of very high quality. It is unfortunate that, over the past thirty years, it has not been possible to bring out volume 1, which covers the critical period to 1939.

    B. "Campaigns" series:
      (i) Kirby, S. W. et al. *The War Against Japan.* 5 vols. London: H.M.S.O., 1957-68.
        I. *The War Against Japan: The Loss of Singapore.* London: H.M.S.O., 1957. Considering its date of publication, General Kirby and his team did a good job on the military aspects of the campaign, but this volume is far from being complete. For one thing, the terms of reference given to the authors by the Cabinet Office precluded a complete examination of the critical civil side of the campaign and its preliminaries, and there was, therefore, no representative of the Malayan administration on Kirby's team. This has produced an

unfortunate distortion in the treatment of the civil government and its affairs. Brooke-Popham and Percival at least
got to publish their own dispatches, but it is instructive (and
depressing) to examine in the Thomas Papers the ex-gover-
nor's vain attempts to get the official historians to even take
into consideration the civil side of the Malayan campaign.
Sir Shenton was never officially notified that the official
history was in preparation, and his request to meet with
General Kirby and his team was turned down. Perhaps he
was too convenient a scapegoat? The materials assembled
for the use of General Kirby and his associates are in the
Public Record Office but are closed until 1987.

II. *The War Against Japan: India's Most Dangerous Hour.* London:
H.M.S.O., 1958.

(ii) Playfair, I. S. O. et al. *The Mediterranean and Middle East.* 6 vols.
to date. London: H.M.S.O., 1954-.

I. *The Mediterranean and Middle East: Early Successes Against
Italy (to May 1941).* London: H.M.S.O., 1954.

II. *The Mediterranean and Middle East: The Germans come to the
Help of their Ally (1941).* London: H.M.S.O., 1956.

III. *The Mediterranean and Middle East: British Fortunes reach
their Lowest Ebb (September 1941-September 1942).*
London: H.M.S.O., 1960.

It is curious that Playfair, who knew a great deal about it, was not
given the job of writing the volume on the fall of Singapore. Perhaps he
was considered too close to the events, or perhaps he would not have
blamed the right people.

(iii) Richards, D. and Saunders, H. St. G. *The Royal Air Force 1939-
1945.* 3 vols. London: H.M.S.O., 1953-54.

I. *The Royal Air Force 1939-1945: The Fight at Odds.* London:
H.M.S.O., 1953.

II. *The Royal Air Force 1939-1945: The Fight Avails.* London:
H.M.S.O., 1954.

These volumes are not part of the "United Kingdom Military Series"
edited by Sir James Butler, and they therefore do not take an interservice point of view. They are well written, but on the Far East the second
volume is, in places, misleading and gives in general the impression of
both incomplete information and a strong desire to get quickly past an
unhappy episode in RAF history.

(iv) Roskill, S. W. *The War at Sea: 1939-1945.* 3 vols. London:
H.M.S.O., 1954-60.

I. *The War at Sea 1939-1945: The Defensive.* London: H.M.S.O.,
1954.

II. *The War at Sea 1939-1945: The Period Of Balance.* London:
H.M.S.O., 1956.

These oft-praised volumes are among the best official histories ever produced, even if they are somewhat biased toward the Royal Navy. Volume 1 is a bit thin on the prewar background to Singapore, but that was inevitable under Captain Roskill's terms of reference.

Woodward, E.L. *British Foreign Policy in the Second World War.* 3 vols. to date. London: H.M.S.O., 1970-.
> Volume I. H.M.S.O., 1970.
> Volume II. H.M.S.O., 1971.

These volumes, which cover Anglo-Japanese relations, 1939-41, are also not part of the series edited by Sir James Butler, and they present the war as seen from the Foreign Office, not always a very relevant perspective. The organization is somewhat confusing and the prose often stupefyingly dull. Still, there is interesting material on the Far East, especially in volume 2, for those patient enough to dig it out.

Indian:

Prasad, B., ed. *Official History of the Indian Armed Forces In The Second World War 1939-45.*

Bhargava, K. D., and Sastri, K. N. V. *Campaigns In South East Asia 1941-42.* Combined Inter-Services Historical Section India & Pakistan, 1960.

> This contains a great deal of tactical detail, but it accurately reflects India's role in the British Empire's war effort that, in his introduction, the general editor had to note: "we had little access to the documents relating to higher strategy and diplomatic developments . . ."

United States:

Morison, Samuel Eliot. *History of United Sates Naval Operations In World War II.* 15 vols. Vol. 3. *The Rising Sun in the Pacific 1931-April 1942.* Boston: Atlantic Monthly Press, 1950.

Diaries, Letters, and Memoirs

Bennett, H. Gordon. *Why Singapore Fell.* Sydney: Angus & Robertson, Ltd., 1944. This apologia by the GOC, Eighth Australian Division, has to be treated with great caution.

Bond, B., ed. *Chief of Staff: The Diaries of Lieutenant General Sir Henry Pownall.* 2 vols.
> I. 1933-1940. London: Leo Cooper Ltd., 1973.
> II. 1940-1944. London: Leo Cooper Ltd., 1974.

Pownall held successively a series of key positions, in which he saw a lot, and these diaries reveal a great deal of it.

Bryant, A., ed. *The Turn of the Tide 1939-1943: A History of the War Years Based on the Diaries of Field-Marshal Lord Alanbrooke, Chief of the Imperial General Staff.* New York: Doubleday, 1957. Composed of extracts from Brooke's wartime diaries, and postwar "Notes on My Life" with linking commentary by the editor, this is a curiously uneven book but has been heavily used, sometimes uncritically, by historians since its publication. Brooke's papers are housed in the Liddell Hart Centre for Military Archives at King's College, London, but will not be available to historians until Sir Arthur Bryant has completed the official biography of Lord Alanbrooke.

Chapman, F. Spencer. *The Jungle is Neutral.* London: Chatto & Windus, 1949.

Churchill, Randolph. *Winston S. Churchill: Companion Vol. 2.* Boston: Houghton Mifflin, 1969.

Churchill, Winston S. *The World Crisis.* Vol. 1. New York: Charles Scribners Sons, 1923.

——. *The Second World War.* Vol. 1. *The Gathering Storm.* Boston: Houghton Mifflin, 1948.

——. Vol. 2. *Their Finest Hour.* Boston: Houghton Mifflin, 1949.

——. Vol. 3. *The Grand Alliance.* Boston: Houghton Mifflin, 1950.

——. Vol. 4. *The Hinge of Fate.* Boston: Houghton Mifflin, 1950. One of the most impressive things about Churchill's war memoirs is the amount of documentary material he made available to historians at a very early date. This is true to a surprising extent even of the Far East, although there are some matters that Churchill glosses over or simply does not mention. It will be interesting to see how much more there is on Singapore in the Churchill Papers when they are eventually opened.

Cooper, A. Duff. *Old Men Forget.* New York: Dutton, 1954. Of his mission to the Far East, Duff Cooper probably preferred to forget.

Cunningham, A. B. *A Sailor's Odyssey: The Autobiography of Admiral of the Fleet Viscount Cunningham of Hyndhope, K.T., G.C.B., O.M., D.S.O.* London: Hutchinson & Co. Ltd., 1951.

Dilks, D., ed. *The Diaries of Sir Alexander Cadogan, O.M., 1938-1945.* London: Cassell & Co., 1971.

Eden, A. *The Memoirs of Anthony Eden, Earl of Avon: The Reckoning.* Boston: Houghton Mifflin, 1965. Eden is less than frank about his part in sending the *Prince of Wales* and the *Repulse* on their doomed mission.

Fergusson, B., ed. *The Business of War: The War Narrative of Major General Sir John Kennedy.* New York: William Morrow and Company, 1958. A very important source of information, and probably the closest we will ever come to the war as seen by Sir John Dill.

Ismay, H. L. *The Memoirs of General Lord Ismay.* New York: Viking Press, 1960 Ismay is, curiously, far less informative about the Far East than Churchill.

Menzies, Robert. *Afternoon Light.* New York: Coward-McCann, Inc., 1967. Sir Robert is curiously bland in his account of the events of 1939-41.

Moran, Charles, Lord. *Churchill: The Struggle for Survival 1940-1965.* Boston: Houghton Mifflin, 1966. This interesting account by Churchill's doctor, based on his diaries, provoked a sharp controversy about both the ethics of its publication, and its historical accuracy. It ought to be read in conjunction with the riposte by a number of Churchill's former staff: Wheeler-Bennett, J., ed. *Action This Day: Working With Churchill.* New York: St. Martin's Press, 1969.

Nicolson, N., ed. *The Diaries and Letters of Harold Nicolson.* Vol. 2. *The War Years 1939-1945.* New York: Atheneum, 1967.

Panter-Downes, M. *London War Notes.* New York: Farrar, Strauss and Giroux, 1971.

Percival, A. E. *The War In Malaya.* London: Eyre & Spottiswoode, 1949. This adds relatively little to Percival's official "Despatch."

Russell-Roberts, D. *Spotlight on Singapore.* Douglas, Isle of Man: Times Press, 1965. This little-known book about the campaign and subsequent captivity, by an Indian Army officer, although written in a somewhat naive style, is revealing, and in places deeply moving.

Slessor, J. C. *The Central Blue: Recollections and Reflections by Marshal of the Royal Air Force Sir John Slessor, G.C.B., D.S.O., M.C.* London: Cassell & Co. Ltd., 1956. Slessor was director of plans at the Air Ministry, 1937-40, and thus RAF member of the Joint Planning Staff. It is what he does *not* say about Singapore, RAF expansion in the Far East, etc., in an otherwise very outspoken book, that is the most interesting.

Slim, Sir William. *Defeat Into Victory.* 3rd ed. London: Cassell & Co. Ltd., 1972.

Smyth, J. *Before the Dawn: A Story of Two Historic Retreats.* London: Cassell & Co. Ltd., 1957.

Simson, Ivan. *Singapore: Too Little, Too Late.* London: Leo Cooper Ltd., 1970. Simson's book is one of the most important sources of information on the mistakes made in Malaya, but serious students ought to read it in conjunction with the correspondence between Simson, H. P. Bryson, and A. H. Dickinson in the Bryson Collection.

Sweet-Escott, B. *Baker Street Irregular.* London: Methuen & Co., Ltd., 1965.

Tsuji, M. *Singapore: The Japanese Version.* Translated by M. E. Lake. New York: St. Martin's Press, 1960. Colonel Tsuji was director of military operations of the Japanese Twenty-fifth Army, and his account is the only one in English on the British defeat as seen "from the other side of the hill."

Woods, F., ed. *Young Winston's Wars: The Original Despatches of Winston S. Churchill War Correspondent, 1897-1900.* New York: Viking Press, 1973.

Biographies

Connell, J. *Auchinleck: A Critical Biography.* London: Cassell & Co. Ltd., 1959.

——. *Wavell: Soldier and Scholar.* London: Collins, 1964.

——. *Wavell: The Supreme Commander 1941-1943.* London: Collins, 1969.

Cosgrave, P. *Churchill at War: Alone 1939-40.* London: Collins, 1974.

Gilbert, M. *Winston S. Churchill.* Vol. 4. *The Stricken World 1916-1922.* Boston: Houghton Mifflin, 1975.

Hancock, W. K. *Smuts.* Vol 2. *The Fields of Force 1919-1950.* Cambridge: Cambridge University Press, 1968.

Roskill, S. W. *Hankey: Man of Secrets.* Vol. 3. *1931-1963.* London: Collins, 1974.

Taylor, A. J. P. *Beaverbrook.* London: Hamish Hamilton, 1972.

Tuchman, Barbara. *Stilwell and the American Experience in China 1911-45.* New York: Macmillan, 1970.

Smyth, J., V.C. *Percival and the Tragedy of Singapore.* London: Macdonald, 1971.

Wingate, R. *Lord Ismay: A Biography.* London: Hutchinson & Co. Ltd., 1970.

Secondary Sources

I have included in this section not only works quoted in this book but those that have contributed to my general understanding of the subject.

Attiwell, K. *The Singapore Story.* New York: Doubleday, 1960.

Aster, S. *1939: The Making of the Second World War.* New York: Simon & Schuster, 1973.

Barber, N. *A Sinister Twilight: The Fall of Singapore, 1942.* Boston: Houghton Mifflin, 1968.

Barclay, C. N. *On Their Shoulders: British Generalship in the Lean Years; 1939-1942.* London: Faber & Faber Ltd., 1954.

Barnett, C. *The Collapse of British Power.* London: Eyre Methuen, 1972.

Beloff, M. *Imperial Sunset.* Vol. 1. *Britain's Liberal Empire 1897-1921.* New York: Alfred A. Knopf, 1969.

Burns, James MacGregor. *Roosevelt: The Soldier of Freedom 1940-1945.* New York: Harcourt Brace Jovanovich, 1970.

Calvocoressi, P., and Wint, G. *Total War.* New York: Pantheon Books, 1972.

Clifford, Nicholas. *Retreat From China.* Seattle, Wash.: University of Washington Press, 1967.

Clutterbuck, R. *Riot and Revolution in Singapore & Malaya 1945-1963*. London: Faber & Faber Ltd., 1973.

Divine, Robert A. *The Reluctant Belligerent: American Entry Into World War Two*. New York: John Wiley & Sons, Inc., 1965.

Dixon, Norman. *On the Psychology of Military Incompetence*. London: Jonathan Cape, 1976.

Falk, Stanley. *Seventy Days to Singapore*. New York: G. P. Putnam's Sons, 1975.

Feis, Herbert. *The Road to Pearl Harbor*. Princeton, N. J.: Princeton University Press, 1950.

Gardner, B. *Churchill In Power*. Boston: Houghton Mifflin, 1970.

Grenfell, R. *Main Fleet to Singapore*. London: Faber & Faber Ltd., 1951.

Howard, M. *The Continental Commitment*. London: Temple Smith, 1972.

Johnson, Franklyn A. *Defence By Committee: The British Committee of Imperial Defence 1885-1959*. London: Oxford University Press, 1960.

Kennedy, L. *Pursuit: The Chase and Sinking of the Battleship Bismarck*. New York: Viking Press, 1974.

Kirby, S. W. *Singapore: The Chain of Disaster*. New York: Macmillan, 1971.

Lee, Bradford A. *Britain and the Sino-Japanese War 1937-1939: A Study in the Dilemmas of British Decline*. Stanford, Calif.: Stanford University Press, 1973.

MacKenzie, C. *Eastern Epic*. Vol. 1. *Defence*. London: Chatto & Windus, 1951.

Marder, Arthur J. *From the Dreadnought to Scapa Flow: The Royal Navy In The Fisher Era, 1904-1919*. Vol. 5. *Victory and Aftermath (January 1918-June 1919)*. London: Oxford University Press, 1970.

——. *From the Dardanelles to Oran: Studies of the Royal Navy in War and Peace 1915-1940*. London: Oxford University Press, 1974.

——. *Winston is back: Churchill at the Admiralty, 1939-1940*. London: Longman, 1972.

Mason, P. *A Matter of Honour: An Account of the Indian Army, its Officers & Men*. London: Jonathan Cape, 1974.

Morison, Samuel Eliot. *Strategy And Compromise*. Boston: Atlantic, Little Brown, 1958.

Ogorkiewicz, R. *Armor: A History of Mechanized Forces*. New York: Frederick A. Prager, 1960.

d'Omrain, N. *War Machinery and High Policy: Defence Administration in Peacetime Britain 1902-1914*. London: Oxford University Press, 1973.

Owen, F. *The Fall of Singapore*. London: Michael Joseph, 1960.

Parkinson, R. *Peace For Our Time: Munich the Dunkirk: The Inside Story*. New York: David McKay Company, Inc., 1972.

———. *Blood, Toil, Tears and Sweat: The War History from Dunkirk to Alamein, based on the War Cabinet papers of 1940 to 1942.* New York: David McKay Company, Inc., 1973.

Roskill, S. W. *Naval Policy between the Wars.* Vol. 1. *The Period of Anglo-American Antagonism 1919-1929.* London: Collins, 1968.

———. Vol. 2. *The Period of Reluctant Rearmament 1930-1939.* London: Collins, 1976.

Sherwood, Robert E. *Roosevelt and Hopkins: An Intimate History.* Rev. ed. New York: Harper and Brothers, 1950.

Skidmore, I. *Escape from the Rising Sun.* New York: Charles Scribners Sons, 1974.

Smith, Gaddis. *American Diplomacy during the Second World War, 1941-1945.* New York: John Wiley & Sons, Inc., 1965.

Stewart, I. MacA. *History of the Argyll & Sutherland Highlanders 2nd Battalion: Malayan Campaign, 1941-1942.* London: Thomas Nelson and Sons Ltd., 1947.

Swinson, A. *Defeat in Malaya: The Fall of Singapore.* New York: Ballantine Books, Inc., 1970.

Thomson, G. M. *Vote of Censure.* New York: Stein and Day, 1968.

Thorne, C. *The Limits of Foreign Policy: The West, the League and the Far Eastern Crisis of 1931-1933.* New York: G. P. Putnam's Sons, 1972.

Wilson, Trevor, *The First Summit.* Boston: Houghton Mifflin, 1969.

Articles

Callahan, Raymond. "The Illusion of Security: Singapore 1919-1942." *Journal of Contemporary History* 9 (April 1974):69-92.

Gilmour, A. Article on Singapore in the Singapore *New Nation,* May 3, 1971.

Mc Intyre, W. D. "The Strategic Significance of Singapore 1919-1942: The Naval Base and the Commonwealth." *Journal of Southeast Asian History* 10 (March 1969): 69-94.

Parkinson, C. N. "The Pre-1942 Singapore Naval Base." *United States Naval Institute Proceedings* 82 (September 1956): 939-53.

Roskill, S. W. "Marder, Churchill and the Admiralty 1939-42." *Journal of the Royal United Service Institute for Defence Studies* 117 (December 1972): 49-53.

Scott, R. Article on Singapore in the London *Daily Telegraph,* February 15, 1972.

Vlieland, C. A. Article on Singapore in the London *Daily Telegraph,* February 15, 1967.

INDEX

ABC=1, 99-100, 101, 127, 144

ABDA, 19; creation of, 233, 235, 252-53. *See also* Arcadia Conference; Wavell

ADB agreement, 127, 140, 165

Admiralty. *See* Royal Navy

Air Ministry. *See* Royal Air Force

Alexander, A. V., 156

Amery, Leopold, M. S., 56, 112

Anglo-American relations: and aid to Russia, 153, 155-56; between the wars, 22-23, 34; discussed with Menzies, 83, 84, 85; in Far East, 127, 157, 237; and Matador, 167-70; 1939-41, 41, 53-55, 98-107; seen as deterrent to Japan, 31, 33, 39-40, 41, 44, 51-52, 54, 76, 81, 90, 98. *See also* Arcadia conference; Atlantic conference; Churchill; Roosevelt.

Arcadia conference, 232-37

Army Quarterly, 23

Arnold, Lieutenant General H. H., 142

Asiatic Fleet, 100, 127, 164

Atlantic conference, 139-44, 145, 149, 153

Atlee, Clement, 167, 229, 233

Auchinleck, General Sir Claude J. E.: as commander in chief, Middle East, 93, 94, 97, 150-51, 163, 258, 261; reinforces Far East, 227

Australia, 126, 127; fears Japanese agression, 22; questions Far Eastern strategy, 25; Churchill's relations with, 30-31, 35, 83, 162-64, 165, 223, 229-30, 233-35, 237, 239, 256, 259, 271-72; reinforces Middle East, 32, 35; strategic misunderstandings with, 32-33, 35, 82-90, 103, 163-64, 229-30, 237, 239, 256, 259, 272-73; requests review of Far Eastern strategy, 47, 48-49; desires concentration of A.I.F., 62; reinforces Malaya, 77, 130, 228-30; wants guarantee of American assistance, 97; wants

capital ships in Far East, 143, 148, 157; and Matador, 167; complains about Brooke-Popham's removal, 179, 250; complains about ABDA, 237, 262; withdraws A.I.F. from Middle East, 238, 273; demands defense of Singapore, 259

Australian Imperial Force (A.I.F.), motives joining, 62

Australian Imperial Force, units of: Sixth Division, 238; Seventh Division, 58, 59, 238; Eighth Division, 76, 77, 130, 174, 239, 254; Ninth Division, 163-64

AVG, and defense of Burma, 217-22

Babington, Air Vice Marshal J. T., 28, 69, 95, 122; requests reinforcements, 35; and Singapore War Committee disputes, 64-66; relief of, 110

Backhouse, Admiral Sir Roger, 158

Ballentine, Brigadier G. C., 253

Barstow, Major General A. E., 203, 244

Beatty, Admiral of the Fleet, First Earl, 27

Beaverbrook, First Baron, 50, 120, 153, 159

Beckwith-Smith, Major General M. B., 16, 270

Bellairs, Rear Admiral R. M., 76

Bennett, Lieutenant General H. Gordon, 204, 228, 244, 248, 251, 254; urges surrender of Singapore, 17, 18; leaves Singapore, 19, 270; arrives in Malaya, 130

Bisseker, F. D., 248

Blythe, W. L., 46

Bond, Lieutenant General Lionel, 40, 64, 69, 128-29, 140, 174, 176, 190; on defense of Singapore, 35-36; and Singapore War Committee disputes, 64-66; on Japanese threat, 109; relief of, 110

Bowden, V.G., 229, 238, 248, 270

Bracken, Brendan, 159

Brett, Major General G.H., 219-20, 221-22, 236

British Army: expansion of, 30; attitudes toward Indian Indian Army, 111-12; organization of, 245-46, 246-47

British Army, units of: Eighteenth Division, 211, 212, 219, 230, 238, 258-62, 272; Fifty-Third Brigade, 219, 226, 261; Seventh Armoured Brigade, 227, 258, 262; Second Battalion, Argyll and Sutherland Highlanders, 204, 261

Brooke, General Sir Alan, 87, 93, 222; becomes CIGS, 161, 210; and Far Eastern strategy, 223, 224, 226, 299

Brooke-Popham, Air Chief Marshal Sir Robert, 122, 202, 205, 212; appointed commander in chief, Far East, 62, 66-69; early career of, 66; corresponds with Ismay, 74, 117, 118-19, 120, 121, 123, 130; given inadequate staff, 107-8; of RAF in Far East, 108, 119; cultivates optimistic attitude, 109-10, 171; ends Singapore War Committee quarrels, 110; on civil-military relations in Malaya, 113-14, 117; and reinforcement problem, 118-20, 170-72, 250; and defense of Hong Kong, 119, 176-77; complains of inadequate information from London, 123-24; and coordination with Americans and Dutch, 126-27; and Matador, 128-29, 140-41, 167-70, 180-82, 190-92, 194, 272; relations with Australia, 130, 250; replacement of, 160-62, 178-79, 247, 250, 252; and Malayan campaign, 194, 197; and Far East War Council disputes, 247-49

Bruce Stanley, 163, 167, 171, 228, 229

Buffalo (fighter aircraft), inadequate performance of, 55

Burma, 126, 261-62, 273-74; reinforcements for, 70, 79, 81, 218-19, 223-24, 256; included in Far East Command, 68, 112; transferred to India Command, 212; transferred to ABDA, 236; allied command arrangements in, 236-37

Burma Road, 47, 54, 217

Butler, R. A., 77

Cadogan, Sir Alexander, 141

Caldecote, First Baron, 48, 51, 78

Canada, 29, 82, 90; urges end of Anglo-Japanese alliance, 22; and Matador, 168; reinforces Hong Kong, 176-77

Carter, Squadron Leader T. C., 74, 107, 108, 115, 121; on civil-military relations in Malaya, 113, 122; on Malayan campaign, 193-94; on causes of defeat, 271

Casey, R. G., 32, 229

Cave-Browne, Major General W., 124, 125

Ceylon, 77, 146, 203; and control of Indian Ocean, 51, 52, 145, 147, 231

Chamberlain, Neville, 25, 33, 40

Chaney, Major General James, 105, 142

Chennault, Colonel Claire L., 218

Chiefs of Staff. *See* Far Eastern Strategy; Mediterranean and Middle East; Brooke; Dill; Newall; Portal; Pound

Chiang Kai-Shek, Generalissimo, and relations with British, 218, 220-22

China, 23, 29, 47; as factor in Anglo-American relations, 217, 257-58, 259-60, 273

Churchill, Winston S: orders fight to end in Singapore, 19; reflects on loss of Singapore, 19, 34, 271; and Far Eastern strategy (pre-1940), 21-22, 31-35; and relations with Australia, 30-31, 35, 83, 162-64, 165, 223, 229-30, 233-35, 237, 239, 256, 259, 273; and relations with the United States, 39-40, 51-52, 54-55, 96-97, 106, 139, 141, 142-44, 209-10, 232-37; and Mediterranean strategy, 42, 52-53, 87-89, 90-93, 100, 104-6, 165-66, 211, 213, 238, 256, 261, 271; and Far Eastern strategy (1940-41), 52-53, 58-60, 77-78, 79, 80, 88, 90, 91, 95, 99, 101, 105, 130, 155-56, 164-70, 180, 272; and Indian Army, 55-57, 129, 130, 151, 261-62; and Singapore Fortress, 60-61, 255, 256-57; under-rates Japan, 61; and aid to Russia, 94, 153-54, 155-56, 161, 172, 211; and reinforcements for Far East, 119, 150-51, 272; and creation of Eastern Fleet, 145-49, 156-60; and relief of Brooke-Popham, 160; hears news of Pearl

Harbor, 195; hears of loss of *Prince of Wales* and *Repulse*, 201, 202-3; and Malayan campaign, 212, 213, 223, 245, 249, 255-57, 259-60, 272; and Burma, 213, 258, 259-60, 273; and Far Eastern strategy (after Pearl Harbor), 230-33, 239, 257-58, 259-60, 261-62, 272

CID, 34; on Far Eastern Strategy, 24, 26, 32

Clark-Kerr, Sir Archibald, 95, 113, 172, 250

Clough, A. H., quoted, 87

Combined Chiefs of Staff, created at Arcadia Conference, 235-36

Cooper, Alfred Duff, 202, 253, 272; sent on mission to Far East, 96, 113, 172, 173-74; as resident minister in Far East, 210-11, 229, 240-42, 247-49, 250, 252; 253, 272

Cowan, Brigadier D. T., 253

Craigie, Sir Robert, 271

Cranborne, Viscount, 165

Cripps, Sir Stafford, 260, 261

Crosby, Sir Josiah, 172, 192

Cunningham, Admiral Sir Andrew, 42, 44, 89, 225

Curtin, John W., 163, 244; argues with Churchill over Malayan campaign, 229-30, 237, 239, 256, 259

Daily Herald (Melbourne), Curtin publishes manifesto in, 230

Danckwerts, Rear Admiral H. V., 102

Dawson, Christopher, 242-43, 248

Dennys, Major General L. E., 218, 220, 222

Dewing, Major General R. H., 107

Dill, Field Marshal Sir John, 82, 94, 104, 111, 124, 159, 161; argues with Churchill about strategic priorities, 90-93; defends Middle East commitment, 106; at Atlantic conference, 140, 141, 142; at Arcadia conference, 222, 223, 235, 236

Dobbie, Major General William, 28, 60, 111, 173

Dorman-Smith, Sir Reginald, 213, 221, 236

Duncan, Brigadier H. C., 253, 258

Dutch, *See* Netherlands East Indies

Eastern Fleet: creation of, 144-49, 156-57; arrives at Singapore, 179-80; *Prince of Wales* and *Repulse* lost from, 199-202; withdraws from Singapore, 203. *See also* Phillips

Eastern Group Supply Council, 56-57

Eden, Anthony, 56, 80, 100, 104, 140, 209, 271; on missions to Middle East, 76, 82; and Far Eastern strategy, 156-57, 158, 160, 164, 165, 168-70

Empress of Asia (troop ship), 262

Fadden, A. W., 162-63, 164

Far Eastern strategy: prior to 1940, 23-26, 31-35; and fall of France, 40-42; redefinition of, 47, 48-51, 53; and reinforcement policy, 57-60, 76-80, 81, 149-50; discussed with Menzies, 82-85, 90; priority accorded to, 93, 155, 165-71, 228, 231, 237; and civil-military coordination, 95-96; weakness of, 97, 106-7; discussed with United States, 99, 102-3, 142; and creation of Eastern Fleet, 144-49, 156-57; after Pearl Harbor, 224-25, 228-33, 237-38; summary of 271-72. *See also* Brooke-Popham; Churchill

FECB, 61, 107, 109, 125, 190

Forbes, Leslie, 240-42

Force Z (*Prince of Wales* and *Repulse*), destruction of, 199-203

Forrester, C. S., 139

France: Mediterranean concerns of, 24, 26; defeat of 28, 39-42

Fraser, Hugh, 17

Fraser, Peter, 52, 143

Freeman, Air Chief Marshal Sir Wilfred, 120, 141, 223

Gamelin, General Maurice, 40

Greece; prewar concern over, 25, 26; Italian invasion of, 75; British aid to, 80, 81-82, 83, 153; British evacuate, 86

Halifax, First Earl, 44, 80, 99; as ambassador to United States, 143, 167, 168, 169-70, 211

Harriman, Averell, 195, 223
Hart, Admiral Thomas C., 166, 179, 180
Hartley, General Sir Alan, 259
Heath, Lieutenant General Sir Lewis, 56, 111, 203; urges surrender of Singapore, 16-17, 18; and Matador, 181, 182, 191, 192, 194; and Malayan campaign, 208, 240, 244-45, 247, 250-51, 272
Hollis, Colonel R. M., 80
Hopkins, Harry: mission to London (January 1941), 100-101; questions Middle East commitment, 105; supports unified command in Far East, 233
Hong Kong, 23, 31, 119; defense of 126, 176-77
Howard, Michael, on Churchill and Middle East, 43
Hull, Cordell, 53, 54-55, 100, 143, 167
Hurricane (fighter aircraft), inadequacy in Far East, 55, 257
Hutton, Lieutenant General Thomas, 219

Imperial Conference (1937), 24, 33
Imperial War Cabinet (1917-18), 82, 90
India, government of: and creation of Far East command, 66; and control of Burma 112
Indian Army: modernization of, 30; Churchill's attitude toward, 55-57, 129, 130, 151, 261-62; expansion of, 56-57, 129-30, 151-52, 253; British Army attitude to, 111-112; organization of, 247
Indian Army, units of: Third Corps, 129, 174, 181, 206, 244-45, 254; Fourth Division, 56, 152; Fifth Division, 56, 152; Ninth Division, 129, 244, 254; Tenth Division, 86; Eleventh Division, 129, 176, 181, 182, 190, 194, 205, 240, 241, 244, 254; Seventeenth Division, 211-12, 219, 229, 238, 253; Nineteenth Division, 259; Sixth Brigade, 129, 204, 208, 244; Eighth Brigade, 129, 192, 197, 244; Twelfth Brigade, 36, 129, 244; Fifteenth Brigade, 129, 204, 208, 244; Twentieth Brigade, 86; Twenty-second Brigade, 129, 244-45; Twenty-eighth Brigade, 174, 177, 204, 208, 247; Forty-fourth Brigade, 219, 226, 253; Forty-fifth Brigade, 219, 253, 254, 258; Third Calvary Regiment, 174, 175; 3/17th Dogra Regiment, 193; 3/16th Punjab Regiment, 207; 1/14th Punjab Regiment, 207; 2/1st Gurkha Regiment, 207
Indian National Army, 273
Indian State Forces, 81
Indochina, 31, 69, 97, 165, 232
Ismay, Major General Hastings L., 60, 161, 212, 222, 257, 261, 273; briefs Brooke-Popham, 68; on Churchill-Dill quarrel, 92; corresponds with Brooke-Popham, 117, 118-19, 120, 121, 123, 130; on Phillips, 157-58

Japan: expansionism of, 23-24; demands closure of Burma Road, 47; erroneous Western views of, 61-62, 109-10; Churchill warns, 101, 102; takes decision for war, 166, 167, 170, 179-80
Japanese Army: and tropical warfare, 82, 246; organization of, 246
Japanese Army, units of: Twenty-fifth Army, 204; Fifth Division, 207
Japanese Navy, units of: Twenty-first Naval Air Flotilla, 199; Twenty-second Naval Air Flotilla, 199, 204
Joint Intelligence Committee, 80, 140
Joint Planning Staff, 176; proposes evacuation of Mediterranean, 42; Thomas meets with, 49; on strategic priorities (June 1941), 93; on creation of Eastern Fleet, 144-45; on reinforcements for Malaya, 150; on strategy against Japan, 231
Jones, Stanley, 46; and Singapore War Committee disputes, 65; and Duff Cooper, 249; relief of, 255
Joubert de la Ferté, Air Vice Marshal P. B., 70

Kennedy, Major General John, 104, 146; differs with Churchill over Middle East, 86-88, 89-90, 91, 94
Keswick, W. J., 174
Key, Major General B. W., 16, 192, 193, 244
King, W. MacKenzie, 167, 235
Knox, Colonel Frank, 102, 211

Kondo, Vice Admiral Nobutake, 199, 200
Konoye, Prince F., 156
Kurita, Vice Admiral Takeo, 199, 200

Layton, Vice Admiral Sir Geoffrey, 69,
  127, 164, 172, 178, 180, 190, 191;
  and Singapore War Committee disputes,
  65-66, 110; hands over to Phillips, 194;
  resumes command, 203; and Malayan
  campaign, 224, 247, 253; and evacuation of Penang, 242
Leach, Captain John, 139, 202, 203
Lee, Brigadier General Raymond, 105
Lloyd, First Baron, 65-66
Lloyd George, David, 34, 82
Longmore, Air Chief Marshal Sir Arthur,
  178
Lothian, Eleventh Marquess of; as ambassador to United States, 31, 41, 53, 54-
  55, 98
Lyon, Brigadier C. A., 240-42
Lyons, J. A., 25

MacArthur, General Douglas, 180
MacDonald, Malcolm, 64
McLeod, Lieutenant General D. K., 218,
  219
Madagascar, and control of Indian Ocean,
  231-32
Malaya, 23, 30; vulnerability during monsoon, 28, 172-73; and British war effort,
  29-30, 35, 40, 116; reinforcements
  refused to, 35, 40; fighter aircraft for,
  55; administrative structure of, 62-63,
  112-13, Singapore War Committee's
  role in, 64-66, 110; local commanders
  on defense needs of (1940), 69-70;
  radar coverage in, 70, 122-23; lack of
  antiaircraft cover in, 97; quality of
  military personnel in, 108-9, 177;
  civil-military relations in, 113-18; state
  of garrison in (autumn 1941), 124-
  25, 174-79; Commonwealth command
  arrangements in, 130; postwar problems
  in, 270. See also Brooke-Popham;
  Churchill; Far Eastern strategy; Malayan
  campaign
Malayan campaign (1941-42): and fall of
  Singapore, 15-18, 262-63; opening

moves of, 190-95; British air power
  broken in, 195-98; Prince of Wales and
  Repulse lost in, 199-203; Percival's
  initial dispositions for, 203-6; northern
  Malaya lost in, 206-9; and Far East War
  Council, 210, 240, 241-43; reinforcements for, 211-12, 213, 223-24, 225-
  26, 228; Chiefs of Staff prescribe
  strategy of delay in, 226; and fall of
  Penang, 240-43; central Malaya lost in,
  244; mainland evacuated in, 261; losses
  in, 270. See also Churchill, Far Eastern
  strategy
Maltby, Air Vice Marshal Paul, 178
Margesson, David, 87
Marshall, General George C., 100, 127,
  141, 222; and creation of ABDA, 233,
  236
Matador (seizure of Kra Isthmus): evolution
  of plan for, 69, 84-85, 128-29, 140-41,
  167-70, 180-82; failure of, 190-91, 194,
  272
Mediterranean and Middle East: pre-1940
  concern over, 24, 25-26; dominion
  contribution to defense of 32, 35, 48;
  proposal to evacuate (1940), 42-44;
  reinforcements for, 58, 59, 150-51,
  152; deepening British commitment in,
  75-76, 80, 81-82, 83, 86-89, 150-53,
  211; argument over priority given to,
  90-94; aircraft reinforcements for, 95,
  152, 154; Hopkins reports Churchill's
  views on, 100; American doubts about,
  104-6, 142; and British seapower, 224-
  25. See also Churchill.
Menzies, Robert G., 52, 99, 102, 120, 171;
  on mission to London, 82-85, 88-89,
  90; wants capital ships in Far East, 143;
  loses office, 162
Moore, Vice Admiral H. R., 223, 224
Murray-Lyon, Major General D. M., 181,
  202, 206, 209, 244

Nagumo, Vice Admiral Chuichi, 146
Netherlands East Indies, 126, 127; British
  involvement in defense of, 47-49, 51-
  52, 77, 79, 101-2, 103-4, 106, 164,
  166-70; Japanese threat to (February
  1941), 80-81; economic importance of,
  81; American support for, 100, 142-43,

144, 168-69; strength of forces in, 164, 274; and ABDA, 237, 262; fall of, 274

Newall, Air Chief Marshal Sir Cyril, 69

New Zealand, 21-22, 23, 127; agrees to reinforce Middle East, 31, 32, 35; and Far Eastern strategy, 47, 48-49, 167; and relations with Britain, 82, 179, 234, 237, 262

Nicolson, Harold, 202-3

Noble, Wing Commander C. H., 193

Noble, Admiral Sir Percy, 64-66

Nomura, Admiral K., 143, 145

Norway, proposed British operations in 154, 269

Nye, Lieutenant General Sir Archibald, 161

oil, British concern over, 43, 75

Pacific War Council, 262

Page, Sir Earle: on special mission to London, 157, 164, 165-67, 168, 172, 228; and final defense of Singapore, 258-59, 260-61

Paget, General Sir Bernard, 161, 178, 179

Palliser, Rear Admiral A. F. E., 159-60, 190, 191, 199, 200

Paris, Brigadier A. C. M., 204, 244

Penang, 32, 129; fall of, 240-43, 248

Percival, Lieutenant General A. E., 124, 140, 174, 178, 253, 270; discusses surrender, 16-18; appointed GOC Malaya, 111; and Indian Army, 111, 247; and Brigadier Simson, 173, 175-76, 251-52; and Matador, 181, 182, 191, 192, 194; and Malayan campaign, 203-6, 208, 226, 228, 240-41, 244-47, 250, 251-52, 254, 257, 261, 272

Philippine Islands, 31, 127, 273

Phillips, Admiral Sir Tom, 106-7, 120, 140, 156, 161, 164; and vulnerability of capital ships, 157-58; meets with Smuts, 159-60; arrives in Far East, 179, 180; and Malayan campaign 194, 197; and loss of Force Z, 199-203

Pilgrim (attack on Spanish and Portugese Atlantic islands), 155, 159

Playfair, Major General I. S. O., 107, 126, 182, 210; on Far East command's problems, 107, 108, 112, 113, 117; on vulnerability of Malaya during monsoon, 173; on arrival of Eastern Fleet, 179

Poorten, General H. ter, 275

Portal, Air Chief Marshal Sir Charles, 69, 83, 142, 167, 222, 233; on aircraft reinforcements for Far East, 120, 149, 150

Pound, Admiral Sir Dudley, 42, 67, 140, 141, 222, 232; and defense of Netherlands East Indies, 49, 51, 52, 80-81, 104, 169; and creation of Eastern Fleet, 145-49, 150, 156-57, 160; and Churchill, 149, 158-59

Pownall, Lieutenant General Sir Henry: on Far Eastern strategy, 24-25, 140-41, 158, 219; replaces Brooke-Popham, 162, 179, 210; and Malayan campaign, 250-51, 252, 253, 254, 263; reflects on defeat, 270-71, 272

Pulford, Air Vice Marshal C. W. H.: replaces Babington, 110; and prewar buildup of RAF in Malaya, 121, 122, 125, 172, 173, 178; and Malayan campaign, 181, 191, 193, 196-98, 199, 200, 240, 247, 250, 253; death of, 270

Pye, D. R., 70

Queen Mary (troopship), 130

Reynaud, Paul, 39, 42

Roberts, Field Marshal, first earl, 112

Rommel, General Erwin, 86, 88, 89, 93, 211, 258, 269

Roosevelt, Franklin D., 94, 155, 236; and aid to Britain 39-40, 53, 98-99, 101; and Atlantic meeting, 96, 106, 139, 141, 142-44, 145; and Middle East commitment, 104-5, 151; agrees to support British and Dutch against Japan, 168-70; and Arcadia conference, 210, 233. *See also* Anglo-American relations; Churchill

Royal Air Force: and prewar Far Eastern strategy, 27-28; and defense of Malaya, 49-51, 55, 80, 149-50, and Middle East, 95, 152, 154; state of, in Far East, 108, 109, 119, 120-21, 125-26, 162, 172; and aid to Russia, 121-22, 154, 161,

211; in Malayan campaign, 195-98, 240, 257, 261, 262

Royal Navy: and prewar Far Eastern strategy, 23, 25-26, 27, 34; unable to form Eastern Fleet, 51, 84, 85, 130; and creation of Eastern Fleet, 144-49, 156-59, 179-80, 199; and control of Indian Ocean, 224-25, 231-32

Russia: German attack on, 89, 91, 152-53; aid to, 94, 153-54, 155, 161; and RAF operations, 121-22, 154, 161, 211; possible Japanese attack on, 155-56, 172

Scarf, Squadron Leader A. S. K., 198

Simmons, Major General F. Keith, 17, 18, 204, 251

Simson, Brigadier Ivan: and state of Malaya's defenses, 124, 173, 175-76, 249, 252, 272; and defense of Singapore Island, 251-52, 257

Sinclair, Sir Archibald, 165-66

Singapore: final defense of, 15-18, 262-63; decision to build base at, 23; defense of, 26, 27-28, 35-36, 70, 76, 82, 123, 130, 251-52, 257; considered a "fortress," 60-61; radar coverage for, 70, 122; Middle East takes priority over, 90-93; strategy conferences at (1941), 127, 172; first air raid on, 193. See also Churchill; Far Eastern strategy; Malaya; Malayan campaign

Slim, Field Marshal Sir William, 112

Smith, Air Commodore, S. W., 28

Smuts, General J. G., 82, 159-60

Smyth, Major General Sir John, 253, 262

South Africa, 82, 167

Stalin, Marshal Joseph V., 94, 153, 161

Stark, Admiral Harold, 98, 127, 141, 142

Stewart, Lieutenant Colonel Ian MacArthur, 204

Stilwell; Lieutenant General Joseph W., 236-37

Straits Times (Singapore), 248

Tennant, Captain, W. G., 202, 249

Thailand, 36, 69; Japanese threat to, 128, 140-41, 144, 155, 167, 169

Thomas, Sir Shenton, 115, 250, 255, 257, 263; urges surrender of Singapore, 17-18; asks for RAF reinforcements, 35, 49; tour as governor extended, 63-64; and Singapore War Committee disputes, 64-65; and evacuation of Penang, 241-43; and Far East War Council, 247-49, 251

Torrance, Brigadier K. S., 175-76

Transport aircraft, 126-27, 246

Trenchard, Air Chief Marshal Sir Hugh, 27, 28

Tobruk, 86; Ninth Australian Division withdrawn from, 163-64

Turkey: as factor in Mediterranean strategy, 25, 26, 44, 75, 80; aid promised to, 97, 152-53, 164, 228

United States: and relations with Japan, 98, 106, 144. See also Anglo-American relations; Churchill; Roosevelt

Vlieland, C. A., 64-65, 110, 129

Volunteer Forces (Malaya), 115, 129, 243, 262

Wards, Colonel G. T., 109, 110

warships (British): Ark Royal, 144, 147, 159, 212; Barham, 144, 212, 256; Duke of York, 147, 212, 232; Eagle, 144, 159; Furious, 159; Hermes, 147, 149, 212; Hood, 139; Indomitable, 158, 159, 212, 213, 224, 261; King George V, 99, 147, 222; Nelson, 147-48; Prince of Wales, 106, 139, 147, 156-60, 164, 165, 166, 179, 191, 199-203, 207, 211, 212, 221, 269; Queen Elizabeth, 225, 238, 256; "R" class, 85, 144, 145, 146, 148, 212; Renown, 84, 85, 144, 147-48; Repulse, 27, 147, 149, 156-59, 164, 165, 179, 191, 199-203, 207, 211, 212, 221, 269; Rodney, 147-48; Tenedos, 201; Valiant, 144, 225, 238, 256

warships (German): Bismark, 93, 139; Gneisenau, 269; Prinz Eugen, 139, 269; Scharnhorst, 269

Wavell, General Sir Archibald: and final defense of Singapore, 19; as commander in chief, Middle East, 76, 81-82, 86, 93, 107, 150; as commander in chief, India, 151-52, 161, 175, 177-78, 212, 218; and Burma, 218-19, 221-22, 262; at Chungking conference, 218, 219, 236; and ABDA, 235, 237, 252; and Malayan campaign, 253-55, 257, 260, 261, 262-63; reflects on defeat, 270
Welles, Sumner, 141
Wilson, Sir Charles, 202, 233, 234

Wimperis, H. E., 70
Winant, John, 195
Wynter, Lieutenant Colonel H. D., 23, 33

Yamashita, Lieutenant General Tomoyuki, 18
Yu Fei-ping, General, 227

Zero (fighter aircraft), performance of 55, 125